Studies in Social Protest

Studies in Social Protest

Shyam Lal
Vice Chancellor
Patna University, Patna
Bihar

RAWAT PUBLICATIONS
Jaipur • New Delhi • Bangalore • Hyderabad • Guwahati

ISBN 81-316-0331-8

Published by
Prem Rawat for **Rawat Publications**
Satyam Apts, Sector 3, Jawahar Nagar, Jaipur 302 004 (India)
Phone: 0141 265 1748/7006 Fax: 0141 265 1748
E-mail: info@rawatbooks.com
Website: www.rawatbooks.com

New Delhi Office
4858/24, Ansari Road, Daryaganj, New Delhi 110 002
Phone: 011 2326 3290

Also at Bangalore, Hyderabad and Guwahati

Typeset by Rawat Computers, Jaipur
Printed at Chaman Enterprises, New Delhi

To my mother
(Late) Smt Bhani Bai

Contents

Foreword

Nothing satisfies me more than to see the ability of one of my old students, Shyam Lal, being recognized in academic circles of colleges and universities, both in the national and international arena. Though scholarly activity is of paramount importance to him, Shyam Lal, in recent years, has also evinced a high degree of administrative leadership in the governance of universities and centres of higher learning. As the Vice Chancellor of J.N. Vyas University, Jodhpur, and the University of Rajasthan, Jaipur, he had rendered outstanding services, wherein by his ways of thinking, scholarship and good intentions, he was able to secure applause from everyone. He is, at present, the Vice Chancellor of Patna University, Patna (Bihar) which is one of the 7th oldest university in the country. Despite tremendous responsibilities of the office of Vice Chancellor of Patna University, where work keeps piling up every day, it is astonishing to see that Shyam Lal's perseverance to his studies has never been diluted with.

Earlier, he has held the post of Chairman, Drafting Committee, Ambedkar Foundation, Department of Art, Literature and Culture of the Government of Rajasthan. He had also served as Professor and Head, Department of Sociology, University of Rajasthan, Jaipur, and Chairman, Institute of Social Research and Applied Anthropology, Kolkata. He had also been the Director of Social Science Research Centre of the University of Rajasthan for a number of years. He has been the recipient of ICSSR's Dr Ambedkar National Fellowship during the years 2003–05.

An erudite scholar of sociology, Shyam Lal is a prolific writer. He has to his credit 18 books and more than 50 research papers published in reputed journals and volumes from time to time. He is a well-known authority on Dr B.R. Ambedkar and on the Dalit struggles and movement, in the erstwhile princely states of Rajputana. His work on *Ambedkar and*

Dalit Movement, published in 2008, is a masterpiece of sociological writing, and perhaps, the only one of its kind.

The key ideas contained in the works of Shyam Lal can be better gauged if one is, to some extent, familiar with his background. By referring to that part of his life, I might hurt his feelings but that is certainly not my intention. Born and bred in a very poor, depressed class family, Shyam Lal, if I may say so, had battled in all ways against conditions of adverse fortune. Placed as he was in a difficult situation, where escape seemed impossible, Shyam Lal stood fixed and unmoving, without abandoning either his hope or determination. Struggling against heavy odds, facing all sorts of indignities, even enduring the taunts of caste Hindus, Shyam Lal carved out his way, slowly and steadily, by the sheer dint of his own merit and resoluteness. And it is suffice to say that today he is a brilliant scholar and is everywhere recognized as brilliant.

What a remarkable spectacle it is to see Shyam Lal raising himself, step by step, so to speak, from nothing by his own toil, exertions and knowledge; dissipating, by the light of reason that he acquired, all the thick clouds in which he was by birth enveloped; struggling alone himself against insurmountable difficulties but bore no malice against anybody; neither repining at misfortune nor fretting against it; going back into himself he has always stood there rooted to the land of his birth: soaring in home-brewed ideas, developed a capacity to drive a point or an argument home, all-out; a man capable of breaking a path, and make one by pushing or beating aside obstacles; a brilliant mind wherein a taste for ostentation prevails in abundance with a taste for probity; a man alien to materialism and luxury, who speaks nothing about commerce and money; neither escapism is known to him, nor he makes a hole and let the water get away; his external appearance and the innermost recesses of his heart synchronize well; and what is still greater and more wonderful in him is that since learned man appeared in him, honest man in Shyam Lal did not go in eclipse. He has all the trappings of high office, but never yielded to temptation. All these qualities are miraculously built in Shyam Lal and reflected in one way or the other, in his works.

The present work titled *Studies in Social Protest*, is a new feather in Shyam Lal's cap. Being the outcome of a scholarly mind, who is thoroughly acquainted with the untouchable castes and possesses a profound knowledge in the field, the work is definitely authoritative. The focus of attention in the work are the Meghwals and their struggles and movements in the erstwhile princely states of Rajputana since 1916. The Meghwals, earlier known as Chamars, are one of the dominating untouchable castes in western Rajasthan, living in thickly scattered population, in almost all the villages. The present work of Shyam Lal is a quite new and novel, as he has examined the ideology, programmes, mobilizational strategies and spread of Meghwal movement against the backdrop of two important changes witnessed in Marwar (Jodhpur) state since 1916, that is, a wave of Dalit assertion and grass-roots activism. While tracing the socio-political history of the Meghwal movement for over 92 years, Shyam Lal has provided a dispassionate account of the growth of social and political awakening amongst the Meghwals, and the various endeavours and encounters they had undergone.

Conscious of the fact that the Meghwal movement in the Marwar (Jodhpur) state was not an isolated affair, Shyam Lal has examined, in an admirable way the external factors and forces that has activated the said movements. The most important amongst them was the impact of Dr B.R. Ambedkar's speeches and his role in various agitations that he had carried out in British India at that time. This had greatly helped in the growth of Meghwal awakening in Rajasthan.

The credibility of Shyam Lal's work is further enhanced because of his vast knowledge and realization of the various issues involved in the Meghwal movement of the period. The information contained in the work can be trusted as it is derived from reliable sources. Based upon realism, knowledge, interviews, and extensive fieldwork, Shyam Lal's work is unique. Being of an inquisitive mind, his attachment is more with veridical knowledge, derived through search, investigation, and occasionally the use of heuristic method. He is an enemy of retrogression, a vehement critic of status quo, and an iconoclast of the Varna system. His sociology, rooted in reason, has compelled him to dismantle the untruths contained in the Brahaminical writings, such as Rigveda and Manusmriti. He idealizes and identifies himself with total change and building up of a new social order based on equality, liberalism and social justice.

What I have witnessed in the present work is that Shyam Lal is one of the leading spirits of the reform movement of the period! He is, in my opinion, a dogged traveller, who has made arduous journeys in his life, often carrying on with a baggage overloaded with miseries and sufferings. He is a social rebel too, but at the same time a pioneer of new sociological thinking, directed against all forms of human exploitation and graded inequalities that still cling to the Hindu social fabric. He stands to root out caste system, and would not hesitate to dig or pull it up with the roots. This vision of new sociology is emphatically reiterated by Shyam Lal in his present work.

The present work, *Studies in Social Protest*, if I may say so, is yet another instance of Shyam Lal's scholarly caste and fertility of mind. Teeming with bright ideas, connected with what is happening, his work has the quality of being relied or depended upon so far as the Meghwal awakening in western Rajasthan is concerned. Neither he has plunged into scientific jargon, nor in external ornaments; the strength of the work lies in using reliable tools, interviewing witnesses, and supplying the fact and information relevant to the case. For this sort of accomplishment, which is so much accurate and so much connected with verification of events that Shyam Lal deserves congratulations.

Being the only and singular scholarly work on Meghwal movement in Rajasthan, I have no hesitation in saying that it will be of great interest to sociologists, anthropologists, political scientists and others who are genuinely interested in Dalit studies.

L.S. Rathore
Emeritus Professor, Political Science
Former Vice Chancellor,
J.N. Vyas University, Jodhpur

Preface

I began my study of 'Bhangi: A Sweeper Caste and its Socio-economic Portraits' when I was lecturer and preparing for my Ph.D. thesis. I read all I could for three years from 1976–1979. The study of the lowest of the low untouchable castes was then not a novel thing for sociologists and anthropologists. Most sociologists and anthropologist had worked on select dominating low castes and studies of Mahar Movement, Chamar and Jatav castes were published by scholars. My study, however, took me further back into the history of Rajasthan trying to find the roots of this most unusual movement among the untouchables.

Although I have published books on other Untouchable Castes of Rajasthan namely, *Untouchable Movement in India: The Bairwa, Samajik Nyaya Avam Dalit Rajniti; Untouchable Saints of India; Untouchable Caste in India: The Raigar Movement, Ambedkar and Dalit Movement*; and *Ambedkar and Nation building* (ed.) and more than fifty articles on many socio-educational and occupational subjects for national and international repute journals, my life has continued to be dominated by Ambedkar and his socio-political thought. In Rajasthan no other scholar has studied the untouchable caste as a whole.

The publication of my books on Bairwa, Bhangi, Bhil, Raigar and convert Buddhists and Christians of Rajasthan has brought the life of these castes/communities in a very positive way into academic world. An important development for me took shape just after one year of the publication of *Untouchable Caste in India: The Raigar Movement* (2006), when I was asked by some highly educated, political elites and social activists of Meghwal and cognate communities, if I was going to pen a book on Chamars, since this group resented the term 'Chamar' as negative, derogatory, defiant and abusive, even demeaning. I replied that I would do so. As long as there is a group or groups of chiefly untouchable castes, who is/are the victim of caste oppression and atrocities, there must be a term to describe them and the literature they create to tell their past and present stories. The rejection of 'Chamar' by those who are able to take their destinies in their own hands is understandable, and in many ways a good sign, a sign of progress. The efforts made and literature published by the community also reflects a reality, to bridge the gap between all the 46 communities to an umbrella organization namely 'Rashtriya Meghwal Mahasangh'. The community fellows are positive and this view of their's makes it hopeful.

All over Rajasthan the low untouchable castes are organizing themselves to fight against inequality, discrimination and deprivation. They often agitate for their legitimate share in economic opportunities, educational privileges and political power. Widespread collective mobilization centred around such interests has led to organized social movement with defined ideologies and leadership, which have brought out significant organizational changes in the community where they originate.

This is a study of one of the dominating low untouchable castes—the Chamar in Rajasthan in the wider context of sociology of social movement. An attempt is made to analyse the genesis, growth, dynamics and socio-cultural and political consequences of the movement among the Chamar of Rajasthan.

I have had fruitful discussion on parts of the book with Indu Mathur and S.L. Verma, University of Rajasthan, Gopal Bhardwaj and K.S. Saxena, J.N. Vyas University, Jodhpur, and I am grateful to all of them for their valuable comments and encouragement. I must place on record my special thanks to my friend Jagdish Roy who made extensive comments on the manuscript which led to the sharpening of focus.

I have pleasure in acknowledging with thanks to all social workers, social activists, political elites, writers and masses of Meghwal Movement who shared their knowledge, their spirit and their feeling for the community with me and have extended their continued cooperation for a period of four years. I cannot adequately thank them for the insights they have given me into the dynamics of mass movement. They number in hundreds but among them a few must be singled out for their constant help: Hanuman Prasad Kataria, Gulabchand Jindal, Late Acharya Guru Prasad K.P., Puranmal Bairwa, Ram Murti Meena, Kamlesh Kumar Sarsar, Late B.L. Chirania, Kusum Maghwal, Prakash Meghwal, Jamna Devi, Pannalal 'Prem', Ashu Ram, M.L. Dudwal and Jethwal Pawar.

Shyam Lal

I
Background

1 Recognition of Untouchables' Sacrifice at Last

An account of dim and distant antiquities of Jodhpur has little place here, but a brief discussion of early political structure of the region will facilitate our understanding of the pattern and process of the late 14th and early 15th centuries that informed the founding of Jodhpur. Until about 1459 the state known as 'Mandor' was held by a succession of dynasties including Rao Jodha.[1] At the same time Vishveshwarnath Reu had mentioned that earlier to this period (Year, 1459), the internal and external political order of the region was characterized by political upheavals. The studies of Marwar during the 14th century has significantly revealed the changing political scenarios. The picture that had emerged are one of significant continuities of conflict between Rana of Mewar and Rathores of Mandor, featuring relentless raids and an unremitted looking of conquered lands, a portrait of chaos and anarchy, devastation and doom.

In about 1438[2] Mandor was conquered by a Mewar ruler, who belonged to the Rana dynasty.[3] Rawat Chunda, uncle of Maharana Kumba ruled Mandor from 1438 to 1453.[4] After one and a half decade of internal intrigues and alliances between the members of Rao Jodha family and others, Rao Jodha succeeded in recapturing Mandor from Rawat Chunda. Thus, Mandor came under the direct rule of Rao Jodha again and in 1458; coronation ceremony of Rao Jodha was held. In the second half of the 15th century Rao Jodha's clan divided into two branches: The older branch continued to rule Mandor and now Rao Jodha founded Jodhpur, a separate principality with its capital at Jodhpur, 6 miles away from Mandor and constructed territorial unit. From 1453 to 1489 Rao Jodha ruled over Jodhpur.[5]

The foundation of Jodhpur in the second half of the 15th century helped to forge a new identity for the Rathores of Jodhpur. The late 14th and early 15th centuries were a period of change in the region. Jodhpur—a new city founded, Mahrangarh fort was constructed and the old capital Mandor, ruled by Rao Jodha shifted to Jodhpur. The various political and administrative measures of Rao Jodha and his successors, who ruled Jodhpur during this period, had several political and socio-cultural consequences for the Rathores of Jodhpur. In this wider context in the middle of the 15th century the main features of Jodhpur were sketched.

The large geographical and linguistic region of Marwar lies in western Rajasthan. The term 'Marwar' has been interpreted in a number of ways. Local tradition regarding the origin of Marwar is recorded in the book of Pandit Vishveshwarnath Reu, entitled *Marwar-ka-Itihas* (in 2 volumes) published first in 1940 and revised in 1999. According to him, it has been derived from word 'Maru' + mad'.[6] The name of the eastern part of Jaisalmer was 'Mad' and it also touched the western part of Marudesh. In the course of time, the term 'Mad' was transformed into Vad. Thus the term 'Marwar' according to Reu was used for western region. Etymological issues aside, what is clear is that the term has been widely used over several centuries. In basic topographic terms, the region is covered by the sandy area which is called 'Thar desert' and lies in Jaisalmer and Barmer districts and joins with Sindh (now in Pakistan) in which its major part is situated.[7]

It is true that untouchables have been persecuted and marginalized through history by the upper caste Hindus. But what most people do not realize is that besides this truth, there is also a big sacrifice that is grim and tragic. What is kept from view is the unpleasant fact that it is the untouchable castes who were and continue to be, the worst perpetrators of caste atrocities in rural India. When a big lie conceals a big truth, it is like marrying off a woman in Purdah.

More than five hundred years ago, when the construction of Jodhpur fort was commenced in the year 1459, the rulers had a socio-religious tendency and performances of religious rites to invoke good fortune on the defenders and to ensure its impregnability. Therefore, to satisfy their socio-religious needs they followed this practice and moved quickly to the Pandit. As per advice of the Pandit, Rao Jodha performed the religious rituals of the foundation of the fort.

Dahima Brahman (late) Mahamahopadhyay Vidral Pandit Ram Karan Ashopa, an official of Marwar state, in his book *Marwar ka Shankshipt Itihas* published in 1933, commented:

"----किले (जोधपुर) की नींव देने से पहले गणपति दत्त ज्योतिषी को मुहूर्त पूछा गया तो उसने अर्ज किया कि सं. 1561 ज्यैष्ठ सुदी 8 बुधवार को बलिदान दिया जाकर ज्येष्ठ सुदी 11 शनिवार के दिन नींव खुदवा कर गढ़ को बनाना आरम्भ किया जाये और ज्येष्ठ सुदी–13 को दरवाजे का फासला बनाया जावे। नींव खोदने और उसे बूरने का मुहूर्त प्रातः काल में है उससे पूर्व दो मनुष्य जो अपनी रूचि से नींव में गडने के लिये तैयार हो बलिदान के निमित्त नीवं में गाडे जायें"।[8]

In this regard, there is a popular Doha (couplet); it runs as follows:

"पनरा सो पनरोतरै, जेठ मास में जाण
सुद इगियारस वार शनि, मंडियो गढ मेहराण।"[9]

There were problems of sacrifice of persons as advised by Pandit Ganpati Dutt, astrologer, but Pandit Ramkaran Ashopa in his narrative directs us towards voluntary sacrifice of two untouchables of Bhambhi community to invoke good fortune on its defenders and to ensure its impregnability in the Jodhpur Fort.

Pandit Ramkaran Ashopa later described the unlettered men who sacrificed themselves.

"---- दो भांबी रतना (कहीं राजिया) और कालिया नीवं में गडने को राजी हुए उनको रावजी (जोधा जी राठोड) ने मन वांछित देकर प्रसन्न किया। उनके वंशजो की इज्जत अन्य भांबियों की अपेक्षा अधिक है।"[10]

The sacrifice of Bhambhis was not featured in detail in historical manuscript compiled around 1459 and onwards which dealt with the history, inhabitants and institutions of Jodhpur. Pandit Vishveshwarnath Reu, a keen observer, also did not mention in details the sacrifices of the Bhambhis in his book *Marwar ka Itihas* written in 1940 and also revised in 1999. It only mentions in a footnote on page 92 of the book penned by noted historian (late) Reu:

"प्रचलित प्रथा के अनुसार जोधपुर के किले की दीवार के नीचे दो जीवित पुरूष गाडे गए। ये जाति के चमार थे इसकी एवज में उनकी संतान को कुछ खास सुविधाये और भूमि दी गई । किसी ख्यात में किले की दीवार के नीचे राजिया नामक चमार गाडा जाना लिखा है।"[11]

... but failed to highlight their sacrifice. India's intellectual, has not given any briefing on their remarkable and unforgettable sacrifice. It is not top historians alone to be blamed, but for the Rajputana historians, this too was not worth investigation. That this is an issue not investigated either due to bias, prejudice or discrimination. It is a problem faced by

Indian academia today that it is almost never talked about. Call it the dark side of globalization or sheer governmental apathy or academic apathy, the untouchables are seeing the dwindling of their past. It is this every day brutality of deliberate academic neglect.

Now untouchables in Jodhpur and in other parts ask certain fundamental questions. Why is the historian so reticent in describing their sacrifice? Why have untouchables remained so neglected? Is this not academic neglect, then what is?

Four centuries later, Rajia Bhambhi's first reference found mention in 1874 when Jodhpur state published a book entitled *The Jodhpur Fort*. In this book it had been stated:

'Its (Jodhpur) foundation was laid in 1459 AD, when a man Bambhi Rajia, was interred alive in the founds to invoke good fortune on its defenders and to ensure its impregnability".[12]

We get a fuller description of sacrifice of Bhambhi Rajia in *Guide to Jodhpur* published on the auspicious occasion of the visit of His Royal Highness Prince Albert, Victor of Wales. The *Guide to Jodhpur* was published by the order of H.H. Maharaja Jaswant Singh, CCSJ and Maharajadhiraj Col Sir Pratap Singh, KCSJ, Jodhpur.

"The Fort (Jodhpur) ... when the foundation was laid, a man Rajia Bhambhi by name was interred alive, as an auspicious omen, in corner over which were built two apartments, now occupied by the treasury and the Nakarkhana (country band). In consideration of this sacrifice, Rao Jodha bestowed a piece of land Raj Bai Bagh near Sursagar on the descendants of the deceased and exempted them from 'Begar' or forced labour".[13]

Another account by Administrative Medical Officer in Rajputana, Jodhpur, Dr Adams, JMS, MD, Meh. FRJPH, FRCSS, in his book *The Western Rajputana States*, published in London in 1900, described the sacrifice of untouchable under the landlord rule.

"The fort (Jodhpur) was built by Rao Jodha, the founder of Jodhpur city in 1459 A.D., and a man Rajia Bhambhi was interred alive in the foundations to invoke good fortune on its defenders and to ensure its impregnability".[14]

Similarly, another fuller picture of sacrifice of Rajia emerges in an account written by higher official of Jodhpur state and Political and Judicial Magistrate, Rai Bahadur Sukhdev Prasad, B.A., CIE around the second half of 1927. In his book *A Short Account of Jodhpur: Its History and Places of Interest* he described the incident:

"Its foundation was laid in 1459 AD when a Bhambhi named Rajia was interred alive in the founds to invoke good fortune on its defenders and to ensure its impregnability".[15]

I recall here two descriptions—one by Pandit Mahamahopadhyay, Rai Bahadur, Sahitya Vachaspati and another by an eminent Rajputana historian, Dr Gori Shankar Heera Chand Ozha, D Lit., of the sacrifice of Bhambhi Rajia in his book *Jodhpur Rajya ka Itihas* published in 1928 and other by another leading Rajputana historian Jagdish Singh Gehlot, *Jodhpur Rajya ka Itihas va Bhugol* published in the year 1938.

"---- राजूपत लोगो में यह विश्वास है कि यदि किले की नींव में कोई जीवित आदमी गाड़ा जाये तो वह किला उसके बनवाने वाले के वंशधरो के हाथ से कदापि नहीं निकलता। इसलिए इस किले की नींव में राजिया नामक भांबी (बलाई) जीवित ही गाड़ा गया। जहां वह गाड़ा गया था उसके उपर खजाना तथा नक्कारखाने की इमारतें बनी हुई हैं। भांबी के सहर्ष किये हुए इस आत्म त्याग और स्वामिभक्ति के बदले में राज्य की ओर से उनके वंशजो को भूमि दी गई, जो अब भी उनके अधिकार मे है और वह 'राजबाग' के नाम से प्रसिद्ध है।"[16]

"इस किले की नींव राव जोधा जी राठौड़ ने सम्वत 1516 की ज्येष्ठ सुदी 11 शनिवार को रखी थी और उस नींव में राजिया मेधवाल गाड़ा गया था क्योकि राजपूतो में एक विश्वास चला आता है कि यदि किले की नींव में कोई व्यक्ति जीवित (पुरूष) गाड़ा जाय तो वह किला उसके बनाने वालो के अधिकार मे सदा अभय रहेगा। इस विचार से ही जोधपुर के किले की नींव में एक हरिजन (अछूत) जीवित गाड़ा गया था। उसके ऊपर खजाना तथा नक्कारखाने की इमारते बनी हुई है भांबी (बलाई) के इस सहर्ष किये गये आत्म त्याग और राज भक्ति की एवज में राव जोधाजी ने उसके वंशजो को जोधपुर किले के पास सूर सागर खेंडा में कुछ भूमि दी जो आज भी उनके अधिकार में है और वह "राजबाग" के नाम से प्रसिद्ध है। इस अपूर्व त्याग के कारण राज्य की ओर से प्रकाशित हुई कई पुस्तकों में राजिया भांबी के नाम का उल्लेख श्रद्धा से किया है और होली के त्यौहार पर भांबियों की गैहर (जुलूस) को किले में गाजे बाजे से जाने का अधिकार प्राप्त है जो अन्य किसी जाति को नही है।"[17]

Besides, there are other references that too describe the sacrifice of Bhambhi Rajia. Instead of providing here a detailed catalogue I will take references occurring in some of the important studies which also have wider significance. During 1938, state administration had published, *Jodhpur Illustrated*. The book added:

"Its (Jodhpur fort) building was commenced in 1459 A.D. when a Bhambhi named Rajia was buried alive in the founds to invoke good fortune on its defenders and to ensure its impregnability".[18]

Nine years later, just before the independence of the country, the state administration again published a book/report entitled "National

Anthem of Jodhpur State" in the year 1947. The report on princely state, Jodhpur, in context of the foundation of Jodhpur Fort in 1459, noted:

"On Saturday, May 12, 1459 when the foundation of the fort (Jodhpur) was built a religious rite was performed and a Bhambhi Rajia was interred alive to invoke good fortune on the defenders and to ensure its impregnability".[19]

Was there More than One Bhambhi Interred Alive in the Founds of Jodhpur Fort?

As has been noted earlier that the historical reference over the past several decades, had significantly cleared the picture. The historical references in various studies, reports and also in the history of Jodhpur state confirm the sacrifice of Bhambhi Rajia, but some of the existing writings on the subject also had different views. What one has to do when there is different opinion about the number of persons buried alive in the foundation.

There are some questions which are to be answered when someone writes on "Recognition of Untouchables' Sacrifice at Last".

How many Bhambhis were interred alive in the foundation of Jodhpur Fort under Rao Jodha's reign? Indeed, if Rajia Bhambhi alone was buried, then it was a single one and not others. But if we go by other eminent historians, it was more then one Bhambhi's sacrifice.

Here is what some of the country's top historians have to say. Asserts renowned historian and author of *Marwar ka Itihas* (revised in the year 1999) Pandit Vishveshwarnath Reu,

"प्रचलित प्रथा के अनुसार जोधपुर के किलें की दीवार के नीचे दो जीवित पुरूष गाड़े गये। ये जाति के चमार थे इसकी एवज मे उनकी संतान को कुछ खास सुविधाएं और भूमि दी गई। किसी किसी ख्यात में किले की दीवारो के नीचे राजिया नामक चमार का गाड़ा जाना लिखा है।"[20]

It is true and certain that two Bhambhis were buried in the foundation of Jodhpur fort, but their names have not been mentioned anywhere. Only Rajia Bhambhi's name has been mentioned.

Another historian Pandit Ramkaran Ashopa corroborates Reu's views. It is only he, who in his book *Marwar ka Itihas*[21] mentions for the first time that there were two Bhambhis namely Bhambhi Ratna (elsewhere called Rajia) and Kalia, whom Rao Jodha buried alive in the foundation of Jodhpur Fort. He also refers to some of the concessions granted to their families.[22] Others like Prem Bhandari[23] says that two persons were buried in the foundation of the fort. They were Chamar by caste. But their names have not been mentioned anywhere.

However, there is another twist in the tale of history. *Agyatdarshan* a special issue of 1984 published by Pandit Bhoj Raj Twivedi[24] clearly states that due to difference of opinion amongst the historians, someone mentions "Ratna, Nalia and Rajia's name who were buried alive in foundation''.

Besides, the rulers also maintained the records through ख्यात and ताम्रपत्र (Tamrapatra) issued to their royalists. Geneologists (Bhatt) maintained the caste and community records.

Naval's speculative history is corroborated by other sources also. Here is what other sources such as ख्यात, ताम्रपत्र and archives have to say.

We get a fuller description of the establishment of Jodhpur Fort that had been constructed over the fifteenth century in an essay "Jodhpur Durg ki Isthapana" written by eminent historian Dr Mahaveer Prasad Gehlot which was published in *Agyat Darshan*, Vol. 7 No. 2, 1984. Mahaveer Prasad Gehlot referring to the writings of late historian Jagdish Singh Gehlot described the horoscope of Jodhpur Fort.

"13 years back Rajputana's top historian (late) Jagdish Singh Gehlot published his book "Marwar ka Itihas". On page 119 of his book, he mentions about the laying of foundation stone of Jodhpur fort along with नक्षत्र map. The records of horoscope of Fort and ताम्रपत्र issued to Bhambhis were available in Jagdish Singh Gehlot's library. But now these documents are missing".[25]

However, a copy of the most important old historical document lying with the Meghwals of Shahpura was obtained by Naval. According to him this is a most reliable document. He also mentioned for the first time that the copy of the same document was also available with Mahaveer Singh Gehlot. He got an idea from this document as to how many Bhambhis were buried in the laying of foundation of Jodhpur Fort.

''सायपुरारा बांभियारै कनै हकीकत पुराणा पाना में लिखी है तिणरी नकल श्रीरामजी सयछै

श्रीगढ जोधपुरा वांभी कडेलांरी मुरजाद री वीमतः मुरजद राव जोधाजी बांधीः तिणारी नकल

गढ मंडोडर रा चूंडाजीरा वांभी हुआः कडेलो छतौः राजोः मानोगःराव चूंडारा वांभी वसोरा हुआ। अमर वांभ लाग मुरजाद कर दीनीः राव जोधाजी जोधपुर वसायो समत 1515 रा जेठ सुदी 11 ईग्यारस वार षुक नक्षत्र अभीज भौमसीग पहाड़पर चीडीयानाथजी री

धूणी हुती नीवंर धकै सो धुणी उठाई नही नीव तौ बांकी भली भली तिण समं आतस करी। जिद नाथजी धुणी चादर मै धाल नै कोस नव पीयाणो कीनो जीद लारै गया। नाथजी कीयौ बतीसौ लागे तो नीव सूंपरण हुवै तिण समै कडैलो मोहणसी बेटी देवस देवसीरी माता इण तीनां ने नीव में दीना संमत 1515 रे काम आया तीण समै मोहणसीरा बेटा मी माणकनं वधारो दीनो देवसी जूंझार हुवा, वादादरी विगत''–[26]

''भीचरडी गांव पटै, बारे कोसांरी पड़त खालझंरी अमर वांभ, वारै मीनां मै दोय सिरपाव, होली दीवाली, सोनो रूपौ पेरणनै पेटिया 6 छाटाक हमेस, नासाण झंडा रूपे जरां रूपीयो 21 दसरावे ससतर तुटे जीकोः सेर मे कांसा भांणा च्यारः चुंगीः अटल पंचायती वांभिंयांमं जोधपुररी सियाही ढुले जितरी दूरमै धणीरा तेज प्रतापसूं सही छैः चाकरी वादे छडो रथ, धारारेः नगारो नोपतः चांतरांरी चाकरीः सही छे सेर मैं सायपुरारो वास वांभीयांरो छेः अमरपटैः धणीरां तेज तपे सहीः वांभी मैगे नाडी मेगोलाई खिणाई गावं भीचरडी शनै तीणरी सीवं 200 हलांरी राव जोधजी बगसीस कीनीः कडोला मेधा ने सीचं वांभीयारी छे नाडी रो नांच डेडोलोई छे स्मत 1530 बरस तीसे''[27]

In his book *Marwar ka Amar Shahid Raja Ram* published in 1994, Naval had clarified on page 14 that to verify the fact stated above, he himself perused and examined the genealogical records (Bhato ki Bahiya) of Raja Ram's family maintained by Rao Prahlad (a community of genealogists) a resident of Pali Marwar, Jodhpur, who corroborates the Shahpura documents' version. The version is as follows:

''सेहर जोधपुर : साहपुरा स्मत 15 वर्ष जेठ सुद 11 षनीवार श्री जोधोजी जोधपुर कीला री नीवं देवण रो मोहरत वेदीयां ने पूछैःजदे जोतसी केवेः नीवं में मनीष जीवतो बतीसो दिरावो तो ठीक रेसीः जेदे राव जोधीजीः कडेला ने बांकारिया तो कडोलो : मोहणस ने मोहणसी री जोडायत और उणरो पुत्र देवजीः देवजी ने राजु कवे है। देवगती पाई ने देवजी नाम हुं वो राजु नाम है एकण धर रा तीन जीव नीव में चुणी जीया है, कोला रे उतराद मे इण तीनो रो थडो थाने पुजीजे है। मोहणसी रा पुत्रः माणकः मेगाने 3 तीन गांव पटी सुदा पटे कर दीना गावं भीचरडी 1, वीनायकियो 2, डेढोलाई 3, और 12 बारे कोसरी मुवाडा डोर रो पालडीः और होली दीवाली आषातीज रा दसरावो सवा सवा रूपियो तेवार दोठ कडेला नैः और सेहर में कांसा भाणां अठल कडैला नै जोदपुर री सीहाई सीच है जठे तक भांभी जीत जात में कडेला री पंचायती ने कमर धुलाई रो सवा रूपियो ने पाट शीचांणो कडेला ने मील सी और अमर वाभं है बारे मीना में दो सीरोपाव कपडा ने0 6 पेटियां सुतरीः कडेलो मेगाराम नाडो रो नाम मेगोलाई है ढेडोलाई भी कैवे है।''[28]

He confirms this when he says "three persons were buried alive in the foundation of Jodhpur Fort, but nowhere their names had been mentioned".

शाहपुरा रे भांबियो रे चाकरी री विगत' is reproduced below as it is:

''शाहपुरा रे भांबियो रे चाकरी री विगत–राव जोधाजी अटे धर बसायो तरे श्री चिडियानाथजी धुणी किला री नीव में तीन मीनख दीरोजे ता किलो वरदायक हुओ तरा

मेधवाल एक मेधवाली एक बेटी एक जुमले तीन मारे बढेरो ने नींव में दिया तरे उपर नीवं चाली। महाराज जसंवसिंह जी काबुल पधारिया तरे कासीद हलकरा रो जावण रो सबुब नही तरे मेधवाल गोरधानियो कागद समाचार के साथ रो भेष करने काबुल गयो। बडा महाराज श्री अजीतसिंह जी गुणरोध पधारिया तरे मेधवाल चार साथे चाकरी मे था सो दोय तो उठे ही सरसावु हुआ दोय पाछा आया। बडा महाराज श्री अभयसिंगजी गुजरात पधारिया तरे मेधवाल चार साथे हा सो उठे ही सिरसदक हुआ। देशनोक री माता ने बतीसो चढायो। रोतडा रे वरस दीखणियारो धेरो थो तरे किणी सावणी सुकुनी कयो बरस एक रो भैस मारने उणो रे पगने माथे दीखणी री फोजरी पायगो मे गाडने आवे उधर दार दारू री धार देवो तो फौज नास जावे तारे इस तरे मारे बुढे रा रू करी–महाराज श्री विजयसिंगजी खुशी खुशी पधारिया चाकर साथे था सम्वत 1863 रा वर्ष मे था सो ढेरो तो गमायो ने श्री दरबार रो जीडो पछै घेरो मायूस नगारा रे वास्ते हेटे उतरिया सो बारला पकड लिया सो दीयों ने तो मारनाकिया दोय जालोरी में जावतां वचिया सम्वत 1864 रा वर्ष में सोवणी सिन्धु मारिया गया गए गढ उथली थी तरे श्री खांचद सु पाछी मालम हुई तरे श्री खांवदा पखानी कर दियो तीका हाजर छै इस तरे री मांरी चाकरी छै कोटवाला भोलावे सुं बेगार काडां और नगारखाना रा चाकर हां ने फिरंगी री बैठ बेगार काडा हां और सारा बढेरा बंदगी चाकरी मोकली पूगा तरे श्री दरबार सुं आजमी ने पेटिया श्री दरबार सुं दरिजिया सो 27 पीढी रा चाकर हां आज पेला तो मांरी उधर रही ने हमे आगे उपर रे छे ज्यो ही धणी राखी चाइजे में तो खांवदां री कीडी मकोडी हां मांरा वढेरा इस तरे री बन्दगी पूगा हा हमे खांवदा री मरजी में आवे जुं कर जो मांरो वढेरा बतीसो तीन दिन नीवं में दिया तरे उण वक्त राजख्त माने पेटिया राज दिया।"[29]

The various sources describing the sacrifices of Bhambhis could be seen as reliable. They have also confirmed that more than one Bhambhi were sacrificed. They also praised the sacrifices made by the Bhambhi community.

Amidst these unanswered questions, there are other pertinent issues. Did poor Bhambhis really surrender voluntarily for being interred alive in the foundation of the fort or were they pressurized under Rao Jodha's administration? The evidence is extremely fragmentary. Here is what some of the country's top historians and others have to say. In the last decade of 1890 the Jodhpur state published a book *The Jodhpur Fort*, commented.

"In consideration of his (Rajia's) sacrifice Rao Jodha bestowed a piece of land 'Raj Bai Bagh' near Sursagar, on the descendants of the deceased and exempted them from 'Begar' or forced labour".[30]

The book did not however specify the willingness of Rajia. Instead, the book merely described the concession granted to his family members. At the same time the writings indicate about the voluntary surrender of Rajia.

There are other scholars who corroborated the Jodhpur state's version. In the year 1928 Gori Shanker Heera Chand Ozha, a Rajputana Brahmin, whose acquaintance we have already made earlier, clarified:

"भांबी के सहर्ष किये हुए इस आत्म त्याग और स्वामी भक्ति के बदले में राज्य की ओर से उनके वंशजों को भूमि दी गई जो अब भी उनके अधिकर में है और वह "राजबाग" के नाम से प्रसिद्ध है। इस अपूर्व त्याग के कारण राज्य आदि की ओर से प्रकाशित होने वाली कई पुस्तिकों में राजिया के नाम का उल्लेख श्रद्धा के साथ किया गया है।"[31]

Similarly, Pandit Ramkaran Ashopa another Rajputana Brahmin confirms this when he says:

"नींव खोदने और उसे बूरने का मुहूर्त प्रातःकाल में है। उससे पूर्व दो मनुष्य जो अपनी रूचि से नींव मे गड़ने के लिये तैयार हो, बलिदान के निमित्त नींव मे गाड़े जावें।"[32]

Also there is a definitive reference in "कमठां री विगत" wherein it is clearly noted:

"राव जोधाजी बतीसो एक भांभी रो राजीयो ले नै हमार खजाने रै सामीं जूनी बुरज है, तिण में बलिदान दे छाली है।"[33]

The founder of Rajasthan Meghwal Parishad, a great social reformer and eminent social activist, Swami Gokul Das published his book *Meghvans Itihas* in Vikram Samvat 2050. In his discussion of "Raja Ram (Rajia) ka Vratant" Swami had stated:

"राजिया के इस सहर्ष किये हुए आत्म त्याग एवं स्वामी भक्ति की एवज में राव जोधा जी राठौड ने उसके वंशजों को जोधपुर किले के पास सूर सागर खेड़ा में कुछ भूमि दी जो आज भी उनके अधिकार में है। यह राजबाग के नाम से प्रसिद्ध है और होली के त्योहार पर भांबियो की गेहर को किले में गाजे बाजे के साथ जाने का अधिकार है जो अन्य किसी भी जाति को नही है। परन्तु उस वीर के आदर्श बलिदान के सामने यह रियायत कुछ भी नही है।"[34]

At the same time he had emphasized that in comparison to the concession granted, the sacrifice of Bhambhi Rajia was more greater.[35]

We have noted that in consideration of his sacrifice, Rao Jodha promised a bonanza of concessions including the land 'Raj Bai Bagh' near Sursagar to the descendants of the deceased. According to Naval, 'Raja Ram Park' in the present day was founded around the eighth decade of 20th century by Urban Improvement Trust, Jodhpur. The inscription on the hoarding states as under:

"सूर्य नगरी जोधपुर की स्थापना के लिए किले की नींव में अपने आपको सहर्ष जीवित बलिदान देने वाले स्वामी भक्त शहीद राजा राम जी की अमर यादगार में नगर

सुधार न्यास द्वारा निर्मित शहीद राजाराम पार्क–राज बाग जोधपुर शहीद राजाराम की याद को स्थाई बनाने के उददेश्य से इस पार्क का निर्माण करवाया गया"[36]

Finally, evidence from other writings, corroborates and confirms the perception of earlier scholars, when Naval says:

"बल पूर्वक बलिदान किसी एक व्यक्ति से करवाया जाना सम्भव हो सकता है, मगर यहां तीन व्यक्तियो का और वह भी एक ही परिवार के लोगो का बलिदान हुआ है। इसलिए यह स्वैच्छिक ही हो सकता है।"[37]

What was the Situation of the Untouchables including Bhambhis within Hindu Social Hierarchy in the Erstwhile State Administration?

The main feature of the Hindu social system in the late 19th century has been elaborated in detail in chapter 20. The socio-economic difficulties of untouchables were compounded by the principles of its subordination within the caste order. Instead of providing here a detailed catalogue, I will take references which occurred in some of the important studies, administrative reports, Gazetteers, census reports, and in ethnographic description which have wider significance. The untouchables including Bhambhis and Chamars were not allowed to enter temples of higher castes and worship since it was believed that their touch would desecrate Hindu gods and goddesses and their presence would pollute the priests and devotees at the place of 'puja'. Similarly, their children were not admitted in the schools. The houses of the Bhambhis and Chamars were located in a separate neighbourhood, invariably situated at a distance at the end of the village and condescendingly referred to as 'Chamar Para' or 'Bhambhi Para' by the upper castes. In the village too they were made to sit at the down side, separately. The upper castes would shout 'Ded' or 'Chamar' or 'Bhambhi'. They had a separate ghat in the village pond to bathe and wash their clothes and Bhambhis and Chamars drew their water from separate wells. They could not carry an umbrella nor wear a turban. They were forbidden to ride a horse. The restrictions were geared towards maintaining the rites of rank within the village.

If Bhambhis wore shoes and crossed the Rajput village, they (Rajputs) would say "Ded, take off your shoes". They (Bhambhis) had to take them off and carry them in their hands when passing in front of Brahmins and Thakurs. It is clear from the above description that they (untouchables) were living in terror.

All this raises important questions about the willingness of the untouchables within a rigid and discriminating social system. Did poor

Bhambhi, Rajia have any option other than to surrender himself to Raj order? We have noted that there was nobody to hear the complaint of the untouchables including Bhambhis against the upper caste Hindus as the caste character of Raj administration was weighed against untouchables. It is significant that opposing the Raj order required courage. A series of questions remain. Was the opposition of Raj order by the untouchables in general and Rajia in particular possible at that time? Was violation of social order, customs and ritual by untouchables not to offer the severe punishment for them? Were the untouchables offensive? In almost every area, it was necessary for untouchables to cope with the prevailing system.

In the last decade of the twentieth century Rajasthani historian, Jagdish Singh Gehlot, who in his essay "जोधपुर के किले की नीव में राव जोधाजी ने राजिया भांबी की बलि चढाई थी" described the terrible conditions of the untouchables. The essay was published in the local daily newspaper '*जनगण*' Jodhpur, on October 27, 1991. In his discussion Gehlot had exposed the hypocrisy of rulers, the Rajas. He had depicted the conditions of untouchables.

"प्राचीन इतिहास में पृष्ठ उलटकर देखे तो वे हरिजनो और दरिद्र प्राणियो के शोषण, उत्पीडन और उन पर सामन्ती तत्वो द्वारा किये गये पाशविक अत्याचारो की दु:खद धटनाओ से रक्त रंजित मिलेगे। सामन्ती काल में देशी राज्यो में हरिजनो की बड़ी शोचनीय दशा थी। इस मानव मेदिनी की दयनीय दशा पर किसी ने ध्यान नही दिया। अपितु उन्हे समाज से तिरस्कृत किया गया। उन पर नाना प्रकार की पाशविक यातनाएं ढाई गई। यहां तक कि उनकी नरबलि देना सामन्ती तत्व गौरव समझते थे... पुराने समय में इनकी क्या दशा थी, इस विषय में यह लिख देना काफी है कि विक्रम सम्वत 1516 (ई0सं0 1459) में मोर की पूछ के आकार वाले जोधपुर किले की नीवं जब सिन्धु के पुष्करणा ब्राहमण ज्योतिषी गणपत दत्त उपाध्याय के मन्डोर के राजा राव जोधा जी राठौड के हाथ से रखवाई गई तब नींव में बांभी(बलाई) राजिया मेधवाल ज्येष्ठ सुदी 11 शनिवार (12 मई) को जीवित चुना गया था।"[38]

From the available description, there is doubt about the sacrifices. But why alone untouchables and not any other? Since they were weak, feeble and helpless, I feel that is why they had selected to be interred alive in the foundation. A similar trend could also be seen in other regions of the country.

Acharya Guru Prasad K.P., a well-known writer of Delhi brought out some more incidents where the untouchables were interred alive in other regions of Rajputana and also in neighbouring states. He described various incidents as manifestation of the sacrifices of the Bhambhis or

Meghwals. We get a small description of the buried Bhambhis or Meghwals that had occurred in the 12th century in an essay entitled "राजस्थान में पूर्व सामंतो का आतंक हटाना जरूरी"[39] published in *Hakdar*, Bikaner, November 2005 (second half). According to him, by 12th century, the sequence of events had increased.

In Vikram Samvat 1114 in the state of Ajmer, Mahachand Meghvanshi[40] used to graze his cows and other animals. The place where he used to take animals for grazing was surrounded by small mountains. The descendants of the then Maharaja Prithviraj Chauhan, namely Raja Nahar Singh of Ajmer, faced an acute shortage of water in that area. To overcome this problem, digging of the ponds in that area was begun by the Raja. A few months later, Raja was told that due to rock earth water had not emerged in the pond. Brahmins advised the Raja, Nahar Singh that if someone surrendered voluntarily to be interred alive in the pond then water would come up. An appeal was made by Raja, but nobody turned up. Recognizing and respecting the will of Raja, Mahachand Meghwanshi surrendered himself voluntarily to be buried alive in the pond. Soon after this, water emerged in the pond. The famous pond is known as Pushkar. A ghat called Gau ghat was dedicated in the sweet memory of Mahachand Meghvanshi.

Similarly, we recall here two complementary descriptions, one related to Udaipur and other to Bikaner. Both were the then princely states.

"In Vikram Samvat 1439 Maharana Lakha of Chittorgarh began the digging of Pichhola Zheel at Udaipur. After digging of Pichhola Zheel, here again water did not emerge. This attracted the attention of Maharana. Then Manna Meghvanshi surrendered himself voluntarily to be interred alive in the Pichhola Zheel. Soon after this, the water emerged".[41]

"When Maharaja Bikaji founded Bikaner city, a daughter of Charan namely Karni, (later called Karni Mata) and her Guru Bhai Dashrath Meghwal—both took voluntary Samadhi at Deshnok, 18 miles away from Bikaner. The family of Maharaja Bikaner accepted the Karnimata as Kuldevi, i.e., family goddess. It is important to note here that here too Dashrath Meghwal was the first man to be worshipped by His Highness and then Karni Mata'[42]

Besides, Acharya Guru Prasad K.P. describes another important incident from a neighbouring state, Gujarat.

"In Vikram Samvat 1194, North Gujarat in general and in particular Patna (Unhalwad) touching the Thar desert of Sindh (now in Pakistan) was facing acute shortage of drinking water. Realizing the pitiable conditions in that area and also the effects of the frequent famines, Sidha Raj, the then Maharaja of Gujarat, began the digging of Sahastraling Talab. The feudal administrators were worried about the not emerging of water because of the sandy area. The worried Maharaja began consultations and invited Brahmins. Whenever and wherever Brahmins were invited, they suggested the performing of certain rituals. In this case too, the same story was repeated. The Brahmins advised the Maharaja to sacrifice a person who possessed 36 qualities if he desired to establish a Sahastraling on the pond. The water will soon emerge only after the performance of this ritual. It was, therefore, of paramount importance that a person must be searched who could sacrifice himself. His Highness's administrators began the search. The administrators did not find even a single person amongst the public and they found all the 36 qualities only in two persons, viz., the Maharaja himself and Veer Meghmaya, a Meghwal boy. The parents of the boy were approached and were requested by the Maharaja for sacrificing their son to satisfy the thirst of the public. What could be the parents' response to The Maharaja in the feudal system and in view of their low social status in the village life. Soon the parents gave their consent. At about the same time Veer Meghmaya was summoned also. After his consent and willingness the Meghwal boy,—Veer Meghmaya, sat on sacrifice stage. Soon after this, Sahastraling Talab was full of water. Several centuries have passed since the incident occurred but Gujaratis remember the sacrifice of Veer Meghmaya even today". In this regard, there is a popular Doha (couplet) which runs as follows:

"वीर मेधमाया नो आप्यो बलिदान पांच करोड गुजरातियो नो आस्मिता नो प्रतीक"[43]

Thus, Meghwals at different places during the feudal system sacrificed their lives in the public interest.

The problem lay with illiteracy and ignorance. As noted earlier, untouchables were the most backward community. Illiteracy was the root cause of their backwardness. Their children were refused admission in the schools. Untouchables' ignorance also meant that they were forced to work for others either for very low wages or without payment and that members of the community could not intervene through the agency of law courts, which were ineffective in redressing their grievances. Finally, the attitude of high caste Hindus, who reacted to religious, social and political awakening among the untouchables of the region by continuing practising social boycott and imposing further hardships compounded the problems and sealed the fate of the untouchables.

What were the solutions offered by the society? The society had already approved the solutions to cope with the social system at all levels.

In the year 1994, Naval published a book *Marwar ka Amar Shahid: Raja Ram*, whose acquaintance *we* have already made earlier, commented that self-sacrifice views cannot be confirmed. According to him the descriptions given by Gehlot could be seen as reliable that Bhambhi's might have succumbed to a rigid and discriminating[44] Hindu social system.

Rajia Bhambhi: A Sociological Profile of Illustrious Son of Mohansi

Now let us turn to the biographic sketch of Rajia Bhambhi. We get a fuller biographical sketch of Rajia through description of Bhambhi community, contribution of his parents and bonanza concessions and many other issues that had been raised in the 20th century in an account of a 92-page book entitled *Marwar ka Amar Shahid: Raja Ram* written by Chandanmal Naval and published by the Rajasthani Granthagar, Jodhpur, in the last decade of 20th century (1994). It is only he who has featured in details for the first time in this book. It is true that historians and other writers had mentioned for the first time Rajia Bhambhi whom Rao Jodha interred alive in the foundation of Jodhpur Fort, but was not described in detail anywhere.

It may be noted here that the sacrifice of Rajia Bhambhi which arose in 20th century amongst the untouchables attacked and bitterly criticized the upper caste historians and other intellectuals through the path of researches. Still these efforts by untouchable scholars did not jeopardize the monopolistic position of the upper caste historians with respect to the sacrifices of Rajia Bhambhi. Naval, however, tried to bring the socio-historical fact on surface through his writings. Thus, Naval became the first to write in details on all aspects of the incident.

Rajia Bhambhi was the illustrious son of Mohansi, who was at that time residing in Shahpura Bhambhi (Meghwal) Basti, Jodhpur. Initially his forefathers lived/resided in Jailsalmer in traditional style. Later on they shifted to Gujarwala for a brief period and then again moved back to Shahpura (also called Shaipura). Some of the relatives settled down in villages namely Khudiyala, Charai, Chamu and Jehlura situated a few miles away from Gujarwala.[45]

Shahpura, where Rajia's forefathers settled down permanently during 14th century and lived until 1549, had become the centre of attraction for Meghwals. Shahpura is situated near the old Municipal Council, Jodhpur (now Jodhpur Nagar Nigam) in the walled city. Shahpura is dominated by Bhambhis. According to old Bhambhi residents, when this Bhambhi Basti came into existence, it was isolated and was encircled by dense forest. Now this is still known as 'Bhambhio-ki-Basti, Shahpura'.

In Shahpura Bhambhi Basti, there is an old place called as 'Kadelo kee Khirki' (KKK). It is believed that it (KKK) was the old residential place of Rajia's parents and grandfathers where they lived until 1549. KKK is still in existence but in a very dilapidated condition. An old small Mandir (temple) is still there. It is known as 'Shri Dada ka Mandir'. A regular worship is performed. After marriage, couples visit this temple and offer prayers (जात देना) and good wishes to Mandir and it is said that these prayers are fulfilled. In a Chowk (open space) there is an old big Neem tree. Besides, there is another small Mandir of Chamunda Devi in KKK, where Rajia and his family members used to worship the Mandir which was their own.[46]

From a description of the family background of Rajia Bhambhi, his parents and forefather's life, as given by one of his biographers, Naval (1994), it has been mentioned that Rajia Bhambhi was born in Kadela gotra of Bhambhis. Another name by which Rajia Bhambhi was called was 'Deva' or 'Devshi'.[47] Similarly, historians and other writers called Raja Ram as 'Rajia' in local dialect.[48] His father, Mohani, a poor untouchable was passing his life in the traditional style. His mother, Kesar was a house wife. She was the daughter of Jiwan, a resident of Parbatsar. Manak was the elder brother of Rajia.[49] Megha was his younger brother and he took to public services. He constructed a pond (Talab) for drinking water for poor fellows in Bhichardi, a village situated a few miles away from Jodhpur, in Vikram Samvat 1530. It is called Magholai.[50] According to Gokuldas, the writer of 'Meghwanshi Itihas', Rajia was married to Gorabai.

The foregoing description of Rajia's family background shows that all historians and other writers including Naval maintain that Rajia was a Bhambhi, but nowhere it has been mentioned about his date of birth. The lack of education amongst untouchables of Marwar state and other regions of Rajputana can be explained in terms of certain interrelated factors. First, the upper caste Hindus treated Bhambhis and other castes as untouchables. They maintained their distance and did not admit their children in the schools and this made the Bhambhis and other untouchables lose all hopes of getting rid of discrimination. Hence, they were unable to get the benefits of education. Second and last, socio-economic and religious restrictions imposed upon them were so rigid that they were passing through dissatisfactory lifestyle and world-view, within the framework of orthodox Hinduism.

Notes and References

1. Pandit Vishveshwarnath Reu, *Marwar ka Itishas* Vol. I (in Hindi), Jodhpur, Maharaja Man Singh Pustak Prakasan, Mehrangarh Fort, 1999, p. 92
2. Ibid., p. 83
3. Ibid., p. 84
4. Ibid., p. 83, 84 and 87
5. Ibid., p. 84–85
6. Ibid., p. 1 Foot Note
7. Dasharath Sharma—general editor, *Rajasthan through the Ages*, Vol. I, From the earliest times to 1316 A.D. Bikaner, Rajasthan State Archives, 1966, p. 2.
8. Quoted by Swami Gokuldas in *Meghvanshi Itihas, Vikram Samvat 2050*, Ajmer, Arya Brothers Book Seller. p. 232
9. Chandanmal Naval, *Marwar ka Amar Shahid: Raja Ram*, 1994, Jodhpur, Rajasthan Granthagar, p. 86
10. Quoted by Swami Gokuldas, Ibid., p. 232
11. Pandit Vishveshwarnath Reu, 1999, Ibid., p. 92
12. Quoted by Swami Gokuldas, VS 2050, Ibid., p. 229
13. Ibid., p. 229
14. Ibid., p. 230
15. Ibid., p. 231
16. Ibid., p. 233
17. Ibid., p. 234–35
18. Ibid., p. 231
19. Ibid., p. 235
20. Pandit Vishveshwarnath Reu, 1999, Ibid., p. 92
21. Quoted by Swami Gokuldas, VS 2050, Ibid., p. 232
22. Ibid., p. 232. Also see Chandanmal Naval, Ibid., p. 11–12
23. Chandanmal Naval, 1994, Ibid., p. 12

24. Ibid., p. 12
25. Ibid., p. 12
26. Ibid., p. 13
27. Ibid., pp. 13–14
28. Ibid., p. 14
29. Ibid., pp. 14–15
30. Quoted by Swami Gokuldas, VS 2050, Ibid., p. 229
31. Ibid., p. 233
32. Ibid., p. 232
33. Chandanmal Naval, 1994, Ibid., p. 19
34. Swami Gokuldas, VS 2050, Ibid., p. 228
35. Ibid., p. 228
36. Chandanmal Naval, 1994, Ibid., p. 19
37. Ibid., p. 18
38. Ibid., p. 21
39. For more details, see, Acharya Guru Prasad K.P.'s essay entitled, "राजस्थान में पूर्व सामंतों का आतंक हटाना जरूरी" in *Hakdar* (Fortnightly paper), Bikaner, November 2005.
40. Ibid.
41. Ibid.
42. Ibid.
43. Ibid.
44. Chadanmal Naval, 1994, Ibid., 20.
45. Ibid., p. 6.
46. Ibid., pp. 7–9.
47. Ibid., p. 5.
48. Ibid., p. 5.
49. Ibid., p. 5.
50. Ibid., pp. 5–6.

2 The Mode of Existence of the Chamars in Traditional Rajputana Society

Untouchable Past

In the Hindu social system a large number of castes are outside the fourfold hierarchical varna division of the society. These exterior castes comprise a number of untouchable castes, whose physical contact is regarded as ritually polluting by the clean 'interior' castes and who are by and large, economically the poorest section of the country's population. The untouchables themselves are divided into many distinct castes and even have a complex hierarchical organization and some of them even practise untouchability in relation to the other untouchable castes.[1] The Chamars are also untouchables in Rajasthan and are placed at the lower end of the caste scale.

The Chamars are a caste of leather workers, village menials and agricultural labourers. Chamars, handling dead cattle and working in leather, have a low ritual status. Like the other castes working in leather in other parts of Rajasthan, the Chamars are also untouchables and placed at the lower end of caste scale. They correspond in status to Mochi, Khatik, Raigar and Jatia of Rajasthan distributed all over Rajasthan.

In Rajputana a number of terms are generally used for the untouchables. They are variously known as Panchama, Achhut, Asprashya, Dhed, Harijan and Dalit. In Rajasthan the term Achhut is used generally for untouchables. Achhut, Asprashya, Dhed and Harijans apply to persons whose touch causes pollution and directly refers to the 'untouchable' status of the caste. The term 'untouchable' was in use for many decades though it was regarded as a degrading appellation by the untouchables themselves. This was replaced by the name 'Harijan'. The word Harijan, meaning the children of God was popularized by Gandhi in

1932 as a new appellation for untouchables. However, this name also was found objectionable by the untouchables. In 1935, the name was changed to the scheduled castes by the British government, while Mahatma Gandhi preferred to call them Harijans meaning, the 'children of God'. The term 'scheduled castes' (SCs) was in use for many years. This was replaced by the name 'Dalit'—a term used for all those who formed one of the major groups of the untouchables.

The castes coming under this category are to be found in different parts of Rajasthan and are known by several other names such as Chamar, Meghwal and Balai in Marwar and western region, Meghwal in Mewar and Bikaner region, Chamar, Bhambi and Ramdasia in Jaipur, Bharatpur, Sawai Madhopur, Alwar, Ajmer, Jhunjhunu and Kota region. Their counterparts are Chamar, Balai, Jatav, Ramdasia and Meghwal in Delhi;[2] Chamar, Megh, Ramdasi and Ramdasia in Punjab and Haryana;[3] Meghwal, Jatav, Bhambhi, Chamar and Satnami in Madhya Pradesh;[4] Chamar, Bhambhi, Chamadia, Satnami and Meghwal in Maharashtra;[5] Balai, Chamar and Jatava in Uttar Pradesh;[6] Chamar, Bhambhi, and Meghwal, in Gijarat;[7] Madiga and Chamar in Andhra Pradesh;[8] Chamar in Bihar;[9] Chamar, Megh, Ramdasia in Jammu & Kashmir;[10] Bhambhi, Chamar, Chamgar, Chamadia, Madiga and Meghwal in Karnataka;[11] Chamar, Valluvan and Madiga in Kerala[12] and Tamilnadu;[13] Chamar, Ramdasi and Ramdasia in Himachal Pradesh;[14] Chamar Satnami and Madiga in Orissa;[15] Chamar in Tripura;[16] Chamar, Rabidas and Charmakar in West Bengal;[17] Chamar in Dadra and Nagar Haveli;[18] Chambhar in Goa, Daman and Diu[19] and Madiga in now Pondicherry.[20]

Throughout this book we shall use only the name Chamar to represent an ethnic category including the cognate castes of Rajasthan.

One thing is common to these cognate castes. Many castes in this category have a set of occupations centring around tanning and curing of hides and skins and as the castes following these occupations are to be found in almost all parts of India, the Chamar category encompasses a whole range of related castes. The name Chamar has been interpreted in a number of ways. It is argued that term 'Chamar' is derived from Sanskrit word 'Charmkar' meaning a worker in hides and the communities which compose of this group are variously known as Bhambhi, Meghwal and Balai, etc.

Classification of Scheduled Castes

Referring to the classification of castes of this level, the *Ethnographic Atlas of Rajasthan*, 1969[21] (based on Census of India, 1961) with reference to the scheduled castes and scheduled tribes said, in the last census the castes under the category of untouchables were under the category of 'scheduled castes' in the caste classification. Their present designation is 'scheduled castes'. They were grouped into five main classes and also under category of miscellaneous castes and unidentified castes.

1. Castes traditionally associated with leather:

1. Chamar	2. Meghwal	3. Balai
4. Khatik	5. Bola	6. Bairwa
7. Dhed	8. Jingar	9. Dabgar
10. Pasi		

2. Castes traditionally associated with scavenging:

1. Bhangi	2. Mehtar	3. Valmiki
4. Chura		

3. Castes traditionally associated with crafts:

1. Koli	2. Sargara	3. Mehar
4. Gawaria	5. Salvi	6. Ghancha
7. Tergar	8. Kooch band	

4. Castes traditionally associated with music and entertainment:

1. Dom	2. Kalbelia	3. Nat
4. Dholi	5. Rawat	6. Bhand
7. Kamad	8. Badi	9. Bazigar
10. Bansphor		

5. Castes traditionally associated with criminal activities:

1. Bawaria	2. Bagri	3. Sansi
4. Kanjar	5. Bedi	

6. Miscellaneous Castes:

1. Thori	2. Majhabi	3. Dhanak
4. Garoda	5. Dhobi	6. Aheri
7. Santia	8. Chandal	9. Sar Bhangi
10. Singiwala		

7. Unidentified Castes:

1. Birgi	2. Bajgar	3. Adi Dharmi
4. Bidakia	5. Gandia	6. Godhi
7. Khangar	8. Mangarodi	

The first group consists of castes working in leather and curiously included: Chamar, Meghwal, Balai, Khatik, Bola, Bairwa, Dhed, Jingar, Dabgar and Pasi.[22] In Rajasthan the term Dhed is used for untouchables in general. It is also used particularly for the Chamars who skin dead cattle, cure the hide and also make shoes. They are agricultural labourers and village menials. Some of the castes such as Meghwal, Balai and Bairwa in this group are definitely regarded as Chamars in Rajasthan. Khatiks are butchers who slaughter goat and other sacrificial animals. They also specialize in the processing of the skins of sacrificial animals for the purpose of mounting them on hand drums etc., used as accompaniment to the devotional songs sung during religious ceremonies. Pasi is believed to be an offshoot of Khatik. Jingar and Dabgar are manufacturers of leather saddles and other accessories required for riding purposes and leather vessels and jars for storing oil. Bola's traditional occupation is skinning the dead animals and tanning and curing of hides and skins.

The second group consists of castes associated with sweeping and scavenging and includes Bhangi, Mehtar, Valmiki and Chura.[23] Bhangi and Mehtar are night soil removers and also practise their traditional occupation of sweeping and scavenging. Also allied to the Bhangis, the Valmiki and Chura have practically left their traditional occupation of sweeping and scavenging.

Some of the castes such as the Koli (weaver of coarse cotton clothes and also artisans), Sargara (makers of arrows), Mehar (spinners and weavers of coarse cotton clothes), Gavaria (makers of comb out of wood and sometimes from the horns of animals), Salvi (weavers of silk), Gancha (makers of baskets), Tirgar (manufacturers of bows and arrows) and Koochband (makers or binders and repairers of indegeneous brushes used in the process of sizing of cotton yarn and weaving of coarse cotton clothes by the Koli and Mehar communities of weavers have been classified in third group[24] consisting of 8 castes associated with craft.

The fourth group[25] includes those castes that were associated with music and entertainment, such as Dom (singers and entertainers), Kalbelia (popularly known as the Saperas or the snake charmers). Their traditional occupation is begging by exhibiting reptiles, which they rear. Nat (also called Nuts associated with singing, dancing and performing acrobatics), Dholi (musicians and drummers), Rawal (entertainers particularly for the community of Charans), Bhand known for their ready wit and humour, their art of storytelling, jokery and buffoonery, the Bhands provide entertainment and fun to the people on festivals and feasts with the aid of their exciting fables and satires, Kamad (also called Kamadia, singing songs in the praise of Ram Deo to the accompaniment of the Rawanhatta or Tamboora), Badi akin to Nats. They show their acrobatic feats only to Meghwals or Bhambhis, Bazigar (also called Madari Bazigar, the musicians) and Bansphors (musicians who provide company on Dholak, Sarangi or the Rawanhatta to the dancing girls).

The fifth group[26] consists of castes associated with criminal activities such as Bawaria also known as Baoni (notorious for its criminal activities), Bagri, Sansi, Kanjar (also called Kunjar) and Bedia (also called Beria) wandering criminal tribes.

The sixth group[27] consists of miscellaneous castes such as Thori (also called Nayak—professional thieves), Majhabi (mostly of the Sikhs but socially possessing an inferior status in caste hierarchy, as having been recruited from low or exterior Hindu castes), Dhanak (also called Dhankia—grooms and menial servants who used to carry out the work of general scavenging), Garoda (also called Garo, Garuda or Gurda—a community of priests of Bhambhis and other low castes), Dhobi (washerman), Aheri (also known as the lower class Thoris, once used to live solely as hunters and fowlers and beg with the Bhangis on the occasion of an eclipse), Santia (traders in cattle, specially in the trade on exchange basis), Chandal (associated with the Hindu crematorium, where they receive some of the articles from bier such as shroud, certain utensils and cash), Sarbangi (also known as Aghories, Sarbhagi was once notorious as a caste of gang robbers and nuisance makers) and Singiwala (indegeneous surgeons who treat people by taking out the impure blood out of the body with the aid of an animal horn called 'Singi'). It is not clear as to how some of the castes, such as Majhabi, Dhanak, Garoda and Dhobi in this group were lumped together. They should have been grouped with the first or second groups and should have been placed with other unrelated castes. Some of the castes such as Dhobi in this group are definitely not regarded as untouchables in Rajasthan.

The lumping together of castes in a group of seven[28] appears still more confusing. Some of the small castes such as Birgi (also called Vargi or Bargi, engaged in cultivation and worked as agricultural labourers) Bajgar (engaged in cultivation and as agricultural labourers), Adi-Dharmi (appear to have taken to their present name only a few years ago after having completely dissociated themselves from their traditional occupation, i.e., tanning and curing of hides and skins), Bidakia (engaged mostly in cultivation), Gandia (engaged in cultivation), Godhi (engaged in cultivation), Khangar (engaged in cultivation) and Mang Garodi (associated with the arts of showmanship, jugglery and magic). Mang Garodi, a caste of magicians who should have been grouped with music and entertainment group, have been placed with other unrelated castes. Defects in the above classification were soon realized and these castes were reclassified into two groups: scheduled castes and scheduled tribes. Chamars are one of the scheduled castes.

To the above (Census of India, 1969) list of fifty-five, were gradually added many more castes so that the total number added up till now has risen to eighty-two.

Popular Traditions, Hegemonic Hierarchies and Communities of the Chamar

An attempt is made in this section to present a generalized picture of the position of Chamar caste as an individual and identifiable unit of social organization.

Considerable confusion still exists in regard to the use of the terms caste and sub-caste in the anthropological and sociological literature concerning Rajasthan. No clear indices have so far been developed to classify a group definitely into one or the other of these categories. For the purposes of the present work the twin criteria of identification and acceptance as the main determinants governing the recognition of the caste have been used. When a group identifies itself as a caste and is so accepted by other communities, it has to be called a caste. It is in this sense that this term has been used throughout.

As stated earlier Chamars are known by several other names, such as Meghwal, Bhambhi and Balai. Details for these categories are given in succeeding paragraphs.

Chamar

The Chamar do not have any written history. Their legends and traditions too do not take us very far. History throws very little light on their origin or on the development of their society.

The Chamar is one of the major communities found in almost all the states of Northern India as well as in other regions. They are known differently in different areas and as such include many sub-groups. Their community name is derived from the Sanskrit word Charmkar, meaning leather worker. The name Chamar has been interpreted in a number of ways. Some earlier writers like Geo. W. Briggs also believe that the tanners of leather, the preparers of skins, the manufacturers of leather articles and makers of shoes belong to a well defined class in the Indian social order. Most of these workers, in upper India, are today included under the general term 'Chamar'. This occupational group can be traced back to very early times. Tanners (Charjamna) are mentioned in the Rig-Veda, in the later Vedic literature and in the Brahmanas. Tanning, Mlamna, is also spoken of in the Rig-Veda and certain details of stretching and wetting hides probably refer to the process of manufacture.[29] Writers like Ibbetson also believe that the name Chamar is derived from Sanskrit word 'Charmkar',[30] meaning a worker in hides.

Some earlier writers like Ibbetson, Crooke, Elliot, Briggs etc., have dealt with all castes found in Hindu society. There are different legends dealing with the origin of the Chamar. Some of the important are as follows. According to this legend,[31] in the beginning, there was but one family of men and they were all Brahmins by caste. In this family, there were seven brothers. Once they were preparing food in the field; it so happened that a calf of cow fell down into fire and died immediately. The six older brothers agreed that their youngest brother should carry away the dead body. After much pulling and hauling, he managed to drag the dead body to the jungle. When he returned from jungle his brothers refused to accept him and outcast him. They told him that henceforth he was to do the work of a Chamar, that is, to skin the animals that died and to make leather and implements of leather. The brothers promised to take care of him in return for these services. Thus, Chamar caste came into existence.

Sir Henry Elliot represents[32] them as a dark race and a fair Chamar, he says is a rare object as a black Brahmin. The Marwari Chamars have the reputation of drinking water very often, as a saying runs: 'Ghoran ghas ne Chamaran Pani', i.e., the Chamars drink water as constantly as the horses eat grass.[33] A slightly different version of this legend of cow is given in Geo.W. Brigg's,[34] *The Chamar*. In this version also the central theme is that of carrying away the dead cow. Briggs writes: "Men say that, in the beginning, there was but one family of men and they were all of the highest caste (Brahmin). They worked in the fields and followed other callings. In this family there were four brothers. It so happened that a cow died one day and the body lay in the courtyard until evening. Since no one could be found to remove the carcass, the three older brothers agreed that their youngest brother should carry away the carcass and that afterwards, when he had bathed, they would receive him on the old footing of equality. To this he agreed. After much pulling and hauling, he managed to drag the carcass to the jungle. When he returned from his bath, his brothers refused to accept him as their brother, but compelled him to live at a distance from them. He made a great fuss about it, but his complaints were of no avail. They told him that henceforth he was to do the work of a Chamar, that is, to skin the animals that died, and to make leather and implements of leather. The brothers promised to take care of him in return for these services. Thus, the Chamar caste arose".

Another explanation connects the caste name to the group's practices of dealing with leather as their profession. Chamar means Charmkar. Charma means leather. Thus, they came to be known as Chamar. Still another popular legend related by many Chamars also incidently explains the origin of their name. According to this legend, five brothers, Brahmins, while out walking one day, saw a carcass of a cow by the roadside. Four of the brothers passed it by, but the fifth removed the body. Thereupon, he was excommunicated by his brothers. His descendants continue to remove the carcass of cattle.[35]

A slightly different version of term Chamar is given in H. Kotani's (ed.), *Caste system, Untouchability and Depressed* (1999). In this version also the central theme is that of disposing and skinning of dead animals. Masanori Sato writes,[36] "they (Chamar) were engaged either in the traditional/hereditary occupation of disposing of dead animals and its related tasks as their main occupation or in agriculture along with their main occupation".

A reading of Hindi translation of the Urdu book entitled, "Chahar Gulshan: Mukaddama" by Sahibjada Shokat Ali Khan and translated by Mohammad Riyajuddin Khan reveals the fact that "Chamar means who prepares the shoes".[37] The Chamars were unclean and untouchable community. Yet they had a sort of warrior right. For instance, they had conquered Kashmir and ruled for decades, together. According to Sahibjada Shokat Ali Khan, the Chamars ruled Kashmir for 38 years. Sukharman was the last Chamar Raja who reigned for 6 months and 7 days. Sahibjada Shokat Ali Khan also mentions that the son of Shanker Verya was the first Raja who ruled for nearly 18 years. According to

Dainik Bhaskar,[38] June 29, 2004 "Itihas ke Aaina Mai: Kashmir"- the Chamar, ruled Kashmir between 855–883 and 883–902 AD.

A certain Brahminical tradition give the Chamar a respectable ancestry and attributes his outcaste condition to the violation of Aryan laws. Risley[39] writes that, according to the Puranas, the Chamar descended from the union of a boatman and a Chandal woman. But scholars identify them with the Korawara or leather worker mentioned in the tenth chapter of Manu's Dharma-Shastra. The father of the caste was Nishada (the offspring of a Brahmin father and a Sudra mother) and the mother of Vaidehi (offspring of Vaisya father and a Brahmin mother).

The clan of Chamars is divided into several parts/groups. Thus, according to Devi Singh,[40] the Chamars of India are divided mainly in 83 gotras. They are:

1.	Ramrana	2.	Rana	3.	Kataria
4.	Balia	5.	Sahogal	6.	Santhal
7.	Paliwal	8.	Paraliya	9.	Puraliya
10.	Parle	11.	Rathore	12.	Rathariye
13.	Khevriye	14.	Khobar	15.	Patiyan
16.	Jaijhariya	17.	Kureel	18.	Jawalia
19.	Munkhia	20.	Patel	21.	Notiyal
22.	Dabre	23.	Dabse	24.	Sidhde
25.	Joshia	26.	Jenania	27.	Maurya
28.	Gaur	29.	Sindhe	30.	Sindgva
31.	Sakarwal	32.	Maliyan	33.	Chawreliye
34.	Pataliye	35.	Lakarpad	36.	Lamba
37.	Kathale	38.	Morchave	39.	Bhukhade
40.	Bhaskar	41.	Kapardwal	42.	Kapale
43.	Mitharia	44.	Bamnia	45.	Peguwal
46.	Karnutadiye	47.	Babre	48.	Baraswal
49.	Kaliyan	50.	Adliyan	51.	Chandehal
52.	Pundeer	53.	Kurian	54.	Jatav
55.	Buliyan	56.	Sanwal	57.	Jindwal
58.	Chichariya	59.	Satparia	60.	Thaparwal
61.	Baliban	62.	Bhistiyan	63.	Rawat

Cont'd...

Cont'd...

64.	Daharwal	65.	Mature	66.	Bhenswal
67.	Kuchaliya	68.	Dhirwania	69.	Badodiye
70.	Hiranwal	71.	Sihanmar	72.	Kaliyan
73.	Datiya	74.	Muger	75.	Diwana
76.	Chapediya	77.	Jantarparia	78.	Menwal
79.	Tejaypan	80.	Gupade	81.	Madtale
82.	Mandel	83.	Rana		

Altogether different number of class/groups were given by Swami Gokuldas.[41] According to him the Chamars of India were divided into 552 clan groups.

Alphabetically they are as follows:

S.No.	*Alphabet*	*Number of Gotra*
1.	A, AA	22
2.	E, EE	7
3.	U, UO	10
4.	AI	1
5.	KA	57
6.	KHA	20
7.	GA	15
8.	GHA	6
9.	CH	14
10.	CHHA	10
11.	JA, JHA	25
12.	TA	16
13.	DA	14
14.	DHA	7
15.	TA	6
16.	THA	5
17.	DA	13
18.	DHA	5

Cont'd...

Cont'd...

19.	NA	30
20.	PA	34
21.	PHA	6
22.	BA	77
23.	BHA	30
24.	MA	27
25.	RA	19
26.	LA	22
27.	SA	37
28.	HA	17
	Total	552

Altogether different number of clan groups were given by Ramesh Chandra Gunarthi.[42] According to him the Chamars of Rajasthan were divided in 84 gotras. Actually he has named only 64 clans. They are:

1. Gehlot	2. Chauhan	3. Pawar
4. Sisodiya	5. Rathore	6. Padiyar
7. Patodaya	8. Gharavanya	9. Ghamandiya
10. Yadav (Jadu)	11. Puwariya	12. Cheral
13. Kumari	14. Bhihanjaya	15. Bargada
16. Bagrri	17. Jogchand	18. Bamnia
19. Vajad	20. Gava	21. Tatiya
22. Kalera	23. Khonda	24. Bhamar
25. Rajodia	26. Tukadiya	27. Mandavaria
28. Khelwar	29. Rangota	30. Ishlanya
31. Koyla	32. Barakala	33. Bharkanya
34. Bhibanya	35. Rayakwal	36. Khatriya
37. Ratdiya	38. Shihanya	39. Jatava
40. Mahar	41. Talvalaya	42. Bhakhand
43. Aakodiya	44. Gomlad	45. Marmat
46. Meemrot	47. Nagvada	48. Barchunaya

Cont'd...

Cont'd...

49.	Bansanval	50.	Jeenwal	51.	Bohra
52.	Paralaya	53.	Jaharwal	54.	Vandwal
55.	Junwal	56.	Charvandiya	57.	Khapariya
58.	Tafvariya	59.	Rasval	60.	Bathara
61.	Gadwal	62.	Banjara	63.	Damdiya
64.	Barala				

Further, altogether different number of sub-castes, were given by Crooke. According to him (1896), there were sixteen major sub-castes with eleven hundred and fifty-six, subdivisions among the Chamars in the North-Western provinces at that time.

Meghwal

Some writers like Hardayal Singh, Bajranglal Lohia and others have tried to trace the origin of the term 'Meghwal' from Megh Rishi. According to these writers the Meghwals take their name from their Rishi—Megh. In some regions of Rajasthan, Megh or Meghwal is synonymous with Bhambhis. Hardayal Singh writes:[43] The origin of supremacy of Brahmin Megh Rishi is obscure and shrouded in legend. According to one of them, once upon a time a cow died in heaven. To remove the carcass the great God then rubbed his body and from the perspiration a strong man arose. The great God then named him Meghchand. In Meghchand family, there were four sons namely Ranghi, Joga, Chand and Adra. The great God then directed all the four sons of Meghchand to collect the dead cattle and skin them in the Mratlog (earth). They obeyed. Thus, Meghwal sprang.

According to another legend,[44] it is true that Meghchand was a Brahmin by caste and was called Megh Rishi. It so happened that during a social crisis Megh Rishi ate flesh of the dead cow. The Brahmins were very angry with Megh Rishi. Thereupon, he was excommunicated by his caste fellows. He was to have a degraded life and was to earn his livelihood by handling dead cattle. Since then his descendants continue to remove the carcass of cattle. The caste still follows the occupation which their ancestors got as a curse from the castes.

In Rajasthan there were several clan groups. The total number of clans, among Balai and Meghwal, according to Ramesh Chandra Gunarthi, are 84. Altogether different number of clan groups were given by Heeralal Janagal. According to him the Meghwals of Rajasthan/India were divided into 293 clan groups. Altogether different number of clan groups were also given by the same writer. According to him[45] (Heeralal Janagal), the Meghwals of India were divided into 723 clan groups. Alphabetically they are as follows:

S.No.	*Alphabet*	*No. of clan group*	*S.No.*	*Alphabet*	*No. of clan group*
1.	A, AA	32	2.	E	7
3.	U	10	4.	A	1
5.	Ka	81	6.	Kh	39
7.	Ga	33	8.	Gha	6
9.	Ch	24	10.	Chh	13
11.	Ja	30	12.	Jha	10
13.	Ta	16	14.	Da	15
15.	Dha	9	16.	Ta	11
17.	Da	24	18.	Dha	7
19.	Na	41	20.	Pa	40
21.	Pha	6	22.	Ba	90
23.	Bha	35	24.	Ma	35
25.	Ra	21	26.	La	24
27.	Sa, Sha	46	28.	Ha	17

Source: Meghvans Ismarika, 1997, pp. 96–98.

Altogether different number of gotra groups was given by Naval.[46] According to him the Meghwals of Rajasthan were divided into 542 gotra groups. The prime gotras of Meghwals are as under:

Amloha, Ahniya, Amoor, Amlaee, Arodhya, Aalriya, Aafriya, Aalyan, Aaglecha, Adanaya, Aayach, Aasarmya, Atraya, Aavla, Aagrale, Aadwa, Aashrawat, Anitya, Aatedaya, Amaratya, Aadam, Aasavera, Indlaya, Ilayachya, Indoliya, Indorya, Echoraya, Inkiya, Idiwal, Ulawat, Ugrava, Ucholaya, Umarchaya, Umardhya, Ujaraya, Uchal, Uthya, Ukhlaya, Umedha, Apea, Katala, Katariya, Kalsana, Kakarwal, Kakradya, Kalesanya, Kanwas, Kahosarpa, Kadayala, Kalsiya, Karoriwal, Kerwadya, Kaleva, Kablya, Kuchawal, Koorwadya, Kamya,

Kalu, Kalavat, Kantiwal, Kandi, Kagiya, Kajalya, Kadiyan, Kakran, Kagliya, Kasriya, Kirad, Kardiwal, Kikralya, Koocharya, Kilanya, Kachhawa, Kasumba, Kadvasara, Kardala, Kudas, Koodasara, Kooladiya, Koolariya, Kuntiya, Kundalwal, Kunawat, Koodiya, Kochwan, Kudkiwal, Kukadwal, Keshwal, Kelodiya, Kakedya, Kelvadya, Keloya, Kekavada, Kolda, Kolya, Karelya, Khati, Khareta, Khatana, Khajuriya, Khari, Khardiya, Khathan, Khkhad, Kharakval, Kharavdya, Khajvanya, Khapdiya, Khagunya, Khakdya, Khatavalyan, Khurtalya, Khada, Kherasa, Khalya, Ganthiya, Gadodiya, Gangali, Gadher, Gadhawal, Gujraniya, Gugarwal, Gujriya, Guneshar, Gunagunawat, Gothiya, Gorawat, Godara, Godeta, Gothan, Gadiyal, Gashiya, Ghatiya, Gotan, Gotewa, Ghorbar, Chandaniya, Chaniya, Charan, Chamaliya, Chitiya, Chitodiya, Charaniya, Chopdar, Chunbhuk, Chunva, churan, Chananiya, Chatarwal, Chandsona, chachiwal, chachiya, Choganwal, Chalkhal, Chagniya,. Chichliya, Chowana, Chochowal, Chogan, Chaparwal, Jaswal, Jalwaniya, Jamanwal, Jalava, Jharwal, Jhakad, Jhantiwal, Jorasiya, Jogal, Joran, Jooraya, Jhotwal, Jod, Jajhodhya, Jola, Jadam, Jethwa, Javir, Jharcha, Jhalmalya, Jasmera, Jhadela, Jaipal, Jethaniya, Josidhya, Tatvadaya, Takanya, Tidal, Tidwal, Tikawat, Tidlaya, Takadiya, Togdiya, Tandalya, Tatlodhya, Tabodaya, Tankba, Takanaya, Tardaya, Tikalwal, Tandiya, Dadwashi, Dahonwal, Dadwal, Dadwana, Dalan, Dangi, Dumolaya, Dahanwal, Dahwal, Dangar, Dalwadi, Doondlodhya, Dangolaya, Doongoliya, Dhadalwal, Dhaywal, Dhabana, Dhakoliya, Dhanwal, Dhiciwal, Dhotwal, Tanan, Toondwal, Todya, Tolawat, Taji, Talaniya, Tharanya, Thuvariya, Tharalya, Jhadoda, Danodhya, Doogriya, Dookhariya, Dujrana, Depu, Debu, Dasdeya, Dewan, Doobariya, Dakriya, Daslanya, Doraya, Darig, Datarbal, Dharavana, Dhodhavat, Dhaniya, Dhanavat, Nardiya, Nagar, Nolsaya, Nimoreya, Naraneya, Nar, Naharwal, Nagri, Nemasaya, Nafriya, Nebhal, Neemrod, Neemranaya, Neemoil, Kuniwal, Nan, Nanakwal, Nakhal, Nalaya, Napa, Neemchal, Needawat, Nagoriya, Naralaya, Narada, Naravada, Nagoda, Narnoliya, Pathriwal, Palayana, Patlayan, Panchal, Parin, Pindar, Pachariya, Padhya, Palariya, Pariya, Pokharwal, Pahariya, Pahadhya, Paliwal, Padir, Pakhadya, Pannu, Panva, Pakhariya, Padot, Parasatival, Pudiwal, Punya, Peeguniya, Panoriya, Parwal, Paluchya, Parala, Pipralya, Paperwal, Palasya, Parela, Patoriya, Poonad, Phatolaya, Phanan, Phasal, Phadan, Phool, Phakar, Badar, Bayawat, Borana, Bofla, Badolya, Bakri, Burala, Bajaniya, Bariya, Barbar, Barundana, Bagchi, Barmaniya, Bunara, Basarwal, Barayala, Barulaya, Basunaya, Banwal, Barumandiya, Baru, Basar, Badundhya,

Bagar, Bindawat, Bariwal, Baseer, Bahiwal, Bavar, Boonya, Barala, Badgotiya, Baservadiya, Bal, Baderwal, Bajad, Banodiya, Bandholiya, Bagarwal, Bardiya, Badboliya, Brahmhote, Baniya, Bagra, Bagotiya, Bagoriya, Basudhya, Braundhya, Basu, Bootya, Basanya, Bagana, Bavalya, Basanwal, Bayala, Beesor, Beeroda.

Areawise Gotras of Meghwals

Areawise gotras of Meghwals are Gehlot (Gahlotya), Ostiwa, Goda, Devgava, Khiwansara, Kansad, Karsand, Kalsad, Karsindhu, Kardiya, Khayati, Khand, Kholari, Gahlotra, Sisodiya, Chuhada, Bikundhya, Gora, Khadpa, Ghoghawat, Ranwa, Talpa, Kachhwaha, Singla, Chadwal, Khohwal, Kanhad, Rathore, (Rathorya), Loyama, Mahayach, Bandra, Jodha, Bagra, Ajeriya, Yadav, Bhati (bhatiya), Kadela, Kilanaya, Kaliravan, Kalecha, Kalwa, Kadwasara, Kalera, Kahanival, Kohli, Kharivas, Khudival, Jaam, Khobada, Gardva, Janagal, Dava, Dewala, Dehravariya, Depan, Pateer, Patodhya, Barvad, Saun, Leelad, Poonad, Kanwalya, Singhmor, Khamiwal, Jhatiwal, Khokhar, Palasaya. Boodiya, Aayach, Ankhya, (Inkhaya), Khuvara, Khatri, Tanwar, Boodagava, Moladhya, Lahkara, Javalya, Gothan, Godanwal, Saloriya, Godhiya, Gorawat, Goyal, (Gohil), Gorkhya, Dhal, Kelwal, Dhaiwal, Gorva, Chauhan (Chuhanaya, Chunya), Idiwal, Gothwal, Momtya, Karkediya, Narnolaya, Bhatanaya, Jevariya, Sogan, Kala, Pateer, Khathi, Jeeloya, Jeenwal, Neemadya, Barolia, Narvan, Solera, Nijranyan, Nirval, Nirbani, Khichi, Khardya, Nalya, Chahil, Sendariya, Panwar, Morodya, Daypanoo, Jatawath, Barla, Lojadiwal, Suvatwal, Ladna, Mahranaya, Kathoriya, Tikawat, Bochaya, Seela, Bhavratia, Shakhala, Chaniya, Sada, Saravata, Gunpal, Seju, Khamb, Jatiwal, Siyal, Subal, Solanki, Shyalva, Suvaliya, Bavalya, Padihar, Kadnochaya, Kalshi, Kadvasra, Kavadiya, Kerad, Kardiwal, Kikraliya, Kadecha, Kadeliya (Kadola), Kulriya, Gurahiya, Gujraniya, Jethaniya, Nathdiwal, Goud, Gandera, Gadeh, Gevan, Gathir, Chandel, Pavatwal, Chandela, Makwana, Makana, Dahiya, Adanaya, Bhungariya Johiya, Gharat, Badgujar, Padvadiya, Nagwa, Tak, Chawara,

Meghwals' Brahmin Gotras

These are Aratwal, Ajmera, Avarwal, Antariwal Antariwal, Inaniya, Kannad, Kalshi, Karda, Kasanwa, Kaslaya, Koothwal, Gandhi, Bamaniya, Basiwal, Layadiwal, Dahima, Taddhiya, Pareek, Garva, Kirat,

Gudesar, Dagwal, Bambhi, Ludar, Sahajwal, Mahad, Vashist, Shaliwan, Bhirat (Bharat), Singra, Patodhaya, Bandar, Sindarya, Bhuwal, Itodhya, Kuradwa, Jajodhya, Didwanya, Malodhya, Jadlaya, Mundel, Karasa, Aashopya, Halsura (Harsulaya), Sirgota, Raithala, Balaya, Dehwal, Suvatwal, Guru, God, Saraswat, Dhananjaya, Bhati, Bayala, Gadwal, Surela, Guglaya, Jalera, Rasguwal, Gang, Bharadwaj, Bavalya, Shandil, Bhamboriya, Dayala Bhigotaya, Patodhya, Bagara.

Meghwals' Vaishya Gotras

These are Aashwara, Goyal, Khandelwal, Chopra, Chaparwal, Jhawar, Dhudhya, Dhakar, Baniya (Banya), Baldwa, Rathi, Maheshwari, Chorda, Chapuniya, Chitrolaya, Buradiya, Somani, Naharwal (Nahar), Nogja (Nogava).

Bhambhi

The Chamar of Western Rajasthan are also called Bhambhi. They have a wide geographical distribution. They are scattered all over Rajasthan. A considerable number of them are found in every village of Rajasthan.

The name, Bhambhi has been interpreted in a number of ways. Some writers like Ramesh Chandra Gunarthi and others believe that the name 'Bhambhi' means 'Cryer' shouter or 'Dhundi Pitanewala'. According to a well established custom prevailing in those days they (Bhambhi) had to convey the message of Darbar to villagers orally. Those who conveyed the Darbar's message by shouting, were called Bhambi. A slightly different version of the term "Bamb" is given by Gunarthi's *Rajasthani Jatio ki Khoj*. In this version also the central theme is that of conveying the message of the Darbar. Gunarthi writes: that 'Bamb' means drum[47] and those who used to inform the villagers through drum beating the Darbar's order/message, came to be known as Bhambhi. Chamars, like other lower social groups, were also appointed as lower village officials. Colonel Walter[48] writes that from each village Darbar appointed a head Bhambhi in a village to whom Darbar presented a Pagdi (पगड़ी) and stick (लाठी) as token or symbol of his appointment which he usually kept with him. Thus 'head Bambhi' was popularly known as 'Gaon Bhambhi' (village head Bhambhi). Another name for Gaon Bhambhi was "Gaon Balai"[49] or 'Raj Balai'. In some other places they were summoned with following words: "Chhadidar" or 'Chofdar'. These were the honorific titles for them. They functioned as messengers, taking letters and documents from the village headmen to Pargana offices and neighbouring villages, helped the revenue officials in measuring fields with *doris* (ropes or chain) and in serving government officials when they visited the village on tour. Such officials were authorized to obtain services from village Bhambhi free of charge. Thus, such a person as rendered services to the villagers free of charge, came to be called 'Vamb'[50] ('Begar', forced labour). Thus he came to be called Bhambhi.

In the olden days the persons of Balai caste did spinning and weaving work. Thus, they (Balai) were also called Bunkar. Naval[51] says that Bunkars are also known as Bhambhis. 'Bhambhi' in colloquial Marwari means a 'person caller' or 'डोडी पीटने वाला'. In fact they summon or call the persons. 'Bhambha' also means Dhol (drum). Some scholars have tried to trace the origin of the term 'Bhambhi' from their traditional business of apprising the villagers (common men) about the Thikana's message through drum beating. Bhambhi means: those associated with this work, namely apprising the Thikana's message through drum beating. The Bhambhis did so in Marwar region and elsewhere, and had been operating for past several hundred years.

In Punjab and Jammu & Kashmir, they are called 'Megh'. They have tried to trace the origin of the term 'Megh' from Megh Rishi and their traditional business is weaving. Another title for Balai is Salvi in Gwalior and Bhopal in Madhya Pradesh. They are so called because they prepare or wear the रेजा (a cloth) and साल (shawl). Similarly, in Uttar Pradesh and Haryana, Balai are known as 'Chandor' weaving the clothes, had traditionally been the task of untouchables and those who performed this kind of work are known as 'Chandor'.

Bhambhi received[52] many dues for their work consisting of allowances in kind per plough, well or field or in kind at every harvest. They were given food at the time of marriage. In addition to this they were also given some money or goods by the government officials as a token of favour for the services rendered to them during their stay.

Besides the Chamar, there are numerous references showing that Bhambhi were also engaged in skinning of dead animals. Weaving has been the occupation which they are even practising at present. The social status of the Bhambhi has been the same as of the Chamar. Another name for Bhambhi is 'Balai'.[53] Likewise those who engage themselves in low grade profession such as removing and skinning of dead animals in villages were called 'Dhed'.[54]

It seems that they obtained a considerable income through their work. They were sometimes landowners or landholders, some of whom may have been granted land by village or village headmen.[55] They were so extensively exploited privately as well as officially under the patronage of village headmen that they were regarded as village servants by the British.

Now we shall briefly discuss the Chamar, Bhambhi, Meghwal and Balai of Rajasthan. In Rajasthan, from the early period, traditional Chamars admitted the outsiders into their fold. Gunarthi[56] writes that for Rajasthan the Chamars are grouped into two main categories—Adak and Sadak. The term 'Adak' was used for the traditional Chamars in general, whereas the term 'Sadak' was used particularly for those converted Chamars who were recruited in the Chamar caste from higher castes. This conversion is elaborated in Munshi Hardayal Singh's description of how members of Brahmin, Rajput, Jat and Charan castes in Rajasthan were lowered. Munshi Hardayal Singh[57] says: 'In times past, when Marwar was troubled by foreign invaders, a large number of Rajput, Jat and Charan joined the Bhambhi caste and thus in the course of time, there arose five sub-divisions among the Bhambhi which are as follows:

1. The Adu or unmixed Bhambhi.
2. The Maru Bhambhi comprising Rajputs.
3. The Bamnia Bhambhi comprising Paliwal Brahmins.
4. The Jata Bhambhi including Jats—1,128 males and 1,029 females have separately retained themselves under this head.
5. The Charnia Bhambhi including Charans.

It would thus be logical to say that in the case of Chamars, who seem to have been recruited during medieval times from several higher castes like Rajputs, Brahmins, Jats and Charans, cultural differences exist between the sub-castes. In fact, the Chamars like Jata Bhambhi in Rajasthan, do not intermarry within these sub-castes. These groups are more conscious of maintaining their old traditions and customs. Not only this, there is also considerable diversity in dress habits between different Chamar groups. In 1891 when Munshi Hardayal Singh wrote about the Bhambhi, Raigar, Meghwal and other castes of Marwar state, he observed:[58]

> The first two divisions (the Adu or unmixed Bhambhi and Maru Bhambhis) are very closely connected and intermarry, while the last two divisions only marry in their own community respectively. The Bhambhis are not allowed

to wear gold and silver ornaments, but an exception is made in the case of head village Bhambhi and his wife. There is striking peculiarity in the dress of men but the Maru Bhambhi women generally wear Ghagra or petticoat of country chintz, while the Jata Bhambhi dress themselves like the Jata women and are distinguished from the latter only by the use of lac Churas instead of ivory ones. The women of the Charnia Bhambhi wear the dress of yellow colour like the Charan women.

Traditionally, all the castes included in the category of Chamar do not enjoy equal status and have a hierarchy of sub-castes. Chamars in Rajputana have conventional matrimonial relations. Chamars followed patriarchal system of inheritance.

The clan of four sub-divisions among the Bhambhi were divided into several clans/groups. Thus according to Lohia,[59] the Bhambhi of Rajputana are also divided into 84 clans. They are:

1. Clans of Adu Bhambhi:

1. Rangee	2. Chandel	3. Aadra
4. Jogchand	5. Mechand	6. Jogad

2. Clans of Maru Bhambis:

1. Palecha	2. Parmar	3. Dangi
4. Sulankhi	5. Bamnia	6. Barari
7. Parihar	8. Thanavlecha	9. Bagani
10. Kudnecha	11. Palasash	12. Ranva
13. Mangariya	14. Aankhiya	15. Leva
16. Sonal	17. Kerala	18. Chavaniya
19. Loha	20. Charniya	21. Leya
22. Aaych	23. Bagdi	24. Muvarcha
25. Madru	26. Rawal	27. Ghilotiya
28. Achal	29. Aapa	30. Daiya
31. Karupa	32. Parghi	33. Gopal
34. Dadlia	35. Kachava	36. Pata
37. Hatela	38. Lukra	39. Khandiya
40. Magra	41. Sendu	42. Makwana

Cont'd...

Cont'd...

43	Barupal	44.	Sundal	45.	Ranghi
46.	Agrecha	47.	Chalndniya	48.	Agri
49.	Chikhra	50.	Mandoka	51.	Bhavru
52.	Kochiya	53.	Rida	54.	Mujariya
55.	Gada	56.	Varvara	57.	Gwdar
58.	Vagrecha	59.	Churiyala	60.	Shavela
61.	Vaniya	62.	Jaipal	63.	Lilar
64.	Makhan	65.	Janvaliya	66.	Vorana
3.	**Clans of Jata Bhambhi**				
1.	Depam	2.	Marankha	3.	Sakha
4.	Joram	5.	Chateliya	6.	Bamnia
7.	Vikuniya	8.	Jodha	9.	Chavaniya
4.	**Clans of Charnia Bhambhi**				
1.	Inda	2.	Champa	3.	Nagiya

Altogether different number of clan groups were given by Munshi Hardayal Singh.[60] According to him, Adu Bhambhis were divided into 6 clan groups, Maru Bhambhis 128, Jata Bhambhis 21 and Bamnia Bhambhis 3 clan groups respectively. Thus, the total number of clan groups according to Hardayal Singh are 158. The names of their clan groups/sub-divisions refer either to their ancestral villages or are related to their specific occupations. Some of these groups are territorial. These exogamous divisions are meant to regulate marriage alliance. They are patrilocal. Divorce and remarriage are socially sanctioned. The members of each group having similar patronymics are believed to have a common ancestry. They belong to the same family. Therefore, intra-clan marriages are forbidden.

Balai

The Chamar, Meghwal and Bhambhi of Rajasthan sometimes like to be called Balai also but they do not appear to claim any connection with any Rishi or king. There are several references to Balai and his duties and functions. Some writers like Hardayal Singh (first published in 1896, reprinted in 1997), Ramesh Chandra Gunarthi (1950) B.L. Lohia (1954).

T.S. Kataria (1964), U.B. Mathur (1969) and others have not discussed the origin of the term 'Balai' in detail because Balai corresponds to Meghwal or Bhambhi of Rajasthan in many respects. According to these writers, in some places or regions, they are called Balai, meaning the offspring of Meghwal. A version of the term 'Balai' is given in Swami Gokuldas's *Meghvans Itihas*. Swami Gokuldas writes:[61] "In village community of Rajputana princely states, there was a well-established tradition in those days which indicates the very presence of Balai in Thikana. Whenever the Thakur/Jagirdar/Jamindars or government officials required the presence of a particular person urgently, Balai went round the village, searched out and took him to the Thikana. Thus, the one who used to summon or call the person/s came to be called 'caller'. His descendants are called the Bulai which later corrupted into Balai".

Another explanation related by some writers also incidently explains the origin of their name (Balai). According to Gunarthi,[62] when something fell down in a well, a local instrument with large number of Panja called 'Bilai' is dropped into the well. This instrument has the quality to search and is meant only to get out the goods which fell down in the well. To search out the fallen down goods and to take them out of the well, Bilai is dropped. The moment the Bilai is dropped, it searched to help in bringing out fallen down goods. Likewise, according to the customs prevailing in those days whenever 'Thikana' or 'Darbar' required the presence of a particular person urgently, Darbar directed the person to search him out. Then he searched out and took him to Darbar/Thikana. Thus, like Bilai, the one who searched out the person came to be called Bilai. His descendants were called Bilai which later corrupted into Balai".

And what does Balai mean? Acharya Guru Prasad K.P.[63] an eminent Balai scholar, explained the term, as follows:

> During the period of Mahabharata, Kunti's sons (Karan and Pandav) were called Kontaya. Similarly, king Bali's (Aauras) and Manasputra were called Balayas: Later on it was corrupted or due to regional variation they were some where called Balai, Balahi, Barahi, and some where they were known as Rajbalai. Their main occupation was spinning and preparing both cotton and woollen clothes. Also they did agriculture work. Being a spinning community, they were also called Bunker, Vankar, Salvi, Kori or Koli and also some where Makwana. During the pre-historic period they worked as 'पदाति सैनिक' hence they were known as Megh (Meghwal) and Meghvanshi. Likewise, to encourage the पदाति सैनिक, persons who used to

beat the drum, played on Toorahi and Ranbheri, were called Vami or Bhambhi. Now all these castes are included under the category of scheduled castes.

As noted earlier, during the pre and post independence period, Garibdas Sahib had introduced the term for the first time and also encouraged the untouchable caste of Balai to adopt the term, viz., 'Sootrakar'. This initiative had been followed by the disciples of Garibdas Sahib and members of Akhil Bharatiya Sootrakar Mahasabha (ABSM). Under the guidance of Garib Saheb, ABSM was formed. A Constitution ABSM was drafted—ABSM placed a premium on the term 'Sootrakar' in its legal efforts to redefine Sootrakar identity. The constitution of ABSM, 1949[64] which discussed the aims and objectives of Mahasabha, powers of President, had explained the term 'Sootrakar' as follow:

"The descendants of pre-historic Rishi Kashyap, framer of Sootra of Vedas and other ancient Granths and manufacture of Sootra or Soot (Khadi) as specified in Vedas are called Sootrakar".

Traditional Rajputana Society and the Chamars

In Rajputana, as in other parts of India, however, the social life of the people was and also continues to be more directly restricted by customs and practices of smaller communities or Jatis. Iravati Karve,[65] a prominent sociologist, characterizes a Jati as a group "in which there is marriage only among the members of the group (endogamy) that used to be spread over a contiguous small area, the members of which generally had one or more interconnected occupations and that used to have a rank relative to all smaller group".

The Hindu population of the Rajputana may broadly be divided into following three caste clusters:[66]

1. Savarnas or caste Hindus from Brahmin to Vaishya,
2. Artisans—Blacksmith, Suthar, Nai, tailor etc., and
3. Untouchables—Meghwal, Chamar, Bhambhi, Balai, Khatik, Mochi, Bhangi, etc.

Besides these groups, there are Christians, Muslims, Sikhs and others who did not fit into any of the caste divisions of the Hindus in Rajasthan.

According to the social hierarchy, Brahmins were regarded as the highest caste and the Bhangis as the lowest of the low.[67] Since the

Bhangis and other lower untouchable castes, as has been mentioned earlier, fall outside the fourfold division of the Hindu social system, Hutton[68] has designated them as 'exterior caste'.

Most of the lower castes listed were usually thought of as being separate from varna system. But these lower castes were closely tied with caste system under the Jajmani system. The remuneration, in kind or cash was paid for the services which were rendered to upper caste Hindus by lower castes. The upper caste Hindus and other castes who received services were called Jajmans and castes who offered services to them (upper castes) were called Kamin. Thus, the right to obtain it was popularly called the Jajmani system. These groups which were generally called Kamins were: Suthar (carpenters), Lohar (blacksmith), Kumbhar (potters), Nai (barbers), Chamar, Meghwal, Balai, Bhambhi (all leather workers), Mochi (also shoe makers), Bhangi and Mehtar (sweepers) etc. Most of their services were essential to everyday life of villagers.

Of the lower castes, Meghwal, Chamar, Balai, Khatik, Mochi, Bhangi etc., were ranked as untouchables. The residing area of these castes called, for instance, Chamarwada or Chamaro-Ki-Basti, Bhangiwada or Bhangio-Ki-Basti were in most cases located outside the villages.

In Rajputana villages, as mentioned earlier the Chamar like other untouchables had their Bastis at some distance from the main settlement inhabited by upper castes. The fact that they cure hide and work in leather makes it necessary for them to build their huts at a place where they do not cause inconvenience to the upper castes. The fact that leather, specially uncured hides, pollutes the upper castes is significant. Leather ritually pollutes the atmosphere as well as persons working in leather and also the place where the work is done. The upper caste people who fear pollution from physical touch of Chamar and their place of work make it compulsory for them to choose a site which no clean caste person may have to frequent. The Chamar Bastis often give an impression of extreme poverty. Thatched huts huddled together, narrow and muddy lanes, children moving about in rags and tanning pots emanating revolting smell are a common experience there. The dwellings are unplanned, the lanes are narrow, zigzag and dirty. Children relieve themselves in the lanes. Hides, cured and uncured are hung on walls or on the trunks of nearby trees.

Seeing a Bhangi or Mehtar as the first thing in the morning or at the time of commencing a journey is considered a good omen by the upper castes including the Brahmin. But in case of other untouchables including

Chamar is considered an ill-omen. This is believed to bring bad luck. The upper caste persons so placed feel that they may have to go without food for the day or may have to encounter difficulties and hardships on the way. This makes it necessary for the upper caste people to have their houses at a considerable distance from them to avoid accidental encounters in the morning.

The scheduled castes in Rajasthan are composed of eighty individual communities. Of these communities eight communities are numerically major scheduled castes.[69] They are: (1) Chamar or Bhambhi or Jatav (2) Megh or Meghwal (3) Balai (4) Thori or Nayak (5) Koli or Kori (6) Khatik (7) Bairwa or Berwa and (8) Bhangi. These eight major scheduled castes together constitute the bulk of the scheduled castes population of Rajasthan for as much as 84 per cent of their castes total population is contributed by these communities.

Table 2.1 shows the distribution of the population belonging to these eight major communities with details of their main concentration and their proportionate strength in total scheduled castes population of the state.

According to 1971 census, the Chamars were classified into four major groups: Chamar or Bhambhi, Megh or Meghwal, Balai and Bairwa or Berwa. Of them the Chamar, i.e., the caste bearing this particular name, alone numbered 15,85,000 forming 38.9 per cent of the total population of the scheduled castes. The above figures, however, did not include some of the satellite castes which are dependent on and attached to the Chamar. The following are their figures according to 1971 census:

Attached castes	*Population*	*Percentage of total Scheduled Castes population in State.*
1. Megh or Meghwal	6,08,000	14.9
2. Balai	3,39,000	8.3
3. Bairwa or Berwa	1,40,000	3.4

Thus, on the basis of 1971 census figures the total number of Chamar including the attached castes would roughly work out to 26,72,000 forming 65.5 per cent of the total population of Chamar.

It is said that there is almost no village in Rajasthan in which there are no Chamars. A considerable number of them are found in the major districts of Rajasthan state. In Rajasthan they are concentrated mainly in

Table 2.1

Distribution of Major Scheduled Caste Communities

	Major Scheduled Caste Communities	*Population (in thousand)*	*Percentage of total Scheduled Caste population in state*	*Districts of main concentration (% share in brackets)*	*Percentage distribution in remaining districts*
1.	Chamar or Bhambi or Jatav	1,585	38.9	Bharatpur (14.0), Alwar (9.9) Sawai Madhopur (9.4) Jaipur (9.2), Jhunjhunu (5.5), Ajmer (5.2), Bhilwara (4.7)	42.1
2.	Megh or Meghwal	608	14.9	Jodhpur (14.9), Barmer (13.0), Sri Ganganagar (12.7), Pali (8.8), Bikaner (8.5), Nagaur (8.2), Churu (7.4)	26.5
3.	Balai	339	8.3	Jaipur (25.0), Sikar (17.1), Bhilwara (11.6), Udaipur (7.8), Nagaur (6.8), Chittorgarh (5.8), Kota (5.6)	20.3
4.	Thori or Nayak	221	5.4	Sri Ganganagar (39.4), Churu (12.0), Nagaur (11.6), Bikaner (7.9), Jhunjhunu (4.9)	24.2
5.	Koli or Kori	191	4.7	Jaipur (18.0), Sawai Madhopur (16.5), Bharatpur (16.2), Kota (9.4), Alwar (8.3), Sirohi (7.4)	24.2

Cont'd...

Cont'd...

6.	Khatik	152	3.7	Jaipur (14.7), Udaipur (9.9), Bhilwara (9.6), Ajmer (8.5), Alwar (6.4), Chittorgarh (6.3), Sikar (5.7)	38.9
7.	Bairwa or Berwa	140	3.4	Kota (28.5), Sawai Madhopur (21.4), Jaipur (20.8), Tonk (14.3), Bundi (9.8)	5.2
8.	Bhangi	182	4.5	Jaipur (11.2), Alwar (10.4), Ajmer (6.4), Bharatpur (8.2), Sawai Madhopur (5.9), Kota (6.9), Nagaur (6.8), Jodhpur (4.4).	39.8

Source: Census of India 1971, Rajasthan Series 18, p.x.

Table 2.2
Distribution of Scheduled Castes Population

State/District	*Population of Scheduled Castes*	*Proportionate strength (%)*	*Growth Rate (%)*
Rajasthan	40,75, 580	15.8	21.31
1. Sri Ganganagar	3,35,037	24.0	12.67
2. Bikaner	88,700	15.5	34.43
3. Churu	1,51,825	17.5	27.43
4. Jhunjhunu	1,30,054	14.0	31.17
5. Alwar	2,40,713	17.3	24.06
6. Bharatpur	3,11,305	20.9	26.72
7. Sawai Madhopur	2,52,578	21.2	19.73
8. Jaipur	3,99,525	16.1	23.50
9. Sikar	1,35,329	13.0	17.73
10. Ajmer	1,98,274	17.3	13.28
11. Tonk	1,23,174	19.7	16.47
12. Jaisalmer	22,612	13.6	19.39
13. Jodhpur	1,54,898	13.4	23.61
14. Nagaur	2,20,656	17.5	35.23
15. Pali	1,45,787	15.0	1.14
16. Barmer	1,11,429	14.4	23.51
17. Jalore	1,08,675	15.3	19.88
18. Sirohi	70,611	16.7	5.21
19. Bhilwara	1,67,031	15.8	19.17
20. Udaipur	1,39,976	7.8	9.82
21. Chittorgarh	1,28,910	13.6	26.44
22. Dungarpur	21,115	4.0	13.04
23. Banswara	24,774	3.8	14.17
24. Bundi	83,710	18.6	35.38
25. Kota	2,06,920	18.1	34.59
26. Jhalawar	1,01,962	16.4	22.78

Source: Census of India, 1971, Rajasthan, Series 18, Rajasthan Part V p. ix.

the districts of Bharatpur, Alwar, Sawai Madhopur, Jaipur, Jodhpur, Ajmer, Bhilwara etc. Although they are found in large number in other districts also.

The services they were required to do for villagers were enormously diverse. In the various administrative reports on the then princely states of Rajputana and also studies on the social structure of Rajputana cities and villages, point out various kinds of duties imposed on Chamars, which included encouraging or calling the villagers to pay the land assessment, to assist the Patwari in measuring the land in villages, to entertain the government officials on their visit to the village, carrying the official message to Pargana office and removing of the dead bodies of the animals left on the road. It can be said that, unlike other untouchables, they did not have any specific skills through which they could maintain their livelihood. Many Chamars engaged in agriculture as labourers had to leave their villages for neighbouring states to earn their livelihood.

The second largest untouchable community in Rajasthan is that of Thori or Nayak. Kolis or Koris, Khatiks and Bhangis are also in large numbers.

Besides these, the censuses listed some other untouchable castes, none of which, however were numerically large. One more aspect to be noticed about untouchable caste groups in Rajasthan is, as pointed out time and again, that there existed mutual animosity and discriminatory feelings against each other. An untouchable can himself be polluted by the touch of another untouchable belonging to a lower caste. Thus, idea of untouchability among the untouchables has been developed with much elaboration in Northern India. A century ago Blunt[70]—the then census superintendent of 1911 wrote about a few untouchable castes in Northern India.

"Eleven castes will not touch a Bhangi, seventeen will not touch a Chamar, ten will not touch a Dhanka, sixteen will not touch a Dhobi or Dom".

Among those castes mentioned earlier, for instance, there was a sort of hierarchy in which Chamars claimed the top list with Dholi, Koli, Nayak, Sansi, Kalvelia, Jatia, Bola and Bhangi below them claiming a higher position than others. T.S. Katiyar[71] reported that Chamars of Rajasthan claiming a higher status themselves do not accept food and water from them (other low untouchable castes). All Chamar castes eat food and drink water from Brahmin, Bania, Rajput, Bhil, Gujar, Mali, potter, barber etc.

In his detailed study on the Bhangis of Rajasthan, Shyamlal,[72] an eminent sociologist, notes that Bhangis have the lowest social status. Bhangis eat food cooked or handled by all the untouchable castes except by Dhobi and Dholi. They strictly refrain from food touched or cooked by them. They claim that Dhobi and Dholi are inferior to them and all other untouchables are inferior to the upper castes. Thus, Bhangi not only claim but maintain superiority over Dhobi and Dholi by refusing to eat food cooked or touched by them. Bhangi argues that they do not render their traditional services to these castes and therefore they are superior to them. The Dhobi and Dholi are the lowest of the low. Dhobi and Dholi are not allowed by Bhangis even to use the public latrines which are cleaned by them. A Dhobi and Dholi must not touch the Bhangi, for his physical contact or even his shadow is very polluting. If a Dhobi or Dholi touches a Bhangi, the latter becomes impure and has to take bath or sprinkle the Ganga Jal over his body to become pure. If a Bhangi elicits with a Dhobi or Dholi girl, the former is excommunicated forever. Their right to claim being superior to Dhobi or Dholi has been firmly established in the Bhangi mythology and tradition.

Devendra Pal Singh Tomar[73] a lecturer in Sociology at Janta Vedic College, Badot (Bagupt), Uttar Pradesh carried out a detailed study on five untouchable communities namely—Khatik, Chamar, Bhangi, Bahelia and Dom residing in Meerut Nagar Nigam Corporation, Uttar Pradesh during 1991–92. His study on untouchability among untouchables, points out that even after India's independence, Chamars claiming a higher status themselves do not accept food and water from the Khatik and Bhangis. The same study further gives us an example of the intense rivalry dividing Harijans (Bhangis) and Jatav seeking social superiority. Besides these, the study also listed some other cases. Tomar refers a case of excommunication from the caste. In 1972 in a marriage ceremony of a Khatik, Harijans and Jatavs who were the members of marriage band party, were served food along with the Khatiks. When this fact was brought to the notice of the Khatik Samaj later on, the Khatik Panchayat criticized bitterly and condemned it. Later on, the family of Khatik who had violated the social norms was excommunicated from the caste.

The low untouchable castes including Chamar appear to have suffered from mutual social discrimination more severely in native states.

In his study on "Anti-Untouchability Ideologies and Movements in Maharashtra from the late Nineteen Century to the 1930's", Masanori Sato,[74] quoting V.R. Shinde—a social worker, reported his bitter experiences on mutual animosity and social discrimination feelings against each other. Shinde points out that, "in a free boarding house built for untouchable students in Pune by the Government of Bombay, Mahar and Chamar opposed each other in demanding a separate cook from their own community .... "

Even after India's independence, a village survey reported that Chamars claiming a higher status for themselves, refused to mend the shoes of Mahars and Mangs and that a Chambhar who tanned hide was excommunicated from his community. In another village, Mangs who were engaged in work of carrying dead bodies of animals and also tanning, but unlike Mahars did not eat dead flesh, considered themselves higher in rank than Mahars. The same survey report gives us an example of the intense rivalry dividing Mahars and Mangs seeking social superiority. In a village marriage ceremony a Mang, who was served food after a Mahar rejected taking it, and another Mahar preceded by a Mang also did not receive food.

According to the description given in various administrative reports, Gazetteers, ethnographic description, census reports, books, newspapers etc., forms of discrimination against untouchables in Rajputana as a whole seems to have been so severe that 'untouchable' problem has assumed an important position in the socio-political life of Rajputana. The actual condition of the forms of discrimination and degree of discriminating consciousness are not difficult to gauge. In our context, it is true that types of discrimination experienced by untouchables are mentioned as bitterly as are by Ambedkar. The Chamar community, with which the present study deals, was the largest untouchable community in Rajputana.

As has been noted earlier, the Chamars were untouchables and as such, they were obliged to perform those tasks which were considered polluting Hinduism.

The integration of the Chamars into the traditional Rajputana society meant, therefore, that they were obliged to perform those tasks which were deemed polluting and unclean by the Hindus. As an untouchable, Chamars existed in the realm of the impure and this required their performing the most unpleasant tasks of the village. Their position also demanded that contact between them and the caste Hindus were strictly controlled and regulated by the norms of caste Hindu society. The position of the untouchables contained within it a curious circularity. They were impure by birth and therefore, were constrained to perform the most impure social duties. Yet the very act of performing these duties confirmed their untouchability and sealed the distance between them and the upper caste Hindus. One of the important issues of the Chamar reform movement consequently had been to reject the traditional tasks of Chamars especially pertaining to the handling and disposal of dead animals. This rejection had also figured prominently as a symbol and theme in the reform movement. Therefore, the refusal by Chamars to perform their traditional duties in the villages of Rajputana had significant socio-political repercussions. It had even occasioned violent conflicts between Chamars and high caste Hindus, particularly the Brahmins, Jagirdars, Jamindars who predominated in the village community.

Yet as long as the Chamars performed their traditional duties without reservation or complaint and as long as they accepted the stigma of their birth and behaved accordingly, the social order of the traditional Rajputana guaranteed their continued existence, if not their prosperity. During the princely states an individual Chamar was not permitted to follow other occupations, through which he could improve his position. Indeed the relationship between caste and occupation was rigid.

The state power maintained the socio-economic position of the untouchables and ensured that they did not deviate from their prescribed duties. Bhairulal Meghwal cites several cases from different areas which reveal the extent to which the upper castes supported the prevailing division of labour. Thus in several cases, the Chamars who had started non-traditional work were given punishment. The social and ritual order of caste, therefore, had socio-religious consent and the caste system acquired under the Rajput regime was directly related to the kind of decisions made by the socio-religious authorities.

Contact between Chamar and the caste Hindus took place within well specified and circumscribed limits. Like other untouchables Chamar could not live within the village proper or even too close to the village. They had to maintain discreet distance from the caste Hindus. Therefore, they had to reside either in some block (Mohallas) on the outskirts of the village or in their own hamlets away from village. Thus, it can be said that 'Residential pattern in a village'[75] has been an indication of caste discrimination. This discrimination may also have been true in the case of other untouchable castes in Rajputana.

This will be evident from the following two statements on the condition of untouchables which also appeared in the *Hindustan Times*. The first appeared in the issue of March 8, 1945, written by one Kesarilal Bordia,[76] Head Master of a school called 'Vidya Bhawan' in Udaipur. It reads as follows:

> Many are the disabilities under which the Harijans in Mewar live. They cannot enter in temples, nor can they draw water from the public wells. They cannot join the caste Hindus in festivals and processions. They have to take out their Rath Yatra or Doll procession through a different route and on a different day. And they cannot ride through the village.
>
> Even silver ornaments, let alone gold ones on their person are resented by the caste Hindus. The result is, they have to content themselves with the tin and brass articles. Age-old usage prevents them from using butter or gur in wedding feasts.
>
> In schools and other public places Harijan boys cannot sit with the children of caste Hindus. They are asked to absent themselves on the inspection day in order to save the Inspector from embarrassment.
>
> A Memorandum has been submitted to the State Government. If the Government chooses to declare in unequivocal terms the disapproval of these disabilities, the hands of Non-official bodies which are fighting untouchability will be strengthened.

The second was in the form of a statement issued by the President of the Harijan Sevak Sangh and refers to the condition of the untouchables in the state of Mewar. It reads as under:

> The Mewar Harijan Sevak Sangh has sent a Memorandum to the Mewar Government drawing their attention to the various disabilities of the Harijan in the State and their consequent hardship. The Memorandum brings out how civil liberties of Harijan are curtailed in several ways by the orthodoxy and prejudices of the caste Hindus.
>
> I enumerate below some of the unjust practices which still persist in the State and for the rectification of which the State has taken no effective measures. They are as follows:
>
> 1. Harijan have no liberty in the selection of clothes to wear. The form of dress must follow the age-long pattern; personal tastes and desires have no place in the choice of the dress.

2. At wedding feasts they have no choice in the selection of food materials. Even on payment they cannot use costly articles.

3. They cannot ride on a horse in the village.

4. They are not allowed accommodation in public vehicles.

5. On religious festivals they cannot take out procession of their idols except through the specified routes.

6. They have no access to wells and temples.

The President of the Harijan Sevak Sangh adds:

> Three years ago in company with Thakur Bapa, I travelled all over the State and placed before the Government and public my impression of the conditions prevailing there and pleaded for reform. On perusal of the above mentioned memorandum and other reports sent to me, I find that the past few years have hardly brought any change and conditions are more or less static.
>
> It is heart breaking to find that passage of time cuts no ice with us. The result is that there is hardly any change in our age-long practices and prejudices. This perversity which binds us to the tyranny and injustices of our ways also makes us impervious to the incalculable harm we have already suffered as a result of it. Even if the ignorant prejudice of the common-man is unshaken the enlightened Governments of the Twentieth Century ought to be more alive to their responsibilities.

The dates of these communications are important. They are of the year 1945. None can say that this Hindu established order is a thing of the ancient past. The fact that these latest accounts refer to the Indian states should not be understood to mean that the established order has vanished from free India.

They could not use the village well nor could their children be educated in the village schools. Education in those days was in the hands of the upper caste, particularly Brahmins who taught to higher caste children and the untouchables were forbidden to study there. In pre-independence period, therefore, the Chamar community like other untouchable communities were overwhelmingly illiterate. To acquire an education, in order to enhance ability to think critically about themselves and about society in which they lived, was restricted.

The untouchables could not take water from the Hindu well at all. They could not build a pucca brick well for themselves even though they might have the money to do so. For having a pucca well for themselves means an attempt to raise themselves to the status of the Hindus which was contrary to the established social order. Not only this, according to the social rules, the untouchables must not remain seated on a cot in the presence of an upper caste Hindu. Untouchables standing in front of them was beneath the dignity of caste Hindus. It must be observed by untouchables. If untouchables defied these rules, they were seriously tortured by caste Hindus.

In the traditional Rajputana society other forms of social contacts were also denied to the untouchables. In some cases free use of the village streets was forbidden. If lower caste people saw someone from upper castes coming along the same street or road from the opposite direction they were supposed to step aside for them. Penalties for transgressing caste norms were severe and were used with devastating effect against transgressors. As a corollary to the pollution customs, the lower castes were not allowed to enter the temples frequented by the caste Hindus. They were also forbidden to wear good clothes, their women were not allowed to wear any gold or silver ornaments', they were not allowed to construct 'pakka' houses like Hindu castes. They were allowed to build only 'kachha' houses and required to call the houses in which they lived as 'huts' whereas Brahmins called their houses, as 'house' and Rajputs as 'Rawla'.

The untouchables must not wear decent and clean clothes and they must not wear gold or silver ornaments. If the untouchables defied these rules, the Hindus would not hesitate to bring them to book. The untouchables have been trying to defy these rules. What were the consequences can be seen from the following incidents which have been reported in the newspapers.[77]

Until 1922, the untouchable caste of Dalai in Berar district of Bundi, were forbidden to eat wheat. In February 1922, a Chamar woman was put in the dock in Sakatgarh, Jaipur, simply because she was wearing silver ornaments on her feet. The reason given was that only men of the high castes were allowed to wear silver or to eat wheat. The low caste people should not dare to aspire for these things."

The *Times of India* in its issue of January 4, 1928 reports the tyranny and oppression practised upon the Balais who form an untouchable community in central India for their daring to wear clean clothes and golden ornaments. Observes the *Times of India*:

"In May (1927) high caste Hindus, viz., Kalotas, Rajputs and Brahmins including the Patils and Patwaris of villages Kanaria, Bicholee

Hafsi, Bicholi Mardana and of about 15 other villages in the Indore district informed the Balais of their respective villages that if they wished to live among them, they must conform to the following rules:

1. Balais must not wear gold lace bordered pugrees;
2. They must not wear dhotis with coloured or fancy borders;
3. They must convey intimation of the death of any Hindu to relatives of the deceased—no matter how far away these relatives may be living;
4. In all Hindu marriages, the Balais must play music before the procession and during the marriages;
5. The Balai women must not wear fancy gowns for jackets;
6. Balai women must attend all the cases of confinement of Hindu women;
7. The Balais must render the services without demanding remuneration and must accept whatever a Hindu is pleased to give;
8. If the Balais do not agree to abide by these terms, they must get out of the villages.

The Balais refused to comply and the Hindus proceeded against them. Balais were not allowed to get water from the village wells; they were not allowed to let their cattle graze. Balais were prohibited from passing through land owned by a Hindu so that if the field of a Balai was surrounded by fields owned by the Hindus, the Balai could have no access to his own field. The Hindus also let their cattle graze down the fields of the Balais.

The Balais submitted petitions to the Darbar of Indore against these persecutions, but as they could get no timely relief and the oppression continued, hundreds of Balais with their wives and children, were obliged to abandon their homes in which their ancestors had lived for generations, and to migrate to adjoining states, viz., to villages in Dhar, Dewas, Bagli, Bhopal, Gwalior and other states."

The untouchables must not eat rich food even if they can afford it. It is an offence for the untouchables to live above their status in life.

The *Pratap* in its issue of 26 February, 1928 relates the following occurrence:

"In the State of Jodhpur at a place Chandayal, you will still see men who do not think that the Harijans have even the right to eat Halwa. One of the untouchable castes is that of Sargaras. Sometime back on the occasion of the marriage ceremony of two or three girls, Halwa was prepared for the members of the marriage party. For this purpose, Maida (white flour) was also brought from the Thakur Sahib. At meal time, the marriage party came for meals but just at that time the Kanwar Sahib of Chandayal sent orders to the Sargaras that they could not eat Halwa. Some cringing sycophants negotiated a compromise in this way that the Kanwar Sahib be presented with Rs 200.00 and then a permission will be given to eat Halwa. At this the Sargaras got infuriated and refused to pay the money."

To lead a marriage procession through the main streets of the village is the right of every caste Hindu. It is also in evidence that the community which enjoys this right is accepted as a respectable community. The untouchables have no such right.

One of the major benefits received by the landlords, Jamindars, Jagirdars and upper caste Hindus was the access to free labour (Begar) and services from the untouchables including Chamar. They could be summoned for sowing or harvesting the lands of these castes, and could also be required to tend public land for which they were not paid.

The Hindus treated the untouchables as having been born to serve the Hindu castes. It being his duty to serve, the untouchable could not refuse to serve the Hindus whenever the latter called upon him to do so. The Hindus of the village held the belief that they could command the labour of untouchables. The system was known as Begar or forced labour. The untouchables of rural areas were seriously tortured by the upper caste Hindus for refusing Begar.

Within the existing socio-religious framework, therefore, the untouchables had very few means through which they could alter their position. As we have seen, challenges to the existing social order by the untouchables were not tolerated. Defiance of caste norms resulted in massive punishment in the form of Bahiskar. Mobility within caste system in Srinivas', phrase 'Sanskritization' was also not available to the untouchables, they were too low and impure for that to be feasible. Moreover, the material prerequisites for Sanskritization, the generation of an economic and political base was also beyond their reach. The untouchables did not possess the economic resources which could be translated into power and thus could not make a convincing case for raising the social status.

The only recourse open to Chamars on the socio-religious plank was to become followers of Kabir sect, which had as a central tenet the abolition of caste. With the establishment of Arya Samaj in Rajasthan in the twentieth century some sections of the Chamar's community had also become the followers of Arya Samaj.

With the advent of the Brithsh Raj the traditional order was disrupted fundamentally; with the establishment of Arya Samaj in India in 1875, the initiative of political movement offered new modes of socio-political activities and finally provoked an intellectual ferment within Indian society which questioned the very principles of Hinduism and the social structure which embodied them.

Notes and References

1. Devendra Pal Singh Tomar, *Hindu Achhut Jatio-Mai Chhuvachhut: Ek Samaj Shastriya Adhiyayan*, Delhi, Commonwealth Publishers, 2003. pp. 29–82. For more details, also see Ramesh Chandra Gunarthi, *Rajasthani Jatio-Ki-Khoj*, Ajmer, Vedic Yantralaya, 1950; Bajranglal Lohia, *Rajasthan-ki-Jatia*, Calcutta, Vishal Bharat Book Depot, 1954; E.A.H Blunt, *The Caste System of Northern India*, Delhi. S. Chand and Co, 1969; Stephen Fuchs, *At Bottom of Indian Society: The Harijan and other Low Castes*, New Delhi, Munshiram Manoharlal Publishers, 1981; Harkishan Santoshi, *Dalito-Mai Dalit*, New Delhi, Nav Sahitya Academy 1990; Bindeshwar Pathak, *Road to Freedom: A Sociological Study on the Abolition of Scavenging in India*, Delhi, Motilal Banarsidass, Publishers, 1991; Shyamlal, *The Bhangi: A Sweeper Caste and its Socio-Econmic Portraits*, Bombay, Popular Prakashan, 1992; National Seminar on Action Sociology and Liberation of Scavengers, New Delhi, February 8–10, 1992, Sponsored by Indian Association of Action Sociologists and Sulabh International; Hardayal Singh, Marwar Census Report 1891, Reprint 1997 (first published in 1896); Puranmal, *Ashprashyata Avam Dalit Chetna*, Jaipur, Pointer Publishers, 1999; Bharat and Rajaram Bhadu (ed.) *Mukhiadhara Shiksha Mai Dalit-Bhed*, Panchkula (Haryana), Aadhar Prakashan, 2007.
2. Census of India, 1971, Series-1, Paper 1 of 1975, *Scheduled Castes and Scheduled Tribes*, New Delhi, Government of India Press, 1975 pp. 94–95.
3. Ibid., p. 52.
4. Ibid., pp. 60–62.
5. Ibid., pp. 63–65.
6. Ibid., p. 86.
7. Ibid., p. 49.
8. Ibid., pp. 45–46.

9. Ibid., p. 48.
10. Ibid., p. 56.
11. Ibid., pp. 68–70.
12. Ibid., pp. 57–59.
13. Ibid., pp. 82–83.
14. Ibid., p. 53.
15. Ibid., pp. 72–74.
16. Ibid., p. 85.
17. Ibid., p. 90.
18. Ibid., p. 94.
19. Ibid., p. 95.
20. Ibid., p. 96. Also see, "Meghwal-Ki (counterpart) Samkaksh Jatio-Ki-Rajyawar Talika" in *Meghwal Keerti: Ismarika*, New Delhi, Meghwal Mahasangh, 1998, p. 5. Devi Singh, "Chamar Jati-Ka Itihas" in Sohanpal Sumnakshar (ed.) *Adim Jati Chamar: Itihas, Dharm-va-Sanskriti*: Delhi, Bharatiya Dalit Sahitya Academy, 2002, p. 57. For more details, see K.S. Singh, *People of India*, National Series, Vol.II. *The Scheduled Castes*, Delhi, Oxford University Press, Delhi. pp. 302–21.
21. *Ethnographic Atlas of Rajasthan,* with reference to Scheduled Castes and Scheduled Tribes, New Delhi, Government of India, Gandhi Centenary Year 1969, pp. 4–113.
22. Ibid., pp. 4–22.
23. Ibid., pp. 24–31.
24. Ibid., pp. 34–48.
25. Ibid., pp. 50–69.
26. Ibid., pp. 72–81.
27. Ibid., pp. 84–100.
28. Ibid., pp. 102–113.
29. The most important source for the early origin and situation of Chamar in Rig-Veda and other old literature is provided in Geo. W. Briggs, *The Chamar,* Calcutta, Associate Press, 1920.
30. Bajranglal Lohia, *Rajasthan-Ki-Jatia*, Calcutta, Vishal Bharat Book Depot, 1954 p. 218. Chamar writers and others have given many interpretations and analyse of the origin of the word 'Chamar'. For more details, see particularly, Sohanpal Sumnakshar, *Adim Jati Chamar: Itihas, Dharma-va-Sanskriti*, Delhi, Bharatiya Dalit Sahitya Academy, 2002.
31. Ibid. p. 213.
32. Ibid., p. 213.

33. Ibid., p. 213.
34. Geo. W. Briggs, 1920. Ibid., pp. 15–16.
35. In his book entitled, *Tribes and Castes of North-Western Provinces and Oudh*, Vol. II, W. Crooke has dealt with all castes found in the Hindu society. There are a few legends dealing with the origin of the Chamar. Out of them, one important has been narrated above, p. 170.
36. Masanori Sato, "The Chamar of South-Eastern Rajasthan 1650–1800 A.D". in H. Kotani (ed.) *Caste System, Untouchability and the Depressed*, Delhi, Manohar Publishers, 1999. p. 31.
37. काश्मीर के चमार?
38. "Itihas ke Aaina Mai: Kashmir" in *Dainik Bhaskar*, Jaipur, June 29, 2004.
39. K.S. Singh, *People of India*, National Series Volume II, *Scheduled Castes*, Anthropological Survey of India, Delhi, Oxford University Press, 1995, p. 301. Also see Geo. W. Briggs, 1920, Ibid., p. 15.
40. Devi Singh, "Chamar Jati-ka Itihas", in Sohan Pal Sumnakshar (ed.) *Adim Jati Chamar: Itihas Dharm-Va-Sanskriti*, Delhi, Bharatiya Dalit Sahitya Academy, 2002, p. 58.
41. Swami Gokuldas, *Meghvansh Itihas*, Ajmer, Arya Brothers Book Sellers, Vikrama Samvat 2050, pp. 113–118.
42. Ramesh Chandra Gunarthi, *Rajasthani Jatio-ki-Khoj*. Ajmer, Vedic Yantralaya 1950. pp. 268–69. Also see, K.S. Singh, *People of India*, National Series, Vol. II, *The Scheduled Castes*, Delhi, Oxford University Press, 1995. p. 301.
43. Hardayal Singh, Marwar Census Report, 1891, Reprint, 1997 (Hindi editions) p. 527, (First published in 1896). For more details, also see, Acharya Guru Prasad K.P. मेघों, (मेघवालों) के विषय में ऋग्वेद की साक्षी, in Acharya Guru Prasad K.P. (ed.) *Meghwal Keerti: Ismarika*, New Delhi, Meghwal Mahasangh, 1998. p. 26.
44. Ibid., p. 527.
45. Hiralal Janagal, "Meghvansh Samaj Ki-Utpati-Va-Gotra", in Ram Swaroop Meghvansh (ed.) *Meghvans: Ismarika*, 1997, Ajmer Akhil Meghvansh Mahasabha, Badi Basti, Pushkar Ajmer. The Diamond Jubilee Press, Laxmi Chowk, 1997. pp. 95–98.
46. Chandanmal Naval, *Marwar-Ka-Amar Shahid Rajaram*, Jodhpur, Rajasthani Granthagar, 1994, pp. 60–64.
47. Ramesh Chandra Gunarthi, *Rajasthani Jatio-Ki-Khoj*, 1950, Ibid., p. 258.
48. Bajranglal Lohia, *Rajasthan-Ki-Jatia*, 1954 Ibid., p. 218. Also see, Marwar Census Report 1891, Ibid., p. 527. Ramesh Chandra Gunarthi, Ibid., p. 257.

49. Marwar Census Report, 1891, Reprint 1997 Ibid., p. 527. Also see Ramesh Chandra Gunarthi Ibid., p. 258.
50. Ibid., p. 527.
51. Chandanmal Naval, *Marwar Ka Amar Shahid Rajaram*, 1994. Ibid., pp. 56–57.
52. Ramesh Chandra Gunarthi, 1950, Ibid., p. 258.
53. Ibid., p. 257.
54. Marwar Census Report 1891, Reprint 1997, p. 527.
55. Masanori Sato, "The Chamar of South-Eastern Rajasthan, 1650–1800 A.D", in H. Kotani (ed.) *Caste System, Untouchability and the Depressed*, 1999, pp. 32–33.
56. Ramesh Chandra Gunarthi, 1950 Ibid., p. 267.
57. For details, see, "The Caste of Marwar" (Marwar Census Report, 1891) Munshi Hardayal Singh, Census Superintendent of Marwar, first edition 1894, second edition 1990, Jodhpur Book Treasure, p. 197. Also see, "Meghwal" in K.N. Vyas and D.S. Gehlot, *Rajasthan-Ki-Jatio-Ka-Samajik Avam Arthick Jiwan*, Jodhpur, Jagdish Singh Gehlot Shodh Sansthan, 1992 pp. 220–222.
58. "The Caste of Marwar" (Census Report of 1891) Ibid.,p. 197.
59. Bajranglal Lohia, *Rajasthan-Ki-Jatia*, Ibid., pp. 219–220.
60. *Marwar Census Report of 1891*, Reprint 1997, pp. 534–35.
61. Swami Gokuldas, *Meghvansh Itihas*, Ibid., 59–60.
62. Ramesh Chandra Gunarthi, *Rajasthani-Jation-Ki-Khoj*, Ibid., p. 257, Also see, Swami Gokuldas, *Meghvansh Itihas*, Ibid., p. 61.
63. For more details, see Acharya Guru Parsad K.P.'s Essay "Chakravarti Rajbali: Rajabali-Ke-Vanshaj Balai" in *Rajabalai Samaj*, Indore, Madhya Pradesh, March 15, 2006.
64. For more details, see, "Vedhanic Sabdarth (शब्दार्थ)" in Akhil Bharatiya Sootrakar, Mahasabha-Ka-Vidhan, Published by Dilli Prantiya Sootrakar Sabha, Dilli, New Delhi, 1949, p. 5.
65. Masanori Sato, 'Anti Untouchability ideologies and movements in Maharashtra from the late Nineteenth Century to 1930s" in H. Kotani (ed.) *Caste System, Untouchability and the Depressed*, 1999. p. 171.
66. Shyamlal, *Untouchable Saints of India*. Jaipur, Sublime Publication, 2005, p. 28.
67. D.R. Gadgil, *Poona: A Socio-economic Survey: Part II*, Publication No. 25, Poona Gokhale Institute of Politics and Economics, 1952, p. 94.

68. J.H. Hutton, *Caste in India, its Nature, Function and Origins*, London: Oxford University Press, 1963 p. 47.
69. Shyamlal, *The Bhangis in Transition*, New Delhi, Inter-India Publication, 1984, p. 4.
70. E.A.H. Blunt, *The Caste System of Northern India*, (Reprinted) S. Chand and Co. 1969, p. 99.
71. T.S. Katiyar, *Social Life in Rajasthan: A Case Study*, Allahabad, Kitab Mahal, 1964, p. 26.
72. Shyamlal, *The Bhangi: A Sweeper Caste and its Socio-economic Portraits*, Bombay, Popular Prakashan, 1992, pp. 24–25, also see, Bharat and Rajaram Bhadu, (ed.), *Mukhiya Dhara Shiksha Mai Dalit Bhed*, Panchkula (Haryana), Aadhar Publications, 2007, p. 39.
73. Devendra Singh Tomar, *Hindu Achhut Jation Mai Chhuvachhut*, New Delhi, Commonwealth Publishers, 2003 pp. 87–88.
74. Masanor Sato, "Anti-Untouchability Ideologies and Movements in Maharashtra from Nineteenth Century to 1930"s in H. Kotani (ed.) 1999, Ibid., p. 174.
75. Masanori Sato, "The Chamars of South-Eastern Rajasthan 1650–1800 A.D." in H. Kotani (ed.) 1999, Ibid., p. 32.
76. For most important sources for atrocities on the untouchables and the situation of low castes in Rajputana and neighbouring states is "Untouchability and Lawlessness" in *Dr Baba Saheb Ambedkar: Writings and Speeches*, Volume V, Mumbai, Government of Maharashtra, 1989, pp. 48–59. Other useful studies on tyrannies and oppressions practised by the caste Hindus against untouchables, especially in Rajasthan are those of Girdhar Behari Sharma, "Law as an Instrument for Abolition of Untouchability: case of Rajasthan" in *EPW.* Vol. X. No. 15, April 12, 1975. p. 625 and Sapna Bhatia, "Untouchability and Atrocities: A case study of Rural Rajasthan" M.Phil dissertation, submitted in the Department of Sociology, University of Rajasthan, 1999–2000 (Unpublished). Also, see Shyamlal, *Untouchable Caste in India: The Raigar Movement (1940–2004)*, 2006, Jaipur, Rawat Publications, Bharat and Rajaram Bhadu, (ed.), *Mukhiya dhara Shiksha Mai Dalit Bhed*, Panchkula (Haryana) Aadhar Publications, 2007.
77. *Dr Baba Saheb Ambedkar: Writing and Speeches*, Vol. V, 1998, pp. 48–49 and also 52. Also see Acharya Guru Prasad K.P., President of Meghwal Mahasangh, "Sawarano-Ke-Utpiran-Ke-Virud Balaiyon-Ke-Sangharsh Gatha" in *Meghwal Keerti: Ismarika,* New Delhi, Meghwal Mahasangh, 1998, p. 14.

II
Politics

3 Social Mobilization and Political Development

In the year 1934, the political atmosphere in Udaipur (Mewar) was very suffocating. The people were demanding right to speech, liberty to form an association etc., but the state administration was not prepared to accede to these demands. As such, in the year 1937–1938, a Satyagrah Movement was launched under the dynamic leadership of Manikya Lal Verma, and his associates established 'Mewar Prajamandal' in April 1938. Balwant Singh Mehta and Bhura Lal Baya were elected President and Vice-president respectively. Verma was elected Mahamantri of the Mandal.[1]

On October 4, 1938, the Prajamandal launched a civil disobedience movement. The movement immediately spread all over the state.[2] The Satyagrah Movement also started in Nathdwara, Chittorgarh and Bhilwara and a large number of satyagrahis including Bhura Lal Baya, Balwant Singh Mehta, Amba Lal Joshi, Amrit Lal Yadav (Chamar), Jai Chand (Raigar) and others were arrested.[3] All these satyagrahis were sentenced to various terms of imprisonment.[4]

Amrit Lal Yadav was born on January 9, 1919 at Chhoti Sadri, district Chittorgarh.[5] He was educated at Government School, Chhoti Sadri. He came in contact with satyagrahis and freedom fighters. They made real impression on the 19-year old boy. In 1938 Amrit Lal Yadav became an active member of Mewar Prajamandal[6] and aroused social and political awakening amongst the untouchable communities. Yadav drew inspiration from satyagraha and freedom movement. He, along with other upper caste persons, organized Harijan agitation in Mewar, the then princely state. Public meetings were also organized and dharnas were arranged. For such and other demonstrations, they were severely tortured. Yadav was also one of them who was tortured and beaten up mercilessly by the police on account of his participation in the national activities.[7] According to the *Rajasthan Varsiki 1994*, Yadav took active part in the national movement and satyagrah from 1938 to 1947. Consequently, he was arrested by the police and sent to jail where he remained for a few months.[8]

After independence, an important event took place in Rajasthan. Amrit Lal Yadav formed 'Rajasthan Pradesh Dalit Warg Sangh' (RPDWS). This created a stir in the whole state and like other socio-cultural movements in the state, a new socio-political movement started in Rajasthan too. In this movement the contribution of Yadav as President of RPDWS, was remarkable.

In the beginning of 1951, another important event took place in Jaipur. On April 26, 1951 Jai Narain Vyas formed his first Congress ministry which included Mohan Lal Sukhadia, Tika Ram Paliwal, Bhikha Bhai Bhil, and Bhogi Lal Pandia.

Amrit Lal Yadav was also one of them; his name was included in the list of deputy ministers as a representative of scheduled castes.[9] A wave of jubilation, spread amongst scheduled castes in general and the Chamars in particular, in Rajasthan.

In the first general election of 1952, Yadav contested the election from Bhopal Sagar (Udaipur) a reserved constituency and won the election as a congress candidate.[10] On March 3, 1952 a Congress ministry was formed in Rajasthan under the dynamic leadership of Tika Ram Paliwal, and Yadav was again inducted as a cabinet minister.[11] Again a wave of jubilation spread amongst the scheduled castes in Rajasthan and Jaipur became the centre of the socio-political activities in Rajasthan. Yadav, an associate of Babu Jagjivan Ram, an eminent Congress leader at the centre, took active part in socio-political activities.

In 1952, Yadav was not only elected for the first time to the State Assembly from Bhopal Sagar (Udaipur), Rajasthan but was also elected in the subsequent elections held in the years 1958, 1962 and 1967 respectively[12] without a break except for a brief period between 1957 and 1958. Thus, he was elected four times in a span of 20 years. Since 1951 to 1971, Yadav had been deputy minister or the cabinet minister. During 1965, 1967 and 1971, when Mohan Lal Sukhadia was Chief Minister of Rajasthan, Yadav became a cabinet minister.[13] Thus he was the first Chamar who became a minister in 1951[14] and remained in the ministry till

1971.[15] Thus he made history. During this long period, he took an active part in organizing various kinds of socio-political activities in the state.

Rajasthan Pradesh Dalit Warg Sangh and Untouchable Reform Movement in 1947

Rajasthan Pradesh Dalit Warg Sangh (RPDWS) was founded in 1947 as a state branch of All India Dalit Warg Sangh which was founded under the leadership of Babu Jagjivan Ram at Kanpur in 1935. Since then All India Dalit Warg Sangh had established its several branches in various states of the country.

The main leader of RPDWS since 1947 was Amrit Lal Yadav. Yadav evinced interest in working for the low untouchable castes/communities when his name was included in the list of deputy ministers as the representative of the scheduled castes in the Congress ministry headed by Jai Narain Vyas and from then until 1999 he was closely associated with RPDWS activities. In 1947 he had established state branch of All India Dalit Warg Sangh in Jaipur;[16] however, his connections with Babu Jagjivan Ram dated back to 1947.

Other leaders of RPDWS were: Panna Lal Barupal, MP (Bikaner); Kanwar Jelia; Hari Shankar Shidharth Shastri, MLA (Jaipur); Kalu Ram Hatila (Bikaner); Sampat Ram, Deputy Minister, Rajasthan; Mahadev Prasad Banka, MLA; Dharm Pal, MLA; Lalu Ram, MLA; Smt Narmada Yadav (Udaipur); Smt Laxmi Devi Barupal (Bikaner); Rud Mal Sogan (Jaipur); Johar Mal Barupal (Jalore); Mangal Prakash Arya (Jodhpur); Ganpat Lal Yadav (Kota); Goverdhan Singh Ken (Bharatpur); Rawat Ram Niyawat, MLA (Churu); Atma Ram Garg (Jaisalmer); Kishan Lal Arya (Udaipur); Gulab Chand Valmik (Jaipur); and Har Jeet Lal, MLA (Ajmer).[17]

The main source of income for running the various welfare programmes and activities in the state was government aid. In the beginning, the government aid was Rs 32,000 In 1955, when Panna Lal Barupal became its President, he urged the Government of Rajasthan to increase the grant-in-aid from Rs 32,000 to Rs 65,000.[18]

The main activity of RPDWS was to organize annual conventions in different parts of the state, with a view to popularize untouchability removal campaign and gaining the support of Dalits for its organization. Thus, there was a great zeal amongst the workers and from 1951 until 1954, RPDWS had organized three conferences, one each at Bikaner, Nagaur and Udaipur respectively.

Most of the issues that RPDWS took up were: untouchability removal campaign, abolition of socio-religious disabilities, campaign against social vices, abolition of untouchability observed within low castes, promotion of inter-dinning between Dalits, supporting issues, for instance, on the problem of inadequate lighting, electricity, water supply, roads which concerned many untouchable castes in different parts of the state, passing resolutions urging government to extent facilities to untouchable castes/communities to improve their poor socio-economic conditions, the resolutions also appealed to the Government of Rajasthan to fulfil the SC/ST quota in government jobs.

One of the features in the development of RPDWS was the creation of district and tehsil branches in different districts of Rajasthan. According to a RPDWS's annual report 1957–1967, there were 25 affiliated district units. Their names are: Jaipur, Bharatpur, Tonk, Jhunjhunu, Alwar, Sikar, Jodhpur, Barmer, Pali, Jalore, Jaisalmer, Churu, Kota, Bundi, Bikaner, Sri Ganganagar, Udaipur, Banswara, Sawaimadhopur, Dholpur, Nagaur, Chittorgarh, Bhilwara, Jhalawar and Sirohi.[19]

There were representatives from different castes and communities on various committees of RPDWS, such as organizing committee, executive committee, etc. It is through representation that the RPDWS acquired all castes and communities character. The RPDWS had gained wider recognition and has emerged as the soul of the Dalit movement in general and Meghwal movement in particular.

The foregoing account of RPDWS shows that from the very beginning, the movement was functionally independent. However, it was affiliated to Congress for the achievement of common goals and Congress's ideology which provided a common basis of activity for betterment of Dalits. The RPDWS drew social activists, leaders and 'pracharaks' from different castes and communities to achieve Gandhi's dream. Thus, RPDWS soon grew into an all-Rajasthan organization over a period of 8 years and had spearheaded so many agitations and implemented several programmes.

It should be noted that RPDWS movement during its early years involved two types of workers, volunteers and pracharaks: first, salaried workers as regular employees of RPDWS were directly administered by RPDWs who followed a liberal policy with regard to admission of untouchables to government schools and hostels, entry in hotels and temples, removal of untouchability and social disabilities; second, non-salaried pracharaks with dedication were involved in 1955, which also helped the untouchables. Another factor which gave impetus to Dalit movement was the sending of the non-salaried pracharaks, by All India Dalit Warg Sangh founded by Babu Jagjivan Ram in Kanpur which played an important role in improving the socio-economic, educational and religious conditions of Dalits in different parts of the state.

The First Dalit Warg Sangh Convention, Bikaner, 1953[20]

A major dalit organization dedicated to the cause of educational and social upliftment of the untouchables was Dalit Warg Sangh (DWS) founded by Babu Jagjivan Ram in Kanpur in the year 1935. Babu Jagjivan Ram devoted a major part of his energies to the development of the untouchable communities.

The activities of RPDWS were significant for Chamar movement in that they contributed to the formation of Chamar elite. The aims of RPDWS were to elevate the social, economic as well as educational conditions of untouchable communities by: (a) promoting education, and (b) remedying their social-religious disabilities. A state branch of Dalit Warg Sangh was established at Udaipur in 1947 which sponsored a variety of socio-educational activities for the benefit of untouchable communities. Through this process the consciousness of Chamar community was moulded and it prepared for a political action.

Although many of Rajasthan's untouchable leaders had primarily local appeal and following, yet some leaders became prominent in Rajasthan and the community as a whole. One such figure was Amrit Lal Yadav who had been associated with Babu Jagjivan Ram from early 1947. Moreover, he was the first powerful Chamar minister in the Congress ministry in Rajasthan since 1952. As a social welfare minister, he was responsible for the welfare and development of untouchables. As a member of dominant Chamar caste, and owing to his official position be had become affluent to the extent that he could order to start welfare programmes and activities in various districts. In 1947 he was the nominated state president of Dalit Warg Sangh in Rajasthan which had been established by Babu Jagjivan Ram in 1935.

Another eminent Chamar member of the parliament from reserved constituency, Bikaner was Panna Lal Barupal, who had been associated with Babu Jagjivan Ram since the first general elections held in 1952. From 1952 onwards both Amrit Lal Yadav and Panna Lal Barupal, assumed vigorously active role in the social and political affairs of their people in Rajasthan. They launched a number of welfare activities throughout the state to mobilize the Chamars into a viable and assertive community, increasingly conscious of its human, social, economic and political rights.

To discuss socio-economic issues and to publicize DWS's activities as well as to better integrate the Chamar and cognate communities in particular and other untouchable communities in general, the DWS had called the first convention of Dalits from all over Bikaner, on November 22–23, 1953 at Bikaner. The Sammelan of Bikaner Chamars was interesting and significant in the development of Chamar movement and thus served a valuable communication gap filler for the developing Chamar movement. The chief guest of this Sammelan was Babu Jagjivan Ram. Amrit Lal Yadav presided over the function.

Ram Ratan Kochar, Swagatadhiyaksh[21] (a non-Dalit), while welcoming the chief guest, president and other delegates, pointed out that, what was particularly to note about DWS movement in that region, was that in the field of untouchability, the upper caste Hindus of Bikaner had become a little flexible on their own. He further stated that the overwhelming majority still followed untouchability. Wells, reservoirs, hotels and tea stalls in Bikaner were not open to untouchables in the same way as they were accessible to other communities, that barbers did not cut the hair of untouchables in rural parts of the region was beyond description. He urged the chief guest, president and others to effect change within the system.

Panna Lal Barupal[22] was especially active as leader and organizer after 1952, in which year he was elected a member of parliament from the reserved constituency, Bikaner. In 1953, he was instrumental in organizing the first Dalit Warg Sangh convention which launched a campaign for removal of untouchability in Bikaner region. Barupal, like Ram Ratan Kochar and other Bikaner-based social activists and leaders, spoke against untouchability and supported the views expressed by Kochar over this issue. Accordingly, to his line of thoughts, if untouchables ceased to act like untouchables, if they stopped performing the tasks such as removal of dead animals and other acts which were considered polluting, the caste Hindus will begin boycotting, torturing and harassing them. Barupal, for example, cited the incident of Tonk district where Harijans (Chamars) had stopped removing the dead animals. As a result of this the caste Hindus socially boycotted them. The reaction and message of upper caste Hindus for Harijans (Chamars) was that self-improvement within the Hindu social order is not permissible.

In addition, Barupal spoke that socio-economic conditions of untouchable communities were very pitiable in that region. A larger population of the untouchables were illiterate masses and economically very poor. There was acute need to motivate the government officials to execute sincerely the socio-economic programmes and activities for the betterment of untouchables launched by the government. Simultaneously, caste Hindus should also be persuaded to abandon observing untouchability. As such they could become instrumental in fulfilling the dreams of Mahatma Gandhi, the Father of the Nation, in the removal of untouchability. He urged the untouchables also to abandon the socio-religious evils and vices which branded them as untouchable. The importance of cleanliness for untouchable communities and good habits in particular was stressed at the meeting.

Barupal further urged the government of Rajasthan to establish a state level commission to study in detail, the pitiable socio-economic and educational conditions of the untouchables and tribals in the state. He demanded that establishment of a separate colony for untouchable castes by the government should immediately be stopped. They should be given patta on most nominal price; light and water facilities be provided in their 'bastis'. Thus, in this Sammelan the major issues addressed included, access to government jobs, sanction of more and more scholarships, admission of children of these communities into technical institutions, removable of untouchability, appointment in Nagar Palikas and Nagar Parishad etc.

In the end, Barupal urged Babu Jagjivan Ram to provide more funds to Rajasthan for the welfare of the downtrodden in the state.

Thus, Barupal was really a political mobilizer or organizer of Meghwal movement. His ideas can be considered to have had a socio-political impact on the movement. The focus and scope of his efforts were socio-political and cultural.

As the president of the function,[23] Amrit Lal Yadav supported the issues raised in the Sammelan and assured to take them up at the government level, but included the specific call that there should be inclusion of certain left out untouchable castes/communities such as Meghwal, Jatav, Bairwa, Balai, Khateek, etc., in the list of scheduled castes.

Similarly, the second annual convention for self reform was held by DWS at Chhoti Khatu,[24] Nagaur district on March 28, 1954. The chief guest of the function was Amrit Lal Yadav, the then Minister, Government of Rajasthan. Panna Lal Barupal presided over the function. Other persons were: Chaudhary Bhagirath, the then Speaker, Rajya Vidhan Sabha, Ajmer; Parash Ram, Ganga Ram Bakolia, MLA etc. In this Sammelan the major issues addressed were virtually identical, but included the specific call that untouchability should be removed and measures to open civic water supplies to untouchables be introduced.

Second Rajasthan Pradesh Dalit Warg Sangh Sammelan, 1955 Held at Udaipur

The main leader of Dalit Warg Sangh since its inception in 1947, in Rajasthan was Amrit Lal Yadav. He was a minister in the then Congress ministry headed by Mohan Lal Sukhadia and was closely associated with Babu Jagjivan Ram since independence. Since then the DWS had increased the socio-educational and political activities in various regions of Rajasthan and it also reached a new height during the fifth and sixth decades of the 20th century.

In 1954, the campaign against untouchability and the demand for removal of socio-religious disabilities were at its peak, when it was decided to hold a second annual convention of DWS in the city of lakes, Udaipur, with a view to organize a mammoth conference in 1955. The mammoth conference of DWS, held at Udaipur in September, 1955, was attended by a large number of delegates from different parts of Rajasthan. Govind Vallabh Pant, the then Home Minister, Government of India, Babu Jagjivan Ram, the then Minister, Government of India and National President, DWS; Hari Bhau Upadhiyaya, the then Chief Minister, Ajmer; Mohan Lal Sukhadia, the then Chief Minister, Rajasthan; Amrit Lal Yadav, the then Minister of Cooperative, Rehabilitation and Revenue, Government of Rajasthan and state President—DWS, MPs, MLAs, and many more addressed the convention.[25]

Amrit Lal Yadav, Chairman of the Reception Committee, in his welcome speech narrated in details the various instances of untouchability from the rural areas of Rajasthan to illustrate the pitiable condition of Dalits and how caste Hindus harassed, tortured and humiliated them. He pointed out that even though an Untouchability Offence Act, 1955[26] had already been passed by the parliament, yet untouchables could not fetch water from wells, they could not take out 'baraat' procession in the villages with band party, Groom could not ride on the back of a horse.[27] If they dared to do so, they were brutally beaten in public. There had been a series of such incidents in the rural areas and caste Hindus kept threatening to kill them unless untouchables stopped violating the traditional norms. He further said that earlier removal of dead animals was traditionally performed by Chamar, Meghwal and Raigars.[28] Now they had stopped it.[29] The results had been mostly disastrous.[30] Upper caste Hindus had become annoyed. They had boycotted untouchables; imposed several restrictions on them. At several places they were compelled to leave the villages; their huts were torched; animals were snatched away from them. Harassed, humiliated and insulted by Hindus, they were threatened to be killed by them. This had set off a furious circle of conflicts.

To eradicate social vices, he argued that it was fair to dismiss the fourfold social system because this contrast was the source of grievances among the untouchables. Yadav also stressed the need for inter-caste marriages and inter-dinning between upper caste Hindus and the untouchables.[31] Political equality we have already achieved. Since social equality is the basis of our Constitution, he urged the upper caste Hindus to accept the practical view for acquiring human equality. He too emphasized and urged the Hindus to employee one untouchable in their homes for domestic help[32] to remove untouchability.

At the end, Yadav expressed his gratitude to all and urged the central and state governments to launch more and more welfare programmes for the betterment of the Dalits.

Dalit Kisan Sammelan[33]

In its formative period the Chamar movement was both localized and dispersed. Local social activists took the initiative in convening meetings which were intended to educate quite as much as they were designated to mobilize and organize the Chamar community. Barmer was also locus of Chamar activity in pre- and post-independent period; a few organizations, based on sub-castes/communities, were formed for the purpose of education and reform.

The local leaders in Barmer took the initiative in holding the first Dalit Sammelan in 1954 at Balotra. Amrit Lal Yadav, the then minister in the Congress Ministry and State President of Dalit Warg Sangh was the chief guest of the function and was to address the 1954 Sammelan of

Chamar community, which drew a large number of delegates. A few noted savarnas were: Shatrushal Singh Vakil (Swagata Adhiyaksh), Ram Niwas Sharma (Swagat Mantri), Champatraj Singh Vakil, Dungar Mal Arya, Uma Ram, Kheta Ram Leela, Kalu Ram, Chhoga Lal Arya, Laxman Das Arya, Choga Lal Mochi, Rana Mal and Chimni Ram were responsible for holding the first Dalit Sammelan.

Laxmandas Arya Up-swagatadhiyaksh of this Sammelan mentioned in his printed lecture that Dalits before independence were harassed, tortured and humiliated by caste Hindus. What is particularly noteworthy about Chamar movement in this region is that Chamars after independence had made progress under the leadership of Amrit Lal Yadav. However, Laxman Das Arya called upon the government to support their reform campaign and to make available facilities for that purpose. He pointed out the miserable socio-economic and educational conditions of the untouchable communities and for its pitiable conditions stated that as an evidence:

"मेघवाल, भील, जटिया वगैरह इन धन्धों के सिवाय काश्त भी करते हैं, पर इन लोगों के पास एक तो पैसा नहीं है, इस वजह से हमेशा बनियों के दबेलदार रहते हैं, जो कोई खेती व अन्य धन्धों से मिलता है, बनिये लोग ब्याज में ले लेते हैं, सो अगर ये लोग कितने ही धन्धे क्यों न करें तो भी ये लोग भूखे रहते हैं।

यहां पर कोई भी लड़का अभी मैट्रिक पास नहीं है, जिले में करीब एक सौ लड़के छोटी–छोटी कक्षाओं में पढ़ रहे हैं। हरिजन लोगों के पास धन न होने के कारण पढ़ाई का लाभ ज्यादा नहीं उठा सकते हैं। सो हरिजन लड़कों को ज्यादा से ज्यादा छात्रवृतियां दी जाये और छात्रावास की स्थापना भी की जाये।

हरिजन लोगों को नीचा समझा जाता है, लोग छूना भी पसन्द नहीं करते हैं। मंदिरों में जाने नहीं दिया जाता है, धर्मशालाओं में ठहरने नहीं दिया जाता है, भोजनालयों में हमको खाना नहीं दिया जाता है। होटलों में हमको चाय का कप नहीं दिया जाता है, कुओं पर चढ़ने नहीं दिया जाता है, प्याऊओं में नालियों से पानी पिलाया जाता है, नाई लोग हजामत आदि नहीं करते हैं।

... सब बातें कानून से दूर की जा सकती है, पर सरकारी अफसर लोग हरिजनों का पूरा साथ नहीं दिया करते हैं... इस तरह के ऑफिसरों को हिदायतें दी जावें और जो सरकार के कानून माफिक हमको फायदा न देते हों उनके खिलाफ सख्त कार्यवाही की जाये।

सरकार की ओर से हरिजन दिवस मनाया जाना शुरू किया गया है पर उसका हम लोगों पर बुरा असर पड़ रहा है। उसका कारण यह है कि अगर कोई भी शख्स हरिजनों के हाथ की चाय पीते हैं तो समाज के लोग जात से बाहर कर देते हैं, उस पर अधिकारी लोग कोई भी कदम नहीं उठाते हैं।"

Thus, in this Sammelan, the major issues addressed included protection of small scale industries in the desert and establishment of co-operative societies for loaning, sanction of more and more scholarships, access to government jobs, execution of laws forcefully, measures for stopping atrocities on Dalits, removal of untouchability and socio-religious disabilities.

In this Sammelan, call for the reforms was put within the bounds of an enlightened Hinduism: there was rare suggestion that Chamars should challenge or defy the Hindu order. Rather Chamar leaders exhorted their community to rid itself of those practices which Hindu principles considered unclean. They also urged that Chamars should overcome the prejudices which divided them according to different segments and to become unified.

Social and Cultural Consequences of RPDWS Movement

This is the story of the genesis, growth and dynamics of RPDWS movement over a period of nearly one decade. The questions that arise now are, what are the social and cultural consequences of the movement and how do they characterize the nature of the changes, that have occurred as a result of the movement? We shall address ourselves to these questions in the sections that follow.

During the pre-independent period, some literate Chamars emerged in Bikaner state, who played the role of social activists. The most notable social activist during this period was Panna Lal Barupal, who was one of the initiators of socio-political campaign.

Panna Lal Barupal was born in Bikaner on April 1913 in the family of Barupal of Bikaner. His forefathers had been working as leather workers, his grandfather Anna Ram was working as agriculture labourer and his father Moda Ram Barupal was also working agriculture labourer. Panna Lal's mother, Rami Devi the daughter of Gula Ram Parihar of village Kolasar was a housewife. Panna Lal studied up to 5th class in Bikaner.

Panna Lal's public life started with his association with Harijan Sewak Sangh Reform Movement in Bikaner in 1946. Ram Gopal Mehta was an important leader of the movement and Panna Lal took an active interest in it. He was an active social worker of Harijan Sewak Sangh (HSS) at Bikaner and in 1946 took active part in rural region of the Bikaner state.

With such an experience and background Panna Lal Barupal contested the first general election held in the country in 1952 as a Congress candidate from the reserved constituency, Bikaner and was declared elected. From 1952 onwards, he assumed vigorously the active role in social and political affairs of Scheduled Castes people in Rajasthan. In 1953, he was instrumental in organizing the first Dalit Warg Sangh convention in Bikaner region. Similarly, the second annual convention for self reform was held by RPDWS at Chhoti Khatu in Nagaur district in 1954. Panna Lal Barupal presided over the function.

The role of Panna Lal Barupal in RPDWS campaign was a great event in the career of Meghwal movement. His role had made the people aware of their rights, social equality as citizens and necessity of modern education and government job in order to make progress. RPDWS launched the socio-political agitation and held annual conferences in different parts of Rajasthan. These were the main means of socio-political mobilization. In this, Panna Lal Barupal built his identity. It will be noted that Meghwals and Chamars in many parts of Rajasthan were in general, socially and economically poor yet they were the first to take advantage of protective discrimination policy. Being socially superior as they claimed and numerically dominant, they had access to modern educational and employment opportunities.

Thus, from 1952, Panna Lal Barupal emerged as a powerful leader. He became Member of Parliament (MP) in 1952 and was known for his organizational abilities, oratory in Hindi, honesty and sincerity of purpose. He evinced keen interest in working for his caste when he was elected as MP in 1952 and from then onwards was closely associated with RPDWS activities. In 1956 he became President of RPDWS.

The dynamics of Panna Lal Barupal's leadership lies in the fact that he brought to bear his skills of modern organization on Dalit involvement. He systematized the working of RPDWS and took initiative in encouraging various educational and literacy programmes and cultural activities. He campaigned for removal of untouchability and social evils.

Panna Lal Barupal took the initiative in encouraging more than 30 various programmes and activities.[34] He organized several meetings between untouchables and caste Hindus in different districts of Rajasthan with a view to minimize social discrimination and gaining the support of upper caste people for removal of untouchability. All the volunteers and social workers associated with the activities of RPDWS took keen interest in the affairs of RPDWS with a view to joining the support of Dalits for their betterment. Thus, there was a great zeal and enthusiasm among social workers working in different districts of Rajasthan, and from 1956 onwards RPDWS had toured 2,681 villages in 17 districts (370 villages in Jaipur, 15 in Bharatpur, 80 in Tonk, 1,050 in Jhunjhunu, 200 in Alwar, 230 in Sikar, 25 in Jodhpur, 50 in Barmer, 5 in Jalore, 127 in Jaisalmer, 15 in Kota, 35 in Bundi, 95 in Bikaner, 9 in Ganganagar, 500 in Udaipur and 250 in Banswara).

One of the features in various programmes of RPDWS was the agitation against the ban on the entry of untouchables in temples and hotels and use of public places, such as dharamshala etc. According to Panna Lal Barupal, who was the President of RPDWS in 1956, they succeeded in getting the entry to temples, hotels and 'dharamshalas' in 17 districts. The breakdown of these shows that there were 59 temple entries in 11 districts (11 temple entries in Jaipur, 3 in Tonk, 6 in Alwar, 3 in Jodhpur, 2 in Barmer, 3 in Pali, 5 in Jalore, 2 in Kota, 11 in Bikaner, 3 in Ganganagar and 10 in Banswara), 203 hotel entries in 11 districts (18 hotel entries in Jaipur, 4 in Bharatpur, 7 each in Tonk and Jhunjhunu, 3 in Jodhpur, 20 in Barmer, 14 in Pali, 5 each in Jalore and Ganganagar, 3 in Kota and 117 in Banswara) and 18 dharamshala entries in 7 districts (3 each in Jaipur, Barmer and Jalore), 1 each in Jodhpur, Pali and Banswara and 6 in Udaipur).

An analysis of various programmes and activities initiated by RPDWS under the presidentship of Panna Lal Barupal shows that there were other major issues to focus. First, a number of efforts concerned reformatory measures, such as the abolition of untouchability by filing the 'challan' in courts, persuasion through posters pasting on walls and distribution of pamphlets among the masses, RPDWS directed that social workers and social activists should organize the combined meetings of both upper caste Hindus and untouchables. Besides, abolition of untouchability within untouchables themselves which observed and practised untouchability and a strong plea for inter-dinning themselves. RPDWS directed that social workers should hold meetings of Dalits to remove untouchability. According to Rajasthan Pradesh Dalit Warg Sangh's Report, 1956, there were about 79 challans filed in various courts in 9 districts (25 challans in Jaipur, 2 in Alwar, 15 in Jodhpur, 5 each in Pali and Jaisalmer, 3 each in Jalore and Kota, 21 in Bundi and 2 in Banswara). The workers distributed 1,101 pamphlets and pasted posters on walls in 1 district (1,101 pamphlets etc., distributed in Jaipur).

On the other hand, RPDWS's workers focussed its attention on organizing several combined meetings of upper caste Hindu and dalits and called it 'Sneh Milan' for removing untouchability and systematic bridging social distance at district level and this became a feature in many districts. For instance during the year 1956–1957, RPDWS had organized as many as 39 'Sneh Milans' in 11 districts (16 Sneh Milans in Jaipur, 6 in Alwar, 22 in Jodhpur, 2 each in Barmer and Bundi, 16 in Pali, 3 each in Jalore and Kota and 5 each in Jaisalmer and Banswara).

The social workers and activists associated with RPDWS had a large number of meetings of various representatives from Dalit communities. It was through these meetings that RPDWS succeeded in removing untouchability and maintained its link with representatives by moral support. As mentioned earlier, the meetings of Dalit communities were held in 11 districts involving 1,610 persons (477 persons in Jaipur, 500 in Jhunjhunu, 200 in Jodhpur, 20 in Barmer, 50 in Pali, 55 in Jalore, 18 in Kota, 21 in Bundi, 10 in Ganganagar, 224 in Udaipur and 115 in Banswara). In addition, RPDWS workers also organized 183 Sammelans in 10 districts and called them 'Harijan Sammelan' (2 in Jaipur, 13 in Bharatpur, 6 in Jhunjhunu, 26 in Alwar, 1 each in Sikar and Jaisalmer, 14 in Jodhpur, 11 in Barmer, 105 in Udaipur and 14 in Banswara).

A notable feature under princely rule was socio-religious ban on untouchables. Panna Lal Barupal, like other untouchables, since his childhood was directly affected by inequalities and status of untouchability. He became frustrated and wanted to remove socio-religious disabilities imposed upon them, such as abolition of ban on untouchables' hair cutting, abolition of water taps meant particularly for untouchables at piao and strong agitation against these. There was a concern for the programmes adopted by government, particularly the programme to remove the socio-religious disabilities. Since 1950, there had been agitation in different districts of Rajasthan to abolish the ban. RPDWS had gained good success in removing separate water taps meant for untouchables. The data mentioned in Annual Report 1956–1957 showed that 142 water taps were removed from Piaos, in 12 districts (44 water taps removed in Jaipur, 5 each in Bharatpur and Pali, 10 each in Tonk, Barmer and Udaipur, 8 in Jhunjhunu, 29 in Jodhpur, 13 in Jalore, 2 each in Jaisalmer and Kota, 10 in Udaipur and 4 in Banswara).

As mentioned earlier, the untouchables in general and Bhangi's in particular, drank alcohol or liquor, ate dead animals and indulged in gambling. The Bhangis also used to eat the leftovers, when Panna Lal Barupal became the President of RPDWS in 1956. He was disappointed.

As in the case of removal of untouchability, socio-religious disabilities, agitation for temple, hotel and dharamshala entry, RPDWS directed that the social workers should involve themselves in removal of social vices and evils. In this sphere, a number of reformatory measures, such as administering the oath, persuading the Dalits, hold meetings with them and presenting a strong plea to abandon the social vices were taken. Panna Lal Barupal advocated that untouchables should give up their social vices. He believed that progress in employment and education was the basis for upward social mobility and keeping this in mind encouraged the organization for industrial exhibitions. In Rajasthan, this issue gained a regional focus and RPDWS in its 1956–57 report published the information. According to this report, 7,123 Dalits abandoned drinking alcohol and liquor and eating of left overs in 12 districts (355 persons in Jaipur, 47 in Tonk, 700 in Jhunjhunu, 466 in Alwar, 5,000 in Jodhpur, 100 each in Barmer, Jaisalmer and Udaipur, 150 in Kota, 15 in Bundi and 30 in Banswara). About 1,530 persons gave up gambling in 13 districts (370 Dalits in Jaipur, 20 in Bharatpur, 80 in Alwar, 500 in Jodhpur 180 in Barmer, 10 each in Pali and Bikaner, 15 each in Jalore and Bundi, 5 in Jaisalmer, 25 in Kota, 250 in Ganganagar and 50 in Udaipur) and also 4,159 Dalits took oath to give up the eating of dead animals in 5 districts (2,000 persons in Alwar, 1,500 in Jodhpur, 305 in Jalore, 300 in Jaisalmer and 54 in Kota).

The position of untouchables in traditional social system of Rajputana was such that it was potentially a situation of tension, arising out of deprivation. However, by and large, the untouchables accepted their status and did not rebel against it. Like ban on temple and hotel entry and admission in schools, the untouchables were prohibited from using any public water tanks or wells. Agitation started paving the way for massive social movement, with distinct ideology led by political leadership, all directed towards social transformation. The impact of the social agitation was felt. The RPDWS report of 1956–1957 in Rajasthan, mentioned that 93 public water tanks or wells were opened for Dalits in 10 districts (12 wells in Jaipur, 54 in Jhunjhunu, 3 each in Alwar, Barmer and Pali, 7 in Jodhpur, 5 in Jalore and 2 each in Kota, Bundi and Bikaner) and ban on them was abolished.

Lack of civic facilities, such as road light, cleanliness etc., in untouchable bastis were another source of deprivation. As a result of socio-political awakening, the social activists and workers, especially associated with the RPDWS had approached the local administration. It should, however, be noted that the lack of civic facilities in Bhangi bastis in various districts were more prone than that of other low caste bastis in the state. The untouchable bastis could receive the civic facilities which were possible because of the sincere efforts made by RPDWS, who followed persuasion policy. This had been discussed in 1956–1957 report and later was published in a small booklet (126 pages) which was circulated among government offices, organizations, social workers and office bearers. In 1956–1957 report Panna Lal Barupal, the President of RPDWS discussed that 654 Dalit bastis received lighting facilities in 8 districts (520 in Jaipur, 2 in Bharatpur, 15 in Tonk, 6 in Jodhpur, 3 each in Barmer and Bikaner, 100 in Udaipur and 5 in Banswara). It was also discussed that 388 untouchable bastis were benefited by cleanliness facilities in 9 districts (18 bastis in Jaipur, 5 each in Alwar and Jaisalmer, 20 in Jodhpur, 3 each in Barmer and Bikaner, 2 in Pali, 25 in Udaipur and 15 in Banswara).

During the princely rule, schools were opened by the government. But low caste children were not admitted to those schools because they were untouchables. With the development of educational facilities in the post-independence period, enthusiasm arose among untouchables because of accessibility to the benefits of modern education. The government schools in the state were thrown open to Dalit children which gave a new impetus to modern education. Soon after independence, the untouchable children were admitted to public schools. It is also notable that caste Hindu teachers and authorities had denied then admission in the schools and that they discouraged their children to come up the modern way. This situation explains why the agitation among untouchables started in the state where the discrimination against them in the field of education was severe. Therefore, Panna Lal Barupal was directing agitations against the denial of their admission to schools. It demanded that the untouchable boys and girls be admitted in the schools. The RPDWS report 1956–1957 narrated that 1,454 boys and girls were admitted in various schools of the state (200 children in Jaipur, 10 each in Tonk and Bikaner, 250 in Jhunjhunu, 425 in Alwar, 50 each in Jodhpur and Barmer, 5 in Pali, 401 in Jaisalmer, 20 each in Kota and Udaipur and 13 in Banswara), 141 students were enrolled in government hostels in 4 districts (100 students in Jhunjhunu, 5 in Jodhpur, 1 in Bundi and 35 in Banswara), 1,018 forms for scholarships were filled in, in 7 districts (11 forms in Jaipur, 150 in Tonk, 250 in Jhunjhunu, 425 in Alwar, 20 in Kota, 72 in Bundi and 90 in Bikaner), 25 new schools, including one adult school, were opened by government for the benefit of Dalit boys and girls in 6 districts (2 schools in Jaipur, 1 each in Sikar, Udaipur and Pali, 5 in Jodhpur and 15 in Barmer) and one hostel was started at Banswara.

In order to improve the socio-economic conditions of untouchables, Panna Lal Barupal realized the importance of government loan facilities for various works, such as digging of wells, purchasing agriculture land and tin sheds etc., establishment of co-operative societies, allotment of government land to refugees for their rehabilitation and stopping the displacement of Dalits. He also encouraged the educated boys to apply for government jobs in various government departments. These measures gave the untouchables an opportunity to improve their socio-economic conditions which had been denied to them for centuries. He asked his people to reduce socio-religious ceremonies to minimum and to increase public activities to maximum.

In an attempt to avail loan facilities, purchasing of land etc., RPDWS directed that social activists should tour all over Rajasthan. The report of RPDWS published in, 1956–1957 showed that there were 855 applicants who had applied for government jobs (648 applicants in Jaipur, 35 in Bharatpur, 125 in Alwar, 15 in Jaisalmer, 25 in Udaipur, and 7 in Banswara) 28 co-operative societies were established in 7 districts (8 cooperative societies in Jaipur, 4 in Jhunjhunu, 8 in Jodhpur, 2 in Pali, 5 in Jaisalmer and 1 in Bundi), government land was allotted to 120 refugee families in 3 districts (106 in Jaipur, 10 in Jodhpur and 5 in Barmer), 597 families got relief for displacement in 10 districts (135 families in Jaipur, 8 in Bharatpur, 110 in Jhunjhunu, 17 in Alwar, 25 in Jodhpur, 110 in Barmer, 10 in Pali, 85 in Jalore, 1 in Jaisalmer, 100 in Udaipur and 6 in Banswara), 1,358 families applied for purchasing the agriculture land in 10 districts (11 families in Jaipur, 150 in Tonk, 600 in Alwar, 10 in Jodhpur, 50 in Barmer, 5 each in Pali and Jaisalmer, 2 in Jalore, 25 in Ganganagar and 500 in Udaipur). In addition, a large number of applicants applied for loan for digging their own wells. Their number were 435 in 8 districts (65 applicants in Jaipur, 15 in Bharatpur, 150 in Jhunjhunu, 85 in Alwar, 100 in Jodhpur, 5 each in Jalore and Banswara and 10 in Udaipur).

Panna Lal considered that availing of government facilities would be the real measure which would improve their poor economic condition.

An analysis of various resolutions passed by the Executive Committee held on April 30, 1957[35] under the Presidentship of Panna Lal Barupal, showed that there were 11 points to focus. Some of the major points were as follows: First, the resolution urged the government of Rajasthan to increase its grants-in-aid from Rs 32,000 to 65,000. The resolution also urged the government to sanction the post of Pracharak for each district in the state. Second, looking towards the population ratio of SC in the state, they requested the then Chief Minister, M.L. Sukhadia, for inclusion of at least one minister and two deputy ministers in the ministry. Third, they expressed concern for not implementing the protective discrimination policy in the state adopted by the Constitution, particularly the recruitment of SC candidates against the 12.5 per cent reserved posts. They also regretted that the committee constituted by the Government of Rajasthan for implementation of reservation policy, had not submitted its report so far. The posts reserved for SC must be filled up only by scheduled caste candidates. Fourth, the resolution appealed to the Government of Rajasthan to allot agriculture land to landless SC people residing in rural areas. Fifth, they expressed concern to Government of Rajasthan and criticized bitterly the government machinery, particularly police department, for not implementing the Untouchability Offence Act 1955, rigidly and also alleged for not filing the challan in courts in time. On the contrary, police rebuked the untouchables. The Government of Rajasthan should issue strong direction to police to implement the Act. Sixth, in Rajasthan Pradesh the untouchable basties in various parts of the state were suffering from the basic amenities, such as roads, water and electricity. In cities, the conditions of bhangi basties were more miserable. Therefore, the Executive Committee urged the government to extend these facilities to untouchable basties. They also demanded to construct modern Dalit basties. Seventh, a large number of untouchables were residing in their bastis since several decades without patta. They were being displaced by local authorities. The state government should be directed that they should not be disturbed and pattas should be given to them immediately. Lastly, the resolution urged the Government of Rajasthan to allot land free of cost to Dalits to construct their own pakka house.

Most of the issues that Panna Lal Barupal took up later on with the Government of Rajasthan and the then Home Minister, Govind Vallabh Pant, Government of India, New Delhi on August 6, 1957[36] were similar to those of the resolutions passed in the Executive Committee held on April 30, 1957.

Since we have already discussed the genesis, growth and dimensions of RPDWS movement at the state level, we may now mention a new prominent literature[37] published by President, RPDWS, Jaipur, during the movement. Some of the famous publications may be listed for the sake of illustration.

1. हिन्दू समाज जिनको अछूत मानता है, क्या वे अछूत हैं?
2. छुआछूत कानूनी जुर्म है के हैंडबिल्स
3. अस्पृश्यता निवारक कानून का सचित्र अनुवाद
4. अस्पृश्यता निवारण कानून का सचित्र पोस्टर
5. प्रथम वार्षिक सम्मेलन बीकानेर के स्वागताध्यक्ष श्री कोचर एवं स्वागत मंत्री श्री बारूपाल का भाषण
6. द्वितीय वार्षिक सम्मेलन उदयपुर के अध्यक्ष श्री बारूपाल एवं स्वागताध्यक्ष श्री यादव के भाषण
7. जाति–पांति और वर्ण–व्यवस्था का रहस्य
8. दलितों के सच्चे हितैषी (कलेण्डर्स)
9. 1955–56 की कार्य रिपोर्ट व आय–व्यय का विवरण
10. भजन सामाजिक कुरीतियां निवारण
11. दलितों के आह भरे उपालंभ (हिन्दी व पंजाबी कविताएं)
12. किसी भले आदमी से छुआछूत करना कानूनी जुर्म है–पोस्टर
13. स्मरण पत्र श्री पी. सत्यनारायण राव, अध्यक्ष राजस्थान राजधानी समिति, भारत सरकार
14. आज का बीकानेर, चित्रमय

The Caste Hindus' Reaction towards RPDWS Movement

While working in rural and urban areas, the social workers, social activists and untouchables had faced a lot of social criticism, opposition, social boycott and imposition of socio-economic restrictions on them by the upper caste Hindus. Thus, the reaction of caste Hindus towards RPDWS movement in the state was similar to that of Chamar and Jatavs in Uttar Pradesh, Mahar in Maharashtra, and Nadar in Tamil Nadu. The Rajasthan Pradesh Dalit Warg Sangh's (RPDWS) report 1956–1957 described the occurrence of caste antagonism between the mass of poor helpless and landless untouchables and small group of mighty and wealthy upper caste Hindus. As the movement gathered momentum over a period of years, RPDWS drew more and more members into the campaign especially for removal of untouchability and social disabilities.

Thus, between 1947–1956 the involvement of persons with RPDWS reached a climax. During these years the agitation of untouchables across the state reached a climax and this was the period when atrocities too increased all over Rajasthan. For instance, the caste Hindus in rural areas such as Rashisar, Parva and Thavaria villages in Nokha tehsil, Bikaner, imposed the following restrictions[38] or ban on the untouchables:

1. The moneylenders stopped giving money.
2. The Bania stopped selling food grains, etc.
3. The venders stopped selling vegetables etc. Those who violated these restrictions became the victims of villagers.
4. Untouchables were not allowed to graze their cattle in the fields of savarnas.
5. The savarnas did not allow the untouchables for defecation in the village boundary, and
6. Untouchables were compelled to collect drinking water from the places where village cattle used to drink water.

Thus, the social life of untouchables in rural areas became more miserable. Their bastis became hell as they became dumping place of village dirt, and dead animals. It was difficult to breath in the fresh air, the village panchayats were silent on Dalit issues.

The enlightened persons among the caste Hindus supported and helped the movement by giving moral support and encouragement towards removal of untouchability and social disabilities, admission of Dalit children in schools, entry into hotels and temples etc. For instance, Choudhary Keshu Ram,[39] Sarpanch of Badhanu village in Bikaner had openly supported untouchability removal campaign launched in his village under the auspices of RPDWS. The agitation, thus, spread throughout the village. One of the unique features of caste Hindus' reaction was to boycott the entire untouchable communities in the village and this they had done to teach a lesson to the untouchables. Choudhary Keshu Ram opposed it and he was constantly in touch with untouchables and their campaigners. When this news reached the village, they became very furious. Consequently, his entire family was socially boycotted by village community. Chaudhary Keshu Ram, thus, became the first victim of anger of caste Hindus.

Besides, Keshu Ram Choudhary, there were other upper caste Hindus who supported the welfare programmes and agitation against social vices, such as untouchability. One such was Kani Ram Jain[40] from village Panchu, Bikaner. Kani Ram Jain supported the issue of removal of untouchability and RPDWS's welfare programme and activity in the village. He now advocated amongst the villagers for equal behaviour with the untouchables to promote brotherhood. Thus, he supported RPDWS movement. Subsequently, Kani Ram Jain was also socially boycotted by his own community and became the next victim.

These incidents, however, have not adversely affected the socio-educational and religious dimensions of main RPDWS movement. On the contrary, the RPDWS movement did add to a state level dimension of RPDWS movement.

Notes and References

1. For detailed discussion of 'Mewar Prajamandal' that stresses the agitation for the right to speech, liberty and to form associations etc., in the Mewar region and socio-political consequences of the movement see, in particular, B.L. Pangaria, *Rajasthan Mai Swatantrata Sangram*, Jaipur, Rajasthan Hindi Granth Academy, 1988, p. 50.
2. K.S. Saxena, *The Political Movements and Awakening in Rajasthan (1857 to 1947)*, New Delhi, S. Chand and Co.1971, p. 216.
3. B.L. Pangaria, 1988, Ibid., pp. 51–52.
4. Ibid.
5. *Rajasthan Varsika, 1955*, p. 60.
6. Ibid.
7. Ibid.
8. Ibid.
9. Ibid.
10. Ibid.
11. Ibid.
12. Ibid.
13. Ibid.
14. Ibid.
15. Ibid.
16. *Rajasthan Pradesh Dalit Warg Sangh: Varshik, Karya Avam Aaya-vyaya Vivran (1956–57)*, edited and Published by RPDWS, Jaipur. Year not mentioned.

17. Panna Lal Barupal, the then President of Rajasthan Pradesh Dalit Warg Sangh had discussed many important socio-cultural activities and programmes which were launched in different regions in Rajasthan, see particularly, *Rajasthan Pradesh Dalit Warg Sangh: Varshik, Karya Avam Aaya-vyaya Vivran (1956–57)*. Edited and published by Panna Lal Barupal, RPDWS, Jaipur (Year not mentioned).
18. Ibid., p. 82.
19. Ibid., pp. 119–123.
20. This description is largely based on three printed lectures delivered by two eminent Dalits and one non-Dalit leader namely Panna Lal Barupal, the then Member of Parliament, Amrit Lal Yadav, the then minister, Government of Rajasthan and Ram Ratan Cochar, keenly interested in the SC/ST affairs. For an elaborate and detailed discussion on pitiable socio-economic and educational conditions of untouchables in rural areas particularly, and harassment, torture and atrocities by the upper caste Hindus on them, see the printed speeches "Bhasan" by Panna Lal Barupal, Swagat Mantri, "Abhibhashan" by Amrit Lal Yadav, Adhiyaksh and "Swagat Bhashan" by Ram Ratan Cochar, dated November 22–23, 1953.
21. For discussion on untouchabilities and observance of social disabilities in rural areas, see, Ram Ratan Cochar, 'Swagat Bhashan', dated November 22, 1953, pp. 1–10, Bikaner, Educational Press.
22. This description is largely based on printed lecture. For an elaborate and detailed discussion, see, Panna Lal Barupal, M.P. 'Bhasan' dated November 22–23, 1953, pp. 1–14, Delhi, Tyagi Fine Art Press. It is also important to mention here that title cover of lecture was printed at Laxmi Press, Dariba Kalla, Delhi.
23. For fuller discussion, see, a printed lecture 'Abhibhasan', of Amrit Lal Yadav which was delivered on the occasion of Rajasthan Dalit Warg Sangh Pratham Sammelan, Bikaner, dated November 22–23, 1953.
24. For a fuller discussion, see a printed lecture 'Swagat Bhashan' of Ram Ratan Cochar, Swagata Adhiyaksh which was delivered on the occasion of Rajasthan Virat Dalit Wargeeya Second Sammelan Chhoti Khatu (Marwar) Nagaur, dated March 28, 1954, Ajmer, Vedic Yantralai 1954, pp. 1–7.
25. In his welcome address Rajasthan Pradesh Dalit Warg Sangh Dwatiya Varshik Adhivasan-ke-Swagata Adhiyaksh Amrit Lal Yadav, Mantri, Sahkari, Punarsthapan Avam Pratak Rajasav Vibhag, Rajasthan-ka-Swagat Bhashan by Swagat Samiti, Rajasthan Pradesh Dalit Warg Sangh, Dwatiya Varshik Adhivesan, Udaipur, was published and circulated on September 17, 1955. Printed at Navjivan Printing Press, Udaipur. Amrit Lal Yadav, Minister, in the

Sukhadia Ministry, Congress, devoted a lengthy lecture on the pitiable socio-economic conditions of untouchables in Rajasthan, p. 8.

26. For details, see 'Swagat Bhasan' by Amrit Lal Yadav, September 17, 1955, Ibid., p. 3.
27. Ibid., p. 4.
28. Ibid., p. 5.
29. Ibid., p. 5.
30. Ibid., p. 5.
31. Ibid., p. 2.
32. Ibid., p. 3.
33. This description is largely based on a printed lecture delivered by a Dalit social activist (name is missing). For an elaborate and detailed discussion on the miserable socio-economic and educational conditions of untouchables in desert region of Barmer and atrocities, harassment and torture by caste Hindus on them, see printed speech, *District Barmer: Dalit Kisan Sammelan*, year not mentioned. Jodhpur. Printed at Hindu Sandesh Press, Sojati Gate, pp. 1–12.
34. This description is largely based on a small booklet edited and published by Panna Lal Barupal. For an elaborate and detailed discussion on the miserable socio-economic and educational conditions of the untouchables in desert region of Rajasthan and atrocities, harassment and torture by upper caste Hindus on them, see particularly *Rajasthan Pradesh Dalit Warg Sangh: Varshik Karya Avam Aaya-Vyaya Vivran (1956–1957)*. Year not mentioned. For touring the villages, agitation against the ban on the entry of untouchables in temples and hotels, challan filled in various courts, Sneh Milan, meetings of Dalit communities, removal of untouchability and socio-religious disabilities etc., data have been derived from pp. 1–126.
35. Ibid., pp. 80–87.
36. Ibid., p. 95.
37. Ibid., See last page of book.
38. Ibid., p. 89. Also see, p. 87–90.
39. Ibid., p. 90.
40. Ibid., p. 68.

4 Political Parties and the Chamar/Meghwal Leadership

Perspective/Policy/Strategy

Caste, Party and Political Representation in the State Assembly

Since the political elites form the driving force in any social movement, it is necessary to give a brief account of their growth and strength. Although modern Chamar, Meghwal and Jatav politicians emerged from 1935 onwards when they formed—'Rajasthan Meghwal Mahasabha' (RMS) and launched a campaign against the socio-economic atrocities, untouchability and socio-religious disabilities in Rajasthan, a steady growth of professional politicians occurred only after 1952 general elections.

Since 1952 the Congress party has established nearly complete hegemony over SC/ST politics. Within Congress, supremacy had increasingly been shown towards Chamars, Meghwals, Bairwas, Balais, Khatiks and Raigars. The sentiments within caste/community however were shifting slowly.

A point worth consideration in this respect is the fact that in the State Assembly elections held in 1952 in the state of Rajasthan, which was the first of its kind, the Congress party in all the constituencies reserved seats for Scheduled Castes, fielded large number of candidates from all major castes/communities, such as Chamars, Meghwals, Bairwas, Balais, Raigars, Kolis, Khatiks and Jatias, etc. The fact related to the election of 1952 to the State Assembly revealed that Amritlal Yadav, Chamar, contesting from Rajsamand-Railmagra, district Udaipur, Deen Bandhu Meghwal, from Shayara, district Udaipur, Laxman Hirat, Balai, from Sarada Salumber, Madholal Mehar, Balai, from Jhalrapatan, district Jhalawar and Sampat Ram Meghwal from Laxmangarh-Rajgarh, won the election. All the five candidates[1] were sponsored by Congress.

The 1957 general elections held in the state, marked a further increase in the representation of Chamar, Meghwal, Jatav and Balai communities in the state politics. In this election (1957), one Congress candidate, namely, Amritlal Yadav, from Jalore reserved constituency was declared elected. He was a Chamar. Hashiya, Ram Rajya Parishad, from Jalore, Jethmal Barbad, Congress, from Nava, district Nagaur, Kota, Kalu Ram, Ram Rajya Parishad, from Mandal, Bhilwara, Mahadev Prasad, Congress, from Khetri, Jhunjhunu, Manroop Ram Parihar, independent, from Kharchi, Pali, Rawat Ram, Congress, from Balortara, district Barmer, Rawat Ram, Congress, from Churu, Roopa Ram, independent, from Nokha, district Nagaur and Surajmal, Ram Rajya Parishad, from Phalodi district Jodhpur (all 9 Meghwals[2]); Narain Lal, Congress, from Neem ka Thana, district Sikar and Sampat Ram, Congress, from Tijara, district Alwar (both Balais[3]); Dhannalal, Congress, from Chhabra, district Kota, Goverdhan Singh, Congress, from Bayana, district Bharatpur, Hari Prasad, Congress, from Vallabhnagar, district Kota and Umedilal, Congress, from Karauli district Sawai Madhopur (all 4 Jatavs[4]) were elected to the State Assembly and 12 winners were nominated by Congress, 2 were nominated by Ram Rajya Parishad and 2 were independent candidates. The total number of Chamar, Meghwal, Balai and Jatav had increased from 5 in 1952 to 16 in 1957.

For the first time in the history of Rajasthan in the Third General Elections of the legislative assembly held in the year 1962, efforts were made by some leaders of scheduled castes communities to associate themselves with some other political parties to fight the election to defeat Congress party. For this purpose—Chothmal Verma, Balai, Dayachand Jatav and Hari Ram Chauhan, Balai, contested elections on Swatantra party, Jan Sangh and Communist party tickets from Bhinaya, Baranand and Tijara respectively and were declared elected.[5] Thus, the neglect of Balai and Jatav's interests by the Congress party, created a crisis in Balai and Jatav organizations, which led to a vertical split in the communities. In this process, of course, Bunaya and Tijara Balais and Baran Jatav moved closer to Swatantra party, Jan Sangh and Communist party. Roopa Ram Panwar, Balai,[6] contested from Nokha as an independent candidate and was declared elected.

Amrit Lal Yadav, Chamar, from Bhopal Sagar, Dinesh Rai Dangi from Desuri, Jethmal Barbad from Parbatsar, Jagmal from Rawatsar and

Lala Ram from Phalodi (all 4 Meghwals[7]); Rawat Ram Balai from Sadulpur, Gokul Chand Jatav from Katumar and Shawaliya Ram Jatav,[8] from Roopavash were elected to State Assembly and all the eight were nominated by Congress party.

Although as per the result declared officially, Congress won only 8 seats yet in comparison to the last assembly election (1957), actually Congress lost 4 seats, i.e., reduced from 12 in 1957 to 8 in 1962. This was an indication of political alienation of Chamar, Meghwal, Jatav and Balai elites from Congress as it was a change in political alignment.

On the eve of the Fourth General Elections in 1967 for the state legislative assembly, again a change took place in the attitudes of Chamars, Meghwals, Jatavs and Balais towards Congress. However, most of the Chamars, Meghwals and Jatavs as in the previous election 1962, remained associated with the Congress. Thus, in the election, 1967, Amritlal Yadav, Chamar, from Rajsamand, Virda Ram from Jalore, Birbal from Sangariya, Manphool Ram from Keshrisinghpura, Mahendra Kumar from Padva and Mulkaraj Thind from Raisinghnagar (all five Meghwals[9]); Gokul Chand from Kherthal and Balvant Ram from Badi (both Jatavs[10]) were elected to State Assembly and all the 8 were nominated by Congress party, but the total number of Congress candidates remained the same as in the previous election, i.e., 1962.

It would be noted that during the year 1967 general elections, the number of candidates who were declared elected increased from one to five. These newly elected candidates were from Swatantra party. Thus, Surajmal Chamar[11] from Suratgarh, Kalu Ram from Siwana, Daulat Ram from Desuri and Moti Lal from Revdar (all three Meghwals[12]) and Jasraj Balai,[13] from Bhinaya—all these Chamar, Meghwal and Balai candidates of Swatantra party were declared elected. It is worthwhile to note here that as in the year 1962, again in 1967 Jan Sangh bagged only one seat of Jatav candidate in the State Assembly. It was Ram Charan from Atru. In the 1967 election, the number of independent candidates remained the same, i.e., one in 1962 to one in 1967. He was Rawat Ram Meghwal, from Chhapra. However, it may be added here that Communist party, which had returned 1 candidate in 1962, viz., Hari Ram Chauhan from Tijara could not muster any seat this time.

The 1972 general elections marked a sudden rise in the number of Congress candidates of Meghwal, Balai and Jatav in the state politics. In this election (1972), the number of Congress candidates who were declared elected increased from 8 in 1967 to 14 in 1972. These newly elected candidates were: Jethmal Barbad from Parbatsar, Jethmal Arya from Revdar, Sisha Ram from Siwana, Dinesh Rai Dangi from Desuri, Birbal from Sangaria, Manphool Ram from Keshrisinghpur, Rawat Ram from Chhapra (all 8 Meghwals[14]), Smt Bhagwati Devi from Bhinaya, Mahendra Kumar from Padva and Sundar Lal from Suratgarh (all 3 Balais[15]); Nathi Singh from Nandwai, Bhura Lal from Shahpura and Ramcharan from Atru (all 3 Jatavs[16]). All these 14 candidates (8 Meghwals, 3 Balais and 3 Jatavs) were declared elected. It will be worthwhile to note here that as in 1967, again in 1972 the Swatantra party bagged only two seats of Meghwal candidates in the assembly. They were: Keshav Dev from Laxmangarh and Bega Ram from Raisinghnagar. Umedi Ram Jatav, contested from Hindaun on Jan Sangh ticket and was declared elected.

The most significant feature of the Sixth General Elections of 1977 in the country and in the various states, of general or reserved constituencies, was a general feeling of disappointment in the minds of the people towards the Congress—the ruling party—because of the emergency imposed in the country in 1975.[17] Decades of rule by Congress party had not delivered the expected goods, but casteism, groupism, nepotism and attending rapacious corruption were the order of the day. People were also frustrated by the police atrocities and compulsory retirement of government servants.

All these had made the Congress rule unpopular and this determined the trend of the canvassing done by various political parties who were in opposition, so much so that they amalgamated themselves into a united front. Thus, in May 1977, the Congress(O), the Bharatiya Lok Dal, Bharatiya Jan Sangh, Socialist party, Congress for Democracy and a few independents belonging to the Congress merged in a single party to form the Janta Party. It was because of these reasons that several young canvassers in the different areas were found to be working on behalf of Jan Sangh, Socialist and Congress(O) parties. Their main object was to defeat Congress in any possible manner.

The number of candidates, as per the figures of the Sixth General Elections of 1977, indicates that all the 14 candidates—Rawat Ram Chamar from Sujangarh, Achla Ram from Desuri, Uda Ram Hatila from Nokha, Kailash Chandra Meghwal from Rajsamand, Chena Ram from Siwana, Bahadur Singh from Nohar, Mangi Lal from Gangrar and Sampat

Ram from Kherthal (all 7 Meghwals[18]), Subhash Chandra Arya, Balai[19] Tarachand from Roopavas and Shrawan Lal from Hindaun (both Jatavs[20]) had exclusively won elections as Janta Party candidates.

The 1977 general elections marked a sudden decline in the number of candidates of Congress party in the state politics. In this election five Congress candidates, viz.,—Jethamal Barbad, Meghwal, from Parbatsar, Dula Ram Balai from Raisinghnagar, Narpat Ram Barbad, Meghwal, from Sursagar, Parsha Ram Meghwal, from Laxmangarh and Manphool Ram Meghwal, from Keshrisinghpur were successful, but the total number of Congress candidates had decreased from 14 in 1972 to 5 in 1977. Thus, a crushing defeat of the Congress was a spectacular feature of the Sixth General Elections in the state as a whole.

As stated earlier, it was Janta Party which won the election in 1977, but the mid-term election of 1980s which was due to the failure of Janta Party, changed the picture altogether. Thus, in the mid-term election Congress party improved its position. Thus, Parashram Mordia from Laxmangarh, Jethmal Barbad from Parbatsar, Dinesh Rai Dangi from Desuri, Narpat Ram Barbad from Sursagar, Peeru Ram from TB, Manphool Ram from Keshrisinghpur, Ram Karan Katala from Jayal, Surja Ram from Nokha and Sampat Ram from Kherthal (all 9 Meghwals[21]). One Balai,[22] namely, Dula Ram from Raisinghpur, Ram Prasad from Roopavash and Ram Sahay from Lalsot (both Jatavs[23]) were declared successful. All were Congress candidates. However, it may be added here that Pradal succeeded in sending one Meghwal,[24] namely, Bhanwar Lal from Sujangarh, one Jatav,[25] Bharoshi Ram from Hindaun and Sundarlal Balai[26] from Suratgarh.

The most significant feature of the general elections of 1985 in the country was the general sympathy in the minds of the people towards Congress party because of the assassination of Mrs Indira Gandhi, the then Prime Minister of India, who remained in power for nearly 18 years. The overwhelming victory of Congress was a very spectacular feature of the Eighth General Elections in the country as a whole. The number of candidates in the State Assembly was 13 candidates from Meghwal, Balai and Jatav communities. Congress was at the top who bagged 9 seats, i.e., Narpat Ram Barbad from Sursagar, Manphool Ram from Raisinghnagar, Mota Ram from Siwana and Raj Kumar Jaipal from Ajmer (all 4 Meghwals), Deepchand from Dag, Pokar Lal from Desuri and Sundar Lal from Suratgarh (all 3 Balais), Umedi Lal from Hindaun and Chandra Sheikhar from Kherthal (both Jatavs).

It will, thus, be seen that BJP, which had not returned a single candidate in 1980, could muster 2 seats this time (1985), viz., Chunni Lal Meghwal from Sujangarh and Mangi Lal Meghwal[27] from Patan. It will be worth mentioning here that the Lok Dal candidate, Mohan Lal and Keshar Dev, who won the election from Jayal and Laxmangarh constituencies of district Nagaur and district Sikar respectively belonged to Meghwal[28] and Balai[29] communities.

The elections of 1990 showed a sudden increase in the number of Bharatiya Janta Party candidates belonging to Meghwals in the state politics. The six BJP candidates, viz., Achala Ram from Desuri, Kailash Meghwal from Niwai, Jogeshwar Garg from Jalore, Mangilal Meghwal from Patan, Mohan Meghwal from Sursagar and Hukma Ram Meghwal from Siwana were successful. Thus, the number of BJP Meghwal[30] candidates had increased from 2 in 1985 to 6 in 1990. Two candidates, namely, Ram Swaroop Meghwal from Raisinghnagar and Mohan Lal Barupal from Jayal (both Meghwals[31]), Babu Lal Balai[32] from Suratgarh, Nirbhayalal from Roopavash and Bharoshi Lal from Hindaun (all 3 Jatavs[33]) were declared successful. All 5 were Janta Dal candidates.[34] Congress bagged 3 seats, i.e., Parash Ram Mordia, Meghwal from Laxmangarh, Bhanwar Lal Balai[35] from Sujangarh and Ramprasad Jatav[36] from Ber.

The elections of 1993 were significant because of a sudden increase in the number of BJP professional politicians from Meghwal and Jatav communities in the state politics. The 7 BJP Meghwal[37] candidates, viz., Achala Ram from Desuri, Kailash Meghwal from Shahpura, Jogeshwar Garg from Jalore, Mengilal Meghwal from Keshavrai Patan, Mohan Meghwal from Sursagar, Rakesh Meghwal from Parbatsar and Revat Ram Panwar from Nokha were successful. Two Jatav[38] candidates, namely, Madan Mohan from Kherthal and Moti Lal from Roopavash were declared successful. They were BJP candidates. Two Meghwal[39] candidates, namely, Parash Ram Mordia from Laxmangarh and Mulkraj Thind from Raisinghnagar were declared successful. They were Congress candidates. Two independent Meghwal[40] candidates—Shashi Datta from TB and Sundar Lal from Suratgarh were declared successful.

The elections of 1998 were all the more significant because BJP, which had returned 7 Meghwal candidates in 1993, could muster only one seat this time. He was Ganeshilal Meghwal[41] from Jalore. Thus it was a crushing defeat to BJP in 1998 elections.

It was the Congress party which won the election in 1998 with two-thirds majority (153 seats out of 200 seats). Thus, the overwhelming victory of Congress and defeat of BJP was the main feature of the Eleventh General Elections in the state. Congress being at the top, bagged 29 Scheduled Castes and 20 Scheduled Tribes seats out of 57 seats in the State Assembly in 1998. Congress being at the top bagged 10 Congress Meghwal[42] candidates, viz., Ashok from Phagi, Atma Ram from Desuri, Aadram from TB, Gopa Ram Meghwal from Siwana, Ghasilal Meghwal from Patan, Parash Ram Mordia from Laxmangarh, Bhanwar Lal Meghwal from Sujangarh, Mohan Lal Barupal from Jayal, Revat Ram Panwar from Nokha and Hanuman Prasad from Suratgarh. One Balai[43] candidate, namely, Bhanwar Lal won the election from Sursagar. He was a Congress candidate. Three Congress candidates, namely, Chandra Shekhar from Kherthal, Nirbhayalal from Roopavash and Bharoshi Lal from Hindaun were successful. They were Jatavs.[44]

As stated earlier, it was the Congress party which won the election in 1998 with two-thirds majority (153 seats out of 200), but in the 12th Legislative Assembly Elections of December 1, 2003, the picture radically changed. Thus, the overwhelming victory of BJP with 120 seats (out of 200) and crushing defeat of Congress was spectacular feature of the 12th General Elections in the state. The number of reserved seats in the whole State Assembly is only 57. Similarly Congress at the top who bagged 29 Scheduled Castes and 20 Scheduled Tribes seats of the 57 in the whole State Assembly in 1998, could not muster even 10 seats this time (2003). The number of BJP SC/ST candidates in the whole of State Assembly was 4 (SC-3, ST-1), Janta Dal bagged 3, while there was only one independent Scheduled Caste. The number of Congress SC/ST candidates in the whole State Assembly (2003) is 9 only (SC-5 and ST-4). This is an indication of political alienation of the weaker sections of the society in general and Scheduled Caste and Scheduled Tribes in particular from Congress. The most significant feature of State Assembly election of 2003 was a general feeling of disappointment in the mind of SC and ST people towards Congress—the ruling party because of indifferent attitude of the Chief Minister—Ashok Gehlot. The Scheduled Castes and Scheduled Tribe people were also frustrated owing to the failure of the Congress government in protecting their genuine interest.

The elections of 2003 are all the more significant because BJP, which had returned only one seat in 1998, could succeed in sending 10 BJP Meghwal[45] candidates this time (2003). Thus all the 10 BJP candidates—Lal Chand from Raisinghnagar, Sriganganagar district; Govind Chauhan from Nokha, Bikaner district, Khema Ram from Sujangarh, Churu district, Sundar Lal from Surajgarh, Jhunjhunu district, K.D. Babar from Laxmangarh, Sikar district, Smt Laxmi Barupal from Desuri, Pali district, Jogeshwar Garg from Jalore, district Jalore, Mohan Meghwal from Sursagar, Jodhpur district, Madan Meghwal from Jayal, Nagaur district and Rakesh Meghwal from Parbatsar, Nagaur district were elected. This is an indication of alienation of Meghwal elites from the Congress as it was a change in the political alignments.

As per the result declared officially, one Jatav[46] candidate, namely, Jai Ram from Kherthal, Alwar district and Nirbhaya Lal Jatav[47] from Roopabas, district Bharatpur were declared successful. They were BJP and Congress candidates respectively. Similarly, one Jatav candidate, namely, Laku Ram Jatav[48] from Hindaun, Karauli district was declared successful. He was Indian National Lokdal (INL) candidate. The number of BJP Jatav candidates has increased from zero in 1998 to 1 in 2003. Likewise the number of INL Jatav[49] candidates has also increased from zero in 1998 to 1 in 2003.

It is important to note that Chamar, Meghwal, Balai and Jatav politicians belong to diverse political parties. For instance, in 1967, 15 MLAs out of 184 candidates in Rajasthan were: 8 Congress, 5 Swatantra Party, 1 Jan Sangh and 1 independent. Similarly, in 1980 15 MLAs out of 200 in Rajasthan were: 12 Congress and 3 Pra-Dal. In 1990, 14 MLAs out of 200 in Rajasthan were: 3 Congress, 6 BJP and 5 Janta Dal. In 2003, 13 MLAs out of 200 in Rajasthan were: 11 BJP, one each from Congress and INL.

Thus, Chamars, Meghwals, Balais and Jatavs have been successful in their eneavour to gain caste representation in the State Assembly since 1952. Since 1952 at least 1 or 2 member of state level Chamar, Meghwal, Balai and Jatav in the State Assembly had been member in the Ministry. Table 4.1, shows the position of parties during 1952–2013.

As stated earlier, it was the BJP which won the election in 2003 with a two-third majority (120 seats out of 200), but in the 13th Legislative Assembly Election of December, 2008, the picture changed radically. Thus the emergence of Congress as the largest party with 96 seats (out of

Table 4.1

Rajasthan Vidhan Sabha Elections and Chamar, Meghwal, Balai and Jatav Representation from All Over Rajasthan in the State Assembly from 1952 to 2013

Year	Number of assembly seats				Name of Scheduled Castes/communities (by party affiliation)					Other Scheduled castes/ communities	Total
	General	Scheduled Castes	Scheduled Tribes	Total	Chamar	Meghwal	Balai	Jatav	Total		
1	2	3	4	5	6	7	8	9	10	11	12
1952–57	139	16	6	160	1(C)	2(C)	2(C)	—	5	11	16
1957–62	128	28	20	176	1(C)	5(C) 2(RRP) 2(IND)	2(C)	4(C)	16	12	28
1962–67	128	28	20	176	1(C)	4(C) 1(SP) 1(CP) 1(IND)	1(C)	2(C) 1(JS)	12	16	28

Cont'd...

Cont'd...

1967–72	132	31	21	184	1(C) 1(SP)	5(C) 3(SP) 1(IND)	1(SP)	2(C) 1(JS)	15	16	31
1972–77	132	31	21	184	—	8(C) 2(SP)	3(C)	3(C) 1(JS)	17	14	31
1977–80	143	33	24	200	1(JP)	4(C) 7(JP)	1(C) 1(JP)	2(JP)	16	17	33
1980–85	143	33	24	200	—	1(Pra-Dal) 9(C)	1(Pra-Dal) 1(C)	1(Pra-Dal) 2(C)	15	18	33
1985–90	143	33	24	200	—	4(C) 2(BJP) 1(LD)	3(C) 1(LD)	2(C)	13	20	33
1990–92	143	33	24	200	—	1(C) 6(BJP) 2(JD)	1(C) 1(JD)	1(C) 2(JD)	14	19	33
1993–98	143	33	24	200	—	2(C) 7(BJP) 2(IND)	—	2(BJP)	13	20	33

Cont'd...

Cont'd...

1998–2003	143	33	24	200	—	10(C) 1(BJP)	1(C)	3(C)	15	18	33
2003–08	143	33	24	200	—	10(BJP)	—	1(BJP) 1(C) 1(INL)	13	20	33
2008–2013	141	34	25	200	1 (BJP)	7(C) 5(BJP) 2(CPM)	—	1(C) 1(BJP)	17	16	34

Source: 1. Trimasik Patrika *Vidhan Bodhani*, October 1997, Swarn Jayanti Visheshank, Rajasthan Vidhan Sabha Sachivalaya, Jaipur, pp. 161–216.
2. *Dr Ambedkar Dig-Darshika*, 2004, Dr Ambedkar Memorial and Educational Sansthan, Alwar, 2004, p. 40.

Symbol:

C = Congress	RRP = Ram Rajya Parishad	JD = Janta Dal
SP = Swatantra Party	CP = Communist Party	JS = Jan Sangh
JP = Janta Party	PRA-DAL = Pra-Dal	INL = Indian National Lokdal
BJP = Bharatiya Janta Party	LD = Lok Dal	IND = Independent

200) and the decadence of BJP with a crushing defeat with just 78 seats (out of 200) were spectacular feature of the 13th General Election in the state. The number of reserved seats in the whole State Assembly is 59 (SC-34, ST-25). Similarly, Congress at the top, who bagged 18 Scheduled Castes and 16 Scheduled Tribes seats out of 59 in the whole State Assembly in 2008, could thus muster 34 seats this time (2008). Thus, all the 18 Congress candidates: Dolatraj Nayak from Raisinghnagar, district Ganganagar; Aadram Meghwal from Pilibanga, district Hanumangarh; Master Bhanwar Lal Meghwal from Sujangarh, district Churu; Babulal Nagar from Dudu, district Jaipur, Tika Ram Jully from Alwar Rural, district Alwar; Bharoshi Lal Jatav from Hindaun, district Karauli; Mamta Bhupet from Sikrai, district Dausa; Ashok Bairwa from Khandar, district Sawaimadhopur; Kamla Loda from Niwai, district Tonk, Manju Meghwal from Jayal, district Sawaimadhopur; Kamla Loda from Chohatan, district Barmer, Ramlal Meghwal from Jalore, district Jalore; Shankar Bairwa from Kapasan, district Chittorgarh; Mahaveer Prasad Mochi from Shahpura, district Bhilwara; C.L. Premi from Kesoraipatan, district Bundi; Panna Chand Meghwal from Atru, district Baraun, Madanlal Bairwa from Dug, district Jhalawar and Ganga Devi from Bagru, district Jaipur, were declared elected.

The number of BJP SC/ST candidates in the whole of State Assembly are 16 (SC-14, ST-2). The number of BJP SC candidates are 14 only. Their names are: Vishvanath from Khajuwala, district Bikaner, Sunder Lal Chamar from Pilani, district Jhunjhunu, Pramila Kudera from Chaksu, district Jaipur; Babulal Bairwa from Katumar, district Alwar; Bahadur Singh Koli from Bair, district Bharatpur; Igarsharam Koli from Bayana, district Bharatpur; Sukharam Koli from Basedi, district Dholpur; Anita Bhadel from Ajmer Daksin, district Ajmer, Sukha Ram Meghwal from Merta, district Nagaur, Smt Sanjana Aagari from Sojat, district Pali, Smt Kashma Devi from Bhopalgarh, district Jodhpur, Arjun Lal Garg from Bilara, district Jodhpur, Jagsi Ram Koli from Revdar, district Sirohi and Chandra Kanta Meghwal from Ramganjmandi, district Kota.

2 CPM candidates (SC) namely Prema Ram Meghwal from Dhodh, district Sikar and Pawan Dugal (Meghwal) from Anupgarh, district Ganganagar were declared successful for the first time.

The elections of 2008 were all the more significant because for the first time Meena politicians who has a dominating say in certain general constituencies, returned 5 Meena candidates belonging to diverse political parties in 2008. As per the result declared officially one Meena candidate namely Smt Rohini Singh (BJP) from Karauli, district Karauli, Ram Narain Meena (Congress) from Devli Unniyara, district Tonk; Murarilal Meena from Dausa, district Dausa and Ramkesh Meena from Ganganagar (both BSP) and Galma Devi Meena (independent) from Mahua, district Dausa were declared successful.

Caste and Representation in Parliament—SC

Lok Sabha

Apart from all this, a good number of Chamars, Meghwals and Jatavs became members of Parliament. For instance, in 1952 Panna Lal Barupal,[50] Meghwal, was not only elected for the first time to Parliament from Ganganagar, but he also won the elections four times in 1957, 1962, 1967 from Ganganagar and in 1971 from Bikaner. Thus he was elected MP fifth time and had a long tenure, say 25 years. He was a Congress candidate. In 1952 Manak Chand Jatav[51] was elected MP from Bharatpursawai Madhopur constituency. He was the candidate of Krashak Mazdoor Party. In 1977 Shyam Sundar Lal Jatav[52] from Bayana, Hukma Ram, Meghwal,[53] from Jalore and Bega Ram Meghwal[54] from Ganganagar were declared elected MPs. All the 3 MPs were Bharatiya Lok Dal candidates. In 1980 Birbal Meghwal,[55] was not only elected for the first time to Parliament from Ganganagar, but he also won the elections twice in 1984 and 1991. Thus, he was elected MP a third time. He was a Congress candidate. For the first time Virda Ram Meghwal,[56] was elected MP from Jalore in 1980. He was a Congress candidate. Lala Ram Ken, Jatav,[57] for the first time in 1984, was elected to Parliament from Bayana constituency. He was a Congress candidate. In 1989 Than Singh Jatav,[58] BJP from Bayana and Bega Ram, Meghwal,[59] Janta Dal from Ganganagar were declared elected to the Lok Sabha.

Kailash Meghwal,[60] one of the prominent Meghwals, was not only elected for the first time in 1989 to Parliament from Jalore constituency, but also won the by-election in 2001 from Tonk and in 2004 from the same constituency (Tonk). He was a BJP candidate. In 1996 Paras Ram

Meghwal[61] a Congress candidate from Jalore was elected to Parliament. In 1966, Nihal Chand Meghwal[62] was not only elected for the first time to Parliament from Ganganagar, but also won the election in 1999 from the same constituency (Ganganagar). Thus he was elected MP twice. He was a Congress candidate. Again in 2004, he was elected to Parliament for the third time from Ganganagar. This time he was from BJP. In 1998 Shankar Pannu Meghwal,[63] contested election on Congress ticket from Ganganagar reserved constituency and won the election for Lok Sabha. Table 4.2 shows the position of parties during 1952–2009 in Rajasthan.

The Parliamentary election of 2009 are all the more significant because Congress, which had not retuned a single seat in 2004, could succeed in sending three Congress candidates this time (2009). Thus, all the three Congress candidates—Bharat Ram Meghwal from Sriganganagar, Ratan Singh Jatav from Bharatpur and Khilari Ram Bairwa from Karauli-Dholpur reserved constituencies—were declared elected. This is an indication of alienation of Meghwal, Jatav and Bairwas from BJP as it was a change in the political alignment.

As per the results declared officially, one Meghwal candidate, namely Arjun Ram Meghwal (a retired IAS) from Bikaner was declared successful. He is a BJP candidate. The number of BJP Meghwal candidates has decreased from 2 in 2004 to 1 in 2009.

Although Kailash Meghwal, one of the prominent BJP elites, was not only elected for the first time in 1989 to Parliament, but also won the bye-election in 2001 from Tonk and in 2004 from the same constituency (Tonk), yet in the Parliamentary elections 2009, he was not given the BJP ticket.

Rajya Sabha

Apart from MLAs and MPs, a few Meghwals and Jatavs became members of Rajya Sabha too. For instance, for the first time in 1982 Nathi Singh Jatav[64] was elected to Rajya Sabha. He was from Congress. In 2000, Jamna Barupal, Meghwal[65], daughter of late Panna Lal Barupal, was elected to Rajya Sabha. She was from Congress. Table 4.3 shows the position of parties during 1982–2000 in Rajasthan.

Table 4.2

Parliament Elections (Lok Sabha) and Meghwal, Bairwa and Jatav representation from Rajasthan in Parliament From 1952 to 2009

Year	Number of Scheduled Caste Seats	Name of the Scheduled Caste Communities (by party affiliation)					Grand Total
		Meghwal	Jatav	Bairwa	Total Seats	Other Scheduled Castes Communities	
1952	2	1(C)	1(KMP)		2	—	2
1957	3	1(C)			1	2	3
1962	3	1(C)			1	2	3
1967	4	1(C)			1	3	4
1972	4	1(C)			1	3	4
1977	4	2(BLD)	2(BLD)		3	1	4
1980	4	2(C)	—		2	2	4
1984	4	1(C)	1(C)		2	2	4
1989	4	1(BJP) 1(ID)	1(BJP)		3	1	4

Cont'd...

Cont'd...

1991	4	1(C)			1	3	4
1996	4	2(C)			2	2	4
1998	4	1(C)			1	3	4
1999 and 2001 (by-election)	4	1(C) 1(BJP)			2	2	4
2004	4	2(BJP)			2	2	4
2009	4	1(C) 1(BJP)	1(C)	1(C)	4	—	4

Source: 1. Trimasik Patrika, *Vidhan Bodhani*, October, 1997, Swaran Jayanti Visheshank, Rajasthan Vidhan Sabha Sachivalaya, pp. 260–269
2. Gleaned from local newspapers published after election, 2009.

Table 4.3

Parliament Election and Meghwal and Jatav Representation from Rajasthan in Rajya Sabha (since 1982)

Year	*Name of the scheduled castes/communities (by party affiliation)*		
	Meghwal	*Jatav*	*Total*
1982	—	1 (C)	1
2000	1 (C)	—	1

Source: Trimasik Patrika *Vidhan Bodhani*, October, 1997, Swarn Jayanti Visheshank, Rajasthan Vidhan Sabha Sachivalaya, Jaipur, pp. 255–259.

Caste and Representation in Congress Ministries

Chamars, Meghwals and Balais had also represented in the Congress ministries since 1951 and held different portfolios. Since 1951 at least one or two members of Chamar communities had been members of the ministry. For instance, in 1951, when Chief Minister Jai Narain Vyas was heading the interim government in the state, Amrit Lal Yadav,[66] Chamar, who was associated with the activities of Prajamandal, Udaipur and Congress during the national movement in the early days in the Udaipur region, was inducted for the first time in the Vyas Ministry, as deputy minister with the portfolio of Scheduled Castes, Scheduled Tribes and other Backward Class Welfare. Thus, he remained deputy minister from April 26, 1951 to March 3, 1952.

After India achieved her independence in 1947, when the First General Elections to the state legislative assembly were held in 1952, Yadav contested the election as a Congress candidate from Rajsamand reserved constituency, in Udaipur district and won the election. When Tikka Ram Paliwal, the first Chief Minister of elected government, was heading the state, Yadav[67] was inducted for the first time in Paliwal's Ministry as cabinet minister with the portfolio of Forest, Cooperative, Labour and Rehabilitation. He remained minister from March 3, 1952 to November 1, 1952.

It is noteworthy that on November 1, 1952 a change took place in the state leadership. As a result of this, when Jai Narain Vyas became Chief Minister, Yadav was again inducted in the ministry and became the Minister of Forest, Cooperative and Rehabilitation. He remained minister from November 1, 1952 to November 13, 1954.

As stated earlier, again on November 13, 1954, a political change took place in the Congress leadership at the state level. This time Mohan Lal Sukhadia became the Chief Minister. When Sukhadia was heading the state for four times during the years 1954, 1957, 1962 and 1967, Yadav, except in the year 1957, was inducted in his ministry in the years 1954, 1962 and 1967 as a cabinet minister. Thus, Yadav remained deputy minister and minister from April 26, 1951 to July 8, 1971 nearly more than 20 years.

During the First General Elections to the State Assembly (1952–57), it was a matter of pride that when the Congress party got the rein of power another Balai/Meghwal leader and MLA, namely, Sampat Ram from Tijara reserved constituency was inducted in Sukhadia's ministry initially as deputy minister. He remained deputy minister[68] from November 13, 1954 to April 11, 1957. When the Second General Elections to the state legislative assembly were held in 1957 and Sukhadia was heading the state, he was again inducted for the second time in his ministry as deputy minister with the portfolio of Revenue, Community Development and Excise duty from April 12, 1957 to February 10, 1960. On February 2, 1960 he was promoted as cabinet minister with portfolio of Local Government and Forest. He remained minister from February 2, 1960 to March 12, 1962.

The formal association of Sampat Ram with Congress ended in 1977, when he became leader of Janta Party. In 1977 when the first popular Janta Party Ministry came into power under the leadership of Bhairon Singh Shekhawat, Sampat Ram became one of the ministers. He entered in the Shekhawat's ministry as a cabinet minister and remained minister from June 27, 1977 to February 16, 1980. In 1990, when Shekhawat again formed the government in the state, he was again inducted in the ministry as a cabinet minister. However, he continued only for a few months, i.e., from May 30, 1990 to October 26, 1990.

Another notable leader, who was associated with the activities of Congress party during his early days in district Pali, in western Rajasthan was Dinesh Rai Dangi, born on April 26, 1931 in the village Bali in district Pali in a poor Meghwal family of Budha Ram Meghwal. His mother was Bhiki Bai. Dangi obtained his BA degree from Gujarat. In the elections held in the year 1962, he was nominated as a Congress candidate from Desuri reserved constituency in the same district and he won the election. When Sukhadia was heading the state, Dangi was inducted for the first time in his ministry as deputy minister with portfolio of Community Development, Panchayat, Forest, Printing Press, Khadi and Gramoudhyog, Small Savings, Lottery and Agriculture. He remained deputy minister from March 12, 1962[69] to March 13, 1967. In 1980, when Jagannath Pahadia assumed as the first Dalit Chief Minister of the state, Dangi became Minister of State (independent charge). He remained Minister of State from February 18, 1981 to July 14, 1981. In 1981, when Shiv Charan Mathur assumed office of Chief Minister after the change of guard, Dangi was inducted as a Minister of State (independent charge) and continued up to February 23, 1985.

It is also true that during later years of Congress ministry (after 1967) the Chamar community was also represented in the Sukhadia Congress government. For instance, when Mohan Lal Sukhadia assumed office of Chief Minister for the fourth time, Jasraj[70] became the first Parliamentarian Secretary of Congress party in 1967 and continued up to August 18, 1968. During the later years of Sukhadia's leadership, he also became a deputy minister. He remained deputy minister from August 18, 1968 to July 9, 1971. Besides Jasraj, another Meghwal leader of Congress party was Mulka Raj Thind, who became Parliamentarian Secretary[71] of the Congress party on October 22, 1967 and continued up to August 18, 1968. In 1968, he became one of the deputy ministers and remained as such from August 18, 1968 to June 16, 1970.

Another notable Meghwal leader was Narpat Ram Barbad, elected from Sursagar, Jodhpur. As an elected member of legislative assembly, he became for the first time a cabinet minister with the portfolio of Revenue, Land Reform and Desert Development, when Shiv Charan Mathur was heading the state in 1988. He remained minister[72] from February 6, 1988 to December 4, 1989. In 1989 a change took place in the state leadership. As a result of this, when Harideo Joshi became the Chief Minister, Narpat Ram Barbad again became a minister. He remained minister from December 4, 1989 to March 4, 1990.

In December 1998 Ashok Gehlot became the Chief Minister. Bhanwar Lal Meghwal[73] from Sujangarh reserved constituency in district Churu assumed office of Minister of State (independent charge) with the portfolio of Youth, Games and Sports and Jail. He remained Minister of State from December 5, 1998 to December 4, 2003. Besides Bhanwar Lal Meghwal, Paras Ram Mordia, another Meghwal from Laxmangarh constituency became for the first time Minister of State (independent charge). He remained Minister of State[74] from May 12, 2002 to December 4, 2003.

In December 2008 Ashok Gehlot again became the Chief Minister. Master Bhanwarlal Meghwal from Sujangarh reserved constituency in district Churu assumed office of Cabinet Minister with portfolio of Primary and Secondary Education, Labour and Employment etc. Babulal Nagar, Khateek from Dudu constituency in district Jaipur became for the first time Minister of State (independent charge) with the portfolio of Food and Supply, Dairy, Agriculture, Technical Education etc. Another notable Bairwa leader was Ashok Bairwa elected from Khandar, district Sawaimadhopur. As elected member of legislative assembly, he became a Minister of State with the portfolio of State Insurance, Information and Public Relation etc. Besides, another Jatav leader of Congress party, Bharoshi Lal Jatav became Minister of State with the portfolio of Agriculture, Animal Husbandry, Motor Garage, Fishery etc.

Caste Representation in Non-Congress Ministries (viz., Janta Party and BJP Governments)

As we have noted earlier that the Chamar communal representation was granted in Rajasthan in the year 1951 when Congress formed interim government under the able leadership of Heera Lal Shastri. Hence, Chamar politicians came to occupy such positions as members of legislative assembly through elections based only on limited franchise since 1952. It is also true that during the later years of Congress ministries (since 1952) the Chamar community was also represented in Congress ministries. Thus, the Chamars have achieved a level of excellence in the political field, comparable to any Scheduled Castes/communities in Rajasthan.

There are also a few Chamar political leaders, who have been represented in Janta Party and BJP ministries since 1977 onwards.

Now, we may consider in this selection, the feedback of the growth of Chamar political elites in non-Congress ministries.

After 25 years (since 1952), Jan Sangh (now BJP), veteran Bhairon Singh Shekhawat was for the first time in 1977 sworn in as Chief Minister of Rajasthan heading Janta Party ministry. Kailash Meghwal was an active Jan Sangh worker, who was associated with activities of Jan Sangh during his early days in Udaipur region. He was and is a staunch supporter of Shekhawat in Rajasthan. He was one of the leaders of Dalits who also agitated for the welfare of the downtrodden in the early sixties. In 1977, when Shekhawat became the first Chief Minister of non-Congress government (i.e., Janta Party) in the state, Kailash Meghwal was inducted in Shekhawat Ministry as the first Dalit Minister of State (independent charge) with portfolio of Sheep and Wool, Panchayat and Community Development. He remained Minister of State[75] from June 27, 1977 to February 16, 1980, and later in 1978, he was promoted to cabinet minister with the portfolio of Rural Development and Panchayati Raj, Mines and Cooperative. He remained Minister from February 7, 1978 to February 16, 1980. Kailash Meghwal was the minister with the portfolio of Flood and Draught Relief in 1992 in Shekhawat ministry. He remained Minister from February 17, 1992 to December 14, 1992. Mohan Meghwal, another Dalit leader and MLA from Sursagar reserved constituency, Jodhpur, was also Minister of State in the 1990 Shekhawat ministry. He remained Minister of State from March 14, 1990 to December 14, 1992. Jogeshwar Garg[76] Meghwal, was also leader of BJP and became Minister of State (independent charge) in 1990. He remained Minister of State from May 30, 1990 to January 24, 1992.

In 1993 again Shekhawat formed the Ministry in the state. Kailash Meghwal[77] became the first Dalit (Meghwal) Home and Justice Minister of Rajasthan in 1994. He remained Home and Justice Minister from February 20, 1994 to November 30, 1998. Achala Ram Meghwal[78]—another active BJP leader, became Minister of State (independent charge) in 1993. He remained Minister of State from December 11, 1993 to November 30, 1998. Mrs Shashi Datta[79] (Meghwal/Balai) became Minister of State (independent charge) in 1993. She remained Minister of State from December 11, 1993 to January 17, 1997.

In December 2003, when Vasundhara Raje became the first lady Chief Minister of Bharatiya Janta Party government in Rajasthan, Khema Ram Meghwal,[80] BJP MLA from reserved constituency, Sujangarh, Churu district, was inducted in her ministry as Minister of State with portfolio of Mines.

In addition to MPs, and MLAs, the other Chamar elites who had been the Chairman, Vice-Chairman and members of the Nagar Palika, Nagar Parishad and Nagar Nigam in the state were/are Chandan Ram, Chairman, Sri Ganganagar; Raja Ram, Chairman, Shadulsahr, Sri Ganganagar; Ramesh Dugaria, Chairman, Gajsinghpur, Sri-Ganganagar;

Mrs Mahendra Kaur, Chairman, Anupgarh, Sri-Ganganagar; Hardev Sahay, Chairman, Suratgarh, Sri-Ganganagar; Mrs Krishna Bhatia and Mrs Shanti Meghwal (both Chairperson) Suratgarh, Sri-Ganganagar.

Vice-Chairman

Kalu Ram Hatila, Bikaner

Member: Nagar Palika, Nagar Parishad and Nagar Nigam

Mrs Marvi Devi, Jaisalmer; Mrs Chandni Devi, Phalodi, Jodhpur; Mohan Lal and Harish (both from Bilara) Jodhpur.

Since the introduction of Panchayati Raj in Rajasthan, the number[81] of Chamar Panchas, Sarpanchas, Pradhans and Zila Pramukhs had increased considerably. Their names were/are: Poorna Ram Chauhan, Zila Pramukha, Bikaner; Shankar Pannu, Zila Pramukh Sri-Ganganagar; Mrs Mamta Meghwal, Zila Pramukh, Pali; Mrs Banarashi Meghwal, Zila Pramukh, Churu; Tika Ram Juli, Zila Pramukh, Alwar;

Pradhan, Panchayat Samiti

Manak Ram, Pradhan, Phalodi, Jodhpur; Mrs Geeta, Pradhan, Balesar, Jodhpur; Kirta Ram, Pradhan, Bap; Hari Ram, Pradhan Anupgarh, Sriganganagar; Dharmpal, Pradhan, Bhadra, Hanumangarh; Jagdish Megh, Pradhan, Nor, Hanumangarh; Chiranjee Lal, Sampat Nath, Leela Ram Arya and Lalit Kumar Sogat (all from Alwar).

Member, Zila Parishad

Multana Ram Barupal, Jodha Ram Bambhania, Mrs Kokha, Mrs Nakhatu Devi and Mrs Bhikho Devi (all from Jaisalmer), Ladu Ram (Jodhpur), Ramlal Verma, Hazari Singh and Mrs Saroj (all Jatavs, Alwar), Leela Ram Arya and Mrs Geeta Devi (both Chamars, Alwar).

Member, Panchayat Samiti

Ramji Ram Inkhia, Abu Ram, Mrs Kamla Devi, Jemal Ram Chauhan, Mrs Shayaro, Mrs Phooli and Om Prakash (all from Jaisalmer), Prema Ram Panwar and Bija Ram (both from Phalodi, Jodhpur), Mrs Rukma Devi, Chola Ram and Mooli Devi (all from Balesar, Jodhpur).

Notes

1. The most important source for the First General Election in 1952 and onwards and other relevant information of it, party affiliation of the candidates etc., is given in Trimasik Patrika, *Vidhan Bodhani*, October, 1997, "Swaran Jayanti Visheshank", Rajasthan Vidhan Sabha Sachivalaya, Jaipur, pp. 161–165. The castes of the MLAs, ministers and parliamentarians, secretaries of parties were confirmed from past and present MLAs, ministers, eminent social activists and aged social workers of the regions. For more details, also see Shyamlal, *Samajik Niyay Avam Dalit Rajniti*, Jaipur, Sublime Publications, 2004, pp. 43–48.
2. Trimasik Patrika, *Vidhan Bodhani*, October, 1997, Ibid., pp. 167–171.
3. Ibid., pp. 167–171.
4. Ibid., pp. 167–171.
5. Ibid., pp. 172–176.
6. Ibid., pp. 172–176.
7. Ibid., pp. 172–176.
8. Ibid., pp. 172–176.
9. Ibid., pp. 177–181.
10. Ibid., pp. 177–181.
11. Ibid., pp. 177–181.
12. Ibid., pp. 177–181.
13. Ibid., pp. 177–181.
14. Ibid., pp. 177–181.
15. Ibid., pp. 181–186.
16. Ibid., pp. 181–186.
17. Shyamlal, *Untouchable Castes in India: The Raigar Movement (1940–2004)*, Jaipur, Rawat Publications. 2006. p. 316.
18. Trimasik Patrika, *Vidhan Bodhani*, October 1997. Ibid., pp. 187–192.
19. Ibid., pp. 187–192.
20. Ibid., pp. 187–192.
21. Ibid., pp. 193–198.
22. Ibid., pp. 193–198.
23. Ibid., pp. 193–198.
24. Ibid., pp. 193–198.
25. Ibid., pp. 193–198.
26. Ibid., pp. 193–198.
27. Ibid., pp. 199–204.

28. Ibid., pp. 199–204.
29. Ibid., pp. 205–04.
30. Ibid., pp. 205–210.
31. Ibid., pp. 205–210.
32. Ibid., pp. 205–210.
33. Ibid., pp. 205–210.
34. Ibid., pp. 205–210.
35. Ibid., pp. 205–210.
36. Ibid., pp. 205–210.
37. Ibid., pp. 211–216.
38. Ibid., pp. 211–216.
39. Ibid., pp. 211–216.
40. Ibid., pp. 211–216.
41. Information were gleaned from *Doorbhash Nirdeshika*, 2000, Rajasthan Vidhan Sabha Sachivalaya, Jaipur. Also see, *Rajasthan Sujas*, October 5, 1999.
42. Ibid.
43. Ibid.
44. Ibid.
45. The detailed account of the elected Scheduled Caste Members of Legislative Assembly Rajasthan (MLAs), 2003 and other relevant information provided by B.R. Nimesh, P.M. Bairwa and O.P. Dhavan (ed.) in *Dr Ambedkar Digdarshika*, 2004 Alwar, published by Dr Ambedkar Memorial Educational Sansthan, see Particularly, "Rajasthan Vidhan Sabha Mai Anusuchit Jati Varg ke Vidhayako ki Suchi" p. 40.
46. Ibid., p. 40.
47. Ibid., p. 40.
48. Ibid., p. 40.
49. Ibid., p. 40.
50. Trimasik Patrika, *Vidhan Bodhani*, October, 1997. Ibid., p. 264.
51. Ibid., p. 266.
52. Ibid., p. 268.
53. Ibid., p. 269.
54. Ibid., p. 265.
55. Ibid., p. 265.
56. Ibid., p. 268.
57. Ibid., p. 268.

58. Ibid., p. 263.
59. Ibid., p. 265.
60. Ibid., p. 261.
61. Ibid., p. 264.
62. Ibid., p. 264.
63. Ibid., p. 268.
64. Ibid., p. 258.
65. Shyamlal, *Samajik Niyay Avam Dalit Rajniti*, Jaipur, Sublime Publications, 2004, p. 45.
66. The detailed account of ministries in Rajasthan from 1949 to 2003 and other relevant information was given in *Rajasthan Mantri Mandal (1949–2003)*, published by the Rajasthan Vidhan Sabha Sachivalaya, Jaipur, March 2004, p. 4.
67. Ibid., p. 5, also see, pp. 7, 10, and 24.
68. Ibid., p. 12, also see, pp. 14, 15 and 51 and 102.
69. Ibid., p. 21, also see, p. 58 and 64.
70. Ibid., p. 30, also see, p. 28.
71. Ibid., p. 30, also see, p. 28.
72. Ibid., p. 83, also see, p. 93.
73. Ibid., p. 123.
74. Ibid., p. 122.
75. Ibid., p. 53, also see p. 49 and 99.
76. Ibid., p. 103.
77. Ibid., p. 108.
78. Ibid., p. 110.
79. Ibid., p. 113.
80. Ibid., p. 113
81. Names of the candidates were gleaned from eminent persons of the castes/communities. Also used other sources, such as *Ismarikas*, published by social organizations and communities, newspapers, see in particular—Meghwal Mandal, *Udaipur Ismarika*, 1999; *Meghwal Darshan* 2000, Bikaner; *Meghwal Digdarshika*, 2001, Jaisalmer, *Ismarika*; Rajasthan Meghwal Parishad, Jodhpur, 2004, *Parivar Parichaya Nirdeshika*, Meghwal Samaj, Jodhpur Shahr, 2005. Also see community newspaper—particularly—*Hakdar* (Bikaner), *Meghwal Jagrati* (Jodhpur), *Udai Megh* (Jaipur), *Dr Ambedkar aur Bahujan* (Hanumangarh) etc.

5 Rashtriya Meghwal Mahasangh *A Caste Model of Socio-Political Organization, 1997*

The politics of untouchables underwent a major shift and change after the emergency imposed in 1975. Before 1975, the untouchable politicians had been in control of Indira Congress and there had been limited political activities of other political parties amongst the untouchable communities in Hindi speaking regions. In 1977s, Babu Jagjivan Ram left the Congress party and formed his own party called 'Congress for Democracy' (CFD) and took control of the untouchable communities and opposed the Congress party in the parliamentary election of 1977. To counter the activities of Indira Congress, Babuji brought various untouchable groups to work for his party.

National Sangoshti on 41st Death Anniversary of Ambedkar, Chamar and Cognate Castes and the Formation of Rashtriya Meghwal Mahasangh, 1997

We have seen that every untouchable caste had tried to organize individual socio-political movement or organization and had kept itself limited to one region (Rajasthan) and one community (Meghwal). They had no taste for collective organization. The problem of bringing together all Chamar untouchable communities across North India proved difficult to resolve. By early 1997, an alternate strategy for socio-political organization of Rashtriya Meghwal Mahasangh (RMM) had come to the fore. The idea of the formation of RMM occurred on 41st death anniversary of Ambedkar on December 6, 1997. On this date (December 6, 1997) a sangoshti (seminar) was held in Delhi in which some prominent social and political leaders of Meghwal Samaj from all over India assembled. Thus, the national president of Akhil Bharatiya Sootrakar Mahasabha,

New Delhi, Acharya Guru Prasad K.P., General Secretary of State Meghwal Sabha, New Delhi; Aatam Singh Bhati and also Mantri of the same organization M.L. Bhagat, Meghwal, General Secretary of Balai Mahasabha, Madhya Pradesh, Hari Ram Chauhan (Mhow), President of Meghwal Mahasabha Punjab, Lal Chand Bhalla (Bhatinda) and the General Secretary of Kori Mahasabha, Uttar Pradesh, Ved Ram attended the seminar.[1] Besides these, three more persons also attended the sangoshti. They were: Gopi Chand Salvi (Nimbahera, Rajasthan), Ram Prasad Bunkar (Sabarmati, Gujarat) and Hari Ram Meghvansi (Gagvana, Rajasthan).[2]

The formation of RMM bore out, Gopi Chand Salvi, Ram Prasad Bunkar and Hari Ram Meghvansi's conviction that in different regions in which Meghwal communities live, although they have different names, but they are one. They also made efforts to bridge the gap between Megh, Meghwal, Meghvansi, Balai, Raj Balai, Bhambhi, Bunkar, Kori, Koli, Salvi, Sootrakar, Rishi, Bhagat, Jatav, Jatiya, Maru, Chamar, Satnami and a few other Meghwal communities (in all 46 communities).[3] Hanuman Prasad Kataria, Ajmer; Panchu Ram Rishi Meghwal, Advocate, Kota and Smt Jamana Barupal, Bikaner (all from Rajasthan) took keen interest in matters pertaining to umbrella organization of all the above mentioned communities. They unanimously accepted the views of Gopi Chand Salvi, Ram Prasad Bunkar and Hari Ram Meghvansi. The participants expressed the need for establishing a federal organization amongst Meghwal communities. The feeling among Meghwal, Sootrakar, Kori, Salvi leaders and others was that Meghwal, Sootrakar, Kori, Salvi, Meghvansi and so forth should be organized in their own community organization and should remain part of the federation. Meghwal, Sootrakar, Balai and others had their own interest which were not different from RMM. That is why RMM was necessary to unite them. It was decided, however, to broaden the base and appeal for that proposed federation, as the Meghwals had a large voting strength in areas in which they lived. Through the formation of the federation, the Meghwals' sphere of influence and impact on decision-making process could be expanded. Thus, almost, all the participants overwhelmingly supported the formation of the federation.[4]

It is significant to note here that the basis for the formation of a federation had already been laid by the 1935 campaign, especially in Rajasthan. The subsequent years had been spent in awakening the consciousness of Balai, Meghwal, Sootrakar, Bhambhi, Chamar, etc., to imbue them with the resolve to fight the upper caste Hindus in general and Thakurs, Jagirdars and Jamindars in particular. The span of 42 years from 1935–1977 that Swami Gokul Das Maharaj had spent in arousing the Meghwal, Bhambhi, Chamar, Balai, Bunkar, etc., benefited the federation.[5]

The results of Sangoshti held in Delhi were gratifying for Meghwal communities. The Meghwal leaders were not only the most conscious of their status, but also the most organized among untouchables of north India and with every passing day, it is seen that they are seriously thinking of their emancipation. They are sensitive to their inferior position and are ready to take advantage of any scheme which they think would do them good. Again, there being a number of leaders in the Meghwal communities who are more or less recognized as great leaders, there is greater awakening in that community than in any other. The Meghwals are most conscious about their disabilities to caste barriers.

Thus RMM was formed on December 6, 1997 at the sangoshti of Meghwal leaders held at New Delhi as a separate platform exclusively for the Chamar and cognate communities with the role of seeking greater involvement of regional, state and national level and to provide its members a distinct identity (Meghwal) to ameliorate their conditions and charting a socio-political course independently.

Its aim was also to bridge the gap between the various segments of Chamar communities and pressing the Government of India and state governments to accept their demands on behalf of the Mahasangh. Acharya Guru Prasad K.P., a Sootrakar from Delhi was elected President[6] and Aatam Singh Bhati (Meghwal) from Delhi, National General Secretary. The meeting on December 6, 1997 authorized the President[7] to constitute the executive committee of RMM.

President Acharya Guru Prasad K.P. emerged as a vigorous defender of the formation of RMM. His long association with Babu Jagjivan Ram, Guljari Lal Nanda, Hemvati Nandan Bahuguna, Swami Ram Bax Maharaj and Garib Das Saheb was a masterful experience of work.[8] In addition to his association with these eminent persons, Acharya Guru Prasad K.P. also remained President and National Secretary of several social organizations and institutions.[9]

During this period Aatam Singh Bhati (Meghwal) made strong efforts to form the new executive committee. In consultation with some eminent activists a list of executive committee was prepared which would be acceptable to all others. A delegation headed by Bhati, Meghwal left Delhi for Ganganagar, Rajasthan, in 1997 for consultation with Nihal Chand, MP, and to seek his views. Nihal Chand expressed his agreement with Bhati's list. He lauded the list. Thus, the list of 41 members of the Executive Committee was declared.[10] Finally, an important issue taken up by the delegates was the question of nominating a Working President for RMM. Delegates requested Nihal Chand, MP, if he could become the Working President and he readily agreed to it.

From 1997 onwards Nihal Chand, MP assumed an active role in the social and political affairs of RMM. He requested Home Minister, Rajasthan, Kailash Meghwal and Ayurved Minister, Achla Ram Meghwal[11] to be the Chief Patrons of RMM to mobilize the Meghwals into a viable and assertive community, increasingly conscious of its human, social, economic and political rights.

The first major tour campaign since the inception of RMM occurred in the beginning of 1998. Thus, on January 3, 1998, President, Acharya Guru Prasad K.P., National General Secretary, Aatam Singh Bhati, (Meghwal) Mantri, M.L. Bhagat Meghwal along with some of the executive members visited Jaipur.[12] When they arrived, they were given a warm welcome. Next day on January 4, arrangements for an important meeting of RMM were made at the residence of Ami Chand Bhupesh[13] and the activists made valiant efforts to collect a large number of persons. This meeting proved a great success as a large number of people attended it. Besides the common man, some eminent government officers, who were inspired by Ambedkar also attended this meeting. They were Gopal Denwal, Director, Rajasthan Scheduled Caste Finance Corporation, Government of Rajasthan and P.C. Hadia, Income Tax Commissioner, Rajasthan.[14]

During their 2-day stay in the capital, Acharya Guru Prasad K.P. and his colleagues met the Chief Minister, Home Minister and several other ministers in order to seek their blessings and cooperation. On January 4, the delegation first met Ayurved Minster, Achla Ram Meghwal and expressed their gratitude for his being nominated Chief Patron of RMM. Speaking to the delegates Achla Ram Meghwal[15] very clearly expressed his willingness to extend his full support to RMM. Next day on January 5, Madan Lal Chirania[16] along with the some group of people met Kailash Meghwal, Home Minister of Rajasthan, at his official residence, Civil

Lines Jaipur. Later on, they went to Government Secretariat where they met Hon'ble Chief Minister, Bhairon Singh Shekhawat. The Chief Minster congratulated Acharya Guru Prasad K.P.[17] and his colleagues for the formation of RMM.

These meetings became an event of major significance in the history of RMM movement.

Rashtriya Meghwal Mahasangh and its Object[18]

The formation of cohesive federation or umbrella organization containing Chamar communities have socio-political benefits as well. First, it would strengthen the socio-political union of untouchable Meghwal communities. Second, the incorporation of similar segment of Meghwal communities into one organization would add to Meghwal-power and ability to influence the cause of community events. Third, and last, the Meghwal communities all over north India shared a set of common interests despite the peculiarities of the region and language. RMM, however, did not develop an extensive or deep-rooted organization in the years following its formation. The problem of bringing together all Chamar communities across north proved difficult.

There is no evidence, however, that the interest of RMM to build a strong organization is effectively translated into practice. Indeed the RMM seems to have been in the state of continual disarray with dissension and internecine squabbling threatening its unity. For instance, just after the formation of RMM, Acharya Guru Prasad K.P. became involved in RMM activities and devoted his full time to its development. As a consequence, on June 16, 1998,[19] RMM convened the first Maha-adhiveshan in Jaipur. RMM had also formally booked Birla Auditorium for this purpose. Invitation cards were dispatched to the community-persons to attend the same. To check this movement some opportunist men opposed this Maha-adhivesan. They were of the opinion that this small scale session of Chamar communities would not be sufficient to bring success to the RMM. As a result of all this, since June 1998 to April 2000, those who had earlier opposed Maha-adhiveshan, could not convene a single Maha-adhiveshan.

The distance between RMM and others had grown wider during the years since the formation of RMM, especially since the announcement of first maha-adhiveshan of RMM in Jaipur. On 23 April 2000[20] RMM had also formally dissolved its earlier national executive committee and all state units. President RMM, Acharya Guru Prasad K.P. too had constituted a new national executive committee and nominated new heads of all state units and directed them to form new state units immediately. His decision was perhaps more related to his desire for Meghwal communities to take advantage of the situation in which they could progress.

Regional Association Before the Formation of RMM

We had noted earlier that Swami Gokul Das Maharaj had made an attempt through Rajasthan Meghvansh Mahasabha (RMS) to carry on the agitation and in 1950, he convened the sixth annual meeting of RMS at Ram Deo Mandir, Pushkar, Ajmer.

On November 23, 1950,[21] Swami Gokul Das Maharaj organized a 'Vishal Community Sammelan' as part of the RMS annual conference. Thus, under Swami Gokul Das Maharaj's guidance the RMS received a modern touch.

The main object of the meeting was to address the question of amalgamation of the different names such as: Chamar, Balai, Bhambhi, Sootrakar, Bunkar, Salvi, Choblar, etc., into one name 'Meghvansh'.[22] When the annual meeting was summoned, a large number of eminent religious gurus, social activists, government officials, educationists and scholars participated in the meeting. Some of the eminent names were: Ram Bax Maharaj, Panchva, district Nagaur; Assistant Chief Commissioner Ajmer; Ladu Ram Bagotia, Deputy Inspector of Schools, Ajmer; Nenu Ram Bhatti, Garib Das Maharaj, an eminent Kabirpanthi and Om Prakash, Ujjain, Madhya Pradesh; Mahatma Hanot Ram Kukri, Ganganagar; Bikaner; Mahatma Moji Ramji Maharaj Bikaner Durga Ram, Engineer, Pali; Ghasi Ram, Tonk and many more.

It was stated that as long different names were in practice, the weakness (of the Meghvans) would prevail.[23] It was because of the regional variations that they were called by different names in different regions. Similarly, they pleaded for a change in the attitude of fellows of different communities for adopting a common name 'Meghvansh' for unity, integrity and progress of the "samaj" as a whole.[24] The same question of adopting the name 'Meghvansh' was raised in Mewar region earlier, in 1936 by Bhairu Lal Meghvansh and later in 1948.

Tracing the origin of the term 'Meghvansh' from Megh Rishi, Swami Gokul Das Maharaj also advocated in 1950 that 'Meghvansh' should be adopted for all sub-castes/communities.[25] Thus, the basic question for Chamars was to get rid of their different names and it was for this purpose that they launched a big struggle in Vikram Samvat 1970 under the leadership of Swami Gokul Das Maharaj.

At the Pushkar session of 1950, a resolution was passed unanimously, requesting the community fellows to adopt the name 'Meghvansh' in admission to schools, appointment to public service and revenue[26] records, etc.

It should be mentioned here that this solution evoked some positive response on the part of community fellows.

Rift in the National Federation of Meghwals

The following is an account of the circumstances under which the internal cleavage emerged.

As has been stated earlier, a meeting of National Federation of Meghwals (NFM) was held in Jaipur, where it was decided to organize an NFM convention at Jaipur. The main object of the convention was to honour the gaddi-adhiyaksh of ten most important dhunis of Meghwal samaj along with some other eminent saints, mehants and also 40 leading social activists of Meghwal samaj at convention. Subsequently, National President of NFM, Acharya Guru Prasad K.P. wrote hundreds of letters to all concerned and appealed them to attend the convention positively to be held at Birla Auditorium, Jaipur on June 16, 1998.

Soon after this, the internal cleavage in the NFM emerged. It was based on a clash of personalities between Kailash Meghwal and his group on the one hand and Parash Ram Mordia and his group on the other. The rift to a great extent was also an expression of conflicting ideologies.[27] Parash Ram Mordia, being an important Congress leader, pursued an informal policy of eliminating the rightist element from the forthcoming convention to be held at Jaipur on June 16, 1998. Kailash Meghwal was the Home Minister, in BJP Government, in Rajasthan, headed by Bhairon Singh Shekhawat who was also Patron of the NFM. A few VIPS were invited. The notable ones were: Chief Minister Bhairon Singh Shekhawat (BJP), Governor of Rajasthan, Darbara Singh; Kailash Meghwal, Home Minister; Achla Ram Meghwal, Minister (both BJP), Shankar Pannu, M.P. and Ami Chand Bhupesh (both Congress) were invited. Since majority of VIPs were from BJP, Mordia, therefore, recommended that Ashok Gehlot and Parash Ram Maderna, both eminent Congress leaders be invited to the convention. National President of NFM, Acharya Guru

Prasad K.P. accepted the request. At that time Mordia was also Working President of NFM for sometime and it was he who had booked the Birla Auditorium at Jaipur and on May 10, 1998 deposited Rs 34,500.00[28] for June 16, 1998. Later on, outwardly, it appeared that this convention was a BJP convention and not an NFM convention. This was resented by many of its leaders, the chief of them being Parash Ram Mordia. Rakesh Meghwal was also the state President of NFM for sometime, he too did not support Acharya Guru Prasad K.P.'s views. Similarly, Ami Chand Bhupesh, the staunch supporter of Mordia too opposed it.

The local convenor found that impediment in convening the convention was the dispute about heavy presence of Chief Minister and the ministers of BJP, hence they tried to work toward its postponement. While Acharya Guru Prasad K.P. wanted to hold the convention as decided earlier, the others wanted to postpone or cancel it. The latter group also felt that amongst the invited VIPs, adequate representation to Congress had not been given. It is also alleged that Mordia, fearing the domination of BJP over the NFM, decided to postpone it. This development should also be seen in the context of conflicting rift between the weavers and Chamars. Mordia and his supporters were not in favour of it, they suddenly announced its postponement. Thus, NFM's programme suffered in the state.

When this news reached New Delhi, National President of NFM, Acharya Guru Prasad K.P. was shocked at Mordia's attempt to sabotage NFM's activities to support the Congress. There was also anguish against Mordia regarding postponing the Jaipur convention.

Soon after this sad incident, National President of NFM Acharya Guru Prasad K.P. prepared, published and circulated a lengthy letter containing five-pages entitled *Aalochana, Samalochana-pratiyalochana* amongst the community fellows, explaining the entire episode and attacking the local organizers.

"The first show of NFM went flop. It happened so because we committed a mistake by involving those persons who did nothing for the welfare of the samaj. Through this letter all the misunderstandings regarding the convention has been cleared. My services to samaj are still available through Bharatiya Dalit Sahitya Academy".[29]

As mentioned earlier, there was a sharp criticism on the part of some regional papers published by individual community fellows from distant places. We get an idea of how the NFM convention of June 16, was targeted from accounts of Acharya Guru Prasad K.P. in his 5-page letter.

Jag Ram Singh,[30] editor *Dalit Jyoti* (Weekly, dated May 25, 1998) published from Jhunjhunu, Rajasthan and also advocate was not pleased with Acharya Guru Prasad K.P.'s policy. It may be noted that the idea of celebrating Kabir Jayanti 44 years ago in Delhi by collection of donation was present still in the minds of many community fellows. In this context the paper asked Acharya Guru Prasad K.P. regarding collection of donation. The paper also criticized Acharya Guru Prasad's move for instigating Kashi Ram, the supremo of BSP against Mayavati.

Panna Lal Preme,[31] the Chief Editor of *Hakdar* (June, 1998, first) published from Bikaner, Rajasthan, wrote in his paper: 'NFM convention of June 16 was a political motivated'. Apart from blaming Acharya Guru Prasad's leadership, after a few months, the same paper again made a statement attacking on the formation of NFM and published the news, titled *Meghwal Mahasangh dwara Mahaul*. The paper further wrote:

"Persons sitting in Delhi, from the organization as and when they desired so. But, what is the result of such organization. How many persons turn up to such programmes.[32] There is absolutely, no social obligation on anybody to participate in such activities."

This news was widely publicized.

Another community paper published from Ganganagar, Rajasthan by Satpal Dhammdeep, also played an important part in criticizing and publicizing the motive behind honouring Kailash Meghwal. The paper 'Dr Ambedkar aur Bahujan' (June 27 to July 3, 1998) carried the whole story under the title, "For what purpose, Home Minister Kailash Meghwal is honoured".[33]

Agitation for Communal Representation in the Central Ministries and Party Organization

As has been noted earlier, like other Scheduled Castes/communities, the Chamars and cognate communities had been vote bank of Congress party in Rajasthan, Madhya Pradesh, Punjab, Haryana, Delhi and Gujarat and the Chamars as a whole extended their full support to Congress party in all the general elections in northern India after independence of the country in 1947. It was because of Babu Jagjivan Ram, a prominent Dalit leader in general and Chamar in particular revolted against the Indira Gandhi Congress after the emergency in 1977 and the Congress leadership were against the Chamars. However, through the efforts of Ram Dhan, (U.P.), B.P. Maurya (U.P.) D. Sanjivaya (Andhra Pradesh) and others the Congress changed its attitude and started giving representation to Dalits in party organization and central ministries.

After more than a decade or so, the Congress with the alliance of left parties and others formed the UPA government under the leadership of Dr Man Mohan Singh at the Centre in 2004. Soon after the formation of the government, Man Mohan Singh inducted few Dalit ministers, four of whom were from one particular group (called communities) and this triggered off a major heart burning amongst the other dominant groups. National President of NFM, Acharya Guru Prasad K.P. spoke of the Meghwals as the major group of SC and to the contrary, the Congress leadership have been given much importance to the group whose population is much less as compared to the population of Meghwals. It was also generally felt that the NFM had become ineffective because of the inactiveness and that Meghwals were being neglected in every sphere of political field. Thus, under Acharya Guru Prasad K.P.'s guidance the NFM revived its activities and this time initiated the agitation for political representation in central ministries and party organization.

The argument was further strengthened in 2006, when National President submitted a 3-page memorandum/representation[34] to Smt Sonia Gandhi, the President of AICC and Chairperson, UPA and demanded for inclusion of Meghwals in the cabinet. It may be recalled that national president of NFM had categorized the whole Scheduled Castes/communities into three major groups, namely, Group 'A', Group 'B', and Group 'C'.

Group 'A' of weavers,[35] 10 per cent of the whole Scheduled Caste population includes: Megh, Meghwal, Mahar, Meghvanshi, Balai, Salvi, Sootrakar, Bunkar, Julaha, Kori, Koli, Malai, Malviya, Marwadi, Nimari, Mer, Dhanuk, Sethia, Katiya, Tantuwai, Chobdar (Kotwal), Mala, Pan, Balagai, Adi Dravidar (Paraya), Devendra Kulam (Pallar), Pulay etc.

Group 'B' that of cobblers,[36] roughly form 3.5 per cent of the total S.C. population of India, includes Chamar, Jatav, Raigar, Ravida, Ramdasi, Mochi of Maharashtra and Rajasthan, Madia, Edagai, etc.

Group 'C' under the category of sweepers[37] and others roughly form 3 per cent of the total S.C. population of the country includes: Balmiki, Khatik, Dhobi, Nayak, Nut, Pashi, Dusad, Dhor, Mang, Mazhabi etc.

The argument for inclusion of major groups of S.C., i.e., Group 'A' of weavers in the central ministries and party organization were: First, that the objective and critical analysis and examination of the fact clearly shows that Congress party leadership seems not fair to Group 'A' as other groups, such as Group 'B' of cobblers and Group 'C' of sweepers and others. The weavers had hoped that UPA government at the centre under the leadership of Man Mohan Singh would undo the injustice done by

NDA government headed by Atal Bihari Vajpai. Second, since the cobblers form 3.5 per cent of the total Scheduled Caste population of India, they got four cabinet berths in UPA (2004–09) government. The notable ones are: Smt Meira Kumar, Mahaveer Prasad, Kumari Shailja and Muniappa (all Chamars). Smt Meira Kumar and Mahavir Prasad are cabinet ministers. Kumari Shailja and Muniappa are Minister of State (Independent Charge) and Minister of State respectively. Smt Meira Kumar is now Speaker, Lok Sabha.

Third, since the weavers form 10 per cent of the total population of S.C., Smt Panbaka Laxmi (Mala), the Minister of State, represents the entire Group 'A'.

Fourth, Sushil Kumar Shinde represents the Third Group 'C' whose population is 3 per cent. It may be recalled that all the castes in this group are quite separate ones and independent and not a homogenous group. Among this group the population of Dhor is less than 0.1 per cent of total S.C.

Fifth, majority of Group 'B' people were/are with BSP, whereas, seeing spinning wheel on Congress flag, the spinning and weaving communities felt dignified and joined hands with Congress party emotionally during national movement and to the contrary, Congress has given less importance to the first Group 'A'. Not only this, Group 'B' also took the lion's share in the Congress organization as well as in the government headed by Congress party.

Sixth, all this created a heart burning and disappointment which ultimately resulted into joining the communal parties like BJP and BSP. Last, the NFM presented a memorandum/representation in April 2006, in order to mobilize public opinion for the demand and a delegation headed by Acharya Guru Prasad K.P. met Smt Sonia Gandhi, President AICC and Chairperson of UPA. The weavers hoped that Sonia Gandhi's leadership would do justice. The President of AICC's reply was favourable and this led to their satisfaction.

In the section that follows, we shall deal with the representation of all the three groups on the Congress party organization.

National President of NFM, Acharya Guru Prasad K.P. aptly summarized the different trends of thinking that control the AICC policy. First, so far as their representation in the Congress party organization is concerned, they were mostly neglected.[38] The Congress Working Committee, is the highest policy making body of the party with large number of members, of whom one is Chamar. The notable one is Smt Satya Behan, The group-wise distribution of other 7 posts[39] in the party organization shows that 4 (57.14%) are from Group 'A'. The notable ones are: Mukul Wasnik, General Secretary; J.D. Seelam, Secretary; K. Jaya Kumar, Secretary and Yogendra Makwana, Chairman, SC and ST Cell. The number of the other groups are: 2 (28.57%) from Group 'B'. They are K.B. Krishnamurthy, Secretary and Pravin Rashtra Pal, Secretary and 1 (14.28%) from Group 'C'. He is Jai Kishan, Secretary.

With the growth of NFM, under the leadership of Acharya Guru Prasad K.P., the NFM developed a thought deciding that their best interest lay in supporting the Congress. The meeting of NFM with Mrs Sonia Gandhi also expressed their anguish against the Congress and requested her to take positive steps to regain the lost vote bank of Congress party in North India by patronizing the leadership of the neglected major section of Dalit communities. The Congress made constant efforts to win the Meghwals over to her side by dissociating them from BSP and BJP.[40]

Rashtriya Meghwal Mahasangh (Youth) Rajasthan Pradeshik Karyakarta Sammelan 2006[41]

In order to reactivate the Meghwal movement, as well as to integrate the Meghwal communities better, 8 years later, the Rashtriya Meghwal Mahasangh (RMM), a state unit of Rajasthan, organized a conference of Meghwal and cognate communities all over Rajasthan to consider social and religious matters.[42] This conference was considered to be an interesting landmark event in the development of the Meghwal movement. The state unit of RMM had called a convention on December 17, 2006 at Dr Ambedkar Memorial Welfare Society, near Doordarshan Kendra, Jhalana Doongri, Jaipur,[43] in which people from various districts of Rajasthan, such as Sriganganagar, Bikaner, Churu, Pali, Jalore, Jodhpur, Nagaur, Sikar, Jhunjhunu, etc., participated.[44] The Chief Guest of the function was Nihal Chand Meghwal, MP Sri Ganganagar. Master Bhanwar Lal Meghwal, former minister in the Congress ministry headed by Ashok Gehlot, presided over the function.[45] Among the special guests of honour were: Mrs Jamna Barupal, former Rajya Sabha Member (Congress), Bikaner; Parshram Meghwal, former MP Jalore, Sankar Pannu, former MP Ganganagar; Smt Manju Meghwal, Zila Pramukh, Jalore; Smt Mamta Meghwal, Zila Pramukh, Pali; Kema Ram Meghwal, Minister of State, Government of Rajasthan (BJP); Rakesh Meghwal, MLA Parbatsar; Govind Meghwal, MLA, Nokha and others.[46]

The importance of the convention for the development of Meghwal movement lay in three aspects: (1) to publicize the convention and meetings held by members of the Meghwal communities all over

Rajasthan, (2) to campaign against social vices with respect to the Meghwal communities, and (3) to concern on the nature sub-caste and social differences.[47]

The coverage of the meetings and conventions held among the Meghwals served to counter the isolation in which most Meghwals and cognate communities fellows in rural areas and regions had lived, conveying to them the sense that after a long torpor their communities were on the move and progress was within their reach. Learning about meetings occurring in some sections of the community may have impelled other Meghwals to join the movement, to start a discussion group in their villages. Thus, through publicizing and providing information, the convention directly aided in the organization of Meghwal movement or more directly created a climate of opinion which could be favourably utilized by a leading organization such as RMM. In this sense, the convention contributed to the social mobilization of Meghwal communities.

The issue to abandon their social vices[48] such as drinking of alcohol, child marriages, dowry system and others was particularly important one in this convention. Almost every speaker expressed his concern about the social evils which branded them as untouchables.

Other important issues taken by the convention[49] were the question of girls' education, financial help to the poor and needy students, help for educated unemployed youth and reviving their traditional weaving and spinning work. There was a suggestion that brilliant students should be honoured and encouraged.

During the period of its operation, the most important step taken with regard to the community's betterment and uplift was a fourteen point resolution of December 2006 of RMM, Jaipur, which was later on submitted to the Governor of Rajasthan, Jaipur, by a delegation led by State President, and General Secretary, State Unit, RMM.

The moving spirit behind this convention is the 80 years old Acharya Guru Prasad K.P.

Notes

1. For a discussion of Meghwal and cognate caste movement that stress the role of both individual caste organization and National Federation of Meghwals

and counterparts, National Meghwal Mahasangh (NMM), in the pre- and post-independence period and socio-religious and political consequences of the movement, see in particular Acharya Guru Prasad K.P. (ed.) *Meghwal Keerti-Ismarika*, New Delhi, Meghwal Mahasangh, 1998. Also see, Acharya Guru Prasad, *Megh Rishi Kaun*? *Meghwal Kaise*? *Tatha Vashtro-dak Vayanjivi Samaj-ki-Akta Kaise Hai*, New Delhi, Rashtriya Meghwal Mahasangh, 2003.

2. Ibid., p. 3.
3. Ibid., p. 3.
4. Ibid., p. 3.
5. "Swami Gokul Das Maharaj and his Contributions", especially see Chapter IX on Swami Gokul Das Maharaj.
6. *Meghwal Keerti-Ismarika*, 1998., Ibid., p. 3.
7. Ibid., p. 7.
8. Ibid., p. 3.
9. Ibid., p. 3.
10. Ibid., pp. 4, 5.
11. Ibid., p. 3.
12. Ibid., p. 3.
13. Ibid., p. 3.
14. Ibid., p. 3.
15. Ibid., p. 3.
16. Ibid., p. 3.
17. Ibid., p. 3.
18. Aatam Singh Bhatti, "Rishi, Meghwal, Meghvansh, Bhambhi, Bejara, Bunkar, Salvi, Tatha Kori, Kabir Panthi Julaha, Aadi, Aadi Samaj-ko-Ak Manch-ki-Aavashyakta" in Meghwal *Keerti-Ismarika*, 1998, pp. 12–13. Also see, 2-page circulation prepared, published and circulated amongst the members of NMM and communities fellows, titled "Jinda Kome Samaya ka intjar Nahi Karti", New Delhi, dated April, 23, 2000.
19. For holding the first convention NMM in Jaipur, the capital of Rajasthan that stress on bringing all the Chamar and cognate communities under the one umbrella organization and the socio-political consequences of federation, see, particularly, Acharya Guru Prasad K.P., *Aalochana, Samalochana, Pratayalochana,* New Delhi, Undated.
20. Acharya Guru Prasad K.P., "Jinda Kome Samaya-ka-Intjar Nahi Karti", New Delhi, dated April 23, 2000.

21. Rishi, Sewadas, Jiwan Darshan, Yug Purush Swami Shri Gokul Dasji Maharaj, Doomara (Ajmer), Gokuldham, Alakh Isthan, 2005, pp. 114–115.
22. Ibid., p. 115.
23. Ibid., p. 115.
24. Ibid., p. 115.
25. Ibid., p. 115.
26. Ibid., p. 115.
27. For detailed information on the rift and specially in NMM, see particularly the 5-page letter entitled 'Aalochana-Samalochana- Pratayalochana,' prepared, issued and circulated amongst the members of NMM and communities fellows by Acharya Guru Prasad K.P., National President, NMM, New Delhi, undated. The most authoritative accounts of the development of rift amongst the office bearers and members of NMM and their roles in Jaipur is given in this letter. Reactions and criticism of communities papers also represent reported in detailed in this letter.
28. Ibid., p. 3.
29. Ibid., p. 5.
30. Ibid., p. 1.
31. Ibid., pp. 1–2.
32. Ibid., p. 2.
33. Ibid., p. 4.
34. For most important discussion that all-India Congress party leadership seems not fair to the major group of the Scheduled Castes, i.e., Group 'A' and on the contrary they (Congress leadership) have given much importance to the second Group 'B whose population is much less as compared to the population of Group 'A'. It has created heartburning and disappointment which ultimately resulted into joining the communal parties like BJP and BSP. For detailed information, see Memorandum entitled "Very Humble and Meek Request to Kindly take a Positive Step to Regain the Lost Vote Bank of the Congress Party in Rajasthan, Madhya Pradesh, Himachal Pradesh, Punjab, Haryana, Delhi and Gujarat, etc., by patronizing leadership of the neglected major section of the scheduled caste Communities", submitted to Smt Sonia Gandhi, President, AICC and Chairperson, UPA, 10, Jan Path, New Delhi, by Acharya Guru Prasad K.P., National President, NMM along with his colleagues, New Delhi, dated April 1, 2006. The summary of the Memorandum was later published in fortnightly paper *Hakdar*. See particularly, 'Soniaji Ne Bulaya Guru Prasadji Ko', Bikaner, *Hakdar*, April 2006 (Second-half)
35. Ibid., p. 2.

36. Ibid., p. 2.
37. Ibid., p. 2.
38. Ibid., p. 3.
39. Ibid., p. 3.
40. Ibid., p. 3.
41. This description is based on news appeared in various communities newspapers and also on talks with Acharya Guru Prasad K.P. to whom the author wishes to express his thanks, New Delhi, dated December 30, 2006. For more details, see also the pamphlet published and circulated entitled "Rashtriya Meghwal Mahasangh (Yuwa) Rajasthan: Pradeshik Karya-Karta Sammelan" by Acharya Guru Prasad K.P. (Rashtriya Adhiyaksh), Arvind Danodia (Pradesh Adhiyaksh), and Kashi Ram Meghwal (Pradesh Maha Mantri, Rashtriya Meghwal Mahasangh). ka-17-ko-Jaipur Main Sammelan,' Date not mentioned. For further details also see Rajasthan Meghwal Mahasangh in *Hakdar,* Bikaner, December 13, 2003; "Meghwal Mahasangh (Yuwa) ka Prantiya Karya Karta Sammelan 17-ko", in *Udai Megh*, Jaipur, December 13, 2006, and 'Meghwal Samaj-ke Yuva Warg-ka-Sanghatith-Hokar Samaj main feli Kuritiyon ko Mitane Avam Apni Haki-ke-Liye Sangharsh Karna Chahiya', Bhanwar Lal Meghwal, in *Dr Ambedkar Aur Bahujan*, Suratgarh, December 23–30, 2006.

    It is important to mention here that on December 17, 2006, Acharya Guru Prasad K.P., National President, Rashtriya Meghwal Mahasangh (RMM) also circulated the photo copies of 5-page hand written letter. Copies of the letter were distributed amongst the participants and delegates. It gave a wide publicity to the event. For an elaborate and detailed discussion regarding the socio-historical background of the formation of RMM and various activities and programmes launched by RMM see his letter, 'Rashtriya Meghwal Mahasangh', dated December 12, 2006.
42. Ibid.
43. Ibid.
44. Ibid.
45. Ibid.
46. Ibid.
47. Ibid.
48. Ibid.
49. Ibid.

6 Harijan Mukti Andolan
Rajasthan Anusuchit Jati Sewa Sangh and Reform Movement

In Rajasthan, apart from Gokuldas Maharaj, Garib Saheb, Bhairu Lal Meghwal and Amrit Lal Yadav, Dinesh Rai Dangi also took the lead in spreading social movement. Born on April 26, 1931[1] in a poor Meghwal family of Bali village in Pali district, Dangi from his early childhood was directly affected by inequalities and status of untouchability. His father, Buddha Ram Dangi was a man with progressive ideas. He encouraged the members of his family to go to school. In his bio-data, prepared by his son, Niraj Dangi, and a copy of the same given to the author, he mentions that Dinesh Rai Dangi passed his matriculation examination in 1952 from Bali Government School and Intermediate Examination (Arts) in 1955. Passing Certificate was given by CBSE, Ajmer. He also did his graduation (B.A. Special) in 1958 from the University of Gujarat, Ahmedabad with the following subjects:

1. Ancient and Mediaeval India
2. Political Science
3. Cultural Anthropology
4. Hindi, and
5. Compulsory English.

He was also interested in Law and he appeared in LLB, Previous, Examination in 1959–1960 from University Law College, University of Rajasthan.

A mention has already been made about Dangi's poor economic condition. The need for government job to support the family and to continue his study became apparent and therefore he made several attempts for a government job. Between 1952 and 1959, he served in various capacities in various government departments, such as 'Assistant

Teacher' from October 15, 1952 to April 14, 1954 in Education Department, Government of Rajasthan at Bali, Jalore and Balotra. Attempts were made by Dangi to change his teaching job and in 1954 he joined as Postal Clerk at Sub-post Office, Beawar, Ajmer. In 1956 Dangi was transferred to Accounts Department, GPO Bombay (now Mumbai) and later on to Head Post Office, Udaipur. In 1959, he was appointed as UDC in the office of Accountant General, Rajasthan, Jaipur.

The most significant event during his stay in AG Office, Rajasthan, Jaipur was his meeting with a eminent Congress leader, which resulted in a series of political events. For instance, a Congress ticket from Desuri—a reserved constituency was offered to Dangi by Mohan Lal Sukhadia, the then Chief Minister of Rajasthan in 1962 for State Assembly election. Dangi and Meghwals of Pali district were happy with this decision and so Dangi resigned from the post of UDC and contested the election from Desuri as a Congress candidate and was declared elected in 1962. This was a significant event with indication that Dangi was being groomed for a bigger leadership responsibility and Rajasthan could be his political turf.

The success of Dangi in the State Assembly election in 1962, provided him the first landmark in the beginning of his political career. First, being the emerging untouchable leadership of Dangi in the election of 1962 and second, his induction as Deputy Minister in the Congress ministry headed by Mohan Lal Sukhadia, saddled him with a degree of accountability for the betterment of the state's untouchables and also was a test of his leadership skills. In Rajasthan, where socio-economic and educational conditions of untouchables had been pitiable it was a challenge for him.

Dangi impressed upon the untouchable masses the need for sufficient social and political awakening in order to be able to fight for citizenship rights. He campaigned extensively in rural areas to bring in crowds. He appeared to be injecting a sense of awareness amongst untouchables to overcome the core obstacles of feudally ruled society. Till then (1962) Rajasthan Congress had named only Amrit Lal Yadav as its leader in the Congress ministry, now Dangi was referred to in the list as untouchable Congress leader. The message to Rajasthan untouchables was clear. Indication was that Dangi will head untouchable masses.

On October 2, 1962 Dangi established 'Rajasthan Anusuchit Jati Sewa Sangh'[2] (RAJSS) and made it a regular feature at the annual meetings of RAJSS. From 1963–1987, he established a few Scheduled

Castes hostels and schools of their own throughout the state as part of the Scheduled Castes welfare programmes and had admitted a large number of students. Inmates were provided with all kinds of facilities. Later, the hostels and schools were handed over to the state government. Thus, under Dangi's leadership, the RAJSS received a modern touch. All this created enthusiasm amongst the masses which made him realize that the socio-political awareness was essential for progress in socially and educationally backward communities. Such an organization helped crystalize their consciousness and worked out a programme of action for fighting against the various kinds of discriminations and deprivations.

The campaign for socio-educational reform took a positive turn when Dangi was elected a Member of AICC in 1965. As an elected member of AICC, he voiced the grievances of Rajasthan's untouchables. During State Assembly election in 1972, Dangi was elected unopposed from Desuri reserved constituency in Pali district. His unopposed election was hailed as due recognition of his work. For him this was an opportunity for service to the people of his constituency in particular and masses in general. This was the first time that an untouchable candidate was elected unopposed.

As the Chairman of Scheduled Castes Welfare Committee in Rajasthan Assembly from 1972 to 1974, he pointed out the disabilities of the untouchables with regard to education and how they were forbidden to enter public schools and temples. He pleaded for complete elimination of discrimination against the untouchables. He was also Chairman of Assurance Committee of Rajasthan State Legislative Assembly from 1972–1973. In 1980–1985 when Commonwealth Parliamentary Association (CWPA) was formed by the government, Dangi was nominated its member from Rajasthan.

Dangi is credited with laying stress on education, starting of hostels and schools etc. As a result of all this he was elevated as the state minister twice during 1981–1985.

Dangi also involved himself in the party organization to safeguard the interests of untouchable masses. He was nominated treasurer of the Congress Legislative Party in Rajasthan from 1972 to 1974 and became Joint Secretary, Rajasthan Pradesh Congress Committee from 1978 to 80 and President of Akhil Bharatiya Anusuchit Jati Parishad, Rajasthan State Branch from 1980 to 88. As incharge minister of two districts, namely Pali and Sirohi he campaigned for the party.

Rajasthan Anusuchit Jati Sewa Sangh (RAJSS)—1962

Rajasthan Anusuchit Jati Sewa Sangh (RAJSS), a major Chamar organization dedicated to the cause of educational and social uplift of untouchables was founded by the then Deputy Minister, Irrigation Department, Dinesh Rai Dangi in Jaipur on October 2, 1962. Dangi devoted his energies to the upliftment of untouchables. In his memoir,[3] which provides information about the RAJSS movement in its formative period, Dangi writes that he got inspiration for this work from witnessing the pitiable socio-economic and educational conditions of untouchables in various parts of Rajasthan. Indeed, he dates the beginning of his resolution to better the lot of untouchables to his meeting with common Dalits in rural areas, social workers and activists.

In social and religious matters, Dangi observed that upper caste Hindus strictly maintained untouchability with untouchables. They were not allowed to fetch water from the well and their children were not admitted in the schools. They were not allowed to enter the temples. Thus, a large number of Chamars and other untouchables were affected by the negative attitude of the caste Hindus. This may have been a big hurdle in the upliftment of the untouchables. Dangi also noticed that untouchable communities too observe untouchability within themselves. As a political leader and social reformer, Dangi attempted to persuade the untouchables, as a whole to abandon their belief in untouchability which impeded their social progress. Thus, the content and style of reform campaign were such as to appeal primarily the educated segment of Rajasthani society, caste Hindus and untouchables alike. The mobilization phase of RAJSS movement under Dangi was gathering momentum and 1963 onwards several agitations, Dharnas and Satyagrah were organized. In anticipation of increased political opportunities and representations, the various groups within untouchable communities had begun to folk together and the Chamars were no exception. Two years later, on October 2, 1962 the birthday of Mahatma Gandhi, he founded the Rajasthan Anusuchit Jati Sewa Sangh, Rajasthan, an organization which was to be dedicated to the cause of advancement of Chamars in particular and untouchables in general and which would provide an organizational forum for socio-educational reform as well as to better integrate the Chamar community.

The activities of Dangi's organization were significant for the Chamar movement in that they contributed to the formation of Chamar elite. The aims and objects[4] of the organization were to elevate the social, economic as well as religious conditions of the untouchables by:

1. Promoting education, higher education and technical education.
2. Remedying their social disabilities, removal of untouchability.
3. Campaigning against socio-religious evils, such as drinking of alcohol, child marriage, death feast, Gang Bhoj etc.
4. Uplifting women.
5. Developing of the slum bastis.
6. Preaching to them principles of good religion, personal character and good citizenship
7. Uniting the different small groups or organizations of different castes/communities into one organization.
8. Stopping the socio-economic exploitation of the untouchables by upper caste Hindus.
9. Fighting for securing government jobs for untouchables in government departments.
10. Providing land to landless untouchables for construction of their own houses and also for agriculture.
11. Protecting and promoting traditional handicrafts, arts and domestic trades on the co-operative basis.
12. Providing financial assistance to untouchables and other poor, needy, helpless and the aged people.
13. Propagating and persuading the people to use more and more things manufactured by Khadi Gramodhyog.

The largest membership of RAJSS was that of Chamars and other untouchable communities. The main financial source of this society was through donations as well as some limited government grants. The membership in RAJSS could be classified into three categories.[5] First—ordinary membership—any untouchable youth who had attained the age of 18 years could become a member on paying paise 25 only; second—those who had attained the age of 21 years and above could become the active members by paying Rs 5 and; third and last, other than untouchables, the non-untouchables (caste Hindus) could also become the members by paying Rs 10. Non-untouchable members would be known as 'Sahyogi members'. It is important to note here that they could not become the Office bearers and cast their vote on any issue.

The RAJSS would operate at state level, district level and Panchayat level and had executive committee and sponsored a variety of socio-educational activities for the benefit of untouchable communities. Its socio-educational efforts were channelled through admission of the children of untouchables in government schools. Although the members of Chamars and other untouchables affected by the work of RAJSS may have been small yet its importance in contributing to the development of the untouchable movement cannot be underestimated. Through this process the consciousness of the Chamar community came to be moulded and it got prepared for political action.

It is necessary to point out that emergence of an awareness among untouchables was a gradual process, occurring at different levels with different degree of intensity. For instance, during the Chinese aggression in 1962, Dalit artists notably Ganpat Lal Dangi and Manak Lal Dangi of Jaipur came into contact with Dinesh Rai Dangi, the then Deputy Irrigation Minister, Government of Rajasthan. Dinesh Rai Dangi established the 'Sainik Sahayog Kala Mandal' (SSKM) at Jaipur in 1962. The Dalit artists in Rajasthan were among the first to respond to Chinese aggression. They realized the value of stage programmes and national songs and started to perform several stage programmes. The aims and objects were: to collect donations in the form of kind and cash for National Defence Fund, to think in the national interest, to educate the people to perform their duties during the national crisis, to expose the aggression and negate false propaganda, so that everybody can contribute some thing according to his/her capacity.

Under the leadership of Ganpat Lal Dangi and Manak Lal Dangi the artists took the lead and toured all over Rajasthan and during 1962 organized first drama of "Jai Himalaya"[6] at Jaipur, Pali and Sadri. Former His Highness of Jodhpur, Gaj Singh Maharaj, inaugurated the stage programme at Jodhpur. The collective mobilization of the masses came under the leadership of the Dalits.

SSKM organized the stage programme in five stages. In the first stage, a meeting of the artists was held and they took the oath to play the drama of national service. In the second stage, the aggressor country, China, ordered the Himalaya (symbol of Dharm and unity of India) to leave it. But Dharm and Unity united and took oath to face the aggressor. In the third stage, what are the duties of the citizens during such socio-political crisis was discussed. In the fourth stage, Shankar—a local villager collected the wealth by unfair means. His wife Ganga opposed it strongly. At last Ganga donated all the collected wealth in 'National

Defence Fund'. In the fifth and last stage, a meeting of the Panchayat Samiti is held, where what should be done by the villagers in such socio-political crisis was discussed. An aged woman in the village was worried. The reason of her worries was that there was rumour of her son's death in Indo-China war. Meanwhile the postman handed over a letter which describes the well-being of her son. She criticized the rumours bitterly and blessed her son.

On the advice of Pradhan even children came forward to serve the Bharat Mata. A newly married couple too was ready to serve the nation. Thus, the entire village addressed itself specifically on three issues—donate money, ornament etc., in National Defence Fund and stop spreading rumours.

In 1963, D. Sanjivaya,[7] an English-educated untouchable leader from Andhra Pradesh became the first Dalit President of Indian National Congress. He was an orator and writer in English. In addition to his active political participation in AICC, he was also associated with welfare programmes and activities of downtrodden section of the society. The dynamics of D. Sanjivaya's leadership lies in the fact that when he visited Jaipur in 1963, Dinesh Rai Dangi, Deputy Minister Irrigation and President of RAJSS met him personally and most of the issues that Dangi took up were RAJSS's activities. D. Sanjivaya took an active interest in the affairs of RAJSS.

Notes

1. This description is largely based on 2-page hand written note prepared and given to the author by son Niraj Dangi, State President of Youth Congress, Rajasthan. Dated March 2, 2006. For more details, see, particularly the Bio-data of Dinesh Rai Dangi, Ex-Minister of State, Rajasthan and Member AICC (I).
2. For most important discussion of the origin of 'Rajasthan Anusuchit Jati Sewa Sangh' (RAJSS) and other activities, see, *Rajasthan Anusuchit Jati Sewa Sangh—Ismarika*, Jaipur, RAJSS 1963, page not mentioned. Printed at Madhu Printers, Jaipur. Also see, 'Rajasthan Anusuchit Jati Sewa Sangh: Meri Najar Mai; Dinesh Rai Dangi in *RAJSS—Ismarika*, 1963.
3. Ibid.
4. 'Rajasthan Anusuchit Jati Sewa Sangh-ka Samvidhan' gives an account of aims and objects, area of activities, types of membership, formation of

executive committees at state level, district level and Panchayat Samiti level; election procedure, rights, duties and powers of various authorities, annual convention etc., published by Dinesh Rai Dangi, President, RAJSS, Deputy Minister, Government of Rajasthan, Jaipur. Total pages 8. Year not mentioned. Printed at Diamond Printing Press, Gopalji ka Rasta, Jaipur. pp. 1–2. Also see, 'Rajasthan Anusuchit Jati Sewa Sangh: Udeshya' in *RAJSS—Ismarika* 1963, page not mentioned.

5. Ibid., pp. 2–3
6. For more details, see, particularly, "Jai Himalaya": writer, Manak Lal Dangi and assistant writer and singer, Ganpat Lal Dangi in *Rajasthan Anusuchit Jati Sewa* Sangh—*Ismarika*, 1963, page not mentioned.
7. See particularly, "Bharatiya Congress Adhiyaksh Shree D. Samjivaya ka Anusuchit Jati Sewa Sangh Ke Adhiyaksh Dwara Samman" in *RAJSS Ismarika*, 1963. Page not mentioned.

7 Acharya Guru Prasad K.P.

A Study in Leadership

Coterminous with the earlier period of Gokuldas's and Gareeb Saheb's activity, another important figure in Meghwal movement is Acharya Guru Prasad K.P.,[1] a Balai from Delhi. Born on May 6, 1926 in Delhi, he was the first child of Saint Goverdhandas K.P. and Badambai. His father was an attendant and was attached with the then British Railway Lord, namely Lord Beggaran and was a devotee of Kabir Panth. Originally, the family came from village Jeelopatan in Sikar district of Rajasthan. Puran Prasad (birth name) received his early education at A.B. Primary School, Mori Gate, Delhi and Middle from A.B. Middle School, Kabari Gate, Delhi. He matriculated from Sanatan Dharm High School, Kadewalan at Ajmeri Gate, Delhi in 1942 and Prabhakar in 1944 and graduated (B.A.) as a private candidate from Lahore University, Lahore (now in Pakistan) in 1945. As was the contemporary custom, Puran Prasad was married when he was only 14 years to Ashrafi Devi, then 12 years old.

Puran Prasad went to Allahabad. He received his Sahitiyaratan degree from Allahabad University. In 1968 he went to Bihar to work towards Sahitya Acharya. In 1998, he also attended Banaras Hindu University to qualify as 'Vidhiya Waridhi'. By any account these were outstanding academic achievements, particularly for a member of untouchable Balai caste. His academic brilliance and motivation were extraordinary as was his ambition to work for betterment of his own community through writing and social activities. He had started, his career as a social worker within his community in 1938. He edited a number of periodicals from 1948 onwards to create socio-political awareness among the Balais. These were: *Sootrakar* (1948–49), *Nav Jeevan Path* (1968–1970), *Bandhan-Mukti* (1970–71), *Meghwal Keerti* (1998) and *Sahshtrabadhi Ismarika* (2001).

During 1938, when Gareeb Saheb visited Delhi for the first time, he held religious discourse with some local eminent Arya Samaji scholars, such as Dehlavi. During his discourse, Gareeb Saheb impressed upon Dehlavi and also satisfied him fully by answering all his questions and queries on religious issues. As a result of all this, a large number of community fellows including Puran Prasad became his staunch followers (hence for the called Guru Prasad K.P.).

It was decided there to form an Association which would devote itself exclusively to amelioration and upliftment of the Balai Samaj in Rajputana. Thus, 'Akhil Bharatiya Sootrakar Mahasabha' (ABSM)[2] was formed in 1945 in Jobner, Jaipur. Indeed ABSM was to function in Rajputana, Delhi and neighbouring regions. The aims of the new Association were educational, cultural and economic. From 1938 onwards Guru Prasad assumed an active role vigorously in the socio-religious and political affairs of his people. In 1951, Karpatri,—a leading social activist founded 'Akhil Bharatiya Pariganit Jatia Parishad', an organization which was to be dedicated to the cause of advancement of untouchables and weaker sections of the society. Guru Prasad joined it in 1950. 'Bharatiya Dalit Warg Sangh' was an important organization to push forward the development of untouchable movement in India. It was established by Babu Jagjivan Ram in the year 1984, and was primarily concerned with the untouchable communities and thus served a valuable communication function. Guru Prasad K.P. also joined it.

To carry forward social and religious matters Guru Prasad K.P. established in 1958 'Satguru Kabir Sahitya Avam Aadhiyatam Anusandhan Parishad' (SKSAAAP). He urged his community fellows to abandon social evils and vices. In 1974 and 1984, Guru Prasad K.P. joined 'Bapu Aadarsh Vidhyalaya Shikshan Sansthan' (founded by Mata Rameshwari Nehru in 1951) and Bharatiya Dalit Sahitya Academic established by Babu Jagivan Ram in 1984 respectively.

In 1998, in order to integrate the Meghwal, Bhambhi, Chamar, Balai, Bunkar and other cognate communities under a common umbrella a 'Rashtriya Meghwal Mahasangh' (RMM) was formed. It was a significant development of the Meghwal movement. Guru Prasad K.P. became the first President of it. Thus, Guru Prasad K.P. joined a large number of organizations to mobilize the untouchables into a viable and assertive community, increasingly conscious of its human, social, economic and political rights.

In addition to social and political work of his community and other Dalit communities, he also published more than 500[3] short essays in several Hindi daily, national newspapers, monthly, fortnightly and weekly community papers and periodicals such as *Rajabali Samaj*, *Sootrakar*, *Shaket*, *Vyakti Aur Samaj*, *Aadarsh Muslim*, *Aaj Ka Dalit*, *Hakdar*, *Udaimegh* etc., published form Delhi and other states. In 1966 he published *Shudrarimanu ka Virodh-Samajik Nayay Sangat* which was his first book. A few more books were also published. According to 'Jivan Vrat' (A copy of which is with the writer), there are 5 books in Hindi. Their names are as follows: *Bharatiya Samvidhan Ke Janak Baba Saheb Ambedkar* (1966), *Dahkata Aankade-Bahkata Lok* (2001), *Arya Aakraman Aur Sindhu Sabhiyata-Ka-Dhawansh* (2002), *Samay-Ki-Shilapar Ukeri Anubhutiya* (2002) and *Sabhiyata, Sanskriti, Sahitya Aur Samaj* (2002). Jivan Vrat also revealed that Guru Prasad K.P. who had written more than 500 short essays and articles in various papers, periodicals and magazines, had the mastery over 7 languages, such as Hindi, Braj, Haryanvi, Rajasthani, Punjabi, Avadhi and English.

Guru Prasad K.P. was perhaps the first person from amongst the Balai untouchables from the states of Rajasthan, Delhi and Madhya Pradesh to receive honour and several other awards[4] from 17 organizations working in 9 states for his contribution to social and educational work. His academic brilliance and motivation were extra-ordinary as was his ambition to work for the betterment of his own community through journalism, creating Dalit literatures, books and socio-political activity. The honours conferred on him are: Dr Ambedkar Fellowship (Delhi) 1987, Dr Ambedkar Fellowship (Uttar Pradesh) 1988; Dr Ambedkar Fellowship (Himachal Pradesh) 1989; Humanity Award (Humanity International Mohali (Punjab) 1989; Rashtriya Dalit Lekhakh award, Ujjain (Madhya Pradesh) 1994; Dr Ambedkar Phule Achhutanand Award, Lucknow (Uttar Pradesh) 1995; Gurumat Sewa Samman, Chandigarh (Punjab) 1996; Saint Kabir Rashtriya Samman (Delhi) 1996; Bharat Ratan Dr Ambedkar Samman, Ujjain (Madhya Pradesh) 1997; Saint Kabir Award, Chandigarh (Punjab) 1998; Rashtriya Shrajan Sewa Samman, Ujjain (Madhya Pradesh) 1998; Satya Shodhak Samman (Mumbai) 1999; Rashtriya Akta Samman Jaipur (Rajasthan) 2000; Rashtriya Akta Praman Patra Kulu, (Himachal Pradesh) 2000; Dalit Sahitya Gourav Samman, Ujjain, (Madhya Pradesh) 2001; Dr Ambedkar Sahitya Mahoupadhyaya Samman, Ujjain, (Madhya Pradesh) 2001; Dr

Ambedkar Rashtriya Puruskar (Delhi) 2003 and Sahityakar Samman, Hindi Academy, Government of NCT of Delhi, 2004.

During 1952–55, he also performed several stage programmes,[5] such as Shanti Path (1952), Bhukha (1953), Kala Aur Vashna (1954), Opari Hawa (1954) and Netaji Subhash (1955) in Delhi, for which he was honoured and was awarded several prizes from Kailash Nath Katju, the then Home Minister, Government of India.

On February 16, 1972[6] at Calcutta (now Kolkata) an agreement was executed between Danish Youth Council (DUF) and Bharatiya Grameen Yuvak Samaj (BGYS) in cooperation with Indian Assembly of Youth (IAY) Ravi Dutt, the Chairman of IAY and Ole Simonsen, Leader of DUF, signed the Agreement. The main object was the youth exchange programme between the two countries. The office bearers of the Bharatiya Grameen Yuvak Samaj and Indian Assembly of Youth were:

1.	Chairman:	Ravi Dutt, Chairman, Indian Assembly of Youth and Bharatiya Grameen Yuvak Samaj
2.	Secretary:	O.P. Bharadwaj
3.	Acting Secretary:	Acharya Guru Prasad K.P.

Soon after this, the first Danish Youth Delegation consisting of 57 members (24 male and 33 female) headed by Ole Simonsen arrived in India by SAS special flight at Palam International Air port, New Delhi on July 13, 1973 morning. They stayed in the capital from 13 to 28 July 1973.[7]

The first Untouchable member of Indian delegation was Acharya Guru Prasad K.P. who had been associated with BGYS and IAY. It was in accordance with Danish Agreement that the first delegation of India (including Guru Prasad K.P.) visited Denmark and Germany, in 1976. He stayed in both the countries from August 3, 1976 to September 13, 1976.[8] The expenses were borne by DUF.

It is significant that most of the untouchables, just as Acharya Guru Prasad K.P. were followers of Mahatma Gandhi and whose main objective was propagating his teachings. The philosophy of Gandhi was considered to be a path of social emancipation of Dalits. It was regarded as beacon light of Dalit upliftment. It is also significant that SCs and STs Associations were centred around the teachings of Gandhi. Thus, local associations supported the objectives of the Gandhian philosophy, although a large number of them were not part of the organizations in forties and fifties. Through them the message of Gandhi had spread over the country and reached the masses at village level and every household imbibed the spirit of Gandhi's teachings.

We have noted earlier that Acharya Guru Prasad K.P. also made attempts to organize Dalits to carry on Gandhi's path. However, this did not create any enthusiasm among the masses, which made him realize that the views of Ambedkar were essential for progress in an educationally backward, socially nowhere and economically poor castes and communities and therefore decided to get the blessings of Ambedkar. In 1948 Acharya Guru Prasad K.P. met Baba Sahib Ambedkar with the Dalit social activists Thakur Pratap Singh and Gyanendra Nath at his residence located at Hastings Road (now Tilak Marg) New Delhi. When they reached, Acharya Guru Prasad K.P. was in Khadi kurta, pyajama and white Gandhi cap on his head, which attracted the attention of Ambedkar and he asked who that young man was? Gyanendra Nath, introducing Acharya Gurprasad K.P. said he has come to you for your kind blessings. Ambedkar, first laughed and then remarked, Gandhi is sitting on his head. How can he get my blessings. Acharya Guru Prasad K.P. immediately removed his Gandhi cap and then touched his feet. Putting his hands on Acharya Guru Prasad K.P. head, Ambedkar expressed his feelings 'to serve the society'.

From an account of events in Acharya Guru Prasad K.P.'s life through various pamphlets, hand written letters, short notes etc., it will be seen that Acharya Guru Prasad was associated with the diverse kind of activities including political activities. He took an active interest in the political affairs and fought general elections for MP/MLA, on party tickets in Rajasthan and Delhi respectively. For instance, a detailed note prepared by Acharya Guru Prasad K.P. shows that in 1962, one of Acharya's friends, namely Ghanshyamdas,—a scheduled caste candidate from Jaipur, Rajasthan desired to contest the State Assembly election from Neem-ka-Thana reserved constituency as a Swatantra Party candidate. Dr Ghanshyamdas took Acharya Guru Prasad K.P. from Delhi to party headquarters at Jaipur. Here they met State President Maharawal Laxman Singh of Dungarpur who was also the father-in-law of Maharaja Karni Singh, Bikaner. When both of them reached, Acharya Guru Prasad K.P. who was in sport suit, attracted the attention of Maharani Gayatri Devi and was asked by her, from where you want to fight State Assembly election. In his reply to Maharani Gayatri Devi, he outlined the purpose of his coming over there and requested her for party ticket to Dr Ghanshyamdas. She was so impressed that spontaneous curiosity prompted her to ask him 'so you are also from reserved quota'. His reply was in affirmative. She was so impressed that she offered him the parliamentary ticket from the Sawaimadhopur constituency. Sawaimadhopur constituency was a nurtured constituency of Maharaja Jaipur. On this occasion, Maharaja Karni Singh of Bikaner was also attracted by the Acharya Guru Prasad K.P.'s personality and offered him ticket from Sriganganagar reserved constituency named after his father Maharaja Ganga Singh. Maharawal Laxman Singh of Dungarpur—the State President of Swatantra Party now agreed to allot ticket to Acharya Guru Prasad K.P. from Sriganganagar, Bikaner. By any account this was an outstanding political achievement, particularly, by a member of untouchable Bunkar caste. He was perhaps the first person among the untouchables of Rajasthan to get party ticket from Swatantra Party, then one of the leading party of princes, an uncommon success story even for person of the highest caste in Rajasthan.

In order to understand the part played by Pannalal Barupal, the two times Congress winner candidate from the same constituency, it is necessary to study the influence of Barupal in Bikaner. Since 1952 to 1962 with the winning of elections, Barupal's social activities began to exert his influence. He encouraged various socio-political activities in the desert region of Rajasthan. It was mainly due to efforts, encouragement and political patronage of Barupal that Dalits were able to improve their socio-economic and educational conditions. By 1962' Barupal's influence was widespread and some of the Dalit leaders recognized that it was Barupal who had fenced up lakhs of Dalits from going out to seek refuge in other political parties because of the indignities and humiliations heaped upon them by the upper caste Hindus.

In 1962 election when Acharya Guru Prasad K.P. reached Sriganganagar to fill his nomination papers as a Swatantra Party candidate and submitted his nomination papers along with other required documents before District Collector, Barupal—a strong Congress candidate objected and raised the question of his (Guru Prasad K.P.) being Scheduled Caste and demanded for Scheduled Caste certificate. It is important to mention here that during 1952 and 1957 elections, it was necessary for scheduled caste candidate to submit the caste certificate, but in 1962 the Election Commission had amended this condition. The

Election Commission also said that it was enough to simply mention in the nomination papers that he/she belonged to SC/ST category. However, those who doubted his/her SC category may challenge it by filing a counteraffidavit. When this amendment was shown from election manual to Kalla, the then District Collector, he was satisfied. Thus his nomination was accepted and got cleared by the District Collector.

During the election campaign an unfortunate incident occurred which changed the whole political scenario as narrated by Acharya Guru Prasad K.P. According to him when he was campaigning in Hanumangarh to fight for MP election, one day he stopped at a Nai's shop for shaving and gave his Key Ponch "to a Cobbler to repair it who was sitting under a shadow of a tree". His jeep with party flag was kept in front of the shop. Soon after this, Kunwar Hari Singh of Dungarpur and brother-in-law of Maharaja Karni Singh of Bikaner passed on. When Hari Singh of Dungarpur saw the jeep with party flag, he stopped immediately and took Acharya Guru Prasad K.P. in his arms and said "Oh, Dada Bhai, today where you are going" (अरे दादा भाई आज कठे). Both chit-chatted for a moment and then he went away. The cobbler was watching all this. Spontaneous curiosity prompted the cobbler to ask Acharya Guru Prasad K.P. "are you Rajput by caste"? Archarya Guru Prasad K.P. replied in the negative and said "I am scheduled caste". But the cobbler did not believe and said "you are telling a lie. Actually you are a Rajput, but show as if you were Harijan. Your driver Om Prakash is a Brahmin. His father, Fakir Chand, is a Patwari. Would you and your driver take food and water at my house?"

The misunderstanding for Acharya Guru Prasad K.P. by the cobbler can be explained in terms of certain inter-related factors. First, the upper caste Hindus, and more particularly members from Royal families in princely states, treated the Chamars, Meghwals and other low untouchable castes with contempt. They maintained their distance and did not associate with the Chamars and taking Acharya Guru Prasad K.P. into his arms by Kuwar Hari Singh confirmed that he (Guru Prasad) was not from low untouchable caste. Second, Kuwar Hari Singh addressed Acharya Guru Prasad K.P. "अरे दादा भाई आज कठे". This further confirmed the cobbler's view of his being Rajput. Hence the cobbler was more sure of this rather than by accepting his low caste status. Third and last, Kuwar Hari Singh offered a more satisfactory social view within the framework of caste system. It was this which largely framed the view of caste status.

Within no time Acharya Guru Prasad K.P.'s image as caste Hindu was widespread and recognized that he was a non-Dalit. This incident spoiled the political atmosphere. While Acharya Guru Prasad K.P. worked hard for election campaign and organized several meetings, he withdrew himself from manifest political campaign and thus in 1962 elections, he was miserably defeated.

In 1967 during the Parliamentary election, Acharya Guru Prasad K.P. fought another election from Karol Bagh reserved constituency, New Delhi as an independent candidate. His election symbol was cycle. Indirect effect of growing sabotage activities of his own people, he failed to garner the support of Dalits in different parts of the constituency.

Soon after emergency and leaving the Indian National Congress, Babu Jagjivan Ram, the then sole eminent Dalit leader formed 'Congress for Democracy' (CFD) in 1977 and later became Deputy Prime Minister of India when Morarji Bhai Desai was heading the country. In 1977, Acharya Guru Prasad K.P. again contested the election for MLA from Anand Parvat constituency, New Delhi. Although CFD was formerly not recognized by Election Commission, New Delhi, he was sponsored and supported by CFD and other Dalit organizations but was defeated.

The foregoing account of Acharya Guru Prasad K.P.'s failure shows that he could not provide a charismatic leadership which could give his supporters self-confidence and respect.

In order to understand the part played by Acharya Guru Prasad K.P. in the amalgamation of 'Indian Socialist Party' (ISP) into 'Democratic Socialist Front' (DSF), it is necessary to study the whole episode. As has been stated earlier that soon after emergency and leaving of the Indian National Congress, strenuous efforts were made by Babu Jagjivan Ram and a new party named 'Congress for Democracy' (CFD) was formed in 1977 under his leadership. Hemvati Nandan Bahuguna was the General Secretary of CFD. Bahuguna, an eminent and enlightened politician of the country, realized that Babuji should not join hands with Janta Party (S). Hence, there was anger and frustration amongst Bahuguna and his colleagues. Some of the members from the CFD under his leadership had formed another party called "Democratic Socialist Front" (DSF). Bahuguna was in the process to get it acknowledged formally as a political unit by the Election Commission, New Delhi, but these attempts did not acquire the character of a recognized party. In 1977 both Bhola Prasad Singh, former Chairman and M.A. Hakim, General Secretary of

Indian Socialist Party left the party and joined Janta (S). A small number of members were there. Acharya Guru Prasad K.P. was now the General Secretary of ISP. Some one advised Bahuguna to invite Acharya Guru Prasad K.P. by sending a messenger for amalgamation of his party ISP into DSF. As a result, a man namely Yadav approached Acharya Guru Prasad K.P. with Bahuguna's message. Bahuguna and Acharya Guru Prasad K.P. started their amalgamation efforts in New Delhi. Bahuguna encouraged Guru Prasad for amalgamation of ISP into DSF. Due to his encouragement an application for amalgamation of ISP into DSF was made to the Election Commission, New Delhi in 1977 by Acharya Guru Prasad K.P. and his request was accepted by the Election Commission. In this process Bhattacharya—a Rajya Sabha member and a trusted colleague of Bahuguna was involved. The main object of amalgamation was to get recognition of his party.

The visit of VVIP, eminent politicians and other dignitaries to various Matha, Ashram and Sarai for getting their blessings in past and present period was/is a common thing. Gulzarilal Nanda was no exception to this. When Nanda was heading Navjivan Sangh, Acharya Guru Prasad K.P. was also associated with it. Acharya Guru Prasad K.P. worked as co-editor of 'Nav Jivan Path', a mouthpiece of the Organization in New Delhi. Haryana Government nominated Nanda as Chairman of Kurukshetra Development Board and was invited by the Haryana Government. He then proceeded to Kurukshetra and took Acharya Guru Prasad K.P. with him.

In his brief notes as well as in separate statement to the author, Acharya Guru Prasad K.P. described a few instances. In one such instance, Acharya Guru Prasad K.P. noted that Nandaji was a devotee of a local saint. Both Nandaji and he went to his Ashram. Nandaji had quietly साष्टांग (bowed) before the saint. It was hoped that Acharya Guru Prasad would also do the same. But Acharya Guru Prasad K.P. did not perform their traditional task (साष्टांग). Thus, Nandaji became angry and asked him (Acharya Guru Prasad), why he did not touch the feet? Acharya Guru Prasad K.P. urged that since big leader like you have totally "साष्टांग, this had ensured others involvement. What I do. I am too little to you." He further pointed out that he would come in the evening for साष्टांग. Nandaji then asked another question why in the evening? For according to Acharya Guru Prasad K.P., it would be different in the evening (शाम का आलम ही कुछ और होता है). His brother-in-law who resided in Kurukshetra and was known to the saint, had narrated the realities of the Ashram long back. As a proof, it was decided to go to the Ashram. The saint was in a drunken condition and uttered that he had performed Yagya (यज्ञ) for Nandaji, who had not financially supported me so far. He has claimed himself to be a big man. What big man? Nandaji and Acharya Guru Prasad K.P. listened to all this and returned without any comment.

An International Dalit Sahityakar Conference was held in 1998 at Dharan in Nepal.[9] This convention was attended largely by the Dalit Sahityakars from all over India and neighbouring countries. Bharatiya Dalit Sahitya Academy (BDSA) had been established in 1984 in Delhi by Babu Jagjivan Ram. Under the aegis of BDSA, Acharya Guru Prasad K.P. attended the International Conference. The expenses were borne by BDSA.

To discuss Dalit writings and their significance for Dalit communities, Bharatiya Dalit Sahitya Academy, UK had called a Convention in 2000. Thus, the Second World Dalit Writers Conference, 2000 was held at Ambedkar Centre, 46 Gordon Road, South Hall, Middex, London, UK from October 12, 2000 to October 15, 2000[10] by O.P. Azad, President, Bharatiya Dalit Sahitya Academy. U.K.C. Gautam was the Chairman, Reception Committee, the Second World Dalit Writers' Conference, UK. The Conference was inaugurated by David Webb (former Superintendent of Police) Chief Executive, Federation of Asian Businessmen in Europe. Mata Prasad, former Governor of Arunachal Pradesh (India) presided over the function. Among the guests of Honour were: Dr Dauji Gupta, MLC (former Mayor); Dr Maheep Singh, editor *Sanchetna* (India); Uttam Kumar Parihar, Member Raj Parishad (Nepal); G.S. Brar (USA); H.P. Randhawa (Germany); Sita Ram Ahir (Canada); Bhante Prajyanand (Sri Lanka) and S. Burmaula (Myanmar).

This Conference was attended by 41 delegates of Dalit writers from India, notably, Ramnika Gupta, who is prominent non-Dalit writer from Bihar (India). Besides, delegates from Nepal, Germany, Canada, Sri Lanka and Myanmar came there to participate.

The important issues taken up by the Conference were:

1. History—pre-Vedic, Vedic and post-Vedic period.
2. Literature—pre-Vedic, Vedic and post-Vedic period
3. History—pre-Buddha, Buddha and post-Buddha period.
4. Literature—pre-Buddha, Buddha and post-Buddha period.
5. History—pre-Ambedkar, Ambedkar and the post-Ambedkar period.

6. Literature—pre-independence, after Independence and up to 2000.
7. History—message for future generation.
8. Literature—message for future generation.

David Webb in his inaugural speech tried to spread the message that only two devoted and wise men could alter the whole world. He supported his message with citing the name of Karl Marx and Engle to the effect that they changed the world history. The 2000 Conference proceedings also revealed that S.P. Sumanakshar, President, BDSA (India) also appreciated the Dalit writings. Amongst others who expressed their views were: Ramnika Gupta, Dr Vimal Thorat, Babu Lal Chanwaria, Acharya Guru Prasad K.P., S.S. Bahal, Amrik Singh etc. In all there were 33 speakers. It is important to note that Acharya Guru Prasad K.P., an eminent writer and social activist, conducted the proceedings of the conference, 2000.

After the completion of the Second World Dalit Writers' Conference, 2000 UK, the most important step taken in regard to 2000 conference resolution was a summary report sent by Bhagwan Swaroop Katiyar on return from UK to *Pioneer,* a Hindi daily newspaper published from Delhi. A wide coverage of this conference and its resolutions were published in this paper.

The resolutions were rather long and discursive. And finally the resolutions indicated that Dalit communities rejected the literature created by caste Hindus. In its opinion the Brahminical literature had destroyed their socio-political history. The resolutions passed included the following specific points:

'द्वितीय विश्व दलित लेखक सम्मेलन'[11]

सम्मेलन का महत्व इसमें पारित निश्चयों और निर्णयों की घोषणा से स्पष्ट है–

1. भारत तथा संसार में बसने वाले दलित साहित्य के लेखक सवर्ण मानसिकता से प्रेरित समाज द्वारा हजारों वर्षों से दलित समाज पर निरन्तर किए जाने वाले दमन, उत्पीड़न और मानवीय व्यवहार की अब पूरी तरह पहचान कर चूके हैं और उसका प्रतिकार करने के लिए पूरी तरह कटिबद्ध हैं। हमारा मानना है कि भारत में प्राचीन काल से लिखा जाने वाला सवर्ण मानसिकता से ग्रस्त अधिकांश साहित्य निर्माण इसी वर्ग के लिए हित साधन के लिये किया गया और समानता मूलक वर्ण व्यवस्था द्वारा पोषित दलित जातियों पर निरन्तर किये जाने वाले क्रुरतापूर्ण व्यवहार की पुष्टि करने के लिए सृजन हुआ। हम ऐसे साहित्य को नकारते हैं जो समता, बंधुता और स्वतन्त्रता के सिद्धान्तों से पूरी तरह अवहेलना करके मनुष्य को सम्मान, गौरव और स्वावलंबन से वंचित करता है।

2. संसार भर में बसने वाले दलित साहित्य के लेखक अपने इस नियम को दोहराते हैं कि हम पूरी तरह प्रतिबद्ध होकर ऐसे साहित्य की रचना में संलग्न है और रहेगें जो समानता, बंधुता और स्ववन्त्रता के महत आदेशों से प्रेरित है और सभी प्रकार के मतभेद भेदभाव को नकारता हुआ मानवीय गरिमा की रक्षा करता हो।

3. ढ़ाई हजार साल पहले महात्मा बुद्ध ने उस ब्राहमणवादी व्यवस्था को चुनौती दी थी जो स्त्रियों और शूद्रों को शिक्षा, ज्ञान, आत्मबोध और चेतना से पूरी तरह वंचित रखकर सम्पूर्ण ज्ञान राशि पर एक ऐसी भाषा (संस्कृत) के माध्यम से एकाधिकार जमाये थी जो सामान्य जनता से बहुत दूर थी, महात्मा बुद्ध ने जो जन साधारण की भाषा में ज्ञान के द्वारा सभी लोगों के लिये खोल दिये और बहुजन हिताय बहुजन "सुखाय" का आदर्श प्रतिपादित किया था। इन्हीं आदर्शों को सिद्ध, नाथ, संतों और मध्य युग के नामदेव कबीर, रविदास, नानक तथा अन्य सिक्ख गुरुओं ने प्रतिस्थापित किया था। आधुनिक युग में महात्मा ज्योतिबा फूले, शाहूजी महाराज और डा0 भीमराव अम्बेडकर ने इस मुक्तकामी क्रांति को मूर्त रूप दिया था, ये हमारे प्रेरणा स्रोत हैं।"

4. बाबा साहेब अम्बेडकर ने भारतीय संविधान का निर्माण करके भारत के सभी लोगों को उनके धर्म, जाति, वर्ण, नस्ल और लिंग की विभिन्नता के बावजूद समान अधिकार प्रदान किये, लोकतंत्र के आगमन से उन वंचित लोगों को भी अपनी बात करने, राज्य संचालन में भागीदारी प्राप्त करने और सभी प्रकार के निर्णयों में हस्तक्षेप करने का अधिकार दिया है, हम ऐसे किसी भी प्रयास का भरपूर विरोध करेंगे जो संविधान की उन धाराओं के साथ मिलकर खिलवाड़ करने का प्रयास करेगा, जिससे संविधान द्वारा प्रदत्त इन मौलिक अधिकारों की क्षति होती है।"

Notes

1. This description about his early life is largely based on personal interview with Acharya Guru Prasad K.P. of Delhi. He is over 80 years old and is reputed to be keenly interested in the affairs of Meghwal communities and possesses a great deal of information about their community's history and the case reported here. Delhi. May 5, 2005.
2. For details, see, a two-page computerised "Jivan Vrat" of Guru Prasad K.P. which was given to the author at the time of interview.
3. As told by Acharya Guru Prasad K.P.
4. For details, see "Jivan Vrat".
5. Ibid.
6. For details, see, "Highlights of the Danish Youth Delegation (1973)". Published by the Reception Committee Danish Youth Delegation 1973. Sponsored by Bharatiya Grameen Yuvak Samaj and Indian Assembly of Youth, New Delhi, p. 1.

7. Ibid., p. 2.
8. As told by Acharya Guru Prasad K.P.
9. As told by Acharya Guru Prasad K.P.
10. It is important to mention here that this description is largely based on a 4-page "Invitation" published and circulated by Organizer, Bharatiya Dalit Sahitya Academy, UK, 2000. The invitation provided detailed information about the venue of the Conference, inauguration of the Conference, delegates coming from various countries, discussion on subjects of the Conference, Award ceremony, Cultural programme and UK, Declarations. For an elaborate and detailed discussion, see the 4-page printed 'Invitation', 2nd World Dalit Writers Conference 2000 UK published and circulated by Organizer Bharatiya Dalit Sahitya Academy, UK 2000. Also see, 6-page hand written list of participants from India entitled World Dalit Writers Conference, 2000 UK participants. Nowhere the name of the person who prepared the list is mentioned. The list was supplied to the author by Acharya Guru Prasad K.P.
11. For an elaborate and detailed discussion on Dalit Sahitya and its Implications. see,"द्वितीय विष्वदलित लेखक सम्मेलन" in *Pioneer* (Hindi), New Delhi. Date not mentioned.

and Thakurs came to know about this [illegible] communities, i.e., orthodox opponents of reform [illegible] grew restless and vindictive. [illegible] Meghwals were cruelly beaten [illegible] imposed on them. They were then forced to leave the villages. They were very poor and could not live in such conditions. Swami visited all the troublesome villages in order to listen to the grievances of the community fellows. He criticized and condemned [illegible] self-respect of Meghwals. Swami [illegible] Jagirdars and Thakurs [illegible] compel them for begar. Swami encouraged the masses to continue the agitation and asked his fellow brothers not to yield before pressure.

III
Movement

8 Rise and Awakening of Meghwal and Sootrakar Communities in Western Rajasthan

The period from 1916 to 1947 represents the formative period in the history of Meghwal movement. It was during this time that this first organization dedicated itself to the uplift of Meghwals as an untouchable community and spearheaded by the Meghwals under Ameda Ram Kataria, began to acquire a social presence. This period contained two distinct stages in the development of Meghwal movement which was characterized by a different set of issues, leadership and style.

The first stage dating roughly from 1916 to 1947, may be termed the era of self-reform. During this period, the organizations that were formed, were reformist in orientation and their major concern seems to have been the social uplift and advancement of the Meghwal community. This advancement was to be effected through the medium of education, and by eliminating those practices and customs which branded Meghwals as an untouchable community. Moreover, these organizations accepted the Hindu order as a social as well as an ideological system and did not fundamentally question that order. Change and progress among the Meghwals were to occur within the Hindu framework and that progress demanded the self-reform of Meghwals as well as the transformation of the attitude of the caste Hindus because the destiny of the untouchables was seen as inseparable from that of the larger Hindu society. In the self-directed modernization of the community lay the solution to untouchability. Untouchability was defined largely with reference to cultural ideological criteria, and the attitudinal and behavioural aspects of social life. Varna and Jati were accepted as principles of social organization, hence the progress of the untouchables was to occur within the social and ideological order of Hinduism rather than in opposing it.

It is important to note that these characteristics of Meghwal movement at its inception were not unique, but were indeed common to many untouchable movements emerging at that time. Jaya Shree Gokhale[1] commented that "self-reform within the Hindu framework was the shared perspective of movements among the lower castes and untouchables that arose in Andhra, Karnataka, Tamilnadu, Kerala as well a Bengal. And in their reformist stance, these movements were within the tradition of caste Hindu reformer or modernizers who formed organizations such as Arya Samaj and Prathana Samaj".

Soon after the independence of the country in 1947, the Meghwal movement, however, moved towards a new direction, with the displacement of the old leadership and the appearance of different issues and a new style in the conduct of the movement. The second phase saw the emergence and the predominance of educated politicians as the leaders of the movement. Developments in the Meghwal community were influenced by reflecting the process of social mobilization. The origin of Meghwal movement may be seen as an instance of that process. The larger political context was characterized by the growth of national movements, Gandhi-Ambedkar Pact, Arya Samaj, Praja Mandal Agitation, Rajputana Harijan Sewak Sangh and the socio-political awakening of other communities all of which affected the contours and directions of Meghwal movements.

Meghwal Sudhar Sabha (MSS), Tiwri, 1916

An examination of the early Meghwal movements reveals that it did undergo the kind of changes contained in the concept of social mobilization. The emergence of social reformers who were influenced by the various social organizations and were prepared to exhort their community to reject traditional values and roles, was a particularly crucial development in the Meghwal community and in the growth of Meghwal movement.

The most significant feature of the Meghwal's movement was that Meghwals were essentially rural and were concentrated in a few occupations among which removing of dead animals and their skinning, agriculture labourers and domestic services at the residences of Jagirdars,

Jamindars, Thakurs, etc., were the most prominent. By virtue of their being untouchables, they were naturally exploited economically, socially tortured, harassed and humiliated by caste Hindus. Their position often impelled them to think over their miserable conditions. Sometimes their position required them to get rid of the upper castes' atrocities. During this period the Meghwals were dispersed. The community Panchas occasionally took initiative in convening small meetings secretly which were intended to educate quite as much as they were designed to mobilize and organize the Meghwal community. The rural areas were the major loci of Meghwal activities in the early period, for the purpose of reform.

The community Panchas and panchayat provided a vehicle for communication of new ideas for the uplift of the community. The call for reform was carried out secretly amongst the trusted people. Rarely, there was an occasion when Meghwals could arrange an open meeting and challenge or defy the Hindu order. Rather, community Panchas exhorted their caste fellows to rid themselves of those practices which Hindu principles considered unclean. The Panchas were thus instrumental in mobilizing the Meghwal masses and enlisting their support for the reforms for social action.

While many of the community Panchas had primarily local appeal and following, some leaders became prominent in the region and the community as a whole. One such figure was Ameda Ram Kataria, a resident of Tiwri, 40 km away from Jodhpur state. As an untouchable, Kataria had suffered from social disabilities and had been tortured by the untouchability criterion. He also realized the miserable socio-economic conditions of the Meghwals in rural areas, which could thus be considered responsible for a change in Kataria to act as active reformer within the community after 1915 which was the beginning of the reforms.

In the beginning of the year 1916,[2] he wrote letters to community Panchas of 9 Pattis of Marwar region, requesting them to attend the community meeting to be held at Tiwri. The letter contained the themes which were intended to reform the community. In addition to letters addressed to like-minded Meghwals, he also toured several villages around the region to mobilize Meghwals in order to enlist their support. He urged his community fellows to attend meetings wherein they could discuss and try to find out the remedy for their disabilities. He was thus instrumental in mobilizing the Meghwals and enlisting them into the movement for social action.

A few months later a 'Vishal' community meeting for self-reform was held by Ameda Ram Kataria at Tiwri on March 3, 1916. This community meeting was attended by a large number of Panchas and common men of the community from 9 Pattis areas, notably: (1) Tiwri, (2) Jelu, (3) Cherai, (4) Osian, (5) Nath-thau, (6) Gangani, (7) Keru, (8) Aagolai, and (9) six bastis of Jodhpur city. The crux of Kataria's organizational efforts reached the height when the meeting unanimously passed a resolution to establish a community sabha. Thus, 'Meghwal Sudhar Sabha'[3] came into existence with Ameda Ram Kataria as President and Sugna Ram Bhatia (Rajbagh Jodhpur), as Vice President. Besides, a 7-member Executive Committee was constituted. The members were: Jetha Ram Kadela (Shahpura, Jodhpur), Raju Ram Lilar (Jud), Pratap Ram Kadela (Rajbagh, Jodhpur), Suja Ram Inkhiya (Mathania), Dharam Ram Panwar (Punjala), Jujta Ram Lilar (Cherai), and Sita Ram Kadela (Chamu).

The Meghwal Sudhar Sabha (MSS) was formed in order to effect the social and educational awakening of the Meghwal community. Besides, the major issues addressed included abandonment of evil practices, the necessity of improvement in behavioural pattern, food habits and dress pattern, discarding traditional occupation and accepting the non-traditional occupation, necessity to mobilize and organize the Meghwal community etc. The call for reform was put within the bounds of an enlightened Hinduism. There was rarely the suggestion that Meghwals should challenge or defy the Hindu order. Rather, the Meghwal leaders exhorted their community to rid itself of those practices which Hindu principles considered unclean. They also urged that Meghwals overcome the prejudices which divided them into sub-castes and become a unified and modern community.

In its formative period, the Meghwal movement was both localized and scattered or dispersed. The Tiwri area was a major locus of Meghwal activity in the early period. We should also note that in that year, Kataria, a wealthy Meghwal from Tiwri, spent his own money for supporting Meghwals who came to that town to participate in the community meeting. Thus, in Tiwri area the Meghwal community had shown considerable vitality in producing a leadership and organization which sprang up in urban localities and took the initiative in directing its social educational development.

The MSS activists in Tiwri were not content merely with holding Sabhas, meetings and passing resolutions in order to publicize the need for the social reform. In social and religious matters MSS urged its fellow Meghwals to abandon their belief in untouchability and to give up religious and ritual practices which impeded their social progress. The issue of removing dead animals and their skinning was particularly an important one during this period and MSS played a prominent role in bringing it to caste fellows' attention. The caste fellows were also urged to abandon those practices which branded them as untouchables, such as eating of dead animals and drinking of alcohol. If low untouchable castes were to make progress, it was essential to reform all untouchable communities. During this period, MSS's stand on reform was similar to that adopted by many untouchable communities, especially Bairwa, Raigar and Bhangis who were vigorously persuading community leaders for the reform and regeneration of untouchable communities.

Thus, from 1916 onwards, the Jagirdars, Jamindars, Thakurs and upper caste Hindus, in particular, opposed reform measures on the ground that these measures could only jeopardize the interest of the caste Hindus. On more general grounds, it were the upper caste Hindus who had increased the process of oppression on Meghwals. Besides humiliation, torture and harassment of Meghwals, the upper caste Hindus had boycotted Meghwals and imposed several socio-economic restrictions on them. By doing so, upper caste communities preserved their power and interest at the expense of the lower ones.

In spite of all these hurdles and their effect, the role played by the community leaders and Panchas produced three forces which accelerated the process of social mobilization within the Meghwal community. First, after imposing several restrictions on the Meghwals, there was an increase in the community sentiment and the demand for removal of social disabilities. The mobilization phase of Meghwal movement under Kataria was gathering momentum. Second, due to increased social consciousness among the Meghwals, the Meghwal community had begun to organize. Third, from 1920, Arya Samaj in particular took cognizance of the untouchable problems and attempted to offer a programme for the amelioration of the untouchables.

From 1916 onwards Kataria assumed an active role in the social affairs of his people vigorously.

Rift in the MSS

In 1920, after four years, differences developed amongst the Meghwals in western Rajputana region. The set of factors dividing Meghwals concerned its internal composition. There, the community seems to have been deeply divided according to rural-urban[4] background with much internecine squabbling and rivalry. The division of Meghwal Samaj into two groups sent shock waves amongst the community fellows.

One Panchayat (called group) was largely rural Meghwals in composition, while the other was primarily urban Meghwals. The first Panchayat was made up of largely village dwelling Meghwals amongst whom the village Panchas, Sarpanchas and villagers' contingent was sizeable. It included 14 Pattis[5] (also called Mathara). Aged villagers were instrumental in organizing Meghwals and had also started reform programmes for Meghwal Samaj in rural areas. Thus, old Meghwals took the lead in mobilizing Meghwals in rural regions.

The second panchayat which included 6 urban[6] Meghwal bastis was formed by urban dwelling Meghwals. Later on, the number of bastis increased from 6 to 12[7] and was later on known as '12 basti panchayat'.[8] The names of the 12 bastis were: (1) Shahpura, (2) Rajbagh, (3) Mahamandir, (4) Sahardar, (5) Mandor, (6) Punjala, (7) Emarthi-ka-Bera, (8) Daru-ka-Theka, (9) Kuchaman-ki-Haveli, (10) Kili-khana, (11) Sardarpura, and (12) Bijalighar.

Now, it is necessary to consider in the following sections, the growth of different kinds of organizations and their reform programmes and activities, and participation of different kinds of elites and their roles. The organizations may be classified under two categories as: (1) Sahar panchayat, and (2) Gaon panchayat.

Sahar Panchayat of Meghwals (SPM), 1920

While Meghwal Sudhar Sabha (MSS) was formed in the year 1916, the Meghwals dwelling in cities/towns separated in 1920 under the name 'Sahar (city) Panchayat of Meghwals' (SPM) under the leadership of Bhagwandas Joiya of Jodhpur. The organization was also popularly known as '12 Basti Panchayat'. From 1920 onwards he vigorously took an active role in the social affairs of his urban people. During the 1920s, he constituted an Executive Committee for launching reform programmes and activities among Meghwals in cities/towns dwellers. Thus, a new Executive Committee[9] came into existence with Bhagwandas Joiya as

President, Basti Ram Tanwar as Vice President; Hazari Lal Dhomnia as Treasurer; Bhanu Ram Jodha as Mantri; Udaram Gathela as Prachar Mantri and Puk Ram Lilri as Potedar (Cashier). Bhagwan Das Joiya and his colleagues took lead in mobilizing the Meghwals into a viable and assertive community increasingly conscious of its human, social and economic rights. Indeed the SPM was to function only in the cities and towns.

It is necessary to point out here that in traditional society of Rajputana, public meetings and other forms of social contacts were denied to untouchables. The penalties for transgressing caste norms were severe and were used with devastating effect against the transgressor. The traditional sanction was the 'Bahishkar' (excommunication) or boycott. The Bahishkar was particularly effective against the Meghwal community as it had no means of livelihood, other than as village servants. The Bahishkar continues to be used as a weapon against untouchables even today. After independence of the country in 1947, the community had undergone some momentous changes which were to propel it in the socio-political direction through formation of its own movement.

After the lapse of three decades, SPM organized its first annual Sammelan on September 9, 1951[10] at Mahamandir-Lakha-ji-ka-Ghara, Jodhpur. The main leader of SPM since 1920 was Bhagwan Das Joiya. A large number of Meghwals from various bastis such as Shahpura, Rajbagh, Mahamandir, Sahardar, Mandor, Punjala, Emarti-ka-Bera (well), Daru-ka-Theka, Kuchaman-ki-Haveli, Kili-Khana, Sardarpura and Bijlighar attended the Sammelan. Community Panchas also participated in it. Among other prominent Panchas[11] of the community were: Basti Ram Tanwar, Harji Bamania, Bhanu Ram, Birda Ram Kadela, Puna Ram Lilar and many others. Bhagwan Das Joiya himself presided over the SPM's first Sammelan at Mahamandir. At the 1951 Sammelan of SPM, the main decisions of the Sammelan were to organize annual Sammelan regularly in different Meghwal bastis of cities/towns, with a view to politicizing and gaining the support of the Meghwals for its organization. The Sammelan concentrated its efforts on educational and literary activities as education was the symbol of progress and sending the children to school became the main object. Similarly, it also focussed its attention on reformatory measures, such as abolition of dowry, abandonment of alcohol and eating of meat, ban on child marriage and strong plea for inter-sub-caste marriages among the Meghwal community.

Meghwal Samaj Sudhar Sabha (MSSS), 1920

As mentioned earlier the rift between the Meghwals dwelling in villages and cities/towns was more defined in 1920 and since then there has been a separate village dweller Meghwal organization called, Gaon Panchayat which was later on changed to 'Meghwal Samaj Sabha' and often there was competition between the two to win over the masses. However, the MSSS has gained wider recognition and has emerged as the soul of Meghwal movement.

As stated earlier, Ameda Ram Kataria evinced keen interest in the working of his community from the very beginning. When he formed MSS at Tiwri in 1916 and was elected as its President, on February 6, 1920[12] a Vishal Sammelan of Meghwal Samaj under his chairmanship was held at village Balarwa Bavari. As in the case of SPM, Panchas of 14 Pattis were involved in the various activities of the Sammelan. The names of the 14 Pattis were as follows:[13] (1) Tiwri, (2) Osian, (3) Aagolaie, (4) Gangani, (5) Cherai, (6) Lohawat, (7) Jelu, (8) Indroka, (9) Keru, (10) Belwa (Indrawati), (11) Ketu (Gogade), (12) Santrawa (Devraj), (13) Dechu (Charde), and (14) Mathania.

The chief Panchas of the 14 Pattis were:[14] Ameda Ram Jaipal (Lohawat), Jetha Ram Kadela (Kevra), Rara Ram (Chanu), Chutra Ram Likhania (Belwa), Labhu Ram, Palria (Mathania), Hariga Ram Inkhiya (Indroka), Purkha Ram Bhatia (Narwa), Raju Ram Lilar (Jud), Rawat Ram Lohia (Tunara), Sugala Ram Bhatia (Rajbagh), Shadula Ram Pidiyar (Bhikampur), Parta Ram Panwar (Rajbagh), Magji Pidiyar (Punjala), Suja Ram Inkhiya (Mathania) and many others. However, at the 1920 Sammelan of MSSS, 12-Bastis severed its relations with MSSS due to differences on certain issues.

Most of the issues that MSSS took up were similar to those of SPM, but there were two[15] main differences. First, the MSSS concentrated its efforts on the demand for ban on 'begar' and stopping atrocities on the Meghwals. Second, the MSSS focused its attention to encourage the community fellows to agitate against social injustice collectively.

With such rich experience and background Kataria became one of the leading leaders of the MSSS. He presided over the second annual Sammelan of the MSSS held at Osian Dev-ka-Bera on April 13, 1952.[16] It was the biggest Sammelan of the Meghwals.

Among other chief Panchas were:[17] Ameda Ram Jaipal (Lohawat), Bhiya Ram Inkhiya (Dhevra), Manga Ram Likhania (Panchla), Gorakh Ram, and Naru Ram Pidiyar (Khetar), Bhiya Ram Dhande (Thab), Jodha Ram Kataria (Honia), Mehram Ram Pidiyar (Badla), Moda Ram Bochiya (Osian), Gula Ram Gathar (Osian) and many others.

An analysis of various decisions taken by the MSSS at its annual meeting showed that there were 3 major points[18] to focus. First, a number of decisions concerned reformatory measures. Second, there was a concern particularly for banning the begar (forced labour). Third and the last, they supported the campaign for eradication of social vices. The MSSS also supported the anti-dowry movement.

Another prominent leader of the MSSS was Labu Ram Lilar of Cherai. In addition to his active participation in Meghwal Sudhar Sabha, he was also associated with Sabha established in 1916 in Tiwri. However, in 1920 when rift developed in MSS, he severed his relations with MSS and joined gaon panchayat. He presided over the MSSS's third Sammelan at Shergarh, held on December 15, 1958.[19] Among other leading community figures of MSSS were: Parta Ram Bhakhania (Belwa), Cheta Ram Likhania (Panchla), Peepa Ram Dodhu (Shetrava), Jora Ram (Khiyaria) and many others. Most of the issues that MSSS took up were similar to those taken up in the Sammelan of 1952.

Other leaders of the MSSS were: Poona Ram Kataria (Tiwri) and Shiv Lal (Ghugrawala). They evinced interest in working for their community when they joined MSS at Tiwri in 1916. From then until 1979 onwards, they were closely associated with MSSS activities. They took the initiative in encouraging various educational programmes and literary and cultural activities. On September 17, 1979,[20] when the historical Sammelan of the MSSS held at Tiwri (Headquarters of MSSS), Tehsil Osian, district, Jodhpur, both Poona Ram Kataria and Shiv Lal presided over the function. A large number of Meghwal Panchas, Sarpanchas, educated, old and young from more than 160 villages attended it. Among other prominent Panchas of the Meghwal samaj were:[21] Mootu Ram (Ketukala), Harka Ram (Teehu), Partap Ram Likhania (Belwa), Daya Ram (Balesar), Longa Ram (Shergarh), Mahinga Ram and Khiya Ram (Mathania), Heemta Ram (Lohawat), Sanga Ram (Shetrawa), Budha Ram (Aagolai), Gorakha Ram and Nara Ram (Khetar), Ratna Ram Nathnau, Bhagona Ram (Jellu), Jasha Ram (Keru) and Kunji (Indraka).

It is also pertinent to note that the MSSS's Sammelan at Tiwri in 1979, lasted nearly 15 days and passed three important resolutions. First, the MSSS urged that Meghwals should send their children particularly, girls to schools in large number. Second, MSSS also supported the caste unity movement. Third and last, a number of resolutions concerned reformatory measures such as the abolition of dowry, abandonment of alcohol and eating of meat and a strong plea for inter-sub-caste marriages among Meghwals. In addition to various resolutions passed in the Sammelan the MSSS also unanimously approved 26 rules in 1979 in Tiwri.

An analysis of 26 rules[22] passed by the MSSS at its fourth annual meeting shows that there were four major points to focus. First, most of the concerned rules were reformatory, such as marriages and 'sagai'. They also supported widow remarriage. There was a concern for divorce; the MSSS directed that Meghwals should not divorce their married wives and thus discouraged it. Husband has a right to divorce his wife on certain grounds but in case of a default, he had to pay Rs 21,000 as fine to the samaj. The MSSS has directed that all kinds of disputes regarding sagai, ornaments, marriage, dowry, divorce, etc., should be settled through community Panchas. They also supported the age of marriage of boys and girls as adopted by the government and ban on singing of abusive songs. Second, the MSSS directed that Meghwals should have their own priests and should not depend on Brahmins. Third, the MSSS also supported the government decision, particularly the ban on death feast. Fourth and the last, that there was a concern on the murder of wife by husband. The MSSS urged the samaj to excommunicate such persons. However, such expelled persons can be taken back in the samaj provided they fulfil the following terms and conditions. First, he had to pay Rs 21,000 to the samaj as a fine. Second, he had to go to Haridwar to take a dip in the river Ganga to purify himself. Third and the last, he had to organize 'satsang'. After completion of these conditions, he would be taken back.

It should be noted that Meghwal reform movement, during its early years did not strike roots in Jodhpur region as it occurred in other parts of Rajputana. There were many factors which contributed to such a situation. Tiwri was directly administered by the local thakurs who followed the traditional policy with regard to untouchable communities including Meghwals in social and economic spheres. Second, the Arya Samaj movement was weak, which did not help the untouchables specifically in rural areas. The Marwar Lok Parisad founded in 1938 by freedom fighters gave an impetus to national movement and was active only in cities/towns. Third, it seems that upper castes atrocities, harassment and torture had terrorized their stir in villages. Another factor which accounts for the lack of enthusiasm for reform movement among Meghwals was the move by the upper castes to socially boycott the Meghwals and impose certain restrictions on them in villages; such measures too had frustrated them.

Rajasthan Meghvansh Mahasabha (RMM), Pali 1950[23]

In Vikram Samvat 1977, Rajasthan Meghvansh Mahasabha (RMM) was formed by Swami Gokuldas Maharaj with a view to uniting Chamars, Meghwals, Bhambhis and Balais under one banner and to introduce reforms amongst them. It was also decided to establish district branches of RMM throughout the state. Accordingly, on January 11, 1950 a meeting was convened at Ram Deo-ji-ka-Mandir, Nadi Jodhpuria Darwaja-ke-Bahar, Pali, under the presidentship of Swami Gokul Das Maharaj in which it was declared that the said organization had been formed with Duga Ram Engineer, Pali as its Pradhan, Moti Lal Makwana as Up-pradhan; Hukma Ram, Assistant Teacher, Middle School, Marwar Junction, as Mantri, Kesha Ram as Up-mantri, Jiya Ji Aakaya as Treasurer, Mahatma Sundarnath as Prachar Mantri and Bhura Ram, Sava Ram, Lachha Ram, Daya Ram, Bhura Ram and many others as its members.

The objectives of the organization were:

1. To produce and prepare Khadi garments more and more as weaving of Khadi is the main occupation of the samaj.
2. To promote agriculture too.
3. Not to remove dead cattle.
4. Not to skin the dead cattle.
5. Not to eat flesh of dead animals.
6. Not to repair old shoes.
7. Not to make any difference between Maru Bhambhi, and Jata Bhambhi. All are equal.
8. To stress on reducing the marriage expenditure.
9. Not to use various names such as Chamar, Bhambhi, Balai, Meghwals, etc. To tell and use only name Meghwal.

10. To recognize only the Gaddi of Karandas Meghvanshi of Harnaji-ki-Dhaniwale. It is considered one of the important Dharmic Peeths among the Meghwals' Peeth in the Rajasthan.
11. To educate more and more children.
12. To observe cleanliness while eating food and wearing clothes.

The main stress of the meeting was on observing the norms of RMM by caste fellows. Those who oppose or violate the norms would be fined up to Rs 151 and or excommunicated from the Samaj. In view of the violent attitude of upper caste Hindus, particularly Jagirdars, Jamindars, Thakurs, Brahmins, Banias, etc., the convention appealed to the 'savarnas' not to compel community fellows to remove the dead animals and skinning them. In case they are forced to do so, the organization would take legal action against them.

Both Meghwals—Panchas and Meghwal workers of Pali Mill supported the RMM and favoured the socio-cultural reforms of the community. On January 11, 1950 Hukma Ram Meghvanshi, Mantri, RMM Pali, Marwar published and circulated a pamphlet, condemning the anti-caste activities of Rama (Unvanwala) Purka (Palika) and Ladu (Kushalpura). He further warned the caste fellows to beware of their anti-activities and mis-propaganda.

Sree Sootrakar Meghvanshi Maha Panchayat, Rajasthan (SSMMPR): Jodhpur 1967[24]

In 1967 a few aged Meghwals in Jodhpur region took the initiative to bring together their own caste men. The first meeting of like minded progressive people was convened on April 9, 1957 at Acharya Vishram Sadan, Kaga Colony, Jodhpur, under the leadership of Swami Ram Prakash Maharaj. In this meeting a committee consisting of a few members was constituted to formulate a scheme for an all-round development of the community. Mangi Lal Goel became the convenor. There were more than 42 active members. Some of the notable active members of the committee were: Nathu Ram Gonda, Saint Madhav Ram Maharaj, Roop Nath Panwar, Pancha Ram Banzara, Bhanu Ram Panwar, Daya Ram Pariyar, Shivnath Solanki, Taru Ram Loha, Mangi Lal Goel and many others. After several meetings, it was unanimously decided to form a separate sabha to be called 'Sree Sootrakar Meghvanshi Maha Panchayat, Rajasthan (SSMMPR). Thus SSMMPR came into existence on that day with Swami Ram Prakash Acharya as President, Viram Ram as Vice-president, Mohan as general secretary Mangi Lal as Mantri, and Harji Ram Bhatti as Treasurer. Besides, a 11 Member Executive Committee was constituted. The members were: Shivnath Solanki, Nathu Ram (Mandor), Jethu Ram Parihar (Mahamandir), Pusha Ram (Mahamandir), Mangla Ram Rathore, Achala Ram Rathore and others.

On the same day, SSMMPR constituted a Draft Committee for framing its constitution with Swami Ram Prakash as its Chairman. Besides, there were about five members in the committee. The Committee made sincere efforts in preparing its constitution under the name of SSMMPR, which was approved in the meeting held in 1967 for registration. It was registered under Registration No. 102/67–68 dated December 6, 1967. The Maha Panchayat had promised to ameliorate the lot as also all-round development of the community. Here it will suffice to note a few selective objectives.

1. To eradicate the social vices such as bad social customs and traditions, campaign against untouchability, ban on death feast, drinking liquor, child marriage, dowry, bahu vivaha, divorce, etc., stress on reducing the marriage expenditure. To unite the samaj and strengthen the social solidarity on social issues.
2. To prevent the socio-economic exploitation by the upper caste Hindus, communal tension, atrocities and criminal activities, to cooperate with each other for social cause, to eradicate poverty. cooperative efforts should be made for various trades, small scale industries to be promoted among caste men for eradication of poverty.
3. All-round development of the community in social, cultural, economic, educational and academic fields. To govern the community as per vedic religious padhathi (procedures).
4. This organization will not be a political Dal. To frame new caste norms and to modify old ones. After purification and performance of certain rituals, the Maha Panchayat could re-admit the out caste person in Samaj.

Rajasthan Meghwal Parishad (RMP), Jaisalmer 2000

A few years ago the founding member and lifelong General Secretary of Rajasthan Meghwal Parishad, who was also the founding member and editor of the fortnightly Hindi paper *Hakdar* (Bikaner), Panna Lal 'Premi', urged his fellow Meghwal Mana Ram Baloch,[25] to establish a district branch of RMP—an association which was to be dedicated to the cause of advancement of Meghwals and which would provide an organizational forum for socio-educational activities. M.R. Baloch was at that time serving at Aafri, Jodhpur on deputation. In 1998–99 Panna Lal Premi nominated M.R. Baloch as organizer of Jaisalmer district. From 1998 onwards, M.R. Baloch assumed vigorously an active role in the social affairs of his people. On May 12–13, 2000,[26] as local organizer RMP, M.R. Baloch called a meeting of educated, intellectuals, social workers and activists of Meghwals in order to discuss the formation of the district branch of RMP at Jaisalmer. In this meeting a large number of Meghwals assembled. Some of the eminent persons were: Roopa Ram Dhande, Dr Ramji Ram, Multana Ram Barupal, Jodha Ram, Advocate, Makhata Ram Inkhiya, Dr Bhupendra Barupal and Ulla Ram Rathore. M.R. Baloch's speech in favour of the formation of expressed themes impressed the participants. There it was decided to form a district association which would devote itself exclusively to the amelioration and upliftment of Meghwals in Jaisalmer. The assembled Meghwals expressed support for the RMP. Finally an important issue taken up by the delegates attending the meeting was the question of holding a Vishal Sammelan of the Meghwal community, fixing up its venue, and timing and issuing intimation to the community men. The meeting on May 12, 2000 decided to hold the first Vishal Meeting on May 14, 2000 at Jaisalmer.

The wide publicity of the Sammelan was totally dependent on its workers and volunteers. They intimated on phone their caste fellows for attending the Sammelan. Pamphlets were sent to local newspapers to give this Sammelan wide coverage. A few representatives were sent to Jodhpur, Bikaner, Nagaur and other places in which most Meghwals lived, intimating them of the holding of the Sammelan. Learning about the Sammelan, impelled other Meghwals to join the movement. Some prominent activists and educators travelled all through the rural areas and apprised villagers in order to enlist their enrolment. Thus, through publicizing and providing information, active volunteers directly contributed in the formation of the organization of Meghwal movement or created a climate of opinion which could be favourably utilized by organizers. In this sense, the activists contributed to social mobilization of the Meghwal Sammelan. Punama Ram Baloch claimed that May 14, 2000 Meghwal Sammelan itself was quite a success and more than 600 people attended it.

From May 13 onwards, some political leaders, activists, workers and common men from Jodhpur and Bikaner in particular arrived to participate in the Sammelan. On May 13, Siromani Samajsevi, Roopa Ram Dhande on behalf of his community arranged a dinner in honour of the delegates.

On Sunday, May 14, 2000 a large number of delegates from Jodhpur, Bikaner and Jaisalmer assembled in Ambedkar Bhawan in Ambedkar Colony, Jaisalmer.[27] The first region-wide Meghwal's Sammelan was convened under the chairmanship of Dalla Ram Rathore, an aged social activist. State secretary of RMP, Panna Lal Premi was the chief guest of the function. The other special invitees of this Sammelan were: Moda Ram Likhniya, Subhash Rathore, Jetha Ram Lohia, Dr Ramji Ram, Roopa Ram Dhanda, Jodha Ram, Advocate, Mana Ram Baloch, Hari Ram Panwar and Multana Ram Barupal, ex-MLA. The convention started at 10.00 a.m.

Mana Ram Baloch, a young IFS, who became active as leader and organizer after 1999, was also instrumental in organizing the first region-wide Meghwal Sammelan urged his fellow Meghwals to be united for the cause of advancement of Meghwals as well as better integration of Meghwal community. In the social and religious matters, he also appealed to community's sadhus and sanyasis to teach their disciples about the social reform and persuade them to abandon their traditional customs and beliefs of Brahminical Karamkand and give up religious and ritual practices which would impel their social progress. His major request was to raise themselves above political affiliation, regionalism and personal indifferences for the cause of advancement of Meghwals.

M.R. Baloch could neither be really a political mobilizer, and organizer of Meghwal movement, nor can his ideas be considered to have had a political impact on the movement. The focus and scope of his efforts were rather social, educational and cultural. By providing social forum M.R. Baloch believed that he had offered the Meghwals a platform whereby they could ameliorate their lot. RMP is an organization through which the Meghwals could fight for their rights. More important perhaps is the notion that M.R. Baloch belonged to an educated generation of Meghwal community, which defined the problem of the Meghwals largely in socio-educational forum.

Panna Lal Premi[28] in his speech noted that while Meghwal samaj was the first in order of total Scheduled Castes population of Rajasthan, yet they were still the lowest in respect of socio-educational advancement, surpassed by other advanced communities as well. To ensure that they acquired equal access to social and economic advancement, the Meghwals would have to organize themselves socially only through the establishment of the socio-political presence, could they achieve their rights. Thus, RMP showed signs of being more than a socio-cultural body devoted to the revitalization and regeneration of Meghwal community through social institutions. Meghwal Directory 2001 reports that it was the beginning to take more interest in the politico-economic conditions of Meghwal community in rural areas and in so doing, was coming into conflict with the traditional structure of power in the villages.

Moda Ram Likhniya,[29] president, RMP of Jodhpur district complained to the gathering that Meghwal samaj was being governed by a handful political leaders and that they were selfish too. There was no Meghwal representative in Rajasthan cabinet. The same convention was also addressed by other speakers and all expressed their support for RMP programmes. Finally, the May 14, 2000 convention unanimously elected the executive committee of RMP, Jaisalmer. Thus, RMP[30] Jaisalmer came into existence on the same day with Deshla Ram Jenva (Roopsi) as President, Kana Ram Bandar (Ramdeovra) and Chelu Ram Solanki (Khuiyala) as Vice-presidents, Jodha Ram, Advocate, as General Secretary, Pritam Ram Bambhania (Jaisalmer) and Narain Das (Chandhan) as Joint Secretaries and Mangla Ram Chauhan (Ramgarh) as Treasurer.

It was a surprise for the Jaisalmer public to see Meghwals assembling at Jaisalmer. A grand feast of 700 persons was organized without any problem. It was an historic occasion for the people of Jaisalmer as never before had they witnessed such a heavy assembly of Meghwals. Mana Ram Baloch and his colleagues at Jaisalmer were happy when they saw that all went well at Jaisalmer.

After one month or so Rawat Ram Rathore (Jaisalmer) was elected Organising Secretary, Hanumana Ram Baloch (Hatara) Jan Sampark Secretary and Kevla Ram Hingra (Sankra) Prachar Secretary.

Notes

1. Jaya Shree Gokhale, *From Concessions to Confrontation: The Politics of an Indian Untouchable Community*, Bombay now Mumbai, Popular Prakashan, 1993.
2. For more details, see in particular, a photo copy of 'Shri Meghwanshi Samaj Sudhar Sabha', post Tiwri, district, Jodhpur. This 7-page document was written by Meghwanshi Ram Chandra Kadela and on February 6, 2003 it was obtained by Ashu Ram and later on circulated amongst Meghwals by him. The copy is with the author, p. 1–2.
3. Ibid., p. 2.
4. Ibid., p. 4.
5. Ibid., p. 4.
6. Ibid., p. 4.
7. Ibid., p. 4.
8. Ibid., p. 5.
9. Ibid., p. 6.
10. Ibid., p. 5.
11. Ibid., p. 5.
12. For more details, see in particular a photo copy of 'Shri Meghwal Samaj Sudhar Sabha' 1920. This 16-page document was written by Chola Ram Inkhiya, Gram Post Ghewara via Tiwri, district Jodhpur. Undated. The copy is with the author, p. 1.
13. Ibid., p. 2.
14. Ibid., p. 1.
15. Ibid., pp. 1–2.
16. Ibid., p. 3.
17. Ibid., p. 3.
18. Ibid., p. 3.
19. Ibid., p. 3.
20. Ibid., p. 11.
21. Ibid., p. 11.
22. Ibid., pp. 12–15.
23. For details, see in particular, a cyclostyled pamphlet entitled 'Shri Rajasthan Meghwansh Maha Sabha' written by Humka Ram Meghwanshi, Mantri Panch Committee, Shri Rajasthan Meghwansh Mahasabha, Pali, Marwar and was published and circulated among Meghwals by him. Pali Marwar, 11.1.1950.

24. For a discussion of Sootrakar Meghvanshi movement that stresses the role of Maha Panchayat (SSMMPR—social organization) in the post-independence period and socio-religious consequences of the movement, see in particular, The Constitution of Shri Sootrakar Meghvanshi Maha Panchayat Rajasthan, Jodhpur, published by Mangi Lal Moyal, Mantri, Sootrakar Meghvanshi Maha Panchayat (Regd.) Rajasthan, Jodhpur, 1970, pp. 1–22. Talk with Swami Ram Prakash Acharya, the founder member of organization and eminent scholar, at Uttam Ashram Kaga, Jodhpur, April 12, 2006.
25. For most important sources for socio-economic conditions of untouchable Meghwals in Jaisalmer district, see Meghwal Digdarshika, 2001, Jaisalmer, Mana Ram Baloch, IFS (ed.) 2002, p. 15.
26. Ibid., p. 15.
27. Ibid., p. 16.
28. Ibid., p. 17.
29. Ibid., p. 17.
30. Ibid., p. 22.

9 Swami Gokuldas Maharaj and the Constrained Meghvanshi Movement

Swami Gokuldas Maharaj (henceforth called Swami) was born on Shanivar (Saturday), Phagun Badi 14, Vikram Samvat 1948 in the village Domara[1] a village situated 20 miles away from the then Ajmer state (now a district). It was a Mahashivratri Parva (festival). His father Nand Ram Singhmar, a rich Meghvanshi, was popularly known as a village Jamindar.[2] His mother was Chhoti Devi. Nand Ram Meghvanshi had four sons, Gokuldas being the youngest one. So he was loved by all. From his childhood, he was interested in reading and writing, but he could not receive the elementary education, because there was no school in the village. His father sent him to a nearby village called Somapur,[3] situated six miles away from Ajmer. It is believed that it was Subedar Thakur Jodhaji Pandit[4] who imparted elementary education to Gokuldas.

According to prevailing customs, Gokuldas was married to Ladi Bai, daughter of Devaji in village Palra in the Ajmer state. At that time he was a child of 8 years or so. For a brief period he helped his parents in agriculture work. However, throughout his childhood and youth, he evinced keen interest in listening to religious songs (Bhajans) and sermons and lived with Sadhus and Sanyasis. In the course of his wandering, he came in contact with Saint Ramhans Panwar, who was well known in Ajmer and expressed his desire to become his disciple. Consequently, on Phagun Sudi 2, Vikram Samvat 1960, a Vishal Satsang Samaroh was organized in village Domara. In this large congregation Saint Ramhans Panwar[5] accepted Gokuldas as his disciple. Since then, he had shown his interest in studying Jap, Tap, Sanyam, Vrat, Yoga etc. In order to make the religious changes effective Gokuldas realized the importance of saint, monk, priest and missionary. Thus, he left his wife and on Chetra Sudi 5, Vikram Samvat 1963 he became a monk.[6]

In the course of his wanderings, he came in contact with another untouchable Saint Swami Ramanand Maharaj,[7] who activated Swami Gokuldas Maharaj to initiate the awakening campaign among the untouchable communities in general and Chamar community in particular. Apparently, Swami took up a challenge to awaken the masses. Thus, Swami was active as socio-religious reformer[8] in Vikram Samvat 1970 and he died on October 8, 1977. During a period of about 86 years, the kind of radical changes he ushered in, were remarkable.

Emergence of Leadership

Swami formulated his system of thought oriented towards social transformation and maintained the reformation of untouchables which was a necessary adjunct for the upliftment of the low castes/communities. He made a direct attack on the social vices, bad customs and traditions etc. It was the Brahmins who had denied the Meghwals and other low untouchables, the right to study and the right to enter the temple.

Swami was the first Meghvanshi untouchable to have shown courage in launching a campaign against the prevailing social evils, bad food habits, customs and traditions. This attracted the attention of Meghwal Samaj. Swami urged his community fellows to abandon the social vices, drinking of alcohol, eating of the dead animal, death feast etc.

One of the programmes of action, directed towards the achievement of this goal, was to form a small group of some dedicated workers and volunteers of Meghwals. Actually, in this mission, Swami not only failed to get the support from his own caste men, but, on the contrary he was also bitterly criticized and rebuked by them. For instance, the following incident related to Swami's activities was narrated by Sewa Das ' Rishi' in his book *Jivan Darshan.*

"When Swami initiated the reform programmes, he was opposed by his own men. Wherever and whenever he went, nobody listened to him. He was insulted and harassed. No community man was ready to allow him to stay at night in his/her house. Some caste fellows with the connivance of upper caste Hindus teased him." Sewa Das was of the opinion that this incident did demonstrate that these reforms with regard to domestic rituals enraged the community fellows, ultimately expelled Swami from the community. The masses reacted to the campaign of reform by saying that reform programmes were unacceptable to us and people of Meghwal Samaj. It was the saddest incident of the Samaj; Hence Swami was pained, became nervous and withdrew himself from manifest reformatory activities, but did not lose hope.[9]

The incident of conflict continued for a few years between the reformers and anti-reformers, which made Swami to think again over it.

In order to convince the masses, Swami realized the importance of contact from person to person and house to house visit. Hence, in an attempt to re-start his reform activities, Swami toured all over Ajmer including the rural areas. He brought about a high degree of identity among Meghwals, who shared his views and the newly introduced reform activities. He made extensive tours, propagating his new message, by visiting hut to hut and meeting the common man to influential and elite persons. A few caste men were influenced by Swami and were so impressed that they became his supporters.[10] During this period he became the campaigner of reform in Ajmer and worked hard for unity of the Samaj. According to Sewa Das[11] 'Rishi', persons of the Samaj in Ajmer who earlier opposed Swami's activities to reform programmes, now wholeheartedly supported his efforts and joined his campaign. Withdrawal of opposition had brought much desired respite to Swami's programmes, which had been at the receiving end ever since opposite groups boycotted reform activities a few years ago. A large number of persons were seen coming forward to campaign.

The Whirlwind Tour, 1924

Swami did not rest, nor was he satisfied with these results. He wanted something concrete for Chamar communities and wanted to rouse the conscience of the untouchables against social vices, social injustice and the evil of untouchability. So Swami toured all over Rajputana. He wanted the support of Meghwals in village Aasalpur in Jaipur state for reforms. It was for this reason that on Vaishaka Sudi 14, Vikram Samvat 1980[12] he attended a religious gathering at Aasalpur to coincide with the foundation ceremony of the temple of Baba Ramdeo which was organized by community Panchas. He appealed to the caste Panchas and community people to abandon the social vices which were putting hindrances to the reform movement.

On Jeth Sudi 14, Vikram Samvat 1981, Swami convened a reform Sammelan at village Barlaya[13] in district Ajmer appealing to caste men to launch a reform campaign. It also passed a few resolutions in support of social reform. On Posh Sudi 6, Vikram Samvat 1982,[14] another community convention was organized at village Kachroda in Jaipur state. Here also community fellows announced the launching of agitation. Swami received the signed letter from assembled Panchas and people approving of the social agitation.

On Chetra Sudi 14–15 Vikram Samvat 1988,[15] Swami reached village Kalyanipuri in Ajmer, that is more than one decade after launching of agitation. He attended the death feast ceremony in which the Panchas and villagers from 210 villages participated and addressed the gathering to abandon social evils. In this meeting four resolutions were passed:[16] (1) To ban to serve alcohol and meat in social functions. (2) To ban singing of obscene songs and dance. (3) To stop caste Panchas to interfere in petty matters. (4) To use the money collected as fine from defaulters for the betterment of the Samaj.

Soon the agitation gained momentum all over Rajputana as social workers and activists from distant places joined it. Swami asked his supporters of the movement to carry on the movement without external help. The subscription was collected only from the caste men. Swami encouraged common men to continue the agitation. By this time community fellows had started abandoning the social evils.

The orthodox section, mainly consisting of Thakurs, Jagirdars and upper caste Hindus,[17] grew restless and vindictive. They all were opposed to reforms. In an attempt to suppress the reforms they let loose some goondas to beat up the Meghwals. The upper caste Hindus harassed and humiliated them. Their huts were burnt. They were pressurized to do the traditional work. This news was widely publicized and villagers who were strong enough earned the appreciation and good will of Swami and people.

The villagers and workers of reform movement used to come from different places, met Swamiji and narrated their miserable conditions.[18] Swami encouraged them to continue their agitation. Swami criticized the upper caste Hindus for harassing the Meghwals. It was a serious matter, if untouchables were brutally beaten up by them.

The Panchas of village Bichun wanted Swami to attend the religious Mella as it would add prestige to Sri Samas Rishi Mella. After receiving an invitation from Panchas, approving of reform movement programmes, Swami reached Bichun on Assoj Badi 1–2 Vikram Samvat 1980.[19]

In Vikram Samvat 1989,[20] on the occasion of death feast, a large gathering of Panchas, common men, women and children from 210 villages assembled at village Domara, in district Ajmer. Swami attended this function in order to encourage the caste fellows to continue the agitation. He also addressed the gathering and made the following 10 proposals[21] to advance the community:

1. To stop the unnecessary expenditure on the death feast.
2. Letters inviting the people to attend the death feast should be drafted only by village Panchas.
3. To ban eating of meat and drinking of alcohol on the occasions of death feast and to see that all caste Panchas should eat together.
4. To pay only Re. 1 and 4 Anna on the occasion of Thangaon pag.
5. To ban observing mourning period after 12 days of death.
6. To complete all rituals of death feast within 12 days.
7. To invite only 5 or 7 villages now. On earlier occasions of death feast, Chhammalish and Staesa ceremonies all the residents of 210 villages were invited.
8. At the time of marriage, maternal uncle will perform simple 'pehrawani'.
9. To marry the girl without taking bride price (money) from boy's parents or take maximum Rs 90 only.
10. To take only Rs 210 over a dispute of deceased wife.

Swami's visit had a direct effect on social reform as he was able to establish a dialogue with caste Panchas and common men and had detailed discussions with them. As a result of combined efforts of Swami's and leaders of community, all the above proposals were approved. The positive response of the gathering to abandon the social evils pacified Swami and his supporters who were agitating against the social evils. It was also decided to impose a fine of Rs 51[22] on those who violated the community rules.

Between Vikram Samvat 1991 and Vikram Samvat 2018 Swami visited several places in Rajputana in order to encourage the social activists to continue the agitation. The places were:[23] Degana (Nagaur), Tilonia, Shakhun and Harsuli, Basdi and Lakhani (Jaipur), Khandela Vati, Domara (Ajmer), Merwada Mandi, Miyan, Pushkar, Dantda, Merta, Dangiavas, Ghughari-Ki-Babri Jujala, Baratiya, Marwar Bisas, Bhinaya, Badan Vada Gopalpura (Mewar), Kunhadi (Kota), Begu and Palri

(Udaipur), Kota Datop (Jaipur), Bhareva and Silva (Marwar), Marwar Pali (Pali), Kapren (Bundi) Bhandaheda Sultanpura (Kota).

Swami Gokuldas Maharaj and his Visit to the Neighbouring Provinces, 1926

Gaining confidence by his success in encouraging the masses in Rajputana to continue the agitation for reform movement, Swami concentrated his efforts to mobilize the support of Chamars of other regions of the country, making it a part of wider reform movement. As a promoter of reform, he toured all over Northern India and convened several meetings of untouchables and made the following few proposals: (i) To abandon the social vices, (ii) To ban the use of alcohol, and (iii) To remove untouchability.

On Jeth Sudi 5, Vikram Samvat 1983[24] Swami reached Shiv Rajpur Kala Dogra Mines Company, Baroda, that is nearly six years after the commencement of reform movement. He convened a Community meeting at Baroda and addressed the gathering explaining the necessity of the reform campaign. He appealed to the caste men to abandon the death feast, drinking alcohol and eating meat of dead animals and to ban child marriage. He also urged the gathering to send children to school in large numbers. The assembled persons approved Swami's proposals.

The second meeting of the representatives of the Chamar communities was held at Kasur in the Punjab city, on Magh Sudi 2, Vikram Samvat 1988,[25] under the Presidentship of Swami. Thekedar Ram Chandra and Kalu Ram convened the Community meeting which supported the self-reforms. It also announced the launching of agitation. Swami received a letter from people supporting the agitation.

After a few months of Kasur convention, Swami was invited by the Thekedar Nathu Ram Jarana[26] to visit Lahore, Punjab and to convene a Satsang as it would encourage the community fellows to launch the agitation against the social evils. Swami attended the Satsangh on Magh Sudi 15, Vikram Samvat 1988 and addressed the gathering extolling the virtue of reforms. He then went to Amritsar, Arjun Dev, Tiran Tarni, Gorakha Talla, Multan and Ambala.

His visit had a direct effect on the reform movement as he was able to establish a dialogue with the representatives of the communities and was able to place before them concrete proposals to eradicate the social evils. As a result of Swami's efforts the local Chamars and leaders announced the launching of agitation.

Swami as the chief campaigner of reform movement, paid a good deal of attention to spread its area. Under his leadership, reform agitation acquired the character of a wider mass movement. On Phagun Sudi 6, Vikram Samvat 1988[27] when residents of Narel Katla Delhi convened a Vishal Stasangh Samaroh at Baba Ramdeo Mandir, Swami was invited to attend it. Similarly, on Phagun Sudi 7/8, Vikram Samvat 1988, another Satsang Samaroh was organized at Delhi. The convention was organized by untouchable communities of manufacturers of bricks. Swami attended both the Satsang Samarohs and addressed the gathering appealing them to introduce the domestic reforms amongst their respective communities.

According to Sewa Das 'Rishi' between Vikram Samvat 1983 and 1990, Swami visited several places:[28] Bhagalpur, Raivad, Premnagar, Bhaiker, Jalandar, Panipat, Karnal, Amritsar, Lalakana, Siyalkot and Multan. He then moved to Ahmedabad, Baroda, Bombay, Viramgaon, Nasik, Khandwa, Kanpur, Haridwar, Rishikesh etc. Similarly, he also toured Goma-ki-phel, Gotu-ki-phel, Juni Indore, Sherpura-Tapriya, Pancham-ki-Phel and Gwala Toli, all in Indore.

Fight Against Untouchability and Begar, 1933

Intensive agitation against social evils and practices of bad customs and traditions, marked the first phase of reform movement under the leadership of Swami. From his very childhood, Swami was directly affected by the inequalities, social discrimination and status of untouchability. The inequality between the caste Hindus and untouchables with regard to the use of public wells, water ponds, public inn, admission to schools, entry to temple and recruitment to government jobs, left an indelible impression on his mind.

Before launching agitation against the abolition of all kinds of ritual and civic disabilities, Swami had written hundreds of letters to community Panchas, Sarpanchas and community fellows to attend the Satsangh Samaroh. With all these preparations, a stage was set for the Samaroh to begin on Kartik Sudi 9, Vikram Samvat 1990.[29] Thus on Kartik Sudi 9, a Vishal Satsangh Samaroh was held at Baba Ram Deo Mandir, Pushkar, Ajmer under the presidentship of Swami. On the first day a large number of Panchas, Sarpanchas, men, women and children from Ajmer-Merwara, Rajgarh, Masuda, Ramsar, Jaipur, Kishangarh,

Mewar and Beawar assembled. It was a social function in which some eminent persons from the city, such as Gauri Shankar Bhargava, Chand Karan Sharda, Rai Bahadur Hirachand Ozha and Sohan Lal Pandit took part in the Samaroh in propagation of programmes on removal of untouchability in Ajmer.

On the second day, Kartik Sudi 10, Vikram Samvat 1990,[30] a procession started from Baba Ram Deo Mandir and moved towards the bazaar of the city and reached Gaughat, Pushkar. After performing worship of Baba Ram Deo at Gaughat, they wanted to enter into Pushkar City and reached a point where the orthodox opponents of reform, Pushkarna Brahmins stopped them. The Brahmins were of the opinion that until recently no such procession was taken out by any untouchable community, now Meghwals could not be permitted to do so. They were ordered to go back by orthodox Brahmins. The procession led by Swami and Bhairu Das Maharaj requested the Brahmins to allow the procession, but in vain. In order to avoid the communal tension Swami immediately informed Chand Karan Sharda[31] and Gauri Shanker Bhargava. They reached and tried to convince the agitated Brahmins to allow the procession. City Magistrate Mithan Lal was also informed. Eventually, the procession moved under the leadership of Swami. The processionists behaved with dignity and peace conditions prevailed.

After a few hours or so, when the procession reached at Baba Ram Deo Mandir, it soon turned into a public meeting.[32] Swami addressed the huge gathering, regretting over the most pitiable conditions of the Samaj. He urged his community fellows to abandon drinking of alcohol and eating of meat as it would add prestige to temple entry movement. He also appealed to leave the impure work.

On September 24, 1942,[33] Swami received a letter from Panchas and others who attended the Samaroh from 210 villages authorizing Swami to manage the affairs of Baba Ram Deo Mandir, Ajmer.

On Friday September 24, 1942[34] this authorization letter written originally in Urdu on the stamp paper of Rs 5 was submitted to the Office of Sub-Registrar, Ajmer for its registration. It was registered at Registry Misal No.4, Binder No. 234, ke-khafa No. 39/42, p. No. 210. Dated September 28, 1942.

In Ajmer-Merwara region, economic exploitation, i.e., 'Begar' was the issue of Swami's agitation. The local rulers mainly consisting of Jagirdars, Jamindars, and Thakurs together had suppressed the

पुष्कर की समस्त व्यवस्था, देखरेख, पुजारी आदि की जिम्मेदारी का दायित्व श्री स्वामी गोकुलदास जी महाराज को 5 रूपये के सरकारी स्टाम्प पर दिनांक 24 सितम्बर 1942 को रजिस्ट्रार, अजमेर के समक्ष अधिकार–पत्र दिया गया।

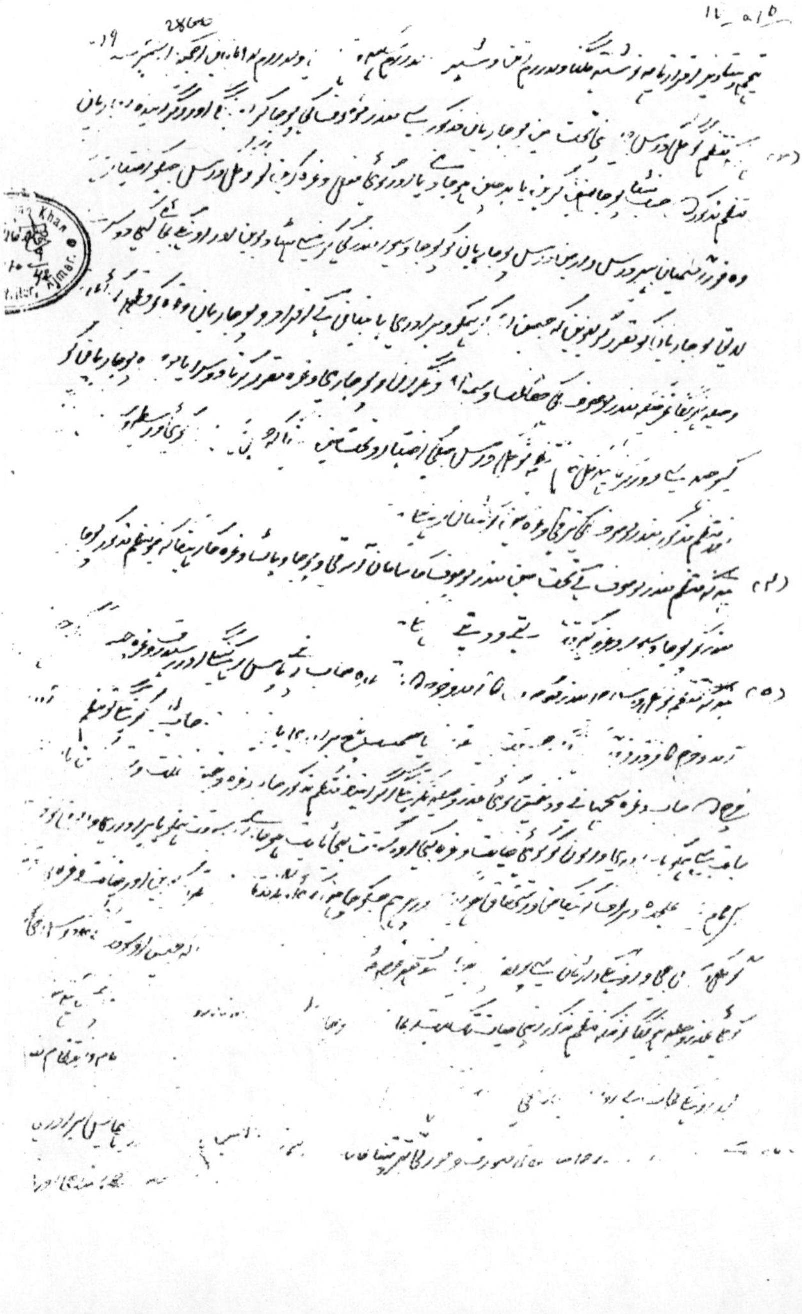

untouchables for centuries. Untouchables were not only suppressed but also economically exploited. Untouchables were employed by Jagirdars, Jamindars and Thakurs in their field as labourers for which they were not paid. This forced and free labour was called 'Begar'.[35] It was a serious offence if untouchables refused to do 'Begar'. In that case untouchables were cruelly beaten by their landlords. They were also harassed. The untouchables were living in a tense atmosphere. Swami, the leader of reform movement, wanted Jagirdars, Jamindars and Thakurs to stop this 'Begar' immediately.

Even before Swami started opposing the economic exploitation of untouchables specifically the Chamars and Meghwals, Bhairu Lal Meghwal had agitated against the 'Begar' in Mewar region. Bhairu Lal Meghwal not only agitated against 'Begar' but also united the Chamars to boycott the 'Begar'.

Before launching agitation against the Begar, Swami wanted details about the legal aspect of Begar. So he in his letter of November 2, 1946[36] to the Commissioner, Ajmer-Merwara, desired to know if there was any provision for Begar.

After nearly one month of the issue of the letter, Sub-Commissioner, Ajmer-Merwara replied vide his letter No. 6687/XXVIII (P) 100 dated December. 11, 1946[37] informing that 'in our Ajmer-Merwara, there are no rules on the subject of Begar'.

On April 5, 1947,[38] Swami then wrote a letter to the Chief Secretary, Government of Jodhpur, requesting him to supply a copy of Begar rules in the state. The Chief Secretary in his letter No. 635 dated April 14, 1947 intimated Swami, 'Begar rules have been totally abolished by the Jodhpur Government.'

Three months earlier to the letter addressed to the Chief Secretary, Government of Jodhpur, Swami, on January 2, 1947[39] sent a letter to Secretary Legislative Sabha, Jaipur state, to supply a copy of Section 374 of Begar rules. Secretary attacking on section 374 and explaining the legal position of section 374, warned "whoever unlawfully compels any person to labour against the will of that person shall be punished with imprisonment of either description for a term which may extend to one year or with fine or with both".[40]

With this legal background, Swami toured all over Ajmer-Merwara region and urged the community fellows to refuse the Begar. This decision was widely publicized in rural area. When Jagirdars, Jamindars

पुष्कर की मन्दिर की सेवा पूजा हेतु श्री पण्डित भैरूं दास जी कड़ैल एवं अर्जुन दास जी भूडोल को नियुक्त किया गया। उन्होंने लिखित में मन्दिर में सेवा पूजा सुचारू रूप से करने की जिम्मेदारी ली।

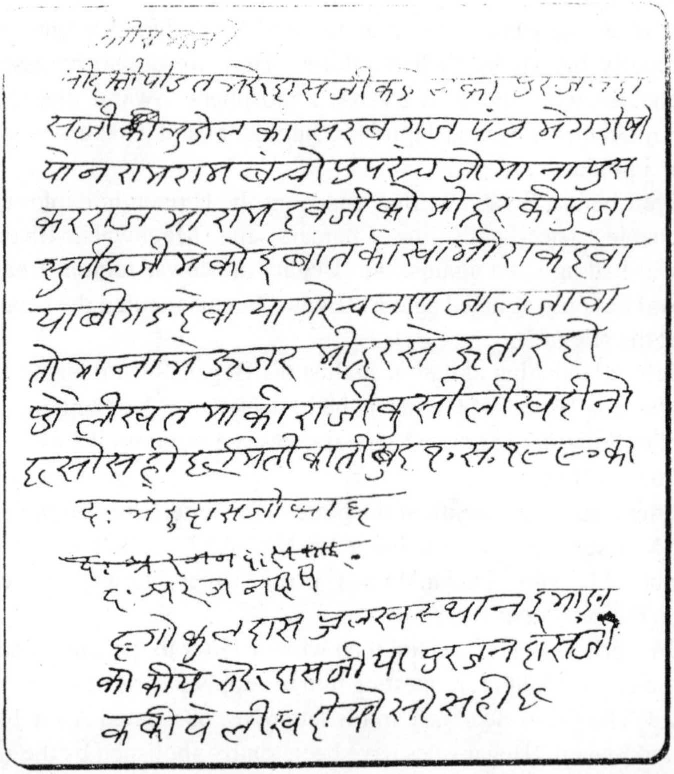

and Thakurs came to know about this decision, the ruling communities, i.e., orthodox opponents of reforms for which Swami had been fighting, grew restless and vindictive. In an attempt to suppress the agitation, Meghwals were cruelly beaten[41] by the landlords. Restrictions were imposed on them.[42] They were threatened to leave the villages. They were very poor and could not live in such condition. Swami visited all the trouble torn villages in order to listen to the grievances of the community fellows. He criticized and condemned their action as harmful to self-respect of Meghwals. Swami expressed hope that Jagirdars, Jamindars and Thakurs will stop atrocities immediately and will not compel them for Begar. Swami encouraged the masses to continue the agitation and asked his fellow brothers not to yield before pressure.

Sub-Commissioner, Ajmer-Merwara's Letter to Swami

No. W6687 /XXVIII(P)100

Dated Ajmer, the 11th December, 1946.

From - The Deputy Commissioner, Ajmer-Merwara.

To - Swami Sewa Dass Gokul Dass,
Village Dumara, P.O. Saradhna,
District AJMER.

Memorandum.

Reference:- Your application dated the 2nd November 1946 to the Chief Commissioner, Ajmer-Merwara, requesting the grant of a copy of Rules for "Begar".

2. There are no rules on the subject of "Begar".

Superintendent,
for Deputy Commissioner, Ajmer-Merwara.

H.S.S.10.12.

Swami Gokuldas, Maulvi Abdul Rahman and Dharmacharyas Questions of Meghwal Link with Muslims, 1933

By Vikram Samvat 1990s, Swami Gokuldas's influence amongst the community fellows was widespread and enlightened caste fellows of Rajasthan recognized that it was Swami who had awakened the community, of thousands of people, from humiliation, harassment and torture and inhuman treatment because of the socio-religious disabilities

The Chief Secretary, Government of Jodhpur's Letter to Swami

J G P 4186-46-10,000 F. M. K. I A.

No 635/FP/G.R.R.9.

FROM
THE CHIEF MINISTER, Secretary,
GOVERNMENT OF JODHPUR,
JODHPUR.

To Sewa Das Swami
Gokul Das,
Alakh Sthan, Dumada,
P.O. Saradhana, Ajmer.

Dated Jodhpur, the 16. 4. 1947.

Sub. Request for supplying copies of Begar Rules etc.

Ref. Your application dated April 5, 1947.

The Begar Rules have been totally abolished by the Jodhpur Government.

Chief Secretary.

m. 11

The Secretary Legislative Sabha, Jaipur State's Letter to Swami

Copy of Section 374
Jaipur Penal Code.

374. Whoever unlawfully compels any person to labour against the will of that person shall be punished with imprisonment of either description for a term which may extend to one year, or with fine, or with both.

True Copy.
Chand Behari Nag

धारा 374 की प्रति।

imposed upon untouchables by the caste Hindus. They also said that community persons should be grateful to Swami for this great work.

The most significant event during his tenure was the question of Meghwals' link with Muslims, which resulted in a series of socio-religious debates. For instance, in Vikram Samvat 1990[43] it was Maulvi Abdul Rahman, a resident of the then Jaipur State, who had tried to establish contact between Muslims and Meghwals. The 14-point argument that Maulvi Abdul Rahman advanced, was to prove the relationship between Muslims and Meghwals. This attracted the attention of the masses in general and Sadhus, Sanyasis, Mehants, Bhats, Jagas, Peers and Kamars of Meghwal community in particular. This incident created a stir amongst them. The Meghwals were angry with this view and opposed it vehemently. There were angry protests also. Contemptuous obsession prompted many Meghwals to refute this point of view, but they were helpless to do so. There was no one in the community except Swami Gokuldas who could solve the problem and for this purpose, it was decided to request Swami Gokuldas.[44] Swami Gokuldas was on tour to Ahmedabad at that time. When Swami Gokuldas received a request, in response to Samaj's call, he reached Ajmer immediately.

In order to understand the part played by Swami Gokuldas, it is necessary to study the whole issue. First, a small group headed by Swami Gokuldas was formed. The main object of this group was to discuss the problems in detail from social and religious point of view. This created enthusiasm amongst the masses which made them realize that refutation of social linkage was essential for untouchable community and therefore, decided to discuss the whole issue with scholars, intellectuals and Sanskrit Pandits of Kashi. Apparently, Swami Gokuldas took it as a prestige issue for the Samaj to challenge Maulvi's thoughts. It should be mentioned here that to meet the travel expenses of Swami to Kashi, funds were collected through donations. For this purpose, the total amount received was in all Rs 900[45] (Rupees nine hundred only). After this decision and with the support of Samaj, Swami Gokuldas went to Kashi. Swami Gokuldas met intellectuals, scholars and pandits, and submitted an application, as also discussed the problem with them. After listening to Swami Gokuldas, it transpired that the necessity for a debate on socio-religious issue was the need of the hour. The pandits of Kashi also directed him (Swami) to submit an application with regard to Meghwals' links with Muslims in Branch office of Kashi organization called

'Rajasthan Sawai Jaipur Moj Mandir', Jaipur. Swami Gokuldas returned to Jaipur with this order and with the support of Advocate Chiranjilal Phojdar[46] and Munshi Mahaveer, Swami Gokuldas submitted the same in Moj Mandir, Jaipur.

The office of Moj Mandir was located near Janana Mahal, where His Highness Sawai Jai Singh lived. The entry of common people was strictly prohibited. The meeting of pandits (of Kashi) was held once a week and that too on every Wednesday, where various socio-religious issues were placed on the table. For instance, intra-religious issues, temples' disputes, caste or community disputes etc., were listened, discussed and settled by Committee consisting of 12 Dharmacharyas:[47] They were: Pandit Niyacharya Hari Nath, Pandit Bakhsudeen, Pandit Kanhaiyalal, Pandit Girdharilal, Pandit Kedarnath, Pandit Suraj Narain, Pandit Nand Kishor, Pandit Madanlal, Pandit Mukundlal, Pandit Purushootam, Pandit Kalyan Bax and Pandit Raghu Nandan.

The question of Meghwals link with Muslim continued for quite a long period, which made the Meghwals impatient. Swami urged the Dharmacharyas for redress and protection, but the issue continued for one year. Swami was the first untouchable to have shown an intellectual ability in challenging the Maulvi Abdul Rahman's views. Swami dismissed the Maulvi's charges that Meghwals were linked with Muslims. This attracted the attention of Sanskrit pandits of Kashi. When Dharmacharyas rejected Maulvi Abdul Rahman's point of views in Vikram Samvat 1991 and issued the certificate to Meghwals on Government Stamp Paper[48] of paisa 8 Anna, the Meghwal Samaj expressed its gratitude to Swami for this historic victory. Thus, under Swami's guidance the Meghwals achieved significant gains. The masses had popularized the decision of Dharmacharyas which gave the movement a distinct identity. Having attained a major success in the field of socio-religious matter, the leaders of the movement turned their attention to fight against another sphere of deprivation, namely the status of untouchables.

Swami Gokuldas Maharaj and Banjara Samaj in Madhya Pradesh, 1940

As stated earlier, Swami Gokuldas Maharaj made extensive tours visiting places in North India, propagating his new message and meeting great people. In Vikram Samvat 1972,[49] when Swami visited Madhya Pradesh,

The Certificate Issued to Meghwals on Government Stamp Paper of Paisa 8 Anna

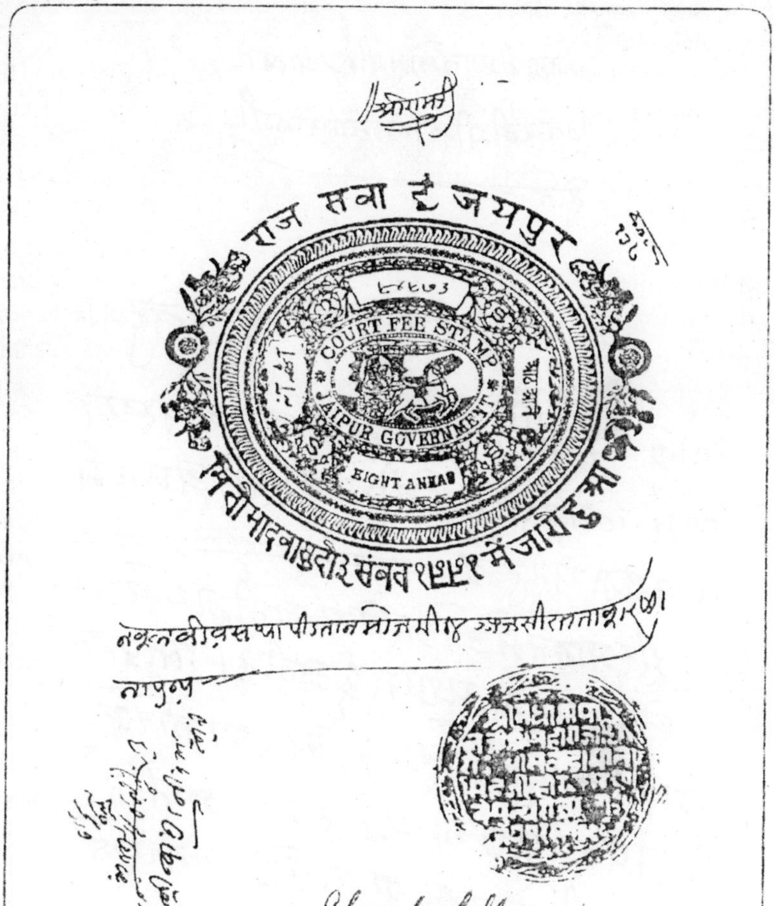

राज सवाई जयपुर का ऐतिहासिक फैसला।

राज सवाई जयपुर का ऐतिहासिक फैसला (पृष्ठ भाग)

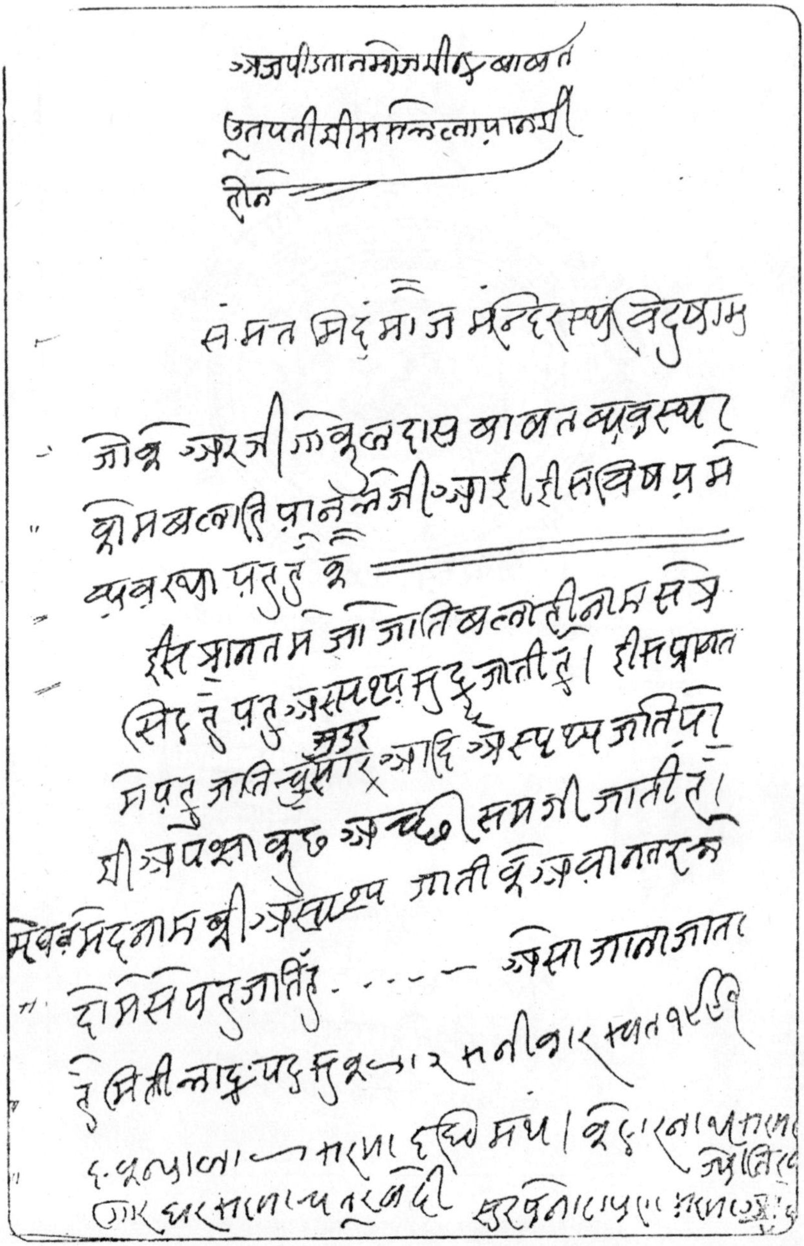

Bhikha Patel, a resident of village Ekjeera, Tehsil Burhanpur, district Khandwa, Madhya Pradesh, urged Swami to visit his village and Swami stayed there for a brief period. During his stay, Swami was able to perceive the deprivation felt amongst the Banjara community. The idea about a social awakening for concerted action, with the intention of redressing them, Swami was able to initiate an agitation against the social vices. A few Banjara men were influenced by Swami, notably, Gopi Ram Kurra (Chauhan), a Nayak.[50]

On February 16, 1940[51] Swami organized a Vishal Sammelan of Banjara community at village Bodarli, tehsil Burhanpur, district Khandwa and appealed to them to abandon social evils. In the social movement amongst the Banjaras that gained a mass character, this was the first set of events of significance. This was the zeal with which Swami spearheaded the agitation, mobilizing public opinion among Banjaras and urging them to give up the social vices, bad food habits and drinking of alcohol. Swami realized that Banjaras had undesirable religious customs and norms. He appealed to his followers to stop animal sacrifice in their traditional temples. He advised them to stop the unnecessary expensive customs, such as detaining the marriage party for two or three days. Swami also pointed out that these customs, traditions, food habits, traditional dress pattern, illiteracy etc., hamper the progress of the community.

Education was another area where the Banjaras perceived their status of deprivation. The education among the Banjaras was nil.

It should be mentioned here that at the Bodarli Sammelan of 1940, Swami envisaged the need for a socio-religious organization to reach the masses. He encouraged them to form a reform organization too and thus, the famous 'Banjara Samaj Sudhar Sabha'[52] (BSSS) came into existence at Bodarli in 1940, which was later on got registered. Swami maintained close contact with the activities of the BSSS in order to strengthen and spread the social reformation that he had initiated.

Due to Swami's encouragement and patronage a large number of community fellows—notably[53]—Bhikha Ram, Pura Nayak, Bhura Nayak and Khari (all from village Ekgeera), Nandu, Gopi Ram, Mangu, Sura, Rashal and Pura (all from village Bodarli) Deshmukh Nayak (from village Peepal Kota), Jai Ram Nayak, Ishar Ram, Bajja Nayak, Sodhar Nayak, Baly Nayak, Than Singh, Dalu Nayak, Prahlad Nayak, Bhikha Ram Nayak, Ganpat Nayak, Naryan Nayak, Ganna Nayak, Prithvi Nayak and Phakira Nayak (all from village Dogar-gaon), Manohar Singh Nayak and Puran Singh Nayak (from village Matapur), Dhom Singh Nayak, Gokul and Chand Nayak (from village Shyampur), Shada Ram Nayak, Jai Ram Nayak, Bheema Nayak and Kama Nayak (from village Golbardi) etc., from different villages joined BSSS.

Each of these villagers, from different villages, had played a significant role in awakening the social consciousness amongst the community fellows.

When agitation evoked a positive response on the part of BSSS, Swami organized another Vishal community Sammelan in February, 1962[54] in Burhanpur, district Khandwa at Gurunanak Dev Gurdwara. A Vishal community procession of men, women and children was taken out under the leadership of Swami and when the procession reached at a point, it turned into a public meeting. In this meeting some resolutions were passed to ameliorate the sufferings of Banjaras in Madhya Pradesh.

In the year 1967, Swami again visited Bodarli and worked hard for community Sammelan, which took place at Bodarli Mandir on February 10, 1967.[55] The Sammelan was presided over by Swami. Swami asked the Banjaras to follow the new message, to give up the social evils, to stop drinking of alcohol and to stop the consumption of meat. In addition to these formal gatherings, the local association too, which was already in existence, assumed the new task of propagating Swami's message.

In the fifth and sixth decades of 20th century a large number of people joined and supported the reform campaign.

Formation of Meghvanshi Mahasabha Pushkar, 1944

While these sporadic efforts did not achieve the character of a movement, Swami's reform programmes created widespread and spontaneous excitement. Influential persons in villages and cities collected volunteers to spread the message of Swami. They urged the people to follow the new domestic rites to stop the singing of obscene songs on Holi festival and marriages, not to consume alcohol and to eat meat. The local people who were already supporting the reform activities took lead to the formation of a social organization for propagating Swami's new socio-cultural programmes.

After nearly 3 decades of intense agitation against social evils, social injustice and practice of untouchability, the local people made an attempt to organize a Vishal Community Sammelan. Before convening of the Sammelan, Swami had written hundreds of letters to Community Panchas and Sarpanchas of 210 village Panchayats, requesting them to participate in the community Sammelan. With all these preparations a stage was set for the Sammelan to be held in Vikram Samvat 1977.

In response to Swami's call, one most significant event occurred on October 31, 1944[56] in village Dorai, Pushkar, Ajmer where a Vishal Community Sammelan was held under the presidentship of Swami Gokuldas Maharaj. A large gathering of people, workers and social activists in village Dorai assembled at the temple. Swami had detailed discussions with the assembled people about the reform programme. In fact he argued that man was the maker of his own destiny. He expressed the hope that Meghwal Samaj will advance towards socio-educational goals which he had placed before them.

The first Sammelan had many important consequences on reform movement as a whole. The people were highly impressed by the efforts Swami had made. They paid rich tribute to Swami. The Sammelan successfully endorsed the reform programme of Swami. Swami supporters secured the signatures of assembled people on stamp paper to approve reform activities.

Thus 'Meghvansh Mahasabha Pushkar'[57] (MMP) came into existence on October 31, 1944 with Swami Gokuldas Maharaj as Chairman, Bhairudas Maharaj as the Vice-Chairman, Ladu Ram Bagotia as Assistant Chairman, Sewadas as Secretary, Bhanwar Lal as Joint Secretary, Bhairulal as Assistant Secretary, Haridev Kayad as treasurer, Nenu Ram as Assistant Treasurer and Mohanlal as Prachar Mantri. Besides, 41 members[58] from various areas were nominated as its members. The main headquarters of the movement was located at Domara and functioned under the general leadership of Swami Gokuldas Maharaj. A branch office was opened at Bhagu Ram's residence at Delhi Gate, Ajmer. Thus, the credit of having started a movement of self-correction among the Chamar communities goes to Swami Gokuldas Maharaj.

In the year 1946, Swami Gokuldas Maharaj published a book entitled *Meghvansh Samaj-ki-Niyamavali*[59] which contained the Constitution of Meghvansh Mahasabha, Pushkar and rules and regulations pertaining to governance of MMP. An application for registering the MMP was made in the office of the Commissioner, Ajmer-Merwara, on April 28, 1945[60] and a certificate was granted by the Commissioner on July 26, 1945.[61] The main object of MMP was to promote and encourage social and educational reforms and industrious habits among the Meghwal community.

Certificate Issued by Commissioner, Ajmer – Merwara, 1945

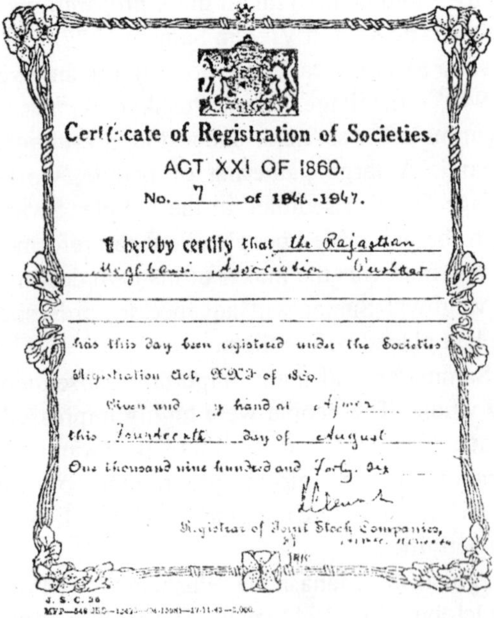

Certificate of Registration of Societies.

ACT XXI OF 1860.

No. 7 of 1946-1947.

I hereby certify that the Rajasthan Meghbansi Association Pushkar

has this day been registered under the Societies' Registration Act, XXI of 1860.

Given under my hand at Ajmer this fourteenth day of August One thousand nine hundred and forty six.

Registrar of Joint Stock Companies,

Rajasthan Meghvansh Mahasabha, Pushkar, Ajmer, launched a campaign for inclusion of Meghvansh in the government's official records, 1950.

Another problem which attracted the attention of RMS, was the inclusion of Meghvansh in government official records.

Meghvansh (also Meghwal) belonged to the broad category of untouchable caste, but since they were not designated as scheduled castes in certain parts of Rajasthan, they were not entitled to enjoy the benefits of protective discrimination policy. For instance, in neighbouring states like Ajmer, Marwar and others in Part 'C', they belonged to the Scheduled Castes SCs category. In other regions of Rajasthan including Udaipur region they did not belong to SCs category and therefore, suffered from political and educational privileges and government jobs.

The RMS sought to overcome this problem by not only claiming SC status, but also by social agitation. As pointed out, Meghwals were referred to both as SCs/non-SCs category.

It is necessary to mention here that emergence of awareness among the Meghwals was a gradual process. Consciousness among the

Meghwals of Rajasthan existed long back. However, after the independence of the country in 1947, many channels of communication were established and RMS took up the issue of inclusion of Meghwals in government official record with the then Udaipur government and this came into focus only when they protested with the state government.

Now we shall examine the socio-political agitation of claiming SCs status in the following section.

One of the first accounts of their efforts in this direction is reflected in the letter written by Swami Gokuldas Maharaj, President, RMS in 1950[62] to the then Udaipur government and urged the government to concede the demand for inclusion of Meghwals in the list of Scheduled Castes.

The demand for inclusion in the list of SCs had some significant effects on the government. In their reply entitled "Request for inclusion of Meghwals in the list of SC', Census Department, Udaipur, wrote a letter dated May 4, 1950[63] enclosing therewith a questionnaire consisting of 54 questions to President, RMS, for early reply and added that RMS must furnish the following information immediately, if government were to accept their demand. They were: (1) Origin of the caste and meaning of the name, (2) Population, (3) Historical and social background, (4) Education (5) Traits and characters, (6) Customs, (7) Religious ceremonies, (8) Deity and profession etc.

Swami Gokuldas Maharaj, President, RMS submitted the required information along with the document to Census Department, Udaipur with the reference to its letter dated May 4, 1950. The furnished information was in the form of detailed report. In 1950, RMS had started a community paper *Prakash* (a monthly periodical) under the editorship of Sewadas. In one of its issues Sewadas had published a report, submitted by Swami Gokuldas Maharaj with regard to Meghwals' inclusion in SCs list (Prakash, No. 50, 1950). After more than five decades, the same replies were reprinted in a book *Jivan Darshan*[64] written by Sewadas, 2005.

The demand for SCs status, as discussed above, had two effects on Meghwal agitation. First, all social activists and leaders among the Meghwals started taking active interest in this matter, as they considered the case worth fighting for. As a result of this RMS emerged as a strong organization representing the population of Meghwals. Second, government had accepted the demand.

Agitation Against Civic Disability, 1951

Drum beating agitation was a stir opposing the ban by untouchables and asserting their right by beating the drum on marriage and on any happy occasion. It was launched in 1951, but before we describe the event, it is necessary to place it in the context of the larger issue of removal of civil disabilities at local, regional and state levels.

It was mentioned earlier that inequality between the upper caste Hindus and low caste untouchables, with regard to use of/or accessibility to water ponds, admission to schools and entry to temples had left an indelible impression on untouchables' minds. Besides, untouchables used to give way to caste Hindu men and women while going to the bazaar by standing on the side of the road. Wearing good and clean clothes, sitting on cot in the presence of Jamindars, Jagirdars and thakurs, beating the drum at the time of marriage and birth of male child were strictly prohibited. MMP was committed to the removal of civil disabilities under the leadership of Swami.

Swami wanted justice and necessity of removing of civic disabilities. It was for this reason that he launched an agitation from his native place Domara. For the first time in 1951[65] he started beating the drums and won the support from community fellows. Soon the orthodox opponents of the reform opposed it and expressed their anguish over it. The atmosphere in the village became tense. Oppression against Meghwals was on the rise during the feudal rule of Jagirdars and Jamindars. Several restrictions[66] were imposed on them, such as: Meghwals were prevented from doing agriculture work in the fields of caste Hindus; the upper caste Hindus refused to engage them as domestic servants; the shopkeepers stopped selling goods to them. Banias and Mahajans refused to lend money on loan for domestic purposes.

The decision to ban the socio-economic facilities to Meghwals was taken unanimously as it had hurt the socio-religious sentiments of caste Hindus. The violation of customs was likely to cause breach of social norms and hurt religious sentiments.

There was a cycle of violence. An atmosphere of fear and insecurity pervaded the areas. A few homes had been burnt and looted. A large number of persons left the village soon after violent caste Hindus grew restless and vindictive. It was not the first occasion when untouchables had locked horns with caste Hindus. It may be noted in this connection that an attempt was made by some caste Hindus to suppress the agitation.[67] Caste Hindus had destroyed the drum and its parts were thrown in a well at the border of the village Saradhana. The tussle between upper caste Hindus and low caste untouchables had witnessed a chaotic scene at the village and untouchables stir appeared to be intensifying this infighting.

It was the monopoly of the caste Hindus to run the shops. Swami saw the point and challenged it. In an instance narrated in Sewadas's book, Swami led a delegation to submit an application to the then Ajmer-Merwara government, requesting for permitting him to open a shop[68] to sell the goods amongst the community fellows. It may be noted in this connection that the idea of opening a shop by Swami was appreciated. He sold and distributed goods amongst caste fellows which strengthened their cause. Opening of the shop angered the upper caste Hindus, specially Bania and Mahajan communities and they intensified the oppression further.

Some of the untouchables began to trace the drum. After a few days of search, they succeeded in tracing it. The drum was taken out from the well.

It was mentioned earlier that it was an agitation against the discriminatory practices and to end the monopoly of the caste Hindus with regard to superior religious goods and services. Later in 1951 Moti Ram Bhambhi[69] and his 16 colleagues filed a court case against Hallu Rawat and other villagers of Hathi Kheda in Ajmer. On April 14,1953,[70] after 3 years, Sub Judge-1st class Ajmer, P.L. Agarwal pronounced the decision in favour of Motilal Bhambhi, prohibiting the caste Hindus from imposing ban on using drum etc. Swami not only broke the ban, but also succeeded in throwing open schools and temples of upper caste Hindus to the low castes communities.

The local press also played an important role in publicizing the news of court decision in Ajmer. The local newspapers carried the following decision:[71]

"सब जज दर्जा अव्वल की अदालत अजमेर
दीवानी दावा नं.0 421 ऑफ (65)
मोती और 16 व्यक्ति दूसरे–कौम भांबी हाथीखेडा (मुददई)
बनाम
हालू रावत और दूसरे ग्रामीण–हाथीखेडा (मुददायलेहा)
फैसला

अगर मुददई को एक काम करने का अधिकार है तो मुददायलेहा को उन्हे रोकने का कोई अधिकार नही है। हमारा कानून सबको समान अधिकार देता है, एक मनुष्य अपनी इच्छानुसार कोई भी कार्य करने को स्वतन्त्र है, जब तक कि वह कानून द्वारा वर्जित कोई ऐसा काम नहीं करे या जब तक वह किसी दूसरे के प्राप्त अधिकारों में कोई हस्तक्षेप नहीं करता ।

मैं ऐसे किसी भी कानून से परिचित नही हूं जो कि एक मनुष्य को उसकी इच्छानुसार शादी विवाह आदि के अवसर पर ढोल या बांकिया बजाने से रोकता है और न मेरा ख्याल है कि इन चीजों के प्रयोग द्वारा मुदायलेहा के किसी प्राप्त अधिकार पर हस्तक्षेप या कुठाराधात होता है अगर मुददायलेहा ने मुददई को पहले इन अधिकारों का उपभोग करने से रोक रखा है तो यह सिर्फ मुददई की कमजोरी ही कहा जा सकता है। लेकिन अब, जबकि यह मामला अदालत में आ गया है, मैं इस तरह के सामाजिक शोषण को जारी रखने में जरा भी पुष्टि नही देखता हूं। इस मामले में मेरे विचार बिल्कुल स्पष्ट है । जैसा कि **उपर** बताया गया है। इसलिये मैं मुददई के दावे का नीचे लिखा हुक्म देता हूं–

(1) मुददई को इस बात की घोषणा की जाती है कि उनको विवाह शादी आदि के अवसरो पर ढोल बांकियां बजाने का हक है।

(2) मुददई के मुकदमे का खर्चा मंजूर किया जाता है।

हस्ताक्षर
पी.एल. अग्रवाल
सब जज दर्जा अव्वल अजमेर

ता0 अप्रेल 14, 1953

Dainik Bhaskar, Jaipur in its issue of June 8, 2006[72] reports the tyranny and oppression practised upon Meghwals in Udaipur region for their daring to ride on a mare. Observes the *Dainik Bhaskar*:

नीमडी गांव में मेघवाल समाज की बैठक बुलवाना समाज के स्थानीय लोगो को भारी पड गया। मेघवाल समाज का हुक्का–पानी बन्द हो गया है।

पंचायत समिति भींडर के गांव अमरपुरा मे पिछले दिनों मेघवाल समाज के दूल्हे को घोडी से नीचे उतार दिया गया था गांव में पुलिस बुलाने की बात पर अब मेघवाल समाज के लोगो का हुक्का–पानी बन्द कर दिया गया है। इसके बाद नीमडी में भी पुलिस पहरे में बिनोली निकाली गई थी। अत्याचार के खिलाफ 4 जून को मेघवाल समाज के समस्त चौखलों की बैठक नीमडी में रखी गई । गांव मे बैठक करने के विरोध में अन्य समाज के लोगों ने रात को बैठक की।

The paper further adds:

(1) इसके बाद से मेघवाल समाज का हुक्का–पानी बन्द है

(2) वे पानी नहीं भर सकते,

(3) चक्की पर पिसाई बन्द है,

(4) किराना स्टोर पर नमक, आटा, तेल, बीड़ी, सिगरेट आदि कुछ भी नहीं दिया जा रहा है,

(5) खेतों में जुताई के लिए ट्रैक्टर किराये पर नही दे रहे है

(6) एस०टी०डी पर फोन नहीं करने दे रहे और

(7) शौच के लिए तालाब की ओर जाने पर भी रोक लगादी गई है।

At the end the paper concludes:

'बहिष्कार का उल्लंघन करने पर 5 हजार रूपये हर्जाना है इसलिए कोई भी हिम्मत नहीं कर रहा'।

Hindustan Times in its issue of 16 June, 2006[73] reports the tyranny and oppression practised upon the Bairwa who form an untouchable community in the Bundi district in Hadauti region. Observes *Hindustan Times*:

"Member of the upper caste opposed the installation of tube well in the Dalit Basti of a village in Nainwa Tehsil of Bundi District. The contractor ran away without installing the tube well sanctioned under MLA LAD Funds.

The Dalits are not allowed to fetch water from the hand pumps and tube wells of the upper caste and rely on the only hand pump in their Basti which is insufficient for meeting their demand during peak summer.

A public contractor authorized by Public Health and Engineering Department (PHED) to install a single point tube well in the Bairwa Basti of Shripura village faced opposition from the upper caste and returned."

When *HT* asked Congress MLA from Nainwa, who is also Deputy Leader of Opposition in the Assembly, Ramnaryan Meena, he said:

> "A single point tube well was sanctioned from his MLA LAD fund for the Bairwa Basti of the Shripura village in his constituency as their hand pump was in bad shape."

The paper adds:

> "No FIR was lodged for not allowing installation of a tube well."

The dates of these incidents are important as they are of the year 2006. Nobody can say that this Hindu-established order is a thing of the ancient past. The fact that, these latest accounts refer to the Indian states, should not be understood to mean that the established social order has vanished from free India.

Building Institutions, Settlement of Age-old Disputes and Swami Gokuldas's Role/Contribution

From an account of the events in Swami Gokuldas's socio-religious transformation campaign given by one of his disciples Swami Sewadas (2005), it will be seen that Swami was associated with the diverse kinds of activities with regard to establishment of Mandirs etc. He took an active interest in encouraging the people for either building or renovating Mandirs and stimulated his followers to organize Melas at different places of Samadhi of saints. In Vikram Samvat 1980[74] Swami laid the foundation stone of Baba Ram deo Mandir at Burhanpur, district Khandwa, Madhya Pradesh and constructed a well. The well is popularly known as Ramkund. Every year, priest Tota Ram, son of Jaga Ram, organized a Mela in which large number of pilgrims participated. The temple provided a focus for religious activities, the most important being the holding of Vishal Satsang Samaroh at night.

In Vikram Samvat 1981[75] Swami constructed another famous temple namely 'Shree Alakhji Maharaj ka Mandir' at his native place Domara, Ajmer, the centre of socio-religious agitation. Besides building temples and boundary walls, Swami also constructed a well, which was built with a view to provide drinking water facilities to common people. The footprints (Padukas) which Swami installed, included both 'Alakhji' and 'Baba Ram Deo Maharaj'. On this occasion, food was served to all assembled Sadhus, Sanyasis, Pandits, Peers and Panchas of the community. The expenses incurred over these items were borne by Swami himself. In this mission, Swami was assisted by a few eminent social activists notably: Ram Narain Kataria,[76] a resident of village Harnada, district Jaipur, who was at that time serving in Railways as SPWJ. Every year on Bhadra Sudi 1, a Vishal Satsangh Samaroh and a Mela is organized. At present Badu Ram Kucheria is the priest of the temple. The temple is also a Gaddi Centre for 'Alakh' missionaries.

Another important 'Dhuni' (a religious seat) was established by Rishi Khivanji Maharaj, a charismatic personality of Meghwal Samaj in Dudu, district Jaipur. Dhuni is the seat of a Sadhu,[77] generally called a Swami or Maharaj, who is incharge of the seat, teaching of Panth in general and Swami's teaching in particular. It is believed that Khivanji Maharaj acquired spiritual power and fulfilled the wishes of his disciples. Thus, Khivanji Maharaj emerged as a charismatic leader. From the account of events in Khivanji Maharaj's life given by Sewadas Maharaj

(2005), it will be seen that Khivanji Maharaj was the first untouchable to have shown spiritual powers to Mohammad Gauri—the then Muslim ruler of Delhi and this influenced the ruler. Sewadas mentions in his book 'Jeevan Darshan' (2005), that in Vikram Samvat 1197,[78] Mohammad Gauri had issued Tamra-Patra and Patta of Dhuni to Khivanji Maharaj's son Hadmal and also allotted 87 bighas of land for its maintenance.

Mohammad Gauri issued Tamra-Patra and Patta of Dhuni to Khivauji Maharaj's Sonhadmal

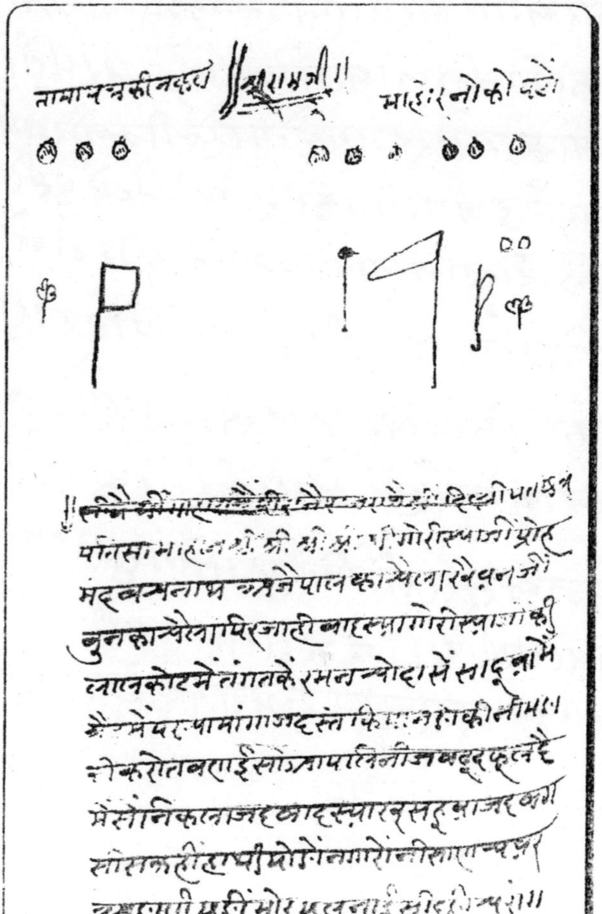

गौंरी बादशाह द्वारा प्रदत्त दूदू धूणी के ताम्र पत्र की नकल

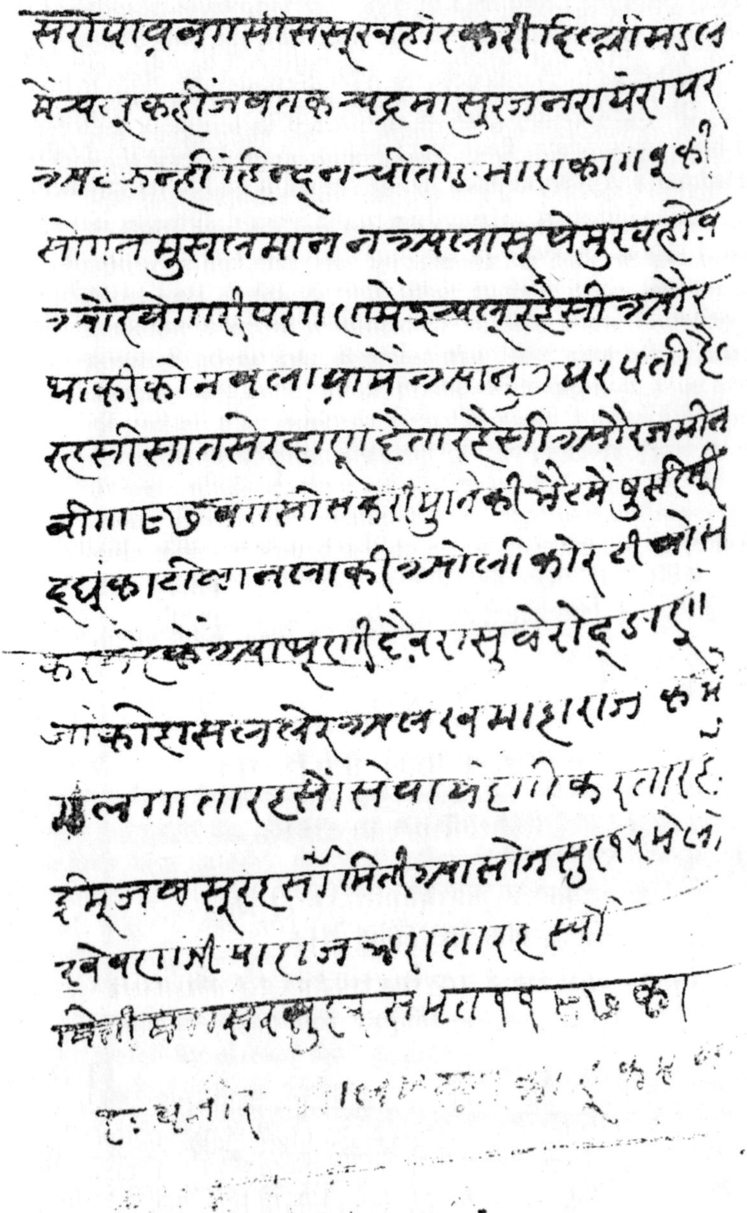

सरोपावबगसीससूरवतोरकरी दिल्लोंमेडल
मेस्वरूकहीजबतक चन्द्रमासुरजनरायेरापर
अमर कन्हीहिन्दुनचीतोउ माराकागनू की
सोगनमुसलमान नअसलसूधेमुरवहोव
अौरबेगारीपरा (तमें रखनू रहैसी अौर
धाकीकोनवलाधामें अमानू अरपती है
रहसीसानसेरहारा देनारहैसी अौरजमोन
बीगा ५५ बगसीसकरीपुनकी मैरमें [illegible]
दृधुंकाटीवाननाकी अमोली कोर दी बास
[illegible] अपापुरी देनरासू बेरोदूडाडू
जोकोरासबनमेर अमलरव माहाराज क मे
[illegible] गातारहसी सेवाबेहागी करतारहे
दोमूजब सूरहसो मिली आसोज सुद १५ मंगल
दवेबरोगी पाराज आरातारर स्थो
मोली [illegible] संमत १९५८ का
[illegible]

Besides, other kinds of facilities, such as to beat the drum, riding elephant or a horse etc., were sanctioned to Khivanji Maharaj. Previously these untouchables had to obtain the prior permission of the government to perform the ceremonies.

In order to popularize the Dhuni (Samadhi) of Khivanji Maharaj, Swami realized the historical importance of having annual Mela and hermitage (Ashram). For this purpose Swami met Jawan Singh—the then Thakur, Dudu Thikana and urged him for his cooperation and support. Hence, Thakur Sahib honoured Swami's feelings. Swami toured all over Ajmer and Jaipur regions and appealed to his community men, his followers and Panchas of community to participate in Community Sammelan to be held at Khivanji Maharaj's Dhuni. In Vikram Samvat 1981[79] Community Sammelan was held under the leadership of Gokuldas Maharaj. In this Sammelan a resolution was passed to organize a Mela every year. Thus, Swami initiated to celebrate the Mela on a large scale and untouchables considered this a prestigious one. It should be mentioned here that on behalf of local Thakur Sahib, food was served to all assembled people. The Thakur Sahib spent a large sum of money on food and other facilities.

In order to strengthen and spread the spiritual reformations that Khivanji Maharaj had initiated, Swami appointed Chaturbhuj Maharaj Gaddi-adhiyaksh of Khivanji Maharaj's Samadhi.[80] On this occasion a procession was also taken out.

Swami organized the fourth Mela at Bichun—15 km away from Phulera railway station, district Jaipur, where 'Samas Rishi', another famous untouchable saint spent his life and where he attained salvation (Samadhi). Swami also took an active interest in organizing a Satsang Samaroh. As a result of this, for the first time on Tuesday, September 5, 1933[81] and another one on Wednesday September 6, 1933, Satsangh Samaroh and a religious Mela were organized respectively. The description of Samadhi at Bichun showed that Rupaji and Ghisaji, both residents of Bichun, built a water tank (Pani-ki-Tanki) to provide drinking water facilities to the pilgrims.

Besides building water tanks and boundary walls, organizing Satsangh Samaroh and Mela, in order to cater to the religious needs of the common people, Swami appointed Garib Sahib,[82] another eminent saint of untouchables and Kabirpanthi, Gaddi-adhiyaksh of Bichun. In addition, to these Mandirs and temples, there is one Samadhi at village Para, 75 km away from district Ajmer and another Samadhi at village Sarsaya, 6 km away from Phagi in district Jaipur. In each of these Samadhis, there is a Meghwal Swami devoted to Peer's work of propagating their teachings.

The Samadhi of Narain Pancha at village Sarsaya took care of the organization of religious aspects of Narain Pancha Dharma. The Samadhi, on the other hand, catered to the religious needs of the common people by holding Satsangh Samaroh and Mela from time to time and enabling them to shed their earlier practices of social vices. Swami took keen interest in procuring 12 bighas of land from Rajputs of the village for the maintenance of the Samadhi. After the death of Rod Das, the Mahent of Sarsaya Dhuni, Swami took initiative in appointing Ramdas Maharaj the new Gaddi-adhiyaksh in the presence of a huge gathering of saints, sadhus and disciples—notably Devdas Maharaj, the Peer of Bichun. Thus, Swami laid supreme emphasis on spiritual strength with a view to gaining self-respect and esteem.

The other issues, which community fellows considered unnecessary, were the disputes between Dudu (Samadhi Isthal of Khivanji Maharaj), Narena (Samadhi Isthal of Ransi Maharaj) and Bichun[83] (Samadhi Isthal of Samas Rishi)—all the three Dhunis are of historical importance and hermitages (Ashrams). The strategy which Panchas of community used in resolving these disputes was to request Swami to resolve these decades old disputes amicably so that social harmony and integrity could be established amongst the disciples and community fellows. Thus, as an attempt to resolve the disputes, Panchas of the community convened a meeting under the leadership of Swami. In this meeting Swami traced the socio-religious history of each Dhuni and analysed their historical importance respectively. He also removed their doubts and misunderstanding in the presence of priests. Swami advocated equal status and importance of each Dhuni. He appealed to the Panchas of the community, officiating priests and intellectual sections of Meghwals to remove the prejudices against one another, and develop better understanding to the maximum. In order to resolve the decades old disputes for ever, Swami realized the need of having a written agreement. Hence, he got a signed agreement which gave them a sense of achievement and fulfilment and in some respect of doing things better than the others.

Swami was active as a socio-religious reformer in Vikram Samvat 1970 and he died on October 8, 1977. During a period of about 86 years the kind of radical changes he ushered in were remarkable. Domara, where Swami established 'Shree Alakh ji Maharaj-ka-Mandir' in Vikram Samvat 1981 and lived until Vikram Samvat 2034, had become a centre of pilgrimage for Meghwals. A marble statue of Swami was prepared by Heera Lal and sons—a famous sculptor of Jaipur, Rajasthan and the statue was installed on May 5, 1982[84] and several religious services were offered to Swami's idol (Pratima). Even today pilgrims make wishes and offer prayers to Swami and these are usually fulfilled. He appears in the dreams of devotees and apparently speaks to them. Three times a year, a Vishal Satsang Samaroh is held in which thousands of pilgrims and devotees come to Domara, Ajmer to partake the blessings of Swami. Thus, even after his death, the spiritual regeneration amongst the Meghwals continues.

Some of the disciples and followers are dedicated to the spreading of Swami's message. For this purpose, they have established more than a dozen institutions including Ashramas, Dhunis, Mandirs, Pratisthan and Dharmshalas in different regions of the country. For instance, in Madhya Pradesh, the first Dham was established by Babulal Maharaj at village Chillars,[85] 45 km away from district Burhanpur, Madhya Pradesh. Later, Babulal Maharaj established six more Dhams,[86] each one at Buldana, Bisampur, Rajakheda, Chhindwada, Medka, and Betul, all in Madhya Pradesh. Besides all these, three statues of Swami were installed in Rajasthan[87] one in Badali Kheda, district Bhilwara and another in Mandi Miyala, district Rajsamand and a third one at Adarsh Nagar, Ajmer, where eminent saints of the Samaj attained salvation (Samadhi). The devotees and followers of Kota region built Dharmshala[88] at village Nayapur, district Kota. Sewadas Maharaj, the present Gaddi-adhiyaksh of Domara, established 'Gokul Dham' at Domara, where Swami spent his life and where he attained salvation (Samadhi).

Notes

1. For a discussion of Meghwal movement that stresses the role of Swami Gokuldas Maharaj and his contribution in social awakening in pre- and post-independence period and socio-religious and educational consequences of the movement, see in particular *Sewadas Rishi Jiwan Darshan: Yug purush*

Swami Shri Gokuldasji Maharaj, 2005, Ajmer Gokul Dham, Alakha Sthan, Domara, p. 40.

2. Ibid., p. 40.
3. Ibid., p. 40.
4. Ibid., p. 40.
5. Ibid., p. 40.
6. Ibid., p. 40.
7. Ibid., p. 61.
8. Ibid., p. 75.
9. Ibid., p. 62 also see p. 64.
10. Ibid., p. 64.
11. Ibid., p. 63.
12. Ibid., p. 75.
13. Ibid., p. 75.
14. Ibid., p. 76.
15. Ibid., p. 76.
16. Ibid., p. 76.
17. Ibid., p. 77.
18. Ibid., p. 77.
19. Ibid., p. 78.
20. Ibid., p. 79.
21. Ibid., p. 80.
22. Ibid., p. 80.
23. Ibid., p. 80.
24. Ibid., p. 76.
25. Ibid., p. 78.
26. Ibid., p. 78.
27. Ibid., p. 79.
28. Ibid., p. 80.
29. Ibid., p. 97.
30. Ibid., p. 97.
31. Ibid., p. 98.
32. Ibid., p. 100.
33. Ibid., p. 100.
34. Ibid., p. 100.
35. Ibid., p. 108.

36. Ibid., p. 108.
37. Ibid., p. 108.
38. Ibid., p. 109.
39. Ibid., p. 110.
40. Ibid., p. 110.
41. Ibid., p. 111.
42. Ibid., p. 116.
43. Ibid., p. 139.
44. Ibid., p. 139.
45. Ibid., p. 139.
46. Ibid., p. 139.
47. Ibid., p. 140.
48. Ibid., p. 140.
49. Ibid., p. 174.
50. Ibid., p. 174.
51. Ibid., p. 176.
52. Ibid., p. 176.
53. Ibid., p. 177.
54. Ibid., p. 176.
55. Ibid., p. 177.
56. Ibid., p. 93.
57. Ibid., pp. 93–95.
58. Ibid., p. 94.
59. Ibid., p. 95.
60. Ibid., p. 95.
61. Ibid., p. 95.
62. Ibid., p. 120.
63. Ibid., p. 120.
64. Ibid., pp. 121–138.
65. Ibid., p. 115.
66. Ibid., p. 115.
67. Ibid., p. 116.
68. Ibid., p. 116.
69. Ibid., p. 117.
70. Ibid., p. 117.
71. Ibid., pp. 117–118.

72. 'नीमडी में भी मेघवालों का हुक्का–पानी बन्द' in *Dainik Bhaskar*, Jaipur, Thursday, June 8, 2006. Also see 'मन्दिर में प्रवेश को लेकर विवाद' in *Dainik Bhaskar*, Jaipur, Monday, August 28, 2006 'मन्दिर में दलितों के प्रवेष का विवाद सुलझा' in *Dainik Bhaskar*, Jaipur, Tuesday, August 29, 2006 'दलितों का मंदिर प्रवेश' in *Dainik Bhaskar*, Jaipur, Wednesday, December 13, 2006. "Dalits fight restrictions enter Rajasthan temple" in *Hindustan Times*, New Delhi, Wednesday, December 13, 2006.
73. "Upper castes oppose installation of tube well in Dalit Basti" in *Hindustan Times*, New Delhi, June 16, 2006.
74. *Sewadas Rishi, Jiwan Darshan: Yug Purush Swami Gokuldasji Maharaj*, 2005. Ibid., p. 153.
75. Ibid., p. 155.
76. Ibid., p. 155.
77. Ibid., p. 158.
78. Ibid., p. 158.
79. Ibid., p. 158.
80. Ibid., p. 161.
81. Ibid., p. 163.
82. Ibid., p. 163.
83. Ibid., p. 172.
84. Ibid., p. 200.
85. Ibid., p. 207.
86. Ibid., p. 207.
87. Ibid., pp. 208–209.
88. Ibid., p. 209.

10 Meghwals, Sootrakars and Chamars Movement in Ajmer-Jaipur

The formation of organizations in the third decade of 20th century led to forging a new identity for the Chamars of Ajmer and Jaipur states. The early 20th century was a period of change in these region. The socio-cultural reform demanded the Gandhi-Ambedkar pact to be implemented and socio-educational activities of Arya Samaj, Praja Mandal, Rajputana Harijan Sewak Sangh etc., expanded among the low untouchable castes and communities. The various socio-educational measures of these organizations in the various regions during this period had positive social, educational and cultural consequences for low caste untouchable communities in general and Chamars and Meghwals of Rajputana in particular. If certain members of Chamar group established their own organizations and successfully resisted the authority of upper caste Hindus, other Chamars were pushed to the margin of village society and faced the growing rigidity of norms of purity and pollution in the region. In this wider context, Swami Gokul Das Maharaj of Ajmer and Garib Saheb of Jaipur, initiated reform programmes primarily among the Chamars of Ajmer and Jaipur, a large cultural region in central and north-east Rajasthan. The socio-cultural endeavour at once drew upon popular traditions and the ritual hierarchy of purity and pollution, rejected the divine and social hierarchies that centred on the Hindu Pantheon and repositioned old signs in a new matrix. It questioned and challenged the ascribed-status of Chamars as low untouchables who were tainted with the stigma of untouchability. The Chamars who joined the organizations were cleansed of their impurity and marks of ritual subordination and reconstituted as Meghwal. At the same time, in the new campaign efforts were made to bridge the gap between the various segments of Chamar community such as Meghwal, Balai, Bhambhi and other sub-castes. The identity of Meghwal was sketched by the middle of the 20th century.

The Formation of Rajasthan Meghvans Mahasabha Pushkar(RMM), Ajmer 1935

Gokul Das was born on Sanivar (Saturday) Phagun Badi Chaudas in Vikram Samvat 1948 at Domara, a village situated 8 miles away from the then Ajmer state. His father's name was Nand Ram Singhmar and his mother was Chhotee Devi. There were four brothers and Gokul Das was the youngest one. From the very beginning he evinced his keen interest in education. At the time, in rural Rajputana, there were no such facilities and moreover the untouchables were not admitted to local Pathshala or schools. However, with the sincere efforts of Subedar Thakur Jodhaji Gokul Das was admitted to a school at Sonalpur, where he learnt to read and write.

When he was about 8 years of age, he was married to Ladi Bai, daughter of Devaji Devagaon of village Palra, but he was not happy. Mohan Lal Kilanya[1] who had given an account of the events in Gokul Das's life, noted that from the very beginning, he had taken keen interest in religious affairs. He used to keep himself in the company of sadhus and sanyasis. During the course of his wanderings, he came in contact with Swami Ramhans Panwar, Ajmer, who was well versed in philosophy. Since then he remained closely associated with Swami Panwar. It is said that after satisfying himself, on Phagun Sudhi Duj, in Samvat 1960, Gokul Das accepted Swami Ramhans Panwar as his guru in a huge religious gathering (Satsang). In addition to his active participation in spiritual affairs, he also disassociated himself from worldly affairs. He wanted to make his life fruitful. His personality attracted the attention of rural masses and thereafter he was rechristemed Swami Gokul Das Maharaj.

He was shocked to see the most miserable socio-economic as well as educational conditions of his community. He concentrated his attention on carrying out a programme of social reform. Later, he toured throughout the country. During his all-India tour he organized several meetings of the local Chamars, Bhambis, Balais and Meghwals. His greatest contribution to Meghwal movement was his severe attack on social evils and vices. He was also a good orator and a good writer in Hindi language. He started the work of reforming his community. He formed a group of a few devotees with the help of whom he attempted to organize the scattered Meghwals in various regions of Rajputana. He travelled throughout the region, holding kirtens (religious discussion) in which he tried to spread the message that untouchability was not a divine creation but was instead a social artefact. Gradually, Swami began to think of the various caste usages particularly untouchability, as humiliating which had otherwise been followed for ages as a natural custom. This was especially so in case of all low untouchable castes in Rajputana.

The major issues addressed by him included the necessity of education, the abandonment of evil practices, discarding the death feast and access to non-traditional jobs. In this way Swami campaigned to persuade his caste fellows to abandon the social evils and practices and created a stir amongst his caste fellows. One of the programmes of action was directed towards the achievement of this goal, and to unite the scattered caste fellows. He was certain that until the Meghwals united, they would not be able to improve their social and economic backwardness. He toured from village to village and from door-to-door, which gave him sense of self-consciousness. He encouraged them to reform themselves. He believed that progress in social and economic spheres was the basis for upward social mobility and keeping this in mind encouraged social unity. To materialize his dream and in order to devote his time and energy to strengthen and to spread socio-religious and spiritual reforms amongst the Meghwals, Swami took a vow to unite the samaj and to make social reform as an object of his life. He concentrated his attention on two issues: (1) formation of an organization, and (2) making it a symbol of identity by submerging the regional names and to carry out a programme of social reform.

With such a background and bitter experiences, Swami discussed social reforms and other issues with some of the caste fellows, such as Moti Ram, Nathu Ram, Hanuman Prasad Kataria (Ajmer), Birdha Ram, Manna Lal, Bhola Ram, Bal Das Balupura, Lumba Ram (Pushkar), Kesha Ram Mukada, Ram Dev, Hari Ram (Beawar, Naya Sahr) and many others.[2] These persons were also interested in the programme of social reforms. They appreciated the contribution made by Swami himself to the reform movement so far. However, Swami himself was dissatisfied with the progress and wanted to form an organization. He thought this would strengthen the community from purely reform organization to an organization bringing about socio-political renaissance among the Meghwals of

Rajasthan. The main decision of the discussion was to organize a Vishal Community Sammelan with a view to unite and to gain the support of Meghwal community for the formation of its organization.

One of the consequences of this thought and programme was its stimulus to the Meghwals of untouchable communities in Ajmer and neighbouring towns and villages under the leadership of Swami. A Vishal Community Sammelan of the representatives from 210 villages of Ajmer state was convened in the year 1935[3] in the village Dorai, Ajmer, as a separate platform for Meghwals with the aim of forming a caste association at the local, regional and provincial levels, ameliorating their condition and charting a socio-cultural course independent of other low untouchable castes. Thus, Rajasthan Meghwal Mahasabha (RMM) Pushkar,[4] came into existence in the same year. Meghwals credit Swami with taking the first step towards creating the caste organization. Meghwal movement was thus welcomed and encouraged. They recount that in the early Vikram Samvat 1977, Swami enlisted the help of caste men to eradicate the social vices amongst the caste fellows. It would be seen that Meghvansh Mahasabha was set up as a result of the joint efforts of Maghana Ram Panwar, Lumbha Ram, Dhanna Ram Gora, Bhogu Ram Panwar, Hanuman Prasad Kataria, Vijay Lal and a few well-to-do Meghwals with substantial support.

The Vishal Community Sammelan discussed several issues.[5] The issue of nomenclature was primary and critical. They appealed to the community fellows that they should now be called Meghwals and not the Chamars, Bhambhis and Balais. Second, in relation to the vexed problem of illiteracy/education, the caste Sammelan requested the local government demanding the admission of children of the untouchables in the schools as they were refused admission in most schools. Finally, the problem of social vices, bad habits and customs, traditions, drinking and unclean occupation by the caste fellows was addressed by the caste Sammelan. The Sammelan requested the Meghwals to abandon those vices, etc.

The members of Rajasthan Meghwal Mahasabha, Pushkar, registered their caste association under the Society Registration Act, 1860.

The members of RMM registered their presence in different provinces of the country by visiting the Punjab, Sanyukt Prant, Delhi; Madhya-Bharat, Maharashtra, etc., with their leader Swami. We have noted earlier that in the course of their tour to above provinces, they had met several local social workers and activists. Mohan Lal Kilanya observed,[6] "it was during this tour that Meghwal brothers from Rajasthan developed close and effective social link with local social workers and were closely involved in establishing various reforms, sabhas and mandals at various places. The leaders of RMM had also recruited large number of volunteers for the purpose".

The RMM launched its first major initiative of a signature campaign of caste fellows in Vikram Samvat 1977. The signature campaign drafted by Swami discussed the deplorable socio-economic conditions of the Meghwals in Rajputana, listed the root cause of their backwardness and suggested remedies and solutions for the upliftment of the caste fellows. The lack of education among them, following bad customs and traditions, drinking habits, unclean occupations, social vices etc., had lowered their prestige. The last statement, in fact, takes us towards the RMM's diagnosis of affliction that plagued the Meghwals.

What were the solutions offered by the RMM? The issue of pure social life was primary. "We request our caste fellows to sign to a signature campaign draft to be issued to the effect that Meghwals would lead a pure social life and would not follow the bad customs, and traditions, social vices, bad habits, unclean occupation, eating of flesh etc. The RMM requested that if it was be followed in toto, it would become accessible to the members of the community to improve their socio-educational and economic conditions".

What was the response of the community to the signature campaign? After the signature campaign draft being circulated amongst the caste fellows by RMM Mohan Lal Kilanya noted:[7] "We do not know how many persons actually signed on the signature campaign draft, but this was to include Meghwals, as distinct from Chamars, where they were found in good number. Indeed, the aged RMM's followers celebrated the campaign as a Charter of Victory. The victory had its costs".

The largely positive response of community fellows in Rajasthan was seen by RMM, which was actively pursuing the policy of encouraging the Meghwals within the framework of RMM reforms. The general impression had been observed to the effect that the group was not to be referred to as Chamar.

The leaders of the RMM did not give up their efforts. They now decided to take up some of the concerns of Swami's project of reform. We have seen that all untouchable communities, including Chamars, had suffered from caste discrimination more severely in Rajasthan. In

Rajasthan, Chamars were not allowed to wear ornaments made of gold and silver, their children were not admitted in schools, they could not use wells, desi ghee, wear the clean and good clothes and sit on khat in the presence of upper caste Hindus, especially Jagirdars, Jamindars, Thakurs, Brahmins etc. Untouchable castes were not allowed to enter in the temple frequented by savarna castes and were restricted in their use of the passage near those temples. At a certain point on the roads leading to temples stood the notice boards or stone which marked the maximum point up to which the untouchable caste could approach. If they saw someone of the higher caste coming along the same road, they were supposed to step aside for them. They were not allowed to construct their own pakka houses and were exploited economically also. In villages they did not receive the traditional services from Brahmin priests, village barbers and washermen.

Besides all this, there were also various ways of torture. An untouchable was harassed, humiliated, insulted and punished when he violated the caste norms. The punishment could consist of a beating with a shoe, along with the imposition of a fine and/or excommunication from village, which involved stopping the services of the village grazier, restrictions on cutting of trees and prohibition on the use of ponds and tanks in the village.

The challenge against the existing caste order aroused strong reaction from the upper castes, especially Jagirdars, Jamindars, Thakurs, Brahmins, etc. From 1932 onwards, the Chamars had started boycotting the handling of the carcasses of the dead animals and their skinning. They had given up eating the flesh of dead cattle. They were disobeying the commands of Jagirdars, Jamindars, Thakurs and upper caste Hindus. This was the second wave of protest against caste norms by a core untouchable group refusing to observe them. At the same time, the emphasis on the initiative was a drive to get the Meghwals recognized not as untouchables, but rather as human beings. In the repetition of this theme, underlay Swami's plan to reform the Meghwals.

At the same time, the upper caste Hindus were not happy. They were outraged. They reacted in several ways.[8] This triggered a confrontation between the upper castes and lower castes. Several caste violences took place and sporadic violent incidents continued in rural areas. A large number of persons were implicated in court cases. A few were killed. Thus, community's effort to reconstruct its status invited upper caste derision, scorn and abuse. Unfortunately, this scenario had been witnessed elsewhere in neighbouring regions as well. Swami's efforts along this line, however, seem to have sometimes confronted the opposition from within his own community. It appears that samaj was divided into two sections. One section of samaj was supporting the agitation of RMM, while the other section held quite opposite views. Condemning all this attack on untouchables in rural Rajasthan, RMM sent out a strong message to upper caste people, saying no force could weaken the resolve of Meghwals. The real question was about social equality at different levels. Swami's effort, as we saw, was to reform the Meghwals.

According to Mohan Lal Kiloniya, after Gandhi-Ambedkar agreement (popularly known as Poona Pact) in 1932, also during the civil disobedience movement in 1942 and following the visit of Gandhi to Rajasthan, his followers had supported the RMM's reform campaign. At the same time Arya Samaj also launched anti-untouchability campaign and initiated some reform measures amongst the various untouchable castes. Mohan Lal Kiloniya wrote in *Meghvansh Itihas* that Arya Samaj supported the reform movement of RMM. This endeavour once again succeeded.

In 1935–36[9] Swami realized that community's historic temples, wells, dharmshalas, etc., were in a very bad shape. These needed repairs and renovation and a few new temples, dharmshalas, etc., had to be constructed through collection of money from donors to give the temples etc., a good look. Money was the big problem. Money for building of temples could be raised in other ways. RMM had sought help from community fellows and approached them. Swami appealed to caste fellows for donation. Collection of donation had begun in 1940. It was a collective endeavour. This was a part of the movement which indicated Swami's efforts to protect community heritage simultaneously. The unique role played by Swami must be considered against this background. As mentioned in the beginning of this chapter, it was the reputation of Swami as a Meghwal 'saint' that reached even illiterate masses. Swami's name thus became a valuable instrument for promoting Meghwal unity. The Meghwal Samaj made Swami their leader and a great Saint.

During his childhood Gokul Das, was discriminated openly in the village. After experiencing atrocities and discriminatory treatment like prohibition from drinking water, etc., of caste Hindus, he decided to launch a reform movement. This was the first ordeal he experienced in obtaining the right to live like a human being.

We would also note that he was a good orator and a writer in Hindi language. In Vikram Samvat 1991 he published *Meghvansh Itihas*, his first book. It is probable that the term Meghwal was used for the first time for Chamar, Bhambhi and Balai. Though, initially the main interest of this book centred on discussion about the genesis and development of castes—Chamar, Bhambhi, Meghwal and Balai and their problems and reforms within these communities, it gradually broadened its outlook to socio-economic conditions of Bhambhi, Balai and Chamar untouchables as a whole. In the same year Swami published another book entitled *Dharma Shastra*.

Similarly, after an interval of more than one decade, in Vikram Samvat 2002, he started *Prakash* (light) his first monthly community newspaper. Though initially the main purpose of this paper centred on highlighting the problem's within the Meghwal community, it gradually broadened its outlook to the socio-economic conditions of the untouchables as a whole. During this period Swami also invited short essays and notes about the prevailing socio-economic conditions, atrocities committed on low untouchables in the neighbouring regions, news etc., for highlighting them in the paper *Prakash*.

When *Meghvansh Itihas* was first published in Vikram Samvat 1991, it was welcomed. At the same time, it also aroused strong criticism and sharp reaction from within his own community. After eleven years, in the V.S. 2002 a revised edition of *Meghvansh Itihas* was published with new facts and information. The second edition was thus welcomed specially by his critics.

Besides these books, Swami actively took interest in writing more books which were later on published by him during Vikram Samvat 1977–1989.[10] Mohan Lal Kiloniya who wrote a brief life sketch of Swami in *Meghwansh Itihas* noted the following books:[11] (1) Bhajan mala, (2) Rishi Puran, (3) Bhajan vilas, (4) Aalakh upasana, (5) Shabad rag-ragini, (6) Shri Ram Deoji ka Vyala, (7) Shri Ram Deoji Maharaj ke Jama Jaran ki Vidhi, (8) Meghvansh Samaj ki Niymawali, (9) Dharumal Roopadedy ki Badi Bel, (10) Dali Bai ka Charit Chitran, and (11) Banjara Bhaskar. In addition to all this, the list of his publications also included books like[12] (1) Manav samaj, (2) Meghvansh Jati ke Rasam-riwaj and Chobis Praman. Thus, he tried to influence not only his caste people and untouchables, but also caste Hindus.

While discharging his duty as social reformer and a good writer his interest moved gradually towards the study of philosophy, purans, vedas, upanisad, smriti and history.

Swami was active as a social religious reformer from the very beginning. During a period of about 86 years, he worked as major moving force of social reform in various ways and capacities till his death in the year 1977.

During the British Raj, the agitation, dharna, arson, protest, rally, stone pelting, etc., by freedom fighters, praja mandals, kisan sabha etc., contributed to anti-British and anti-local rulers sentiments in the then princely states of Rajputana. The holding of meetings by common masses was a problem for rulers for it could only be held with the permission of the government. Without prior permission from government it would mean confrontation. The feeling against British Raj became quite intense and Swami realized that the main obstacles to reform movement of Meghwals was firstly, government ban on holding of meetings and secondly, Swami's opposition from a big segment of Meghwal community as well. Swami's efforts to organize the Meghwals, were however hampered by a group and his colleagues. Swami's meetings also were marred by their supporters. All this enraged Swami and his followers. However, Swami was keen that attempts should be made to expedite the reform programmes amongst the untouchable Meghwals particularly, in Ajmer.

Thus, on April 28, 1945[13] in the office of Deputy Commissioner, Ajmer-Merwara, Swami submitted an application to issue two chapras to MMP. Reasons: the issuing of chapras by Police Commissioner would have social benefits as well. First, Meghvansh Mahasabha, Pushkar (MMP) was a registered social body and had no connection or linkage with any political organization. Second, the issuing of chapras to MMP would also authorize it to organize the meetings to initiate the activities and programmes of social welfare among the untouchable Meghwals in Ajmer. Third, while MMP has been specially concerned with the organization of untouchable Meghwals within Ajmer state, it generally took position of defending the interests of Meghwals as a whole. Swami in particular emerged as a staunch reformer and defender of the rights of untouchable Meghwals in Ajmer. It was, therefore, after issuing 'chapras' as a token of government symbol an opposition person could not disturb or mar the meetings of MMP.

Swami's request was accepted. Thus, the Deputy Commissioner, Ajmer-Merwara vide his letter No. W. 498/XXVIII-P53 dated Ajmer, July 26, 1945 issued two chapras as a token of government symbol to Gokuldas, President, Mandir Panchayat Committee Meghvansh, Pushkar. According to Commissioner's letter:

"There is no objection to the use of chapras of the shape shown in the diagram enclosed with application, i.e., entirely different from those worn by government peons".

The success in obtaining chapras may be attributed to Swami. Sewa Das Rishi states that MMP had a ready-made base on which it could attempt to organize meetings. Two Meghwal workers were not only to wear them around their necks, but also stand among the untouchable masses of Meghwals. Since chapras were issued and recognized by government as such there was a lesser possibility to disturb or mar the meetings of MMP by individuals or group and/or ban by government.

Rajasthan Mahrishi Vashishta Meghvanshi (RMVMSA) Sootrakar Association, Ajmer 1943

The Meghwal Samaj and Balai Samaj had produced two eminent religious gurus in their own communities namely, Gokul Das Maharaj and Garib Das Sahib respectively. They called upon their respective communities to initiate a process of self-reform, to modernize, and cleanse themselves of baneful social practices and above all to educate themselves. Furthermore, neither the Meghwal nor the Balai organizations developed the political thrust of the Meghwal and Balai movements, but remained by and large socio-cultural groups dedicated to internal self-reform.

The divergence in the socio-cultural orientation of the Meghwal movement on the one hand and Balai movement on the other, may be explained by the differing socio-economic development of the two communities under the traditional Hindu caste system. The development of Meghwal elite had been influenced by the ideas of Gokul Das Maharaj and by the directions they took from him. The Balai development of Sootrakar movement reflects the social mobilization among the Balai community.

If the development of Meghwal movement occurred more or less in isolation from other untouchable communities of Ajmer-Jaipur regions, it also did not form close ties with Balai Samaj movement. Despite their common heritage in the ideas, the Meghwal and Balai movements came into conflict over some fundamental issues. Gokul Das Maharaj, Alak-Nami along with hundreds of his followers were active in promoting the term Meghvansh in place of Chamar. He has toured several villages and had also propagated Meghvansh and advised the caste fellows to adopt it. On the contrary, Garib Das, a Kabir Panthi, did not agree with the term Meghvansh, which was especially pronounced by Gokul Das Maharaj. Garib Das Sahib and his followers, therefore, propagated and asked them to call Chamar communities including Balai, 'Sootrakar'. There, the community seems to have been deeply divided according to sub-castes, with much internecine squabbling and rivalry. Community conflict, however, to the terms was also intense. One of the major issues taken by a few intellectuals was the question of inter-division. Gokul Das Maharaj and Garib Das Sahib were urged to end the vitiating effects of the terms in their midst and unite as one community. Thus, the relative comforts of Meghwals as well as their fragmentation into sub-caste may have prevented the development of a more radical social and political consciousness as occurred in other regions.

Thus, in October 1943 in the Vishal Mela of the samaj held at Pushkar, Ajmer, it was decided by some intellectuals to control the damage. This decision, by a few well-wishers of the samaj, was a great event just as it was a harbinger of the things to come for Chamar movement.

Especially, during the Pushkar mela, Mohan Lal Kirnia, Ajmer and Cheesulal Kadela, Ajmer attempted successfully to persuade Gokul Das Maharaj and Garib Das Sahib to work together for the upliftment of the Chamar samaj. They urged them to abandon their differences and to think of Chamar samaj as a united one and to establish a Chamar unity in social, religious as well as political matters. Thus, in their efforts, they succeeded to bring Gokul Das Maharaj and Garib Das Sahib into one group. According to Hanuman Prasad Kataria's undated letter to the author (received on March 1, 2006) Rajasthan Mahrisi Vashishta Meghanshi Sootrakar (RMVMS) Association, Ajmer was formed in October 1943[14] as a result of sincere efforts made at Vishal Pushkar Mela, Ajmer. There it was decided to form a new organization which would devote itself exclusively to the amelioration and upliftment of Meghvansh Sootrakar communities in and outside Rajasthan.

The aims of the new association were:[15]

1. To promote knowledge, literature, science and art amongst the caste fellows.
2. To introduce all social, educational, cultural and economic reforms for the progress of the samaj.
3. To use all legal means and resources for the all-round development of the samaj, and
4. All movable and non-movable properties of the association would be utilized for the association only.

From October 31, 1944 the RMVMS started its function from Ajmer as its headquarters. The office bearers of this association were:[16]

1. Gokul Das Maharaj (Domara)—Pradhan
2. Pandit Bherudas (Kadel)—Sabha Pati
3. Sita Ram (Meharta)—Designation not mentioned
4. Ram Bax (Panchva)—Designation not mentioned
5. Sewa Das (Domara)—Mantri
6. Bhura Lal (Bhavani-Kheda)—Sanyukta Mantri
7. Bhanwar Lal—Designation not mentioned
8. Hardev (Kayad)—Treasurer

In addition, there were in all 22 executive members.[17]

The act also specified that Chamar and cognate sub-castes were eligible for membership but had to pay Re 1 as annual subscription and had to observe the rules and regulations of the association. The act stated that members had to abandon eating of meat and drinking liquor. And finally, it indicated that those members who failed to deposit the fee for three consecutive years could not attend any meeting and cast their votes. It is significant to note that RMVMS was registered under Society Act No. 1860/21, in the office of the Deputy Commissioner, Ajmer.

Akhil Bharatiya Sootrakar Mahasabha (ABSM), Jaipur 1949

During the middle of the 20th century, attempts were made by a few religious gurus to change their current name Balai and these attempts did acquire the character of a movement. For instance, in early 1943 Saint Garib Das of village Bhojpura Kala, in the princely state of Jaipur started advocating adoption of the original name, 'Sootrakar' by the caste men in rural Jaipur. It is significant that Balais' original name centred around Sootrakar. Saint Garib Das thought that the change of the nomenclature of the caste from Balai to Sootrakar would appreciate the importance of original Indian concept and thus in future the community would get rid of the stigma of being called 'untouchables'. Enthusiasm for adopting the name Sootrakar for Balai of North India can be explained as follows:

In order to attain the desired goal, Garib Saheb convened the first community Sammelan at Jobner in Jaipur state on May 10, 1943.[18] In this meeting it was decided to propagate and popularize the original caste name Sootrakar in place of Balai among the rural and urban Sootrakars. Now Sootrakars became aware of their traditional name and got interested in adopting the name Sootrakar. Garib Saheb now started taking active interest in spreading the name Sootrakar in neighbouring states such as Delhi, Gujarat and Madhya Bharat (now Madhya Pradesh). In order to unite the whole samaj under the banner of Sootrakar, Garib Saheb established a Prachar Kendra in Delhi. The Delhi Sootrakars also started taking active interest in spreading the name Sootrakar. The kendra's activities became more social.

On February 15, 1946[19] Delhi Prantiya Sootrakar Karyakarni (DPSK) was constituted. Delhi had a large number of Sootrakar population. The executive committee therefore organized socio-cultural and reformatory activities.

Due to sincere efforts made by active participation of Sootrakar workers and activists, several small Sammelans and/or meetings were organized throughout Jaipur state particularly at Kishangarh Renwal, Bansa, Thani, Aasalpur, Jobner[20] and many other places to propagate its activities and bring about the great consciousness among the Sootrakars scattered in rural areas of Jaipur state. Prachar kendras were established at several other places. The prachar kendras made sincere efforts in propagating the Sootrakar and had promised to ameliorate the lot as also all-round development of the community.

As stated earlier, an internal consciousness grew within Sootrakar movement. Since 1943 onwards Garib Saheb along with a few other social activists, had realized the plight of the community. This realization aroused the consciousness of a large number of Sootrakar activists. Consequently, in April 1948, Garib Saheb organized another Vishal Sammelan of Sootrakar Samaj in Jaipur with a view to discussing the socio-economic conditions of the community. Besides, the main objective of this Vishal Sammelan was to form an all-India level caste organization. This Sammelan attracted many men, women and children, youth or old amongst the Sootrakars. As a result of this, on April 8, 1948,[21] the Akhil

Bharatiya Sootrakar Mahasabha came into existence in Jaipur, the then princely state. A vidhan parishad[22] headed by Kishan Sahay Dumoliya consisting of 15 members was constituted. The aims of the organization were educational, cultural and economic upliftment. Its motto was 'educate, agitate and organize'.

According to Pradhan Mantri, Akhil Bharatiya Sootrakar Mahasabha, Acharya Guru Prasad K.P. who wrote the bhoomika (introduction) in the constitution of ABSM mentioned that the next day, i.e., April 9, 1948[23] a delegation under the leadership of Garib Saheb presented a silver statue/image of Baba Ramdeo Maharaj to His Highness Raj Rajendra Sir Aamde Sahai Hindustan, Major General Sri Sir Sawai Man Singhji Bahadur on the historical occasion of his 25 years of attaining the throne at Albert Hall, Ram Bagh Niwas.

The establishment of ABSM in the year 1948 was a great event in the history of Sootrakar movement. This organization made the Sootrakars aware of their pitiable conditions, their low social status as untouchables and there was a necessity of a change for social reform and fighting against the atrocities in order to make progress. This organization supported the opening of the branches of ABSM whose main activity was to agitate and fight against the atrocities, untouchability and disabilities in different regions of North India. This was the way to garner social mobilization. Thus, this organization got a separate identity due to the development of the activities of Sootrakar movement.

As a result of all this, ABSM became popular among the Sootrakars in Jaipur from 1943 onwards. A notable feature of ABSM's campaign was to spread its activities among the Sootrakars in Jaipur and the adoption of social reforms. It led to violent riots[24] due to boycott of traditional work by Sootrakars. Upper caste Hindus also filed false criminal and civil cases against Sootrakars in the lower courts with a view to harass them.

Thus, ABSM acquired a mass character in northern India, where the Sootrakars started taking an active interest in order to form branches of ABSM and to propagate the reform activities among caste men. Thus on March 18, 1948,[25] 'Gujarat Prant Sootrakar', Ahmedabad came into existence. Similarly, on December 12, 1948,[26] another state branch namely, 'Mahamalva Sootrakar, Indore' (Madhya Bharat) was formed. This became the forum of Maha Panchayat to propagate its activities and bring about greater consciousness among Sootrakars scattered all over northern India. ABSM launched a campaign which later on became an all-India front with growing influence of ABSM also in other regions of the country such as United Province, Himachal Pradesh, Poorvanchal etc. That is why the influence of ABSM increased in those days. Later on, they joined hands together at the national level. With the increasing all-India organizations, social activists now found it necessary to have their own constitutions. That is why, the ABSM repeatedly raised emotive issues for socio-cultural unity. They had prepared the ground both for internal and external campaigns throughout Rajasthan, Delhi and elsewhere against social vices and social disabilities.

With the increasing consciousness, agitation against disabilities and untouchability, discarding of traditional services, Sootrakar outraged the upper caste Hindus, particularly, Thakurs, Jagirdars, Jamindars, Brahmins, etc. That is why severe violent incidents took place in rural areas. Several restrictions were imposed on Sootrakars. In spite of all this odd, ABSM achieved great success as fruits of the campaign were reaching common Sootrakars.

In the beginning of 1949, Rajasthan Sootrakar Sabha constituted a draft committee for framing its own constitution with Kisan Sahay Dumolaya as its chairman. Besides, there were a few members in the committee. The committee made sincere efforts in preparing its constitution under the name of ABSM.

Due to the organizational efforts made by Rajasthan Sootrakar Sabha, a Vishal Sammelan was held on July 26, 1949[26] at Shahpura, Jaipur. In this Sammelan a handwritten copy of the constitution of ABSM was handed over to Pradhan Mantri of ABSM, New Delhi by Pradhan Mantri of Rajasthan Sootrakar Sabha, Jaipur for implementing it in letter and spirit. On August 22, 1949,[27] under the chairmanship of Kisan Sahay Dumolaya, a meeting of Vidhan Parishad consisting of 15 members was convened for detailed discussions on the constitution, at Delhi. After prolonged discussions and with certain modifications, the Vidhan Parishad approved the constitution unanimously in the meeting held on August 22, 1949. Later on it was sent to the press for printing. Thus, on January 26, 1950 the act of ABSM came into force which was applicable to all state branches of ABSM in North India.

The aims and objectives[28] of the ABSM were as under:

1. To protect the ethical, social, economical, cultural and citizenship rights of Sootrakar.

2. To abolish poverty and slavery of underprivileged class in Indian society under the torchlight of Bapujee by promoting of khadi in each village.
3. (a) To embark all Indian Hindu Sootrakars in one garland (unity) according to our religion and history of our forefathers as they have made different classes being residents of different provinces of India. (b) On the economical side, in the interest of industrial unity or organization, everyone who spins the thread (sootra) and prepares khadi can be the member of association.
4. No place for man of communal and revolutionary mind in Sootrakar association.
5. To make free Sootrakar class from Begar (forced labour).

According to the constitution, the organization was divided into state, district, tehsil, city and village units with elected executive committees having president, vice-president, and secretary at each level. State units were formed in Rajasthan, Delhi, Madhya Pradesh and Gujarat. There were two types of membership of Mahasabha: (1) ordinary membership, and (2) representative membership. A person who had attained the age of 18 years was interested in social service and followed the norms of Mahasabha could become an ordinary member by paying 4 Anna as annual membership fee. Likewise, Mahasabha enrolled those as representative members who had done 3 years fieldwork either at village, city, tehsil or the district level.

Meghvansh Prakash Sabha (MPS), Ajmer 1960

In many major towns and cities such as Jodhpur, Jaipur, Udaipur and Bikaner in Rajasthan, the Meghwals had shown a high capacity for social and political mobilization. The leaders of Ajmer-Beawar occupy the leading position. The poor Meghwals and social activists in Ajmer town started organizing themselves for welfare activities.

Bhanwar Lal, Bhura Palasya, Kanmal Gora, Suraj Mal Gora, Jiwan Lal Gora, Jagannath Gora, Kahai Lal Bamnia, Mishri Lal and many others, all residents of Ajmer, took the initiative in working out plans for social upliftment of Meghwals. Thus, on July 23, 1960[29] a Meghvansh organization was formed in the city of Ajmer, called 'Meghvansh Jati Sudhar Sabha (MJSS) Ajmer. Later on its name was changed from Meghvansh Jati Sudhar Sabha to Meghvansh Jati Sudhar Sanstha (MJSS).[30] The main programme of the Sanstha was to propagate the social reforms. In the same year, on October 8, 1960, the Sanstha convened another Vishal Community Sammelan. This time it was held at the village pond in Kalyanpuri, Ajmer district. The Sammelan was attended by a large number of community fellows from far flung rural areas of Ajmer. A few reputed community fellows also participated in it. The main aim of this Sammelan was to think over the new name of the Sanstha once again. After long discussions, not only did the Sammelan change the name of the organization with majority in favour, but it also agitated for poor socio-economic conditions and asked the caste men to minimize their expenditure on marriage, birth of male child, death feast and ban on serving liquor on certain occasions. Thus, 'Mehgwals Prakash Sabha MPS Ajmer' came into existence on the very day, i.e., October 8, 1960.[31]

In this Sammelan, it was also decided to initiate the process of framing the constitution for MPS. As a result of this, the Sammelan constituted a drafting committee[32] for framing its constitution with Bhanwar Lal Anand, a resident of Singar Chori, Ajmer as its Chairman. Besides, there were about 11 members in the committee. It is significant to note that for framing the constitution for MPS, the drafting committee also received guidance and help from some eminent persons, namely, Mauna Lal Jasraj, Sansadiya Sachiv, Vidhan Sabha Jaipur; Prof Dhanraj Singh, Delhi; Hukma Ram, Assistant Registrar, Jaipur; Pandit. Rambhajan Lal Mishra, Dayanand Vidhyalaya, Ajmer and Mohan Lal Kalyana, Mantri, Dalit Warg Sangh, Ajmer. The Committee made sincere efforts and took 6 months in preparing its constitution under the name of MPS, which was approved in the meeting held in the year 1961. It was registered under Registration No. 55/1967–68. The sabha had promised to ameliorate the lot as also all-round development of the community.

From the year 1960 onwards, the MPS assumed an active role and vigorously pursued the social and cultural affairs of its people. The MPS launched a number of activities and programmes to mobilize the Meghwals into a viable and assertive community, increasingly consciousness of its human, social, economic and political rights.

After seven years, on August 19, 1967[33] a large contingent of Meghwals from 210 villages all over Ajmer district attended the Vishal Sammelan of caste Panchas, Sarpanchas, chaudharys, patels, etc., held at Ajmer. Due to organizational efforts made by MPS, election for executive committee was held in this meeting. Thus, a newly elected executive committee[34] came into existence on that day with Ramji Lal Gora as Pradhan Chunni Lal Natya as Up-pradhan, Kanhailal Gora as Mantri, Mangilal Shamriya as Up-pradhan, Ladu Ram Nirmal as Treasurer, Harji Lal Bhati as Nirikshak, Shankar Lal Bamnia as Chairman of Sewa Dal. Besides, there were about 8 members in the Executive Committee. They were: Kishan Singh Sogan, Ram Kisan Gandhi, Ram Dayal Gandhi, Jagannath Gora, Ramji Lal Khinchi, Babu Lal Maluka, Mangi Lal Joram and Mangal Ram Suwal.

The Formation of Meghvansiya Samaj Chetna Sansthan, Rajasthan(MSCSR), 2004

It is necessary at this stage to understand the organization of MSCSR in order to ascertain the Samaj's internal dynamics. MSCSR was formed at Rajasthan level. It consists of members, each of whom pays Rs 100 as an annual membership fee and the administration of MSCSR rests with the executive committee of 11 members including Chairman, General Secretary and Treasurer. While some members are nominated by the executive committee, others are elected by the general body.

MSCSR functions at the district level and consists of 125 branches. Each district unit is managed by a committee consisting of president, general secretary and treasurer and 11 members. In 2005, there were 8 district units. The name of the districts are: Bikaner, Nagaur, Pali, Sriganganagar, Sikar, Churu, Alwar and Jhunjhunu and about 100 members.

As noted earlier, from 1935 to 2004, many local, regional and state level registered and non-registered social organizations came into existence in Rajasthan. However, in January 2004, the social activists made another effort with B.L. Chirania[35] as the leader to establish MSCSR. They were successful.

There were many factors under which the formation of MSCSR took place. The following is an account of the circumstances which led to the formation of MSCSR. First, the then princely states of Rajputana were administered by rigid caste norms with regard to untouchables including the Chamars. Second, during the pre- and post-independence period several socio-political organizations were formed in Rajasthan, which also helped the Chamar communities, but in practice were inactive in the areas and third, the Chamar communities had a numerical dominance and also stronghold in Rajasthan, but they were divided into several segments or sub-castes, which also weakened their social and political position. This was resented to by many of the community leaders. Another factor which accounts for the formation of MSCSR movement was the lack of enthusiasm amongst the community fellows for politicizing the Meghwal movement. They were not particularly interested in the social, economic, educational and political programmes of the samaj. It was because of all this that B.L Chirania and his colleagues on January 14, 2004 called a community meeting as Technological Park, Mansarover, Jaipur. There, it was decided to form a new organization. Thus MSCSR came into existence with B.L. Chirania as the chairman.[36]

According to a 12-page yellow pamphlet published and circulated by B.L. Chirania and Madan Lal Dudwal (undated) the major objectives of MSCSR were as follows:

1. To bridge the gap between several segments of Chamar communities and unite them into one group, i.e., Meghwal.
2. To make the samaj free from the habit of drinking and other bad customs and traditions.
3. To organize group marriages.
4. To work for equality and social harmony.
5. To fight for rights.
6. To inculcate good character amongst the youths.
7. To launch a campaign for modernization.
8. To promote and protect the meritorious students.
9. To educate the girls and empowerment of the women.
10. To publish community paper and to have the interaction with community fellows.

Soon after the formation of MSCSR, it became active. It played an important role in bridging the gap between the Chamars and other cognate castes. It first organized a state level seminar at Pink City Press Club, Jaipur, on June 13, 2004, in which a large number of elite, government officials, social workers and political leaders assembled. It was presided over by legislative assembly speaker Smt Sumitra Singh. The guest of honour was Chairman, Scheduled Castes Commission Rajasthan, Hanuman Prasad, Prof Shyamlal and a few others. It was stated that the MSCSR would launch an intensive campaign to unite all the Chamar communities. On this occasion, 'Meghvan Samaj Parichayatmak Directory', consisting of name, father's name, official designation, home address with telephone number of nearly 1,636 elite members of the samaj was also released. Besides, messages, short essays on history of Meghwals, present-day socio-economic conditions of SCs were published. It also included short biographical sketches of some elite members of the samaj. It was edited under the leadership of B.L. Chirania and contains 140 pages.

Chirania took keen interest not only in bridging the gap between Chamar communities of Rajasthan, but also in the social, educational and political affairs of the samaj, He is the chairman of MSCSR since 2004 to the present day (2006). From 2004 onwards, MSCSR intensified its struggle against untouchability and this led to victimization of Chamars by caste Hindus, in civil and criminal cases. In 2004, MSCSR gave the Chamar the slogan of 'One Name and One Identity—The Meghwal'.

MSCSR, which had spread all over Rajasthan over a period of nearly 2 years spearheaded a few agitations and organized as many as 60 meetings and small Sammelans at several cities and towns of Rajasthan state. Notable cities and towns were: Jaipur, Bikaner, Jhunjhunu, Khetri, Nagaur, Neem-ka-Thana, Bagad, Mukundgarh, Navalgarh, Buhana, Bansha, Sikar, Fatehnagar and Laxmangarh. All these attempts had been made to bring about a reconciliation between the different segments of the communities and on September 12, 2004, a Vishal Community Sammelan was organized at Jhunjhunu to unite them into one group. The Sammelan was presided over by B.L. Chirania

According to organizers more than 60,000 men, women, children including Panchas, Sarpanchas, elites of the samaj; and political leaders assembled. The Sammelan passed many resolutions, the main one being the declaration that there would be one name for the Chamar communities, viz., Meghwal. The term Meghwal is flexible enough to incorporate those who follow the occupations of leather and its products. The practice of holding large funeral feast should be banned with immediate effect. This was considered as a crime and that the poor and needy students should be financially supported and helped. The other resolutions stressed the need to mention Meghwal in caste certificate, electricity and water bills and also telephone bill.

Notes

1. For detailed information, see Mohan Lal Kiloniya 'Lekha ka Sankshipta Jiwan Parichaya' in *Meghvansh Itihas*, by Swami Gokul Das Maharaj, Vikram Samvat 2050, p. Ka-Ja. See also, 'Sewa Das Rishi Sri Sri 1008 Swami

Shri Gokul Das ji Maharaj ka Jiwan Charit' in *Jiwan Darshan*... 2005, pp. 37–41.

2. Swami Gokul Das, *Meghvansh Itihas*, Ajmer, Vikram Samvat 2050, pp. 260–61. For more details also see, Sewa Das 'Rishi', *Jiwan Darshan: Yug Purush, Swami Sri Gokul Das Ji Maharaj*, Ajmer 2005, pp. 65–67.
3. Swami Gokul Das, *Meghvansh Ithash*, Ajmer, Vikram Samvat 2050, Ibid., p. Ga, see also, Sewa Das Rishi *Jiwan Darshan*, 2005, p. 18
4. It is necessary to note here that the name of the organization has become a controversial issue, Swami Gokul Das Maharaj in his *Meghvansh Itihas* writes that: 'Rajasthan Meghvansh Maha Sabha, Pushkar, was formed in Vikram Samvat 1977, whereas Sewa Das 'Rishi', the disciple of Swami Gokul Das and also author of *Jiwan Darshan* ascribes an almost different name. According to him, 'Rajasthan Meghvansh Mahasabha, Pushkar' was formed in Vikram Samvat 1977. For distinction between Swami Gokul Das's and Sewa Das 'Rishi's verdict, see, particularly Swami Gokuldas's *Meghvansh, Itihash*, Ajmer, Vikram Samvat 2050, p. Ga and Gha. Sewa Das 'Rishi', *Jiwan Darshan* , Ajmer, 2005, p. 18. The Rajasthan Meghvansh Mahasabha, Pushkar, mentioned above is based on the writings of Swami Gokul Maharaj.
5. Swami Gokul Das, *Meghvansh Itihas*, Vikram Samvat 2050, p. Gha and Da.
6. Ibid., p. Cha.
7. Ibid., p. gha avam da.
8. Ibid., p. chha.
9. Ibid., p. ja.
10. Ibid., p. Da. Full account of his writings reported in Sewa Das 'Rishi', *Jiwan Darshan* 2005, see particularly, Swami Gokul Das Ji Maharaj Dwara Rachit Granth-Sahitya, pp. 143–152.
11. Ibid., p. da.
12. Ibid., p. yan.
13. For the need of 'chapras' for organizing the public meeting by untouchables during the British Raj, a full account of it, reported in Seva Das 'Rishi', *Jivan Darshan* 2005, see particularly, "Samaj Sudhar Sabhayo ki Suraksha Hetu Chapras Prapta Karna", pp. 106–108.
14. Undated letter from Hanuman Prasad Kataria, Ajmer to the author, Jaipur. Letter was received on March 1, 2006 and is with the author.
15. For a detailed discussion of the aims and objectives, office bearers, members of executive committee, rules and sub-rules, membership, meetings, etc., of Rajasthan Maharishi Vashishat Meghvanshi Sootrakar Association, Ajmer,

see in particular, the Constitution of the Association published in 1946. 8-page documents, pp. 1–2.

16. Ibid., p. 3.
17. Ibid., pp. 3–4.
18. For a discussion of Sootrakar movement that stresses the role of Garib Saheb and social consequences of Sootrakar Mahasabha, see, Akhil Bharatiya Sootrakar Maha Sabha-ka-Vidhan, Dilli, Dilli Prantiya Sootrakar Sabha, 24 page documents, 1949, p. 1.
19. Ibid., p. 2.
20. Ibid., p. 2.
21. Ibid., p. 2.
22. Ibid., p. 5.
23. Ibid., p. 3.
24. Ibid., p. 3.
25. Ibid., p. 3.
26. Ibid., p. 4.
27. Ibid., p. 4.
28. Ibid., p. 6.
29. For most important discussion of the origin of Meghvansh Prakash Sabha in Ajmer, Rajasthan, see, Meghvansh Prakash Sabha, Ajmer-ka-Sangh, Vidhan, 23-page document, Ajmer, Meghvansh Sabha, 1967. See in particular Bhoomika of Kanmal Gora, Mantri Meghvansh Prakash Sabha, Ajmer.
30. Ibid.
31. Ibid.
32. Ibid.
33. Ibid.
34. Ibid., pp. 21–22.
35. The most elaborate account of Meghvanshi Samaj Chetna Sansthan, Rajasthan (MSCSR) is given in the pamphlet published and circulated by B.L. Chirania and Madan Lal Dudwal, Organizer and Maha Sachiv of MSCSR, respectively, see 12-page document, *Meghvanshia Samaj Chetna Sansthan, Rajasthan*, published from office, F 314, Vaishali Nagar, Jaipur, Undated. Also see, White pamphlet of the same name containing 8 pages; Yellow pamphlet containing 5 pages and Green pamphlet containing 4 pages. All undated.
36. Ibid.

11 Some Aspects of the Meghwals Caste Movement in South Rajasthan from Pre-Independence to Post-Independence

Critique of Caste Discrimination

Bhairu Lal Meghwal was born on March 12, 1911[1] at village Majavada, district Udaipur. His father Dev Ram Meghwal was a man with progressive ideas. He encouraged members of his family for education. His mother Vijay Bai was a housewife. His father was a hard worker who manufactured leather goods such as 'Joothiya', boots, chappals, horse bridle and Jean, sandle[2] and earned good reputation in his profession. Orthodox Jagirdars, Jamindars and upper caste Hindus were treating the Meghwals, and other low untouchable castes just like animals. His father from his childhood was directly affected by untouchability. Atrocities, harassment and humiliation by Hindu upper castes left an indelible impression on his mind. As a result of this, his grandfather Ramji, uncle Kishna Ram and others left the village and moved to Udaipur. At that time Bhairu Lal Meghwal was only a 12-year old boy.

One of the most significant events of Dev Ram's life occurred in Udaipur during the princely rule. The then His Highness of Mewar State, Maharana Bhupal Singh, GCS, IKC organized a big exhibition. The craftsmen, who prepared and placed their materials in the exhibition, were from upper caste Hindus. The untouchables of Mewar region were also famous for their goods. Dev Ram Meghwal, with his grandfather and uncle also displayed the leather goods prepared by them in the exhibition, for which his father (Dev Ram Meghwal) was honoured by the then

Maharana by presenting him a Silver Medal.[3] It also gave Meghwal community wider popularity and identity. The credit goes to Dev Ram Meghwal.

While his father was staying in Udaipur, Bhairu Lal Meghwal passed his Primary and then Matriculation examination in about 1927, as a private candidate since the Meghwals, Chamars, Balai and other untouchables were not admitted to the schools. He was not interested in practising the traditional work and he took to non-traditional work.

Having attained measures of success in the field of engineering, he turned his attention towards a suitable job. It was because of the customary rules of pollution that untouchables were not given the jobs in government departments. He made several attempts to enter into government job and at last in 1936 he was appointed as steam plant driver at Devasthan Power House, Rishabh Dev.[4] However, this did not create any enthusiasm in him; it rather made him realize that caste barriers were great hindrances in the progress of the community. Later on he was transferred as a charge man of stations at Chittorgarh, Mahar-Mangra Nathdwara, Udai Niwas, Sajjangarh and Jai Samand, the places where Maharana used to visit, from time to time. He not only worked as steam plant driver and incharge of outstations, but also worked as clerk for the time being in the telephone exchange. Similarly, for a short duration, he also served in a cotton factory at Fateh Nagar, Udaipur. The owner of the factory was Roshan Lal Chatur, who was a man of progressive ideas.

It should however, be noted that while Bhairu Lal Meghwal was serving in a cotton factory at Fatehnagar, Udaipur, it was Pandit Onkar Lal Paliwal,[5] who predicted two forecasts about him. First, he could enter into a second marriage which was possible because Meghwal community and other untouchable communities that followed liberal customs permitted so, whereas the upper castes Hindus did not permit bigamy. Second, in the matter of money he would earn more and more money but would remain from hand to mouth. Both these forecasts, to a considerable extent, came out true for him. First, he married Moti Bai, daughter of Rama, village Baharda, district Udaipur. Again after an interval of 12 years he married Chandan Bai, daughter of Nathu Ram, village Badrana, district Udaipur. Moti Bai gave birth to four sons and one daughter, and Chandan Bai gave birth to two sons and one daughter.

Due to caste prejudices and manifestation of deep jealousy of caste Hindus with respect to untouchables, Bhairu Lal Meghwal started thinking of leaving the government job and later on he did so. Thereafter, he turned to a small business. He started a small shop named Mewar Boot Factory.

Soon after this, he was employed as a member of state cotton ginning and pressing factories at Bhilwara and Chhoti Sadri for four years from 1929 to 1933. In the first year he worked as a Marshall's steam engine oilman, in the second year as a 'hydraulic press valve man', in the third year as a 'fire man' and in the fourth year as a 'steam-engine driver'. Thus, he not only worked in various capacities for six years but also succeeded in gaining the knowledge of engines etc. After gaining six years experience, he started correspondence with Lahore Engineering Board, Government of Punjab (now in Pakistan). As a result of this he was called for interview by Chairman of the Board at Lahore. On October 11, 1935[6] when he appeared before the Board interviewers, he was asked the questions related to the profession. According to the Certificate, "having given satisfactory answers to the questions asked by the Board of Examiners, a third class Engineer Certificate of Efficiency was granted to him under the Indian Boilers Act, 1923".[7]

Thus, the basic question for Bhairu Lal Meghwal was to get rid of their status of low untouchables and it was for this purpose that Meghwals launched a small struggle in 1936 under the leadership of Dev Ram Meghwal. Now we will discuss Meghwal Mandal Movement.

The Formation of Meghwal Mandal Udaipur MMU

The Meghwals constituted a significant proportion of population of Udaipur. The members of the untouchable group either worked as farm labourers, or the ritual association of the community with hides, leathers and carrion meant that collectively it carried the stigma of death pollution of the cattle. The close connections between divine social and ritual hierarchies, located the Meghwals at the margins of the caste order and excluded them from Hindu fourfold system.

An examination of the early Meghwal agitation reveals that it did undergo the kinds of changes contained in the concept of social mobilization. The emergence of new elite which was influenced by modern ideas and was prepared to exhort its community to reject traditional values and roles, was particularly crucial a development in the Meghwal community and in the growth of Meghwal 'Agitation'.

In the third decade of twentieth century, around 1936, an untouchable named Dev Ram Meghwal,[8] village Majawara, district

Udaipur initiated a social organization primarily among the Meghwals (traditionally leather workers) of Udaipur, the then princely state of Rajputana. The beginning of the movement dates from 1936, when Bhairu Lal Meghwal, who had suffered from social disabilities and atrocities perpetuated by caste Hindus and had been greatly influenced by his father Dev Ram Meghwal's ideas and views, began to work to reform his community. To translate his father Dev Ram Meghwal's dream into reality, Bhairu Lal Meghwal started his carrier as a social worker within his community in the year 1935 on a war footing. Before he began his campaign, he travelled the length and breadth of the region and also consulted Meghwal Panchas in order to enlist their support and help. Thus, he toured throughout the Mewar region and held meetings at Jhadol, Gogunda, Rishabhadev, Salumber, Vallabhanagar, Kaved, Malvi, Fatehnagar and villages in Chittorgarh. He urged his fellow caste men to abandon their bad habits and to give up socio-religious and ritual practices which impeded their social progress and lowered the social status. What is particularly noteworthy about Meghwal movement in this region is that a large number of social workers came forward to support the social reforms amongst the Meghwals and worked actively under the leadership of Bhairu Lal Meghwal to mobilize the masses for that purpose. A few noted activists from Meghwal community were: Nathu Ram (Sisve village), Bhairu Ram (Visanwas), Partha Ram (Vallabh Nagar) Narain and Balu Ram (Kapoda), Narain (Manpura), Karing and Limba (Takan), Kalu Ram (Kurabada), Moti Shanker and Narain (Baharda), Moti (Barwada), Prem and Udairam (Badrana), and Onkar (Dabok).

In this way Bhairu Lal Meghwal tried to persuade his community fellows to transform their way of life. In addition to Kirtan and work of his community, he also urged his own men to send their children to schools.

Dev Ram Meghwal, Bhairu Lal Meghwal and other Meghwals residing in Mewar region were among the first to realize the value of reform and started to organize themselves and moved in the right direction to implement the said reforms. Dev Ram Meghwal and his son Bhairu Lal Meghwal took the lead and held a community meeting at Majavada. A large number of Meghwals assembled there. Thus, on Saturday, July 25, 1936,[9] they established "Meghwansh Jati Sudharak Mandal, Udaipur (MJSM)" at Majavada and this was the beginning of the community awakening. The first office bearers of this organization were: Dev Ram Meghwal (Majavada) President, Bhairu Lal Meghwal (Majavada) Patron and Pradhan Mantri, Nathu Ram (Godhana) Up-Mantri, Nathu Ram (Badrana) and Bhairu Ram (Vitanvas) Pracharak and Prem Ram (Udaipur) Treasurer. There were 11 members: Partha Ram (Gorana), Nathu Ram (Malpura), Deva Ram (Godana), Ganesh Bhatt (Udaipur), Uda Ram (Gudali), Kalu (Lurda), Charna (Lurda), Mada Ram (Vijanvas), Amra (Jhadol), Nand Ram (Chota Baharda), and Jeeva (Bagpura). Besides the above, there were 4 helpers also: Tulsha (Badrana), Ghasi (Khermaliya), Smt Pema Bai (Danana), and Smt Magni Bai (Damana). Later on in 1951, the name of this Mandal was changed to 'Meghwal Mandal Udaipur'(MMU).

The activities of Meghwansh Jati Sudharak Mandal (MJSM) were significant for the Meghwal movement in the sense that they contributed to awakening of socio-political consciousness amongst the Meghwals. The aims of MJSM[10] were to 'elevate the social, economic as well as spiritual conditions of the untouchable castes/communities by: (1) Promoting modern education, (2) Remedying their socio-religious disabilities, (3) Encouraging them to abandon the social evils, bad habits and customs, (4) Preaching to them the principles of Vedic religion, personal character and good citizenship, and (5) Protecting their socio-political rights.

A few years later (1970), he started a newspaper *The Drashtikon* in order to publicize the activities of MJSM as well as to better integrate the Meghwal community. It was the first newspaper for untouchable Meghwals in all of Rajasthan. The paper operated on a rather meagre budget and experienced financial difficulties almost constantly. It was published fortnightly in Udaipur and an yearly subscription for Udaipur dwellers was Rs 25 (now Rs 50). The cost of an individual issue was Rs 1.40. As it was totally dependent on its caste men for survival and took no financial support from upper caste Hindus, the paper frequently appealed to its readers and fellow Meghwals to contribute liberally to bring its financial position on track. The cost of putting out a paper fortnightly was Rs 100 and while there are no figures on how many copies were published, it seems that its subscription was not sufficient enough to cover the cost. It ran at a loss for nearly 39 years, from the date of its start and was continuously in danger of being disbanded. The paper's importance for development of Meghwal movement lies in three areas. First, its publicizing all holiday meetings all over the Udaipur region, second, its presentation and promotion of socio-economic issues with respect to the Meghwal community in particular and untouchable castes/communities in general and third, its presentation on nature of caste and untouchability.

The MJSM which was registered in 1945 was the forerunner of reforms. An application for registering the MJSM was made to the then Mewar Government, Udaipur in February 1943 by Dev Ram Meghwal and it was registered on December 31, 1945 under Societies Registration Act No. VII of 1941 and its registration No. is 168. The main object of MJSM was to eradicate social evils and to promote socio-religious and economic reform amongst Meghwals and their physical, mental and spiritual development.

The MJSM was formed at the Mewar regional level. Each member had to pay one rupee as entry fee and two rupees as annual fee. The administration of MJSM rested with an Executive Committee of 16 members including the President, Pradhan Mantri, Treasurer and Prachar Mantri, while some members were nominated by the Executive Committee. Others were elected by the general body.

A branch is the smallest local unit roughly corresponding to the Village level. It is managed by a Committee consisting of a President, Vice President, Secretary and Treasurer and a few members. In 1947 there were 12 branches and about 200 members.

The MJSM rose to the position of unifying central organization around 1951, mainly due to the efforts of Dev Ram Meghwal, Bhairu Lal Meghwal and other social workers and activists. Before this period the MJSM had a strong base mainly in Udaipur and in other areas there were no organizations. Around 1940, a few organizations came into existence in Chittorgarh, Jaipur, Ajmer etc. The MJSM grew in popularity and had a few branches and a large number of members and nearly 60 volunteers. The MJSM made an effort to raise itself to an all-Rajasthan level.

The extent of support Bhairu Lal Meghwal was able to command can be gauged with certainty. There are indications that he succeeded to secure support of Chhagan Singh Choudhary, Advocate, Udaipur who in his essays[11] provides much information about 'Meghwal Mandal' in its formative period. He writes that during the early period of the movement, Bhairu Lal Meghwal was supported by many of the upper caste Hindu social reformists, whom Bhairu Lal Meghwal approached. The financial backing for social activities and programmes was also received by

Meghwal community. What is significant about Bhairu Lal Meghwal's movement is that it represented the first attempt by the Meghwals to organize it on their own behalf and moreover it can be said that such an attempt occurred for the first time in that community of Meghwals which had benefitted most from upper caste Hindus. According to Chhagan Singh Choudhary, there were 24 upper caste Hindus in Udaipur region. The number of upper caste Hindus supporting the reform movement during Maharana's rule, therefore, was of statistical significance.

Salient Features of MMU (erstwhile MJSM)

Though the Meghwal Mandal Udaipur (MMU) had a written Constitution, which prescribed objectives, functions, organizational set-up. procedures, norms, rights and responsibilities etc., yet the leaders hardly took it seriously to adhere to the principles enshrined in it. Except a few, most of the Meghwals, did not even know the aims of MMU as mentioned in its Constitution. To them it was an organization for the development of Meghwals.

According to the Constitution, the organization was divided into district, Tehsil, city and village-level units with elected Executive Committee having president, vice president and secretary at each level. District units were formed in Udaipur, Chittorgarh, and Jaipur. However, they hardly met even once a year except on occasions when MMU's conference was held. Except for a few district leaders who enjoyed state level positions, none cared to enrol members or to send reports of the units regarding their activities to the state office. A regular office with well maintained record was run only by Udaipur district unit.

Yearwise detailed figures of membership were not available for all the years. This only indicates that a large number of Meghwals were not interested in getting themselves enrolled as members of the MMU. In order to know more about the nature of membership the author collected the information through conversation with social and political leaders. During conversation the following points emerged:

1. Membership of MMU was not constant, both in terms of members and individuals. Sometimes it enrolled more than hundred and at other times, it hardly registered any member. Similarly, some individuals did not usually continue their membership from year to year. This was so because the Meghwals took their membership very casually. They paid membership fee only when approached by the leader.

2. The decision-making and executive powers of MMU were concentrated in the president and secretary—the core positions. These omnipotent offices had so far been occupied by two male leaders. For the first four years the offices were held by two leaders—Dev Ram Meghwal, and Bhairu Lal Meghwal. The other office bearers of MMU at the state level were—Treasurer, Organizing Mantri. These chairs were occupied by several Meghwals at a time.
3. An analysis of various resolutions passed by MMU at its annual meetings showed that there were issues which were to be highlighted. First, a number of resolutions concerned reformative measures, such as, the abolition of dowry, ban on death feast, strong plea for eradication of the use of liquor and child marriage, ban on second marriage of women while the first husband is alive and ban on eating the flesh of dead animals. MMU directed that Meghwals should promote the Dharm Vivaha and not to accept Dhapa (bride price) at the time of marriage. Second, there was a concern about the untouchability, particularly in rural areas and they encouraged the anti-untouchability movement. Third, they supported issues that the local units were interested in, for instance, the problem of inadequate educational facilities and job opportunities for SCs which was a matter of concern to many SCs including Meghwals in different parts of the state. In Rajasthan this issue gained a regional focus and MMU in its annual meeting, held from time to time, passed a resolution urging the government to provide more and more facilities to SC candidates.
4. From 1936 onwards MMU remained very active. On November 16, 1999 Bhairu Lal Meghwal breathed his last. Since then MMU remained inactive for some period. However, since then MMU has been energized by wide recognition and has emerged as the soul of Meghwals.

Some Aspects of Dalits and Non-Dalits and their Involvement

It is necessary at this juncture to discuss the role played by some of the upper caste Hindus in the activities of Meghwal Mandal, Udaipur (MMU) in order to fight against the social injustice, removal of the evil of untouchability, atrocities and disabilities.

Chhagan Singh Choudhary

A native of Mewar state, Chhagan Singh Choudhary[12] went to Banaras in the year 1929 for higher education. He was admitted in the 1st year of three-year Degree Course (Arts) in Banaras Hindu University. 'Sarvayaga Andolan' at the national level was an agitation to demand Swaraj for India. It was launched by Gandhi in 1929. During this period Pandit Madan Mohan Malviya[13]—the then Vice-Chancellor of Banaras Hindu University gave a call to the students throughout Banaras to participate in large number in the agitations. In response to his call, every day a large number of batches of students took part in the agitation and courted arrest. The Indian National Congress was committed to the removal of evils of untouchability under the leadership of Gandhi. Soon the campaign for removal of untouchability gained momentum. While M.M. Malviya's call encouraged the students to participate in the agitation, a few Banaras Hindu University students participated in the Harijan upliftment programme. Chhagan Singh Choudhary, as a first year student of Banaras Hindu University was highly impressed by Gandhi's Harijan programme[14] for the welfare of untouchables. Chhagan Singh Choudhary took active part in the propagation of removal of untouchability campaign in Banaras. It was for this reason that he, along with other students, arranged a collective food programme of both the upper caste Hindus and low caste untouchables and wanted the support of upper caste Hindus for removal of untouchability and upliftment of the downtrodden. He succeeded in winning their support. He and his colleagues arranged several public meetings in villages appealing the caste Hindus to throw open the public wells and temples for untouchables. They also launched a campaign to remove untouchability. Thus, with the Gandhian influence, Chhagan Singh Choudhary returned back to Mewar in 1935 as a law graduate from Banaras Hindu University. Nearly 3 months after his arrival, he started his practice at Udaipur. After a few months he came to know about Bhairu Lal Meghwal and his socio-religious agitation from Laher Singh Mehta—a well-known personality of Mewar and later on became a judge in Rajasthan High Court.

Soon after this, he met Bhairu Lal Meghwal in 1936.[15] Bhairu Lal Meghwal had detailed discussions with Choudhary about his ongoing social agitation. He also apprised Choudhary of three things: The pitiable socio-economic conditions of the untouchables in Mewar state, the disabilities imposed by upper caste Hindus on untouchables and atrocities perpetrated by Jagirdars, Jamindars and others on untouchables. Choudhary was highly impressed by the socio-religious agitation Bhairu Lal Meghwal had launched. Thus, Choudhary was prepared to cooperate with Bhairu Lal Meghwal to fight against all this. He was also pleased to find many social activists, workers and a few literate persons among the Meghwals and considered them as good as those from upper castes. He was aggrieved to see that low caste people were treated as untouchables by upper caste Hindus.

Choudhary's involvement had a direct effect on MMU as he was able to place before the Mewar government the real picture to solve their socio-economic and educational problems. As a result of Choudhary's efforts MMU submitted several letters, applications, memorandums, reminders, replies etc., (all in English) requesting the President of Indian Union that Meghwal, Bhambhi and Balai be included in the list of SCs in the state of Rajasthan and constitute all the double-seated constituencies in India in single-seated constituency to enable the SCs candidates to contest.

It may be noted that at last in November 1956,[16] the Government of India announced that Meghwal, Bhambhi and Balai be included in the list of SCs in the state of Rajasthan. The double-seated constituencies were converted into single-seated constituencies in India.

Besides the inclusion of Meghwal, Bhambhi and Balai in the list of SCs, Choudhary as a real sympathizer of untouchables paid a good deal of attention to their socio-economic problems. Under his leadership the MMU became well-organized and acquired the character of a wider mass movement. He prepared an organizational plan to enrol the social workers and activists at the village level. Within no time a large number of volunteers were enrolled. The MMU in the 1936 was however, a more effective organization in Mewar only.

Choudhary served the real cause of untouchables in three ways—first he served as a legal adviser of MMU, second, he worked to get the disabilities removed for the welfare and progress of the low untouchable communities, and third, by involving himself actively in MMU programmes, he championed the cause of untouchables' rights.

Religious reforms movement, started by Arya Samaj, was regenerated by social action of Choudhary. Meghwals gained several privileges such as access to educational institutions, performance of religious sacrifices, Yagya, Havan and use of sacred thread that were being used by the

Brahmins. Choudhary, Bhairu Lal Meghwal and other leaders of the movement had a reference group of Arya Samaj in mind while fighting against the discrimination in the fields of education and socio-religious privileges. The other untouchable communities also had similar grievances against the Hindus. Hence, other untouchable castes joined hands with Meghwals' movement in achieving social justice.

Choudhary also initiated the prohibition movement as an aspect of MMU's activities from 1936. Use of liquor, gambling, child marriage, death feast, Gangabhog, Dhapa (bride price) etc., were the acute problems amongst Meghwal, Bhambi and Balai. There were also many social vices among the Meghwals. Under these circumstances, the prohibition movement among Meghwals was beset with serious problems. Individual leaders like Choudhary, Bhairu Lal Meghwal and others took a leading part in the movement by persuading the Meghwals to boycott these evils. Although the movement had initially some success in certain parts yet it was on the whole not successful.

The agitation for political rights and representation in the Rajasthan state legislature, formed the next activity in the history of MMU movement. The earlier activities of Choudhary discussed above were, first, the social awakening, second, the religious reforms and third, to characterizing it by fighting for the rights of admission to government schools and fighting court cases against untouchabilities under the leadership of Choudhary as a lawyer.

Prabhu Lal Meghwal

Another notable leader, who was associated with the activities of MMU during its early days in Mewar region, was Prabhu Lal Meghwal[17] of Chhoti Sadri. His father, Vala was a very poor man. His mother, Yamuna Bai, was a housewife. Prabhu Lal Meghwal, born in about 1901–02, was from his very childhood, directly affected by disabilities and status of the untouchables. His father was a poor farmer and had 3 bighas of agricultural land and a kachha Tapra (hut) in the village. His father was not a man with progressive ideas. He did not encourage his son Prabhu Lal Meghwal to learn Hindi. B.L. Meghwal, RAS son of Prabhu Lal Meghwal mentions in his essay "Jatiya Gaurav Badhanewale Yashswi Saput: Prabhu Lal Meghwal", that during the regime of princely states untouchables were not admitted in any schools and so his father (Prabhu Lal Meghwal) could not get his childhood education. In another instance narrated in his essay,

B.L. Meghwal mentions that when his father (Prabhu Lal Meghwal) had grown up, he realized and experienced that we are backward because of illiteracy[18] and my father (Prabhu Lal Meghwal) had to go to a Muslim Moulvi's[19] house to learn Hindi at night, because Brahmin and Baniyas did not teach the untouchables. The discrimination between upper caste Hindus and untouchables with regard to the use of public roads, tanks and wells, admission to schools, and entry into temples, recruitment to government jobs etc., had left indelible impression on his mind. After his primary education at Moulvi's house and with the encouragement given by the Moulvi,[20] he started to read *Ramacharitamanas, Satyarth Prakash, Geeta, Mahabharat* and many other books. Prabhu Lal Meghwal had by now gained self-confidence and began to assert his influence. The need to improve the economic conditions of the family became apparent. Such strong economic conditions helped him to work out a programme of action for fighting against the various kinds of discriminations and deprivations. He also purchased 40 bighas of agricultural land and this enhanced his economic condition, which made him realize that strong economic condition and education were essential for progress and therefore, he decided to work along with Bhairu Lal Meghwal. Prabhu Lal Meghwal met Bhairu Lal Meghwal and discussed with him how they could elevate their socio-economic condition and talked about the necessity for social regeneration of Meghwals and for having a strong organizational base all over Rajasthan in order to spread the message.

As a most active worker of MMU, Prabhu Lal Meghwal did much to bring about a new cultural awakening amongst the Meghwals of Mewar by launching a reform movement. Since the MMU was associated with the leadership of Prabhulal Meghwal, it is necessary to assess his contribution to MMU movement. While Bhairu Lal Meghwal pressed to fight the cause of the Meghwals, Prabhu Lal Meghwal led the movement with his boldness and powerful speeches in district Mandsor of Madhya Pradesh, (Kundal, Kanthal, Neemuch and Palsod all in M.P.) and district Chittorgarh, Rajasthan, of which he was a native member. He spearheaded the social movement in these areas and exposed the cruelties of the upper caste Hindus through his speeches. He also challenged the atrocities perpetrated and discrimination thrust upon them.

He led a crusade against atrocities and discrimination to gain sympathy of Meghwal boys and girls along with other untouchable children to get them admitted in the public schools, allow them the use of public wells, entry into temples, to wear ornament made of gold and silver, to ride on a mare and the use of band at the time of marriage etc. It was customary for the caste system that untouchables including Meghwals were not allowed to do so. For instance, the marriage party of Pholchand,[21] son of Prabhu Lal Meghwal was to go from Chhoti Sadri to Mahudiya a Brahmin dominated village through Soniyana village. This Soniyana village was also dominated by Rajputs. Meghwals feared that upper caste Hindus might reprimand them if they break the customary rules. Thus, the basic question for Prabhu Lal Meghwal was to get rid of these rules. It was for this purpose that the marriage party took five guns and 7–8 swords with them so that they might use them at the time of violence. However, there was no clash between Meghwals—Brahmins and Rajputs. Thus, he showed a unique courage which perhaps few would have dared to do. Thus, under his guidance the Meghwal movement received self-confidence. This did create enthusiasm among the masses, which made them realize that courage was essential for progress in educationally and socially backward communities and therefore, decided to oppose the traditional rules. Age-old usage prevented untouchables from using butter or 'gur' in wedding feasts, barbers did not serve them. They were not allowed to sit on a 'khat' in the presence of upper caste Hindus. The leaders encouraged Meghwals to wear neat and clean clothes and use ornaments. Agitation against the removal of untouchability was launched. When Prabhu Lal Meghwal started opposing the ban on the use of good clothes, ornaments, admission to schools, the upper caste Hindus harassed, tortured and humiliated him. He was not only tortured but also involved in false court cases.

The persons of the first generation of leadership besides Bhairu Lal Meghwal at the Mewar Regional level were: Prabhu Lal Meghwal, Moda Ram, Pannalal, Narain Lal Kanod, Bhera Ram, and at the local level: Balu Ram, Partha Ram, Nathu Ram and Narain Manpur (all Meghwal).

Prabhu Lal Meghwal took lead in intense agitation[22] against social evils. Besides the school admission and temple entry movement, he also initiated the prohibition movement, as an aspect of MMU's activities during pre-Independence period. Prohibition was one of the MMU's constructive programmes and was one of the main programmes of reform, which Prabhu Lal Meghwal had initiated in Chhoti Sadri of Chittorgarh district, Rajasthan and Kundal, Kanthal, Neemach and Palsoda areas of Mandsor district, Madhya Pradesh. Consumption of liquor was an acute problem amongst the Meghwals who used to take dowry money from groom's parents before the marriage. At the time of marriages and some other occasions they used to sing obscene songs. There were also many persons who removed the dead animals and skinned them. Eating the meat of dead animals was also very common. Under these circumstances the prohibition movement[23] among the Meghwals was beset with serious problems. A few individual leaders like Prabhu Lal Meghwal took a leading part in the movement by imposing ban and disuading them (Meghwals) from all these evils.

The programme of activities that concerned them were: ban on the use of meat and alcohol in public functions, stopping of Dhapa (bride price), abolition of singing of obscene songs, stopping child marriages, diverting Meghwals from leather work to other crafts, promotion of education among Meghwals, stopping of the removal of dead animals and skinning them. Besides, when Prabhu Lal Meghwal started agitation in Chhoti Sadri areas, the Meghwals had already started calling themselves as descendants of Sant Ravidas.[24] Similarly, since they were dealing with leather they were called Chamar also. Prabhu Lal Meghwal prohibited them from using the term 'Ravidas Vanshi' and 'Chamar'. He not only prohibited them from using the customary terms but also played a leading role and succeeded in popularizing the new term 'Meghwal'[25] from 'Chamar' and descendants of Sant Ravidas, which gave the movement—an ideology and a distinct identity to the community. They sought to reform their way of life by a process of self-withdrawal, organization and protest. Having attained to some extent a measure of success in the field of social reform, the leaders of MMU turned their attention to fight against another sphere of injustice namely Begar—the economic exploitation.

Prabhu Lal took lead in intense agitation against Begar[26] (forced labour) demanding abolition of it. It was an agitation against the economic exploitation by the upper caste Hindus such as Jagirdars, Jamindars, Thakurs and others.

Constructing Reform: The Initiative of MMU and Arya Samaj's Response

By early 1920s the influence of the Arya Samaj on untouchables in Rajasthan was noticed. The assumption was that the aims and objects of the Arya Samajists were unique and distinct from those of caste Hindus and that Arya Samajists all over India should share a set of common aims and objects despite the particularities of untouchable castes and regions.

The increasing influence of Arya Samaj in the form of socio-religious reformers amongst the untouchables was also related to the socio-political situation at that time. For instance the discussion held in the year 1932 regarding Gandhi-Ambedkar pact (popularly known as Poona Pact) for upliftment of untouchables of India and campaign for socio-religious reforms were taking place. Other organizations had launched the socio-reform movement and had organized untouchable communities which represented their special points of view—the most prominent example being, of course, the Rajputana 'Harijan Sewak Sangh' with campaign for abolition of untouchability. In view of social urgency, therefore, it was decided to do the social work amongst the untouchables which would bring them back into the Vedic religion, hence Arya Samajists focussed on untouchables.

It was mentioned earlier that Bhairu Lal Meghwal who was leading the intense agitation against the practice of untouchability and to get admission of the untouchable children to schools was from his childhood days directly influenced by Arya Samaj. In one of his essays, Virendrapal Singh Rana,[27] a freedom fighter of Udaipur mentions that he (Bhairu Lal Meghwal) used to read the literature of Arya Samaj. In the course of his study he came in contact with some of the Arya Samajists who were well-versed in Vedas. Under these circumstances, Bhairu Lal Meghwal came under the influence of Arya Samajists. Thus, he emerged as an Arya Samajist leader by 1948. He formed his own system of thought, oriented towards social transformation and maintained that the reformation of Meghwal community was a necessary adjunct to the upliftment of the masses. He made extensive tours, propagating Vedic religion and meeting his own people. The strategy that he adopted was to abandon the idol worship, and asked his fellow caste men to throw statues of gods and goddesses into rivers, water tanks and wells. He taught his caste men the Vedic religion. It were Brahmins and other upper caste Hindus who had denied the Meghwals and other low caste untouchables the rights to participate in Brahminical Hinduism, including the rights to study the Vedas and right to recite and listen to the Vedic Mantras. His views seemed to have stirred a hornet's nest as he drew references to prove his points, one, in the Ramcharitamanas where it reads "Dhol, Ganwaar, Shudra, Pashu aur Naari, Yeh Sab Taaran Ke Adhikari" (drum, illiterate,

Dalits, animals and women, all are fit only to be beaten)'. The other, in the Manu Smriti where it lays down punishment for Dalits who dare to hear the recitation of the Vedas (pouring molten lead into their ears) and cutting off their tongues, if they recite the Vedas. All such references he argued promoting untouchability and negate social guarantee of equality and social justice. The strategy that he adopted was to perform Vedic Yagya at the village level and chanted the Vedic Mantras at the village level, which provided the social basis for the Brahmin to acquire a high ritual status. This attracted the attention of Hindus of upper castes. Bhairu Lal Meghwal was of the opinion that all men had to study the Vedas to perform Yagya, chant the Mantras and oppose the view that only Brahmins had the right to recite the Mantras. One of the programmes of action, directed towards the achievement of this goal, was to promote Vedic religion among the members of low castes, such as, Meghwals, Bhambhis, Chamars and Balais.

Besides propagating Vedic religion in 1960[28] he also wrote, published and distributed a 36-point programme of moral conduct for socio-spiritual reform and of carrying out action-oriented programmes such as performing Yagya, stopping idol worship and encouraging Vedic religion. In public meetings it was also read out and stressed upon the importance of the 36-point programme of moral conduct which was also appreciated by the Hindus of upper castes.

In the last six decades of the twentieth century, attempts were made by MMU leaders to change their traditional religious beliefs and practices and it was only with the propagation of Arya Samaj ideology that it emerged as a widely spread movement. For instance, on September 27–28, 1966,[29] MMU convened a two-day Vishal Sammelan of workers and social activists at village Jarkhada, Tehsil Badi Sadri of district Chittorgarh, for the welfare of the community. On September 1966 Kulpati Gurukul Chittorgarh, Vartanand presided over the Sammelan. More than 100 workers and activists attended this Sammelan. All the main speakers particularly Vartanand Sarvanand, Balvant Singh, Bhanwar Lal Joshi, Chhagan Singh Choudhary and Madan Lal Mehta addressed the gathering about the socio-educational, economic and political development of the untouchables and won their approval. A procession was taken through the main bazaar of the village. The young social activist, Kailash Meghal, also addressed the Sammelan and Swagat Aadhiyaksh Modi Ram expressed his gratitude for extending support to the Sammelan.

One of the most significant decisions taken in the Sammelan, was the formation of a Committee[30] consisting of 6 members. The names of the members were: Khem Raj Siyal (Dudhalia), Pyarchand Solanki (Bilot), Udai Ram Raloti (Gudel), Ghashi Ram Parmar (Karju), Nand Ram Babal (Geeunli), and Bhairu Lal Kamali (Semada). The main object of the Committee was to convene and manage the Vishal Sammelan at Udaipur and Vishal Dev Yagya at Chittorgarh in 1967 respectively.

Another most significant event of the first day Sammelan was the submission of a four-point memorandum[31] to the state government for taking up positive measures for the betterment of the Samaj.

1. To take hard measures to ban or eradicate untouchability.
2. To issue the directives to Panchayat, block development officers and police personnels to implement the laws in letter and spirit.
3. To appoint a State Vigilance Committee to look after the violation of law in the state.
4. To remove the hurdles in the allotment of the agriculture lands to untouchables.

Addressing the Sammelan Prabhu Lal Sisodia of Chhoti Sadri, Chittorgarh asked the people to abandon the social vices.

On second day, September 28, 1966[32] Prabhu Lal Sisodia of Chhoti Sadri, Chittorgarh presided over the Sammelan. The MMU at its session in Jarkhada village resolved to raise sufficient funds for holding the next Sammelan and Dev Yoga in 1967 at Udaipur and Chittorgarh respectively, to increase the membership of MMU by enrolling boys and girls above 18 years, to publish and circulate the list of the dedicated volunteers of castemen for its wide publicity, to hold as many meetings as possible at different places for wide publicity, to authorize Chairman and Pradhan Mantri, MMU to spend Rs 50 to Rs 100 and Rs 25 to 50 respectively for official purpose and to impart training to those persons who would participate in Dev Yagya to be held in 1967 at Chittorgarh.

On June 30, 1969[33] the first Meghwal Pratinidhi Sammelan was held at Vallabh Nagar, Udaipur and a Charter of the following demands was submitted to the Government of Rajasthan and the Government of India:

1. To provide educational facilities to the weaker sections of the society, more particularly SCs, two hostels accommodating at least 100 boys be opened at each tehsil headquarter and district headquarters of the state.

2. To improve their economic conditions, small scale industries/udyog etc., be started at district level.
3. To provide more and more economic security to low untouchable communities.
4. To appoint a Commission at the state level to conduct the socio-economic survey of these downtrodden people to know the root cause of their economic backwardness and problems connected with lands. Also suggest the measures to improve their conditions.
5. To ensure that Matric, B.A. and M.A. passed SCs candidates be appointed in government jobs.
6. To execute government orders banning the death feast forcefully.
7. To execute the Sharda Act (Child Marriage Act, 1929) vigorously.
8. To impose untouchability offence Act forcefully in the state. Even after 21 years of Independence untouchability is still being observed, untouchables are not allowed to use the public wells and tanks.
9. To employ more and more well educated SCs candidates particularly in the Social Welfare Department, Government of Rajasthan.

After submission of the memorandum, District Social Welfare Officer, Udaipur, Kalu Lal Sukhwal, called Bhairu Lal Meghwal to his office. Bhairu Lal Meghwal went to District Social Welfare Office and impressed upon Kalu Ram Sukhwal the need for providing sufficient education to SCs/STs in order to get them government jobs and to fight for citizenship rights. Thus, under Bhairu Lal Meghwal's guidance the MMU received a modern touch.

From the account of events in MMU's history given by Kusum Meghwal—editor of 'Meghwal Mandal' Udaipur (1985), it will be seen that a two-day Executive Committee from April 22–23, 1970[34] was convened at village Majawada, under the Chairmanship of Balvant Singh and more than 150 workers of Arya Samaj attended it. On April 22, the Committee took an active interest in discussing the issue for social reforms. Besides social reforms, the Committee also discussed plans to carry out action oriented programmes. On second day, April 23, the Committee passed the annual budget of Rs 21,066 for carrying out various programmes and activities. It was also decided to invite Kulpati Gurukul Chittorgarh Swami Vartanand to preside over and Maharana of Mewar Bhagwat Singh to inaugurate the Adhiveshan to be held at Udaipur in 1970. It was also decided to invite Maharaja Sudarshan Singh of Shahpura to inaugurate the Dev Yagya to be held at Chittorgarh. More than 94 years ago, fire was lighted in the palace of Maharajadhiraj

Shahpura by Swami Dayanand Saraswati which is still burning. The Committee took special interest in bringing it in Dev Yagya at Chittorgarh. Thus, the Committee laid emphasis on Vedic strength with a view to gaining self-respect and esteem. Various committees were formed for carrying out different responsibilities.

From December 20–21, 1972[35] a two-day general meeting of MMU was held under the presidentship of Chatar Lal Mundra—Pradhan of VHP, Udaipur at Arya Samaj Bhawan, Udaipur. Krishnanad, Anil Sharma, Bhagirath Joshi, Bhanwar Lal Joshi, Ranjeetlal Agarwal, Chhagan Singh Choudhary, Virendra Pratap Singh and Niral Singh Shekhawat attended the meeting. All the speakers in their address supported the reform movement. Three new committees, i.e., Executive Committee headed by Hemraj Meghwal, Advisory Committee headed by Chhagan Singh Choudhary and Propaganda Committee headed by Ram Lal Meghwal came into existence in December 1972 to manage the forthcoming Sammelan at Udaipur and Chittorgarh.

The foregoing account of MMU's achievement, establishes that MMU provided a Vedic ideology which brought out religious regeneration and gave the untouchables self-confidence and respect.

Vershtiyagya Bhupalpura, Udaipur, 1973[36]

From June 10–17, 1973 the MMU arranged an eight day Vershtiyagya at Bhupalpura, Udaipur. It was held under the aegis of Arya Samaj, Bhupalpura. Prof Prithvi Singh Lama, the then Vice Chancellor of Udaipur University, presided over the function. President of Pesticide, India, Udaipur and also District President of VHP Udaipur, P.P. Singhal inaugurated it. Balvant Singh—former Pradhan of Arya Samaj Udaipur, arranged all Vedic activities at Bhupalpura from the beginning to the end. The programmes of performing Yagya, Havan etc., started in the morning from 4–6 daily. Vedavagish Arya Gurukul Chittorgarh Satyavrat Shastri, Pradhan Arya Samaj Bhupalpura—Bhanwar Lal Joshi, Mantri Arya Samaj Bhupalpura—Shree Krishna Pareek and Virendra Singh Barna attended it. Up-pradhan Arya Samaj Shahpura—Ram Nivas Joshi sat and performed Yagya, Havan etc.

On the first day Laxmi Chand Meghwal—a civil engineer also took part in the Yagya. Besides, Kalu Ram, Nathu Ram, Jivan Ram and Dhan Ram (all Meghwals) participated in Yagya with their wives. Pradhan of Arya Samaj, Udaipur, Uderalal presided over the concluding session,

Chhagan Singh Choudhary, Dr Brij Mohan Jawlia, Up-pradhan Arya Pratinidhi—Rajasthan, Thakur Roop Singh Chundawat, Udaipur, Thakur Lal Singh Shaktawat, Vanprashthi Udaipur, Ramgopal Bhuratia MLA Madhya Pradesh and Thakur Balwant Singh Panchvati Udaipur took active part in the Yagya. They emphasized upon the importance of Vershtiyagya in our life.

Gaining confidence by this success in the equality of citizenship agitation, MMU concentrated its efforts on holding the convention of social activists, making it a part of the equality of citizenship and social justice movement. After five years of Vershtiyagya, MMU arranged another big Karyakarta Adhiveshan from June 11–12, 1978[37] at village Siyarda district Udaipur under the Chairmanship of Hem Raj Solanki. Banwarilal Joshi, Chhagan Singh Choudhary, Virendra Pal Singh Barna, Parmanand Sindhi, Gyarsi Lal Bairwa, Chenna Ram Meghwal, Mota Ram Meghwal and Prakash Chandra Meghwal attended the Adhiveshan and made effective speeches, appealing to abandon social vices. They also urged to strengthen the social organization and persuaded them to agitate for social and political rights. Although they did not get approval from state government and central government for holding the Vishal Sammelan and Dev Yagya at Chittorgarh, yet a resolution for holding them was approved. Bagdi Ram Meghwal as an active social worker of MMU, Chittorgarh moved this resolution and Mota Ram Meghwal (Sanwad) district Sirohi seconded it.

It was resolved that Maharana Bhagwat Singh, Udaipur be requested to preside over the Sammelan and Defence Minister, Government of India Babu Jagjivan Ram to inaugurate it. Similarly, Chief Minister Rajasthan, Bhairon Singh Shekhawat was requested to inaugurate the Dev Yagya at Chittorgarh.

It was further resolved that to meet the heavy expenditure of running the Sammelan roughly estimated from Rs 25–30,000, a special campaign be launched to collect donations.

As stated earlier in the year 1935, MMU had launched a campaign to remove evils of untouchability, to demand the right of admission for the untouchables in schools, use of public wells and tanks and taken initiative in the propagation of the removal of social evils programmes in Mewar state. Since then MMU has still been agitating for the betterment of the down-trodden. Now MMU wants to extend its activities throughout Rajasthan state. It was for this reason that MMU resolved to dissolve the

MMU after the convention of Chittorgarh and to start a new organization namely Garibjan Vikas Mandal (GJVM) throughout the state. This resolution was moved by Virendra Singh Barna, Udaipur and seconded by Gyarsilal Bairwa Kuti, Bandikui, Jaipur. Virendrapal Singh Barna's resolution was passed unanimously for the establishment of Garibjan Vikas Mandal (GJVM). A small committee came into existence to draft the Constitution of the new organization GJVM under the leadership of Bhairu Lal Meghwal, Mahamantri of MJSM and Up-Mantri Virendrapal Singh Barna. Bhairulal Meghwal and others were authorized to move an application for registering the GJVM. They would seek the legal advice and guidance from Advocate Chhagan Singh Choudhary. The main object of GJVM was to promote and protect the interest of the larger untouchable communities.

The formation of two committees provided a landmark in the development of GJVM, the first being the 'Up-samiti' headed by Khemraj Meghwal, village Meharta, Tehsil Mavali with ten members and the second—'the seva samiti' headed by Roop Lal Meghwal, Siyarda, Tehsil Girva with 10 members.

Programme of MJSM/MMU's Movement

A series of meetings, Sammelans, Vedic Yagya, Havan etc., had been held since 1935 onwards entirely in respect of the issue of untouchability. This was a manifestation of social protest of low caste untouchables in respect of social evils and socio-religious disabilities imposed upon them by Hindu upper castes. The untouchables were now agitating for the right of entry into public schools. The MMU was becoming a powerful organization to reckon with, and industrial exhibitions, it organized from time to time in various places, were a success and were widely publicized. The untouchables gained self-confidence and began to assert their independence.

On April 1, 1946[38] MJSM held its first executive meeting at Udaipur which happened to be the headquarters of MJSM, and discussed several issues. The meeting was chaired by Dev Ram Meghwal and 13 executive members attended it. The MJSM at its meeting held on April 1, 1946 at Udaipur, discussed issues regarding registration of MJSM, obtaining registration certificate, to pass the annual budget for carrying out day-to-day activities and programmes in the next year, to collect the donations and also intimate and apprise the caste fellows of all these achievements. The second executive meeting of MJSM was held on October 1, 1946 at Udaipur. In this meeting 11 executive members took part. The meeting was chaired by Bhairu Lal Meghwal—the Pradhan Mantri of MJSM and a few resolutions were passed in the meeting. As a result of this, MJSM managed to publish and distribute 500 copies of pamphlets in the villages giving detailed information about the aims and objects of MJSM and Dhapa was banned. A campaign for social awakening was engineered to create the consciousness among the fellow caste men. Similarly, the meeting also authorized the Chairman and Pradhan Mantri of MJSM to spend some money on publicity.

The First Public Meeting of MJSM

The MJSM held a public meeting after briefing its previous activities; the account of income and expenditure was presented. Later on, budget for the year 1947–48 was also passed.

MJSM also managed to hold the elections of the new Executive Committee in the Sammelan and the result showed that almost all the members of the committee were elected. A resolution to ban the bride price was moved by Bhairu Lal Meghwal and was passed unanimously on this occasion. Dev Ram Meghwal and Bhairu Lal Meghwal expressed their views on how to implement the resolutions. Four students namely: Dal Shankar, Laxman Chand, Prem Shankar and Kailash Chand expressed their feelings regarding the betterment of the Samaj. The Chairman of the Reception Committee, Jalu Ram Dalwada and many others, also supported the resolution for the success of the Sammelan.

The MJSM managed to hold the elections and results showed that Dev Ram Meghwal (President) Bhairu Lal Meghwal (Pradhan Mantri), Balu Ram (Sahkari Mantri) Ghasi Ram (Prachar Mantri) and Narain (Pracharak) and 12 other persons were elected to the new Executive Committee. From the point of view of social awakening movement, this was a great success.

Special Meeting[39]

The MJSM held a special meeting at Udaipur on March 1, 1947 and passed two Resolutions. First, to publish and distribute 200 copies of pamphlets to raise the fund to carry out smoothly, effectively and systematically the various socio-educational programmes, and second, to decide the final date for the first convention at Majavada. Chairman, Pradhan

Mantri and some executive members belonging to MJSM started visiting village after village, and meeting and talking to people from house to house-to-persuade caste men to abandon the death feast as it was an evil and had already been banned.

The MJSM held its third executive meeting[40] on November 21, 1947 at Udaipur under the Chairmanship of Bhairu Lal Meghwal. It was attended by 12 executive members. In this meeting it approved to hold the first convention in February 1948 at Majavada. As a result of this, various sub-committees were formed and different members were assigned responsibilities. Another important decision that was taken by the Executive Committee was to invite as many as 100 to 150 representatives from all over Mewar region. A strategy was adopted by the committee to print a song (composed by B.L. Meghwal) on the invitation card for awakening the Samaj to abandon the social vices and to create unity amongst the Meghwal, Bhambhi and Balai communities. The stanzas of the song are produced below:[41]

सोते जागो मेघवाल भाई, अब सोने का जमाना नहीं है
जाति मण्डल कायम हुआ है, सप्रेम इसको अपनाना है
द्वेष भाव दिल से निकाल, एकता के बधंन मे आना है। (1)
'जाति हित मे तन–मन–धन अर्पण करना अपना धर्म है
जाति सुधार करने में ही, अपना जीवन बिताना है। (2)
जाति की शान बढाना है, पिछडो को गले लगाना है
कुरीतियों को भेंट कर, सुरीतियों की नीव जमाना है
जाति सेवा सुधार करना, गंगा स्नान समाना है
यही आण बाण पालकर , भावसागर से तरना है
भैरूलाल मेघवाल अन्तिम यह सन्देश सुनाता है
जाति निज मे, नव जीवन ज्योति जगाना है। (5)
सोते जागो मेघवाल भाई, अब सोने का नही जमाना है

The main issues[42] to be discussed in the forthcoming convention were:

1. To chalk out a plan to reorganize the MJSM.
2. To review socio-political scenario of the country.
3. To chalk out the plan to eradicate the social vices from the Samaj.
4. To plan the programmes and various activities for the betterment of the Samaj.
5. To discuss religious issues.
6. To elect new Executive Committee.
7. To present the accounts of income and expenditure for the last year.

8. To present the budget for the year 1948, and
9. To present the detailed report on the various programmes carried out among the caste fellows.

First Sammelan at Village Majavada, 1948[43]

The MJSM held a three-day historic Sammelan on February 1 to 3, 1948 at village Majavada, Udaipur. The Sammelan was presided over by Dev Ram Meghwal and more than 125 representatives attended it.

The leaders of MJSM, at its meeting paid floral tribute to late Mahatma Gandhi. The main concern of MJSM now shifted from prohibition to protest, which the Mewar government realized and was concerned about it. The low caste untouchable communities were being discriminated by the Hindu upper castes. MJSM which had protested against discrimination had passed 11 resolutions. Similarly, all the assembled untouchables had signed and put their thumb impressions on an application. Later on the leaders of MJSM submitted the signed application along with resolutions passed by them to the then government of Mewar state. They also submitted the same to Bhupal Singh, the then Maharana of Mewar state.

The campaign of MJSM assumed significant character and created a statewide awakening. The Meghwals, Bhambhis and Balais as a whole were happy by this move of MJSM. The waves of this agitation reached the entire Mewar region and even other regions of Rajputana. The leaders also framed 15 norms in the meeting to eradicate the social evils and vices from their communities and for the betterment of the Samaj. The norms are as follows:

1. To educate their children and to observe the Vedic religion.
2. To abandon liquor and social evils.
3. To take food only after performing the rituals of purification after birth and death.
4. The dead body should not be buried but put on a funeral pyre.
5. To abandon the Dhapa.
6. To observe a fast on full-moon day and the Amavasya; worship God and donate something to poor and needy fellows.
7. To contribute according to his/her capacity for the overall betterment of the Samaj.
8. To improve their economic conditions, to be honest and sincere. Not to steal any thing.

9. Not to exhibit anger and not be proud.
10. To pay respect to parents, saints and guests.
11. Shaving of the head (tonsure) at the burial place.
12. To write letters to the government for allowing the untouchables to wear ornaments made of gold and silver.
13. Not to promote the caste/class conflict.
14. To publish the names and addresses of donors who donate Rs 5 on more in the Annual Report of MJSM.

Imperatives of Education: MJSM/MMU

In the next decade or so the MJSM movement started operating through several forms, primarily in the Udaipur, Chittorgarh and Jaipur districts. The impetus for agitation and mobilization among Meghwals arose largely in response to local forces and at the behest of MJSM. These activities were on literacy. During the princely states low untouchable boys were not admitted in vernacular primary or high schools. Thus, the number of literates among the untouchables in these princely states, was statistically insignificant. It is likely that MJSM was instrumental in mobilizing the Meghwal, Bhambhi and Balai communities and enlisting them into the movement for educational action. While this process of educational mobilization became especially marked after independence of the country, its roots lay in an earlier period. On November 18, 1953[44] a special meeting for educational action was held under the chairmanship of Dev Ram Meghwal at village Majawada in which Bhairu Lal Meghwal, Balu Ram (Kanod), Ghashi Ram (Karju), Narain (Mampura), Bhairu Ram (Vijanvas), Hamer Mal (Badbal), Partha Ram (Vallabh Nagar), Karing (Taken), and others participated. The resolutions passed were virtually related to the deplorable socio-economic conditions of the untouchables but resolved that MJSM should take initiative to start their own 'pathshala' for untouchable boys and girls.

The educational aspects of MJSM's movement programme were implemented through establishment of pathshalas for untouchables in rural areas. Thus, on May 20, 1954[45] for the first time a 'pathshala' called 'Gandhi Pathshala' opened at Vallabh Nagar, Udaipur. The major objective of these pathshalas was the promotion of education amongst the untouchable communities with a particular emphasis on girls' education. In the first year of its operation MJSM expanded the bulk of its energies on the operation of the pathshala. Subsequently, another pathshala,

Table 11.1

Meetings of MJSM/MMU Held Since 1948

Name of the village/place	*Year*	*Date*	*Duration*	*Remarks*
Vijanvas	1948	March 11–12	2 Days	Issues regarding social reforms were discussed in detail.
Uthala	1948	April 15	1 Day	People from 40 nearby villages participated in this meeting, new members were enrolled for MMU. To assist in smooth functioning of the Mandal, a 7-member sub-committee was formed which includes Bheraji, Gad-Ki-Vasni, Khem Raj Dudhalia, Moti ji Badgaun, Heeraji Akodara, Premji, Uthala, Shobhaji Taravat and Kalu Mabhli.
Vijan-vas	1948	May 25–26	2 Days	Passed the resolution against the ban imposed on untouchables by upper caste Hindus regarding not to wear the ornaments made of gold and silver, not to prepare food with Gur and sugar. Also passed the resolution that they would not remove the dead animals, use separate clothes while skinning the animals, to take bath daily. Like this many resolutions were passed. An application signed by participants was later on submitted to Rajpramukh, the Maharana of Udaipur and also sent to the then Government of Rajasthan.
Bohera	1948	June 3	1 Day	A large meeting was held. In this meeting, various enquiry reports were presented. Also alerted the Meghwals not to be misguided. In respect of the expansion of the activities of MMU, and another sub-committee consisting of 11 members was formed.

Cont'd...

Cont'd...

Kanoda	1948	June 6	1 Day	Local social activists namely Narain Lal, Balu Ram and other colleagues organized this meeting. Bhairulal Meghwal and his colleagues were invited to deliver the lecture on removal of Social evils and to encourage the workers to face the atrocities boldly.
Vijanvas	1948	September 16	1 Day	Meeting of the Executive Committee was held in which five resolutions were passed.
Nandiwala	1948	October 27	1 Day	A meeting was organized in which Meghwals from 31 villages took part.
Udaipur (MMU Hqs)	1948	December 1	1 Day	A meeting of the Executive Committee of MMU was held.
Gogunda Sayara	1948	December 4 and 13	2 Days	In order to collect information regarding the atrocities perpetrated on untouchables, several meetings were held in the rural areas of Gogunda Sayara.
Uthala	1948	December.28	1 Day	A meeting was organized. Discussions were held on the preparation of the forthcoming Sammelan to be held at Vijanvas.
Vijanvas	1949	January 22-23	2 Days	A two-day Sammelan was held under the Chairmanship of Ran Ram Meghwal. On this occasion, a procession was taken out under police protection, National flag was unfurled, 5 resolutions were passed.Fight new suggestions were proposed by Meghwal Samaj for the betterment of the Samaj. Nanu Ram Ravidasvanshi, Neemuch, Madhya Pradesh read out poems in respect of reforms to be implemented. Likewise Laxmanchand, Kailashchand and Dal Shanker (all students) also recited poems.

Cont'd...

Cont'd...

Pahad	1949	February 27	1 Day	A Sammelan was held which was attended by a large number of untouchables. A signed memorandum against the atrocities was sent to Pandit Jawaharlal Nehru, the then Prime Minister of India and Sardar Vallabh Bhai Patel, the then Home Minister, Government of India for taking necessary action.
Udaipur	1949	December 18	1 Day	An executive meeting was held to discuss how Sammelan at Kanoda can be organized.
Vijanvas	1950	January 1	1 Day	An executive meeting was held. Detailed discussions took place regarding celebration of the annual function.
Chhoti Sadri	1950	June 11	1 Day	A function was organized to Install the statue of God Radha Krishan at Chhoti Sadri. Total expenditure was borne by the activist namely Prabhu lal Ravi Dasvanshi. All the members of the executive Committee participated in it. According to a rough estimate, 4000 Meghwals assembled. In this meeting a large number of Meghwals became the members of MMU.
Jamlavada	1950	June 12	1 Day	Inspired by previous functions (held at Chhoti Sadri) the local Meghwals also stalled the idols of Laxman and Sita. A procession was also taken out. The social activities of MMU, were propagated amongst the local masses.

Cont'd...

Cont'd...

Amrapuri	1951	January 11 & 12	2 Days	A public meeting was held in which 8 resolutions were passed for the all-round development of Meghwal Samaj. In this meeting Balu Ram Meghwal put up a proposal for change of name, i.e., from 'Meghwal Jati Sudharak Mandal, Udaipur to 'Meghwal Mandal, Udaipur' which was approved unanimously, since then it was called "Meghwal Mandal, Udaipur. In this meeting it was also decided that Prabhu Lal Meghwal (Chhoti Sadri), district Chittorgarh and Ghasi Ram Meghwal Karju, district Udaipur would contest the forthcoming State Assembly Election, either as Party nominee or as Independent. On January 12, 1951 a new Executive Committee was constituted. The members were: Dev Ram Adhiyaksh, Bhairulal Meghwal—Pradhan Mantri, Narain Nanu – Sahkari Mantri and Prabhulal—Prachar Mantri. There were in all 11 members.
Badi Sadri	1951	July 15	1 Day	A meeting attended by a large number of people was held by Meghwals of Badi Sadri to get rid of the atrocities, perpetrated by upper caste Hindus. It was decided unanimously to fight against them collectively.
Badi Sadri	1951	August 27	1 Day	Bhairulal Meghwal with large number of colleagues reached Jodhpur in order to open a branch of MMU. Some new members were enrolled.
Udaipur	1951	September 9	1 Day	A meeting was held at Udaipur headquarters in which representatives from 22 villages assembled. It was decided to meet the authorities of Government of India and Government of Rajasthan for the betterment of Meghwal Samaj.

Cont'd...

Cont'd...

Chhoti Sadri	1951	September 15	1 Day	A meeting with the help of local social worker namely Prabhulal was held. A large number of Meghwals assembled and a decision was taken for social reforms.
Dhuni Mata	1951	September 17	1 Day	Meghwals from 33 villages took part in the meeting. To strengthen the work of MMU and for its expansion a sub-committee of 11 members was constituted.
Bari Sadri	1952	January 15	1 Day	In the meeting special stress was laid for improvement of economic condition of MMU.
Bohera	1952	February 2	1 Day	To make popular the programmes and activities of MMU amongst the Meghwals, emphasis was also given to enrol more and more new members.
Badbal	1952	April 14	1 Day	To protest against the harassment, humiliation and atrocities of caste Hindus, a strategy also was formulated for gaining social equality. In all 17 areas were identified for claiming social equality, such as to wear the ornaments made of gold and silver, to ride on a mare for marriages, to use the public wells, to enter the public temples, to get admission in government schools etc.
Godva	1952	April 13	1 Day	A large number of caste Panchas from neighbouring village participated. Discussion untred around the activities of MMU. How to improve economic conditions was also discussed.

Cont'd...

Cont'd...

Merta	1952	May 4	1 Day	In the meeting Meghwals from village Nadival anami participated. Discussions took place about Social reforms, Programmes and activities of MMU.
Bambora	1952	May 11	1 Day	To enquire about the social inequality, a meeting of 42 villages was convened. Large number of Meghwals attended it. From 11-5-1952 to 1-6-1952, Bhairulal Meghwal and his colleagues, Bhera Ram, Ghasi Ram, Narain and Karing travelled several villages and prepared the list of harassment, atrocities and humiliation perpetrated on Maghwals and other untouchables in villages. A sub-committee of 11 Members was also constituted to propose ways and means to stop all this. The members taken were: Karing, Bhima, Bambora, Deva Ram, Papund, Govind Pilla, Tala Gudal, Manna, Godel, Ram Chotka, Gangala, Moda Khadwa, Ganga Ram Saradi, Gautam, Kotada and Manna Lasakiya.
Padrada	1952	August 19	1 Day	How to promote education amongst the children of Meghwal Samaj was the main issue before the committee. A seven-member Committee of caste Panchas including Mana Ram, Samera, Nand Ram Jemli, Rata Padrada, Chamna, Pipana, Chhana Sayara, Nathu Ram, Bhanpura and Lalu Barvada was constituted.

Cont'd...

Cont'd...

Chhoti Sadri	1952	September 12	1 Day	First Sammelan of Ravidas Sabha was held. Complete arrangements were made by Prabhulal, Keshu Ram, Hemraj Siyoti. Expenditure on food was borne by Smt Mittu Bai Siyoti w/o Prabhulal. The Executive Committee of MMU headed by Bhairulal Meghwal and his colleagues also took active part. The main purpose of this meeting was to awaken the socio-political consciousness among the Meghwals of this region and to persuade them to give up the social evils. Dr Mangal Singh from Chhoti Sadri was the main speaker on this occasion.
Udaipur	1952	September 17	1 Day	A meeting of the inspection committee was held. It was attended by Bhattis (caste genealogists). On the request of MMU, the Bhattis (caste geneologists), namely Gokul Dungla, Bhagirath Bhindar and Bhairudan and others attended it with old records.
Bambora	1952	December 27	1 Day	An urgent meeting was held to discuss certain issues and also to prepare some schemes for future.
Badbal	1953	April 14	1 Day	A meeting under the chairmanship of Pyarchand Bilot was held. Some important issues were raised in the meeting, particularly to improve the economic condition of MMU, and to expand its activities in other areas also.

Cont'd...

Cont'd...

Sayara Pargana	1953	May 2	1 Day	Under the chairmanship of Devi Lal, a meeting of Meghwals of Sayara Pargana was held at Gogunda. Amrit Lal Yadav, the then Forest Minister, Government of Rajasthan also attended it. In his speech Yadav said that there is no need to run the MMU separately and this created flutter amongst the assembled Meghwals. Speaking on behalf of MMU Bhairulal Meghwal said that MMU is not a political organization. It is a voluntary organization rendering its services for the betterment and upliftment of the Dalit Samaj and also awakening social consciousness amongst the untouchables.
Dhashya	1953	December 2	1 Day	This meeting was held to discuss all-round development of the Samaj
Kalibheet	1953	December 8	1 Day	The meeting was held to discuss all-round development of the Samaj.
Loda	1954	January 5	1 Day	Under the presidentship of Dhula Ram Karawali a meeting of Dalits was held. Some of the important social issues such as to oppose the tax imposed on manufactured 'Jutia' etc., were discussed.
Udaipur	1954	January 11	1 Day	Under the chairmanship of Dev Ram Meghwal a meeting of Executive Committee of MMU was held. Last year's income and expenditure account was presented. The budget for the current year was also presented and passed. Application for removable of tax and Theka Pratha (contract system) of Aavla-Chhal was moved to the Home Ministry, Government of India and Backward Class Welfare Department, Government of Rajasthan.

Cont'd...

Cont'd...

Ballabh Nagar Boheda, Badi Sadri, Doongla Mewal, Sayara, Rishabhdev, Kherwara, Phalasiya	1954	April 4 -5	2 Days	To send the information about the plight of the untouchables to Backward Classes Commission, Government of India. Various meetings were held at Vallabh Nagar, Boheda, Badi Sadri, Doongla, Mewal, Sayara, Rishabha Dev, Kherwara and Phalasiya from April 4-5, 1954.
Semdur	1954	July 10	1 Day	A sub-committee was formed to discuss, how to expand its activities in Mewal Pargana.
Udaipur	1954	July 17	1 Day	A sub-committee was formed to expand its activities in Sayara Pargana.
Delvas	1954	Sept. 23	1 Day	A meeting of MMU was held at Delvas- Boheda. In this meeting copies of the orders issued by Government of Rajasthan for abolition of disabilities imposed on untouchables and to protect the interests of Dalits were distributed. Similarly, copies of the Judgement passed in favour of Dalits regarding court cases were also distributed for wide publicity.
Charan Khedi	1954	December 12	1 Day	Under the chairmanship of Omkar Meghwal (Jar Khan) a big Sammelan was held. A resolution was passed regarding the reserved seat. Also a sub-committee was constituted for Boheda, Badi Sadri Pargana.

Cont'd...

Cont'd...

Majavada	1957	January 1-2	2 Days	A Sammelan was held under the chairmanship of Khemraj Dudhalia. Before commencement of the Sammelan, all the workers, participants and others assembled and paid their tributes to first Law Minister of India, Constitution maker and Massiha of downtrodden late Dr Ambedkar. They also discussed various issues concerning their socio-economic life, mainly inclusion of Meghwal, Bhambhi, Balai and other ntouchable communities/castes in the SC list of Rajasthan. To bring the unity amongst the small segment of broad castes-the Chamar/Meghwal, some of the achievements in certain areas. To fight the general election, to do something for the betterment of the same etc. The office bearers also placed before the gathering the comments and opinion they received from political leaders, eminent persons and others about MMU. On this occasion Advocate Chhagan Singh Choudhary and Balu Ram Meghwal, Convener of Propaganda Committee also spoke. A new Executive Committee was constituted for 2 years. This time instead of 11 members Committee, 21 members were elected for Executive Committee under the chairmanship of Narain Lal Meghwal. Bhairu Lal Meghwal was Pradhan Mantri.

Cont'd...

Cont'd...

Majavada	1965	March 10, 11 & 12	3 Days	Under the presidentship of Narain Lal Meghwal, a three-day Sammelan was convened. First day, on March 10, 1965 some of the eminent Arya Samajists—Roop Shanker Sharma, Anil Kumar Sharma, Bhanwar Lal Sharma, Krishna Pareek and Murari Lal Verma participated in the Workshop and later on addressed the public gathering. Chhagan Singh Choudhary praised the services rendered by Bhairu Lal Meghwal. Chhagan Singh Choudhary moved a resolution which was supported by Ghasi Ram Karju. On March 11, Income and Expenditure Account for the years 1962–64 was placed before it. A new Executive Committee, Propaganda Committee and Advisory Committee came into existence on March 11, 1965.

Cont'd...

Cont'd...

Vallabh Nagar	1965	October 10–11	2 Days	A two-day Executive Committee meeting was held at Vallabh Nagar, Udaipur. In all, more than 250 persons took part in the meeting including executive members, Propaganda Committee's members, Arya Samajists and others, particularly Ishwaranand, Dr Radha Krisha Paliwal, Roop Shankar Sharma, Prem Chand Gupta, Hari Narain Sharma etc., addressed the meeting and emphasized the need to reform socio-religion. It was resolved to open MMU's account in the Punjab National Bank, Udaipur, to authorize office bearers to spend Rs 8 for tea and Rs 10 for food, to issue the time tables of the meetings well in advance for public purpose, to authorize the office bearers to spend Rs 5 without submitting the receipt, to collect Rs 10 and Rs 5 from those who will participate in the first Pari and second Pari respectively, to deposit the donation first, and to collect the donation both in kind and cash.

Source: Gleaned from Meghwal Mandal Udaipur *Iswarika,* 1999, edited by Kusum Meghwal. Published and circulated by Bhairu Lal Meghwal, his family members and well-wishers, 1999.

namely, 'Jawahar Pathshala' was opened in 1954[46] at village Majawada and called upon the government to support education amongst untouchable boys/girls and to make available funds for that purpose. The importance of education for untouchable communities was stressed in the other meetings of MJSM, sincerely urged stating that all parents should encourage their children to acquire education and at the same time should taste the sweetness of education themselves. Education had been seen as the panacea which would in the long run cure the ills of Meghwal, Bhambhi and Balai communities.

The workers and activists of MJSM in Udaipur were not content merely with holding meetings in order to publicize the need for education. In 1955,[47] another pathshala for untouchable boys and girls called 'Dayanand Pathshala' was started by MJSM at Jaipur. Thus, MJSM had shown considerable vitality in promoting education and establishing pathshalas in numerous localities and took initiative in directing its social and educational development. What is particularly noteworthy about Meghwal movement in this region is that especially in the field of education, the Meghwals, Bhambhis and Balais had made significant progress on their own.

Inclusion of Meghwal, Bhambhi and Balai, first in the List of Scheduled Castes in the Mewar State and thereafter in the State of Rajasthan

It is necessary to mention here that emergence of awareness among the Meghwals was a gradual process. Meghwal consciousness among the Meghwals of Mewar state existed long back. However, after 1947 many channels of communication were established and Meghwals of Mewar state came to know that other untouchable communities have been enjoying the benefits of reservation policy of the Mewar Legislative Assembly (election) rules 1947, while MJSM was responsible for taking up the issue with the Mewar government, the inclusion of Megwals in the list of SCs came into focus only when protested with the then state government. However, SCs issue were developed among the Meghwals first at the Mewar state level and it was after the formation of Rajasthan state in 1949 that SCs issue emerged at the state level (Rajasthan).

Now, we shall examine the socio-political agitation of claiming SCs status in the following section.

One of the first accounts of their efforts in the direction is reflected in the petition submitted by MJSM to the Government of Mewar in 1948,[48] wherein they urged the government to concede their demand for inclusion of Meghwals in the list of SCs. MJSM affirmed that Meghwals were large in number in low caste inhabitants of the land and were residing in villages scattered all over the state. The petition pointed out that Meghwals had a long history of oppression and that they had suffered at the hands of the upper castes and their socio-economic conditions were so poor that they could not progress by themselves but required aid of the state in order to uplift themselves from their depressed conditions.

The demand for inclusion in the list of SCs had some significant effect on Mewar government. As a result of this, on February 17, 1948, Y.L. Dashora, Election Commissioner, Mewar government issued a notification including Meghwals in the SCs list and added that in exercise of powers conferred by Section 131 of the Mewar Legislative Assembly (Election) Rules, 1947, the following addition is made in the Sixth Schedule. At the end of the list Add '17 Meghwals'. Later on the same modification also appeared in the Mewar Gazette, dated February 23, 1948. Thus, the demand for inclusion of Meghwals in the SCs category was accepted.

The Meghwals belonged to the broad category of the low untouchable caste but since they were not designated as SCs in the Mewar region of south Rajasthan, they were not entitled to enjoy the benefits of affirmative policy. For instance, as a matter of fact in the similar circumstances, this right had been conceded to the people of these castes in the neighbouring sister states like Ajmer, Marwar and others in Part 'C'. In other regions of Rajasthan Meghwals, Bhambhis and Balais did not belong to SCs category and therefore suffered from political and educational privileges and appointment in government jobs.

The MJSM sought to overcome this problem by not only claiming SCs status but also by social agitation. As pointed out Meghwals, Bhambhis and Balais were referred to both SCs and non-SCs category.

It is significant to note that in the beginning of 1948, MJSM held its meetings under the leadership of Bhairu Lal Meghwal who was the founder member of MJSM and also its Pradhan Mantri. The meeting passed many resolutions, the main was that Meghwals, Bhambhis and Balais must be included in the SCs list of Rajasthan. On February 6, 1949,[49] MJSM submitted a petition to Sardar Vallabh Bhai Patel, the then

Home Minister, Government of India, drawing his attention for inclusion of Meghwals, Bhambhis and Balais in the SCs category. On December 26, 1950 Bhairu Lal Meghwal's MJSM submitted a petition to the President of India, requesting him that Meghwals, Bhambhis and Balais of Rajasthan should be included in the SCs category, but no action was taken on the petition. Similarly, they had also submitted a memorandum to the Prime Minister, Law Minister and Election Commissioner of India. Simultaneously, the matter was also brought to the notice of the Government of Rajasthan so that Meghwals, Bhambhis and Balais in Rajasthan could be included in the list of SCs. On October 7, 1951 and again on November 13, 1951, a new petition was submitted to the President of India.

The next effort was initiated in November 11, 1951 when Advocate Chhagan Singh Chaudhary, Bhairu Lal Meghwal, Ghasi Ram Karju and other colleagues met ministers, concerned authorities, political leaders and members of parliament at New Delhi, seeking their support for inclusion of Meghwals, Bhambihs and Balais in the list of SCs category. It is important to note that while they were returning to Udaipur, they dropped at Jaipur. Here they also met the ministers and other authorities and reiterated their demand for inclusion in the SCs list and requested them to take necessary steps to rectify the injustice done to these communities as early as possible.

After three months another effort was made. On March 27, 1952[50] a delegation headed by Bhairu Lal Meghwal went to New Delhi—the capital of the country to meet the Home Minister, Government of India and to impress upon the authorities the immediate necessity of expediting the above matter, for which a representation dated October 7, 1951 was made to the President of India which was forwarded to the Home Minister for necessary action and disposal. During their meeting with authorities in the Ministry of Home Affairs, Bhairu Lal Meghwal presented a copy of the detailed representation for ready reference and requested to do justice to Meghwals, Bhambhis and Balais in the state of Rajasthan.

The demand for inclusion in the list of SCs had some significant effect on the Government of Rajasthan. In his reply entitled 'Request for inclusion of Meghwal, Bhambhi and Balai castes in the list of SCs' Director,[51] Backward Classes Welfare Department, Government of Rajasthan, PC Dave wrote a letter No. 5846/C/116 dated March 29, 1952 to MJSM and directed Bhairu Lal Meghwal to meet Backward Classes

Welfare Officer, Udaipur division, Utsav Lal Sharma and simultaneously a delegation of 23 persons under the leadership of Bhairu Lal Meghwal held several meetings with Utsav Lal Sharma at Udaipur from 7April 1952 to 12April 1952. The other members were: Advocate Chhagan Singh Choudhary, Prabhu Lal, Daulat Ram, Bhairu Ram Meghwal, Kishna Ram, Mana, Sava, Vasha Ram, Limba, Jairam, Bhaira, Ghasi Ram, Pyar Chand, Dev Ram, Akor, Tola Ram, Narain, Ghasi Ram, Narain, Moti Ram, Bagta Ram, Krishna, Moda Ram and Bhairu Ram.

Another significant feature of Bhairu Lal Meghwal's long and detailed discussions with Utsav Lal Sharma was that they all together toured several villages and held meetings with untouchables. Bhairu Lal Meghwal and Advocate Chhagan Singh Chaudhary attempted to show Utsav Lal Sharma, the miserable socio-economic conditions of the Meghwals, Bhambhis and Balais in the rural areas of Udaipur region.

During a week-long discussion, the most important issues in respect of their inclusion issue were customs, rituals, traditions, occupation, living standard, employment conditions, literacy and social status, untouchability etc., of Meghwal, Bhambhi and Balai castes. The discussions were rather detailed. Their major request was for the inclusion in the list of SCs category for the Meghwal, Bhambhi and Balai. The MJSM, as a low caste untouchables, was only requesting for providing the amenities which other castes already enjoyed. Despite repeated efforts, the Government of Rajasthan had not accepted the demand and the issue of inclusion of Meghwal, Bhambhi and Balai in SCs category remained alive.

Similarly, on July 10, 1953 Advocate Chhagan Singh Choudhary, Bhairu Lal Meghwal and other colleagues met central Ministers, Members of Parliament and other authorities regarding inclusion of Meghwal, Bhambhi and Balai in the list of SCs category. The issue of Meghwal, Bhambhi and Balai, inclusion in the list of SCs category is particularly important because during this period, MJSM played a prominent role in bringing this issue to the notice of the masses.

The demand for inclusion in the SCs category as discussed above, had two effects on MJSM agitation. First, Mandal workers and activists among the Meghwal, Bhambhi and Balai started to take active interest in this matter, as they considered the case worth fighting for. Second, it is a fact that political parties, directly or indirectly had supported the MJSM cause in Rajasthan with the result that MJSM did not get disheartened and loose hope. After one decade of harassment and suffering for them, the most important step taken by Government of India with respect to the inclusion of this issue was issuing a Notification. The Government of India also revised the list of SCs and declared Meghwal, Bhambhi and Balai as SCs, and published in the Government of India Extra-ordinary Gazetteer No. 59 dated December 26, 1956.[52] The MJSM welcomed the decision. Subsequently the Government of Rajasthan also included the Meghwal, Bhambhi and Balai in the list of SCs in Rajasthan. A few months later, Government notified a revised list of SCs which has also appeared in Gazette of Rajasthan dated November 29, 1956. MJSM gave this achievement a wide publicity in Rajasthan. Thus, MJSM succeeded in claiming not only social or religious rights/privileges but also civic and political privileges which were absolutely necessary for their upliftment from their most abject conditions of distress and degradation.

Notes

1. The most elaborate account of Meghwal Mandal, Udaipur and discussion of the origin of the Meghwal movement in Udaipur region is given in *Ismarika*, 1999, edited by Kusum Meghwal and published and circulated by Shri Bhairu Lal Meghwal, his family members and well-wishers, see in particular "Meghwal Mandal, Udaipur", *Ismarika*, 1999. For more details, see also "Meghvansh' Jati Sudharak Mandal, Udaipur-ka-vidhan", p. 69–70.
2. Ibid., p. 3.
3. Ibid., p. 3.
4. Ibid., p. 4.
5. Ibid., p. 4.
6. Ibid., p. 4.
7. Ibid., p. 4.
8. Ibid., p. 5.
9. Ibid., p. 5—For more details also see particularly "Meghvansh Jati Sudharak Mandal, Udaipur", p. 68.
10. Ibid., p. 9.
11. Chhagan Singh Choudhary, Advocate, 'Meghwal Mandal, Udaipur-ka-Sewa Karya Kram Avam Uplabdhia', in Meghwal Mandal, Udaipur, *Ismarika*, 1999. Ibid., pp. 8–10
12. Ibid., p. 8.

13. Ibid., p. 8.
14. Ibid., p. 8.
15. Ibid., p. 8.
16. Ibid., p. 10.
17. B.L. Meghwal "Jatia Gaurav Badhanewale Yashswi Saput: Prabhu Lal Meghwal" in Meghwal Mandal, Udaipur, *Ismarika*, 1999. Ibid., p. 23.
18. Ibid., p. 23.
19. Ibid., p. 23.
20. Ibid., p. 24.
21. Ibid., p. 23.
22. Ibid., p. 24.
23. Ibid., p. 24.
24. Ibid., p. 25.
25. Ibid., p. 25.
26. Ibid, .p. 24.
27. Virendarpal Singh Rana, "Dalit Dalan Aur Chetn ka Sanvahak: Meghwal Mandal, Udaipur" in Meghwal Mandal, Udaipur, *Ismarika*, 1999, Ibid., p. 17.
28. Ibid. p. 19. For more details, see in particular "Meghwal Mandal, Udaipur ke Karya Kram ki Roop Rekha". pp. 54–55.
29. "Karya-karta Sammelan"—Jarkhana", Chittorgarh, 27–28 September, 1966. Ibid., p. 84–85
30. Ibid., p. 85.
31. Ibid., p. 85.
32. Ibid., pp. 85–86.
33. "सन् 1969 में मेघवाल मण्डल के तत्वावधान में हुए मेघवाल प्रतिनिधि सम्मेलन की और से प्रस्तुत किये गये मांग–पत्र की प्रतिलिपि ज्यों की त्यों सूचनार्थ प्रकाषित है–मांग पत्र'' in Meghwal Mandal, Udaipur, *Ismarika*, 1999 Ibid., pp. 88–90.
34. Meghwal Mandal, Udaipur, *Ismarika*, 1999. Ibid., p. 86.
35. Ibid., pp. 86–88.
36. "Vershtiyagya", Ibid., p. 90.
37. "Karyakarta Betak—Gram Siyarda" in Meghwal Mandal, Udaipur, Ibid., pp. 90–92.
38. Kusum Meghwal has given analysis of various meetings, Sammelans, Vedic Yagya, Havan etc., of MMU, see particularly मेघवषं जाति सुधारक मण्डल उदयपुर संस्था के पंजीकृत होने के बाद की कार्यकारिणी सभा की महत्वपूर्ण बैठके' in MMU p. 71. For most important sources for socio-educational and other activities in Udaipur region is "Shri Meghwal Mandal, Udaipur-ki General

meetings–ki-Karyawahi", December 21, 1972, published by Bhairu Lal Meghwal, Pradhan Mantri, MMU Rajasthan, pp. 1–13. Also see, Bhairu Lal Meghwal, Pradhan Mantri, "Shri Meghwal Mandal, Udaipur-ke-Karya Karta Sammelan-ki-Karyawahi, 1957". pp. 1–14.

39. Ibid., p. 71.
40. Ibid., p. 71.
41. Ibid., p. 72.
42. Ibid., p. 72.
43. Ibid., pp. 72–74
44. Ibid., p. 79.
45. Ibid., p. 96.
46. Ibid., p. 97.
47. Ibid., p. 95.
48. Ibid., In early 1948, Bhairu Lal Meghwal, Secretary, MMU, submitted representation to then Mewar Government and with subsequent reminders, the Meghwals demanded for their inclusion in Scheduled Castes list of Mewar. As a result of this, the Government of Mewar accepted their genuine demand. For details regarding inclusion in Scheduled Castes list, see specially Notification issued by Election Department, dated February 17, 1948, p. 104.
49. Bhairu Lal Meghwal, Secretary, MMU submitted representation/petition to the President, Indian Union, Government of India, New Delhi and with subsequent reminders, the Meghwals demanded for their inclusion in the Scheduled Castes list, see specifically, Bhairu Lal Meghwal, Secretary, MMU letters dated October 7, 1951 and November 13, 1951 respectively, addressed to the President, Indian Union, Government of India, New Delhi, pp. 97–100.
50. A full account is provided in the representation submitted by Bhairu Lal Meghwal, Secretary, MMU to the then Home Minister, Government of India, New Delhi for their inclusion, on March 27, 1952, pp. 100–101.
51. For more details, see particularly 'मेघवाल, बलाई आदि जातियों को परिगणित जातियों में सम्मिलित की जाने हेतु पिछड़ी जाति कल्याण विभाग, राजस्थान सरकार जयपुर द्वारा जांच' in MMU, p. 77.
52. See specially : 'मेघवाल मण्ड़ल के प्रयासों से मेघवाल सहित कई अन्य जातियों को परिगणित जातियों में षामिल कर लिया गया जिसमें उन्हें संविधान सम्मत सभी अधिकार प्राप्त हुए' in MMU. p. 103. Also see letter dated 2 September, 1995 from Arunan Gashu De, Officer, on special duty, Ministry of Home Affairs, Government of India to Bhairu Lal Meghwal, Mantri, Meghwal Mandal, Udaipur, p. 102.

12 The Organizations of Meghwals and Chamars in Bikaner

The formation of Maha Sangh Meghwal (MSM) by the end of 20th century helped to forge a new identity for the Chamars of Rajasthan in particular and of North India in general. The earlier 20th century was a period of change in the region. The freedom movement expanded, the formation of Prajamandals in the princely states increased, Kisan agitation took place, various socio-educational measures of Gandhi Congress, Rajputana Harijan Sewak Sangh (RHSS), Arya Samaj etc., in this period had positive socio-political and cultural consequences for the untouchables of Rajasthan, in general and Chamars of Bikaner in particular. In this wider context, these organizations initiated reform measures. The reform endeavour questioned the divine and social hierarchy that centred on the Hindu pantheon. It questioned and challenged the ascribed status of Chamars as low untouchables who were tainted with stigma of untouchability.

National Movement, Praja Mandals, Rajputana Harijan Sewak Sangh, Arya Samaj and Chamars in Bikaner

In the beginning of the 20th century, the first special organization for untouchables was established by Swami Gopal Das, the great non-Brahmin reformer in Churu, in 1907.[1] Thus 'Sarva Hitkarini Sabha' (SHS) came into existence in that year (1907). It has a plan to open schools in every untouchable basti that makes a request for the same. As a result of this, SHS established a few Sarva Hitkarini Pathshalas and Kabir Pathshalas separately for all untouchable communities. The expenditure of the schools were borne by SHS. P.C. Joiya reported in his study that

"The schools were opened so that untouchable children could acquire the rudiment of education".

The first stage, dating roughly from 1875, may be termed the era of Arya Samaj reforms. During this period the organizations, that were formed, were reformist in nature and their major concern seems to have been the social upliftment and advancement of untouchable communities. This advancement was to be effected through the medium of education, with the elimination of those practices and customs which branded the untouchables as untouchable communities. Panna Lal Premi mentions in his essay that according to Master Harji Ram Janagal, Jasolai, that it was during 1922[2] that the first school for the children of untouchable communities was opened at Phad Bazar by Arya Samaj. The first school teacher was Hardwari Lal Tanwar, a staunch Arya Samajist from Rampur, Uttar Pradesh. What is noteworthy about Arya Samaj's movement is that after a few months, the school was named as Baba Ram Deo School by the Arya Samajists, as Meghwals are staunch followers of Baba Ram Deo, a 14th century social reformer of Marwar.

In the next few years or so, the school was shifted to Chokuti Railway crossing. During this period, a large number of untouchable students were admitted in the school. Panna Lal Premi, Panna Lal Barupal, Tulsi Ram, Jeth Mal, Hukma Ram, Harji Ram Janagal, Dhura Ram and Arjun Ram Janagal (all Meghwals) were the first who passed middle school examination in vernacular from this school. We should also note that Harji Ram Janagal was the first who, after passing middle school examination, was appointed as teacher in the same school. It happened so because upper caste literate Hindus were not interested to teach the low caste students enrolled in the primary or middle schools of Arya Samaj.

Another significant feature of Arya Samaj's movement was that a few years later Arya Samajists succeeded in getting the financial support for this school. Panna Lal Premi mentioned in his essay that the then His Highness Ganga Singh, Maharaja of Bikaner sanctioned Rs 125[3] as subsidy for the school. The main feature of His Highness's support was that it clearly showed his interest in the welfare of the untouchables and therefore could be considered as the first attempt by him to educate the untouchable children.

We should also note that after His Highness Maharaja Ganga Singh, his son His Highness Shadul Singh Maharaj also took active interest in the welfare and education of the untouchables. To a greater extent, perhaps, than in the other regions of Rajputana His Highness Shadul Singh Maharaj increased the subsidy from "Rs 125 to 150".[4] The untouchable students from various untouchable bastis came there for study. In school, a few years later, His Highness constructed a water tank. All these measures helped to affect the social and educational awakening of the Meghwal community.

In 1932 by the sincere efforts of Ishwar Dayal, a Branch of RHSS was opened in Bikaner. He launched a campaign for admission of untouchable children in government schools, started agitation for opening the doors of temples for untouchables and to allow them to use water of wells and tanks. P.C. Joiya, further reported that 'due to sincere efforts of RHSS, 12 untouchable children were admitted in a school in Pilani.[5] At the same time, throughout this period, some of the native persons supported reform programmes in Bikaner. In early 1935, Seth Ram Gopal Mohta constructed Baba Ram Deo mandir exclusively for Chamars in Kolayat and also appointed a Kamadia untouchable as priest of the temple. On August 28, 1935,[6] Seth Ram Gopal Mohta, the initiator of social reforms held a Vishal Satsangh (religious gathering) for Chamars, in this temple and they were then allowed to enter the temple. Later on Seth Mohta also established separate Ayurvedic dispensary in the premises of the temple and also appointed Dr Nahar as doctor for untouchables. Even though the spread of education among the Chamar community was limited in the early 20th century, it did have an impact on the formation of a social consciousness among some segments of the community.

Another important impetus for the education of Chamars and for the development of consciousness among them was the handiwork done by Vakil Ishwar Dayal in Bikaner. Harijan Hitkarni Sabha (HHKS) was established by Vakil Ishwar Dayal, the great non-Brahman reformer in early 1944[7] in Bikaner. On March 11/12, 1945, the first annual convention of HHKS was held in the premises of Mohta dharamshala. The initiative of reform programme of HHKS had some special effect on upper caste Hindus during this period. In this endeavour there were some supporters from upper caste Hindus also. For instance Seth Braj Ratan Karnani was greatly influenced by HHKS and its programmes and also announced a donation of Rs 100[8] for untouchable school in Shivwadi.

Rishi Meghvanshi Samaj Sudhar Sabha, 1946 (RMSSS)

By 1946s the Chamar community had undergone some momentous changes which were to propel it in the socio-political direction, through the formation of its own movement.

Before they formed an organization, some of the prominent Arya Samajists and untouchable educators recount that they travelled around the region and consulted Chamar leaders in order to enlist their support. P.C. Joiya mentioned that first regionwide Chamars Vishal Sammelan was convened on August 17, 1946[9] at Gulabnath's Ashram—an untouchable saint. The Sammelan was presided over by Gulabnath Maharaj himself. The main objective of the Sammelan was the promotion of education among the Chamar community, with particular emphasis on the formation of the Chamar's organization. Arya Samajists and Chamar activists were to address the 1946 Sammelan which drew a large number of Panchas, Sarpanchas, chaudharies, patels and others. Thus, in Bikaner region, RMSSS was formed in 1946.[10] What is particularly noteworthy about the Chamar movement in this region is that it was a product of local uprising. The second meeting of RMSSS was held on November 11, 1946 at Baba Ram Deo mandir at Kolayat, 52 km away from Bikaner and constituted an Executive Committee[11] of RMSSS with Kedar Dhura Ram as the Pradhan, Master Shrawan Ram as Up-pradhan, Narain Dat as Mantri, Dalu Ram as Up-mantri, Purkha Ram Ganter and Jiya Ram Janagal as Treasurers, Mahatma Hukma Ram Janagal as Prachar Mantri, Dhura Ram as 'Singer', Tulchha Ram Barupal as Pustkalaya Adhiyaksh.

Since the pre-independence period, Bikaner state, which was dominated by Chamars, had introduced a number of changes in the political and social order. P.C. Joiya has described these changes in a narrative form in his article published in the year 2000.

"Neither to remove the dead cattle nor to eat flesh of dead animals, not to drink alcohol, not to do beggar, to promote education and send children to the schools, to eradicate the social vices; to agitate for admission of the untouchables in government schools. Wells, tanks, ponds and public places be made open to untouchables in the same way as they are accessible to Savaranas."[12]

These changes direct us towards an understanding of the major objectives undertaken by RMSSS in Bikaner.

The main purpose of RMSSS was to awaken social consciousness among the rural masses at village level and tehsil level. At that time

RMSSS's efforts were instrumental in creating a climate of reform within the Chamar community. Subsequently, another meeting of RMSSS was held under the presidentship of Dr Hardwari Lal—a Chamar, at Shekhasar and Lunkaransar. The resolutions passed in this meeting were virtually identical but included specifically that, "we accept all the reform measures of RMSSS."[13] According to this line of thought, if a Chamar acts against reform, if he performs the tasks and acts which were considered polluting and if the Chamar caste fellows thinking of reform do not change, the RMSSS would outcaste or excommunicate them and/or impose a fine up to Rs 51.[14] This message and its implications came to have increasing effect on caste fellows. Bikaner, therefore, was an important centre of activity among the Chamar community.

While some of the Churu-Ratangarh organizations and its leaders had primarily local appeal, and following some organizations became prominent in the region and among the untouchable communities as a whole. One such organization was HSS. HSS had shown considerable interest in the welfare activities and its branches were opened in numerous cities and also took initiative in directing its energy towards social and educational development. HSS convened a Vishal Sammelan of untouchables at the Ashram of Baba Shantokdas at Ratangarh. What is particularly noteworthy about untouchable movement in this region is that the untouchables of Ratangarh also approved and accepted the reforms introduced by RMSSS which was very typical. In this Sammelan it was resolved not to drink alcohol on childbirth/wedding and other ceremonies. It was stressed to reduce the expenditure on marriages and other ceremonies. Women were not prohibited from going to upper caste Hindus for singing the songs; they were not allowed to sing songs on the streets. They were asked to send more and more female children to schools for their education.

While Hardwari Lal was a prominent leader in Bikaner region, Panna Lal Barupal was another leader based in Bikaner who received greater attention both within and outside the region. P.C. Joiya notes that 'Panna Lal Barupal was especially active as leader and organizer after 1946, in which year he had joined the RMSSS. Soon after taking the reins of RMSSS, Panna Lal Barupal's community activities, (dated to 1946) started, when he convened a regionwide communities' Vishal Sammelan on November 11, 1946 at Kolayat.[15] The Chamar leaders were to address this Sammelan which drew thousands of delegates. The major issues addressed in this sammelan included equal access by untouchables to educational institutions and government jobs. The demands made by RMSSS at Kolayat on November 11, 1946, are typical. It demanded: "Call for untouchable representation in the interium government of Maharaja, Bikaner; to give voting right to all eligible untouchables who have attained 18 years of age, to give untouchable representation in Dhara Sabha as per their population ratio; to give relaxation in qualifications for untouchable minister."[16]

The Charter of Demands also included a special call that Meghwal Samaj should discard the traditional occupation and rid itself of those practices which Hindu principles considered unclean. They also urged the His Highness that their intention was not to put the state government and savarnas in trouble. They appealed to the government and savarnas to make alternative arrangements. Meghwals as subjects under Bikaner Raj were only requesting amenities which citizens of other castes were already enjoying. P.C. Joiya points out that 1946 Sammelan demands were submitted to His Highness, Bikaner by both Panna Lal Barupal and Hardwari Lal.

The mobilization phase of RMSSS movement under Panna Lal Barupal was gathering momentum after submission of the Charter of Demands for basic amenities and next day on November 12, 1946 again a Vishal Community Sammelan was held at Jasolai to give its demands a wide publicity. Both Panna Lal Barupal and Hardwari Lal group can thus be considered reformers trying to effect change within the community.

Social activists in Bikaner were not merely content with holding meetings and Sammelans in order to publicize the need for reforms. Another branch of RMSSS was formed in the same year at village Muklawa in Raisingh tehsil. Ramraj was nominated the Secretary of RMSSS at Muklawa. As local secretary of RMSSS, he introduced socio-educational measures among the Meghwals.

Similarly, a meeting for self-reform was convened by Meghwals at Muklawa in 1946 which was also attended by Panchas, Sarpanchas and Patels of more than 60 villages. The decision taken was virtually typical. Resolved: "To prohibit the caste fellows from taking food at the houses of muslims".[17]

RMSSS took initiative in holding meetings and Sammelans on May 24–25, 1947 at Gulabnath Bagichi, Bikaner, for apprising the achievement of RMSSS. They also took concrete measures to give wide publicity through the press.

What is important to note about the Meghwal movement in this region is that the call for reform was put within the bounds of an enlightened Hinduism, without any opposition. Rather, Meghwal leaders exhorted their community to rid itself of those practices which Hindu principles considered unclean. They also urged that Meghwals overcome the prejudices which divide them according to Brahminical thought and to become a unified and modern community.

The genesis and development of Meghwal movement was an important one in this period and Panna Lal Barupal played a prominent role in bringing it to the knowledge of the caste fellows. What is noteworthy about Meghwal movement is that it was opposed on the ground that it represented the Meghwals, whose accession to power could only jeopardize the interests of the Bhambhis and other untouchables. But this was obviously not so. The main argument advanced by P.C. Joiya in his article was that Hindus might weaken the unity of RMSSS. As a result of instigation by upper caste Hindus as Joiya mentioned, on June 6, 1947[18] some of the Raj Bhambhis (a section of Chamar community) filed a petition against the members of RMSSS in the court of City Magistrate, Bikaner, under Sections 153, 153C, 504 and 102 of CRPC/IPC. Six social activists namely Panna Lal Barupal, Shrawan Ram, Dhura Ram, Rawat Ram, Mehta Ram and Bhera Ram were involved in this case.

On June 29, 1949[19] an important case was taken up by City Magistrate, Gopal Acharya. While appreciating the progressive views of Panna Lal Barupal and his colleagues for the upliftment and betterment of the Samaj, the City Magistrate rejected the petition. This argument bore a close resemblance to the ones advanced by untouchable reformers such as Ambedkar.

The RMSSS sponsored a variety of reform programmes and activities in Bikaner as well as surrounding areas for the benefit of Meghwal Community in particular and the untouchable communities in general.

In social and political matters RMSSS played a prominent role in bringing to His Highness's attention the issue of Sootrakars. On November 5, 1947[20] a meeting of Sootrakars was organized. The aims of the meeting was to submit a memorandum to His Highness for involving them in social and political matters. Another important issue taken up by RMSSS was the question of untouchability and its eradication. To discuss the proposed issue and its significance for untouchable communities RMSSS had called a meeting in 1948[21] and this meeting passed a resolution urging His Highness to appoint a minister from amongst the untouchables. Thus, on March 3, 1948 the RMSSS under the leadership of Panna Lal Barupal submitted a memorandum to His Highness requesting for appointment of untouchable minister. On August 9, 1948[22] again Panna Lal Barupal submitted a reminder to His Highness. An appeal was also made to all sections of the Meghwal Samaj of Bikaner and other untouchables to take up the issues raised by RMSSS to involve them in the movement.

After independence, the question of untouchability became a political issue which involved not only the untouchables but also various organizations and caste Hindu reformers as well. As stated earlier, the problem of untouchability received the attention of Meghwal movement and on June 1, 1948[23] RMSSS held a meeting at village Garabdesar, tehsil Lunkaransar. Panna Lal Barupal, Dharampal, Hardwari Lal and others delivered lectures. The RMSSS committed itself to launch a campaign for the removal of all disabilities imposed upon the untouchables by customs. The disabilities were of a most vexatious and oppressive character, subjecting these communities to considerable hardship and inconvenience.

Impressed by the views of the untouchable activists, Fateh Singh,[24] the then Thakur of the village, took cognizance of the untouchable problems and attempted to offer a programme to ameliorate the fate of the untouchables. Thakur Saheb depicted himself as the reformer of the untouchables and, he supported the Meghwal movement. By any account this was an outstanding social achievement for the members of Meghwal community.. Panna Lal Barupal assumed the leadership of these movements as well and to some extent was able to impact a political significance to the movements.

The period also witnessed two simultaneous phenomena in the social field. The savarnas imposed certain restrictions that made the life of untouchables miserable. Incidents of violence and atrocities too increased against the poor Meghwals and other low caste untouchables. P.C. Joiya a Research Officer, Archives Bikaner, commented on the restrictions imposed during the year 1948.[25]

"The savarnas restrained them from fetching the water from wells. Similarly they also wanted the shopkeepers and Mahajans (Banias and money lenders) to ban on selling the goods and lending money to them. They had warned the low caste untouchables not to graze their cattle in the savarnas' fields. While imposing several restrictions on untouchables, the savarnas grabbed their land and stolen their cattle too. Their women folk were harassed, insulted, humiliated and tortured like anything."

In addition to Meghwals' reform activities on behalf of RMSSS, Panna Lal Barupal and his colleagues took an active role in promotion of close harmony between low untouchable communities which was relevant not only to the Meghwal communities but to other low castes communities, poor and helpless untouchables as well. Particularly in Bikaner, Panna Lal Barupal and RMSSS attempted to promote class rather than caste issues. RMSSS organized a massive one-day meeting on November 20, 1949[26] at Gulabnath's Ashram, Bikaner, where almost all the low untouchable communities such as Meghvanshi, Gurda, Nayak, Mehtar, Koli, Kuchbandia, Kanjar, Sansi, Satiya, etc., assembled from all over Bikaner. Sincere efforts were made by RMSSS to make the meeting a success. It turned out to be most successful. P.C. Joiya[27] states that in this meeting all the assembled members accepted the tea and water from each other to remove the untouchability prevailing amongst the untouchables themselves.' The meeting also resolved that low untouchable communities would make efforts to fight against internal untouchability. During this period, however, by and large, Panna Lal Barupal and RMSSS made strenuous efforts to broaden the base of the movement and to widen its appeal. Thus, this period marked a high point in the cooperation between Meghwal organization and low untouchable communities. His efforts were largely appreciated.

The year 1949 also produced a fall out between Panna Lal Barupal and the Meghwal community. Panna Lal Barupal faced opposition from a segment of Meghwal community. The Meghwal community showed its disagreement by excommunicating three young Meghwal youths on September 19, 1949[28] in Bikaner. The Meghwal Samaj charged that they ate food with Mehtars and thus violated the social norms. Yet the feeling among Meghwals was that the expelled youths should be taken back in the Samaj. As a result of this, it was, however, decided to take them back. They[29] were asked first to pay Rs 101 as fine for violating the social norms. Second, they must purify themselves by taking a dip in Ganga at Haridwar. All the conditions for readmission were completed by the expelled youth. P.C. Joiya states that "all the three expelled youths were readmitted". Thus Panna Lal Barupal's efforts to remove untouchability within untouchables, however, received a great jolt and division between Meghwals, Mehtars and other low castes continued to widen.

Despite opposition, Panna Lal Barupal continued his efforts to bridge the gap between divided Meghwals and other untouchable communities. Panna Lal Barupal took particular interest in the matter pertaining to Jata Bhambhis and Maru Bhambhis. His efforts to bridge the gap between these two major segments of Chamar Samaj in Bikaner in particular and Rajasthan in general dated from 1950 with the holding of first Sammelan on May 5, 1950[30] at village Bindasar. The feeling among Meghwal leaders was that both sections of Jata Bhambhis and Maru Bhambhis should be united and should remain as one. The formation of a cohesive group constituting Jata and Maru Bhambhis and other similar groups/communities would have social and political benefit as well. First, the main numerical strength of the Jata and Maru Bhambhis together would deny the superiority of the upper caste Hindus. Second, the incorporation of most numerical dominated segments of Chamar community into one organization affiliated to RMSSS would add to the latter's power and ability to influence the course of community events. Thus, RMSSS further attempted to bridge the gap by holding another Vishal Sammelan in 1950[31] at Nokha-Mandi, Bikaner. According to P.C. Joiya, Kana Ram (Aakhasar), Harji Ram (Lumbasar-Kumbasar), Moda Ram (Panchu), Aadu Ram (Jeendesar), Deva Ram, Girdhari Ram, Panna Ram (all Janglu) and many more took active part in protecting Jata-Maru Bhambhi unity, which was relevant to Meghwal untouchables. Particularly in Bikaner they attempted to promote Jata-Maru Bhambhi unity.

Besides Jata-Maru Bhambhi unity, Panna Lal Barupal also made various efforts to bridge the gap between Meghwals and other untouchable communities, such as Sootrakar (popularly known as Balai). Thus, RMSSS had already made groundwork on which it could attempt to organize unity. A meeting of Akhil Bharatiya Sootrakar Sabha[32] (ABSS) was convened on July 29, 1950 at Rajasthan Meghvanshi Sootrakar Sabha, Bidada-ki-Bagichi, Sujangarh. The meeting was chaired by Garibdas—an untouchable from Jaipur and the majority of delegates were Sootrakars. Garibdas made an appeal to unite together and support and also follow the reform programme. Similarly, another Sootrakar Sammelan was organized on February 1, 1952[33] at Jasrasar, Nokha. Here again it was chaired by Garibdas. With the sincere efforts of local natives, such as Mota Ram, Naga Ram, Aadu Ram, Taru Ram, Kalu Ram, Gopal Ram, Hiralal, Ramlal, Uma Ram and Sewa Ram—a resolution was passed by the gathering, unanimously to implement in letter and spirit the reform programme and activities approved by Rishi Meghwans Samaj Sudhar Sabha. The third Vishal Sammelan[34] of Akhil Bharatiya Sootrakar Sabha was held at Nagaur on February 18–19, 1951 and a large number of untouchables were from Bikaner. The leaders also apprised the delegates of the achievement of ABSS. It also appealed, to delegates wealthy caste men, seths, and Maharajas of upper castes and state government to donate liberally in kind for construction at Gogamedi and wells at Bharu Pawa respectively. The Sootrakars including Meghwals supported these developments.

In 1950, after independence of the country, the period also witnessed rapid changes in the field of social and political consciousness. We see that Panna Lal Barupal sought to unite all untouchable communities through 'Dalit Jatia Sangh' (DJS), as Dalit organization. Thus, on November 24–25, 1950[35] the first state level Vishal Sammelan of low castes was convened by Panna Lal Barupal at Bikaner. It was chaired by Seth Ram Gopal Mohta, a well-known Brahmin reformer of Bikaner. Thus, the focus of unity was shifted from local to division and then to state. Panna Lal Barupal, the most dedicated social activists, undertook special measures from 1946 onwards. These meetings/Sammelans increased socio-political unity between low castes and upper caste Hindus. Another important attempt for the uplift of Meghwal community and ensuring that the execution of the reform measures should take place in 1951. This time, on January 1, 1951[36] village Kharbara was chosen by Panna Lal Barupal to convene the Meghwal Sammelan and a large number of Meghwals came from more than 84 villages of 9 Kheda. This time, it was specifically declared that it would be the basic duty of caste-fellows to promote their socio-political interests.

Congress, as a sign and symbol of a well-wisher of low untouchable communities in Rajasthan too worked for the upliftment of poor Meghwals and other low caste men. P.C. Joiya notes that in 1952, the District Congress Committee, Bikaner for the first time held divisional level Harijan Sammelan at Magra in Bikaner. The moving spirit behind this Sammelan were Panna Lal Barupal and Ram Ratan Kochar.

What was the situation of Meghwals and other low untouchable castes under the state government? We have noted that untouchables were still facing social disabilities of upper caste Hindus in everyday life. Subsequently, attempt to enact legal safeguards for the untouchable communities in Rajasthan, the state government on September 11, 1952[37] issued a circular to all the heads of departments and directed them to organize 'prabhat pheris', socio-cultural activities and programmes so that Harijans may enter into the temples, hotels and other public places on Harijan Day. These activities and programmes were the main instruments used for the eradication of the practices of untouchability and prosecution of those who continued to practice it. The power of the state government, therefore, was to be used to reform social and religious institutions of Hindu society.

On the efforts made by the government, P.C. Joiya commented as follows:

"Prabhat pheries were taken out by Harijans themselves within Harijan basties, piao (water huts) were arranged outside public park and Bata shop at KEM Road. Similarly tea was served to untouchables in state owned hotels. Likewise Bhajan-kirtan (religious gathering) were held at Harijan temples".[38]

During these 17 years from 1935 to 1952, the untouchable organizations had spent time in arousing the untouchable masses which benefitted the untouchable leaders and enabled them to strike at the roots. That is why they reacted so strongly against the government programmes. A large number of Dalit organizations in Bikaner in a comprehensive move criticized and condemned the government's drama. At the same time a few organizations protested to the government. All this was done merely to avoid confrontation with upper caste Hindus as far as possible. Nowhere did they (government officials) strictly break wrong practices against untouchables. They described it as 'government drama'.[39]

During this period, however, by and large Panna Lal Barupal and RMSSS made strenuous efforts to broaden the base of the movement and to widen its appeal. Thus, this period marked a high point in cooperation between RMSSS and other untouchables.

In 1952, the First General Elections of free-India showed a further enhancement of Panna Lal Barupal's fortune. Out of 2 reserved seats in Rajasthan for Lok Sabha, Panna Lal Barupal contested as Congress candidate from Ganganagar and was declared elected. The 17 years social work done by him among the untouchable masses in Bikaner played a major role in his victory. Subsequently, Panna Lal Barupal was elected to

Lok Sabha on 5 occasions. After 1952 General Elections, a new Executive Committee of Meghvansh Samaj Sudhar Sabha was constituted. Thus, the new Executive Committee[40] came into existence with Harji Janagal as Pradhan, Arjun Ram Janagal as Up-pradhan, Govind Ram as Pradhan Mantri, Dhura Ram as Khaganchi, Giya Ram Janagal and Rukha Ram Godar as Up-Mantri, Rawal Ram Solanki and Daluram as Nirikshak, Hukma Ram Janagal as Shiksha Mantri, Bhairu Ram Bhadarwal as Pracharak, Shrawan Ram Panwar as Advisor, Narain Chauhan and Surja Ram Devla as workers.

After 1952, RMSSS saw the involvement of Dr Govinda Ram Goel and Ram Ratan Kochar in the reform campaign. In addition to their reform activities on behalf of Meghwals, Goel and Kochar took part in the demonstrations by Meghwals in Bikaner. On November 22–23, 1953,[41] the first convention of a large number of untouchables took place in Bikaner, where untouchables from all over Rajasthan amassed. The Sammelan was attended by Babu Jagjivan Ram, the then Communication Minister, Government of India and Amritlal Yadav, the then Co-operative Minister, Government of Rajasthan. Panna Lal Barupal and Ratan Lal Kochar, representatives on behalf of RMSSS welcomed Babuji and Yadav. RMSSS was also represented by men like Govind Ram Goel, Ram Ratan Kochar, etc. Panna Lal Barupal and other members attempted to highlight the achievements of RMSSS. On other issues, Panna Lal Barupal in his speech urged Babuji to help in promotion of socio-economic and educational programmes which were relevant, not only to Meghwals but to all poor untouchables and landless labourers as well. His main emphasis to all this welfare programme, however, concerned the upliftment of low caste communities in Rajasthan. He hoped that sanction of more and more welfare schemes by both centre and state governments for untouchables would result in their further development. P.C. Joiya states that in this Sammelan pattas of plots were also distributed amongst the untouchables.[42]

The Rajasthan Meghwal Parishad (RMP) 1983

Panna Lal 'Premi' and his colleagues ventured into organizational aspect of Meghwal movement, but it did not seem essentially different from earlier organizations with the movement. 'Meghwals Nav Yuvak Sangh'[43] (MNYS) was formed in 1964 with the sincere efforts of Champa Lal Goel, Panna Lal 'Premi', Aadu Ram Pannu (Bhinasar) and Sugna

Ram Gander (Amar Singh Pura) in Bikaner. There it was decided to form a youth association which would devote itself exclusively to launch a campaign to eradicate the 'traditional customs and social vices' of Meghwals in Bikaner. Indeed the MNYS was to function only in Bikaner. The aims of the new association were social, educational, cultural and economic upliftment; MNYS also organized a number of camps, festivals, etc., to mobilize Meghwals into a viable and assertive community increasingly conscious of its human, social and political rights. Their movements were supported largely by the Meghwal community.

The other major organization involved in Meghwal movement was 'Rajasthan Meghwal Parishad' (RMP), an association founded by some of the eminent social activists in 1983. The leadership of RMP was largely Meghwal caste-fellows and included some active leaders of Meghwal movement in Bikaner division. On February 13, 1983[44] some of the social leaders had appealed to Meghwal Samaj for a public meeting to be held on March 20, 1983 to discuss the formation of a new organization and its significance for the Meghwals. As a result of all this, with the help of Panna Lal 'Premi', Amar Sukh Parihar (Udasar), Lalu Ram Chauhan (Siyana) and others, a Vishal Meeting of Meghwals was convened at the Rawatsar House, Bikaner on March 20, 1983. The meeting was attended by a large number of people and was quite a success. Thus, on March 20, 1983[45] RMP came into existence with Moola Ram Bhadraval as President. As community leaders and in some sense, models for younger Meghwals to emulate, they had perhaps a radicalizing effect on the community.

The aims[46] of the RMP were to elevate social, economic as well as educational conditions of Meghwal Samaj by:

1. Reducing economic expenditure on marriage, birth of a male child, death-feast etc.
2. Neither to give nor take dowry and not to use/serve liquor at the time of marriage.
3. Banning child marriage.
4. Promoting close harmony between Jata Bhambhi, Maru Bhambhi, Sootrakar, Bhambhi, Chamar, Balai and Meghwal.
5. Fixing minimum number of Baratis.
6. Promoting group marriages.
7. Giving only one meal at the time of marriage.

8. Safeguarding self-respect.
9. Outcasting or excommunicating those who go against the social norms.

The activities of RMP were significant for Meghwal movement, in that RMP contributed to the formation of Meghwal elite.

To prepare the constitution, RMP had constituted a Committee under the chairmanship of an eminent social activist. The other members of the Committee were: Hazari Devra, Panna Lal Premi, Bulakidas Devra, and Bhanwar Lal Parihar. This committee was empowered to seek the help of other eminent scholars such as advocates regarding their views on various aspects in the proposed constitution. When the constitution was completed, it was placed before the RMP, where it was approved. At the conclusion of the meeting it was also decided for its registration. Chairman and his colleagues moved an application and it was registered. Its Registration No. is 579/83–84 dated March 30, 1984. The Constitution was printed at Hakdar Printers, Amarsinghpura, Bikaner. A wide publicity campaign was launched especially in Bikaner division. In Bikaner the copies of the constitution were distributed through volunteers.

RMP took lead in opening district branches of RMP all over the state. Panna Lal Premi, an old social activist and also founder member of RMP claimed in his essay: "Meghwal Samaj: Tomorrow and Today", published in 2000 in *Meghwal Darshan*: that they had district branches in more than 50 per cent districts of Rajasthan. From 1983, with the formation of RMP, leaders took active interest to organize the Meghwals in rural areas. The organization of RMP at the village level, tehsil level and district level was an important one, as the majority of Meghwals lived in villages. The membership of this organization was derived from Meghwals primarily from villages.

Notes

1. The most elaborate discussion of the origin of Meghwal and Chamar movement in Bikaner region is given in the *Meghwal Darshan, 2000, Bikaner*, published and circulated by the Megh Mitra Mandal, Bikaner, under the Chief Editorship of Panna Lal 'Premi' and Editor Ganesha Ram Danva. See, P.C. Joya, "Riyasat Kalin Bikaner-ke-Meghvanshi Samaj Mai Samajik-va-Rajnetik Chetna" in *Meghwal Darshan, 2000, Bikaner*, p. 11–14.

2. Panna Lal Premi, "Meghwal Samaj Kal Aur Aaj" in *Meghwal Darshan, 2000, Bikaner*, p. 15.
3. Ibid., p. 15.
4. Ibid., p. 15.
5. P.C. Joiya, "Riyasat Kalin Bikaner-ke-Meghvanshi Samaj Mai Samajik-va-Rajnetik Chetna" in *Meghwal Darshan, 2000, Bikaner*, Ibid., p. 12.
6. Ibid., p. 12.
7. Ibid., p. 12.
8. Ibid., p. 12.
9. Ibid., p. 12.
10. Ibid., p. 12.
11. Ibid., p. 12.
12. Ibid., p. 12.
13. Ibid., p. 12.
14. Ibid., p. 12.
15. Ibid., p. 12.
16. Ibid., p. 12.
17. Ibid., p. 13.
18. Ibid., p. 13.
19. Ibid., p. 13.
20. Ibid., p. 13.
21. Ibid., p. 13.
22. Ibid., p. 13.
23. Ibid., p. 13.
24. Ibid., p. 13.
25. Ibid., p. 13.
26. Ibid., p. 13.
27. Ibid., p. 13.
28. Ibid., p. 13.
29. Ibid., p. 13.
30. Ibid., p. 13.
31. Ibid., p. 13.
32. Ibid., p. 14.
33. Ibid., p. 14.
34. Ibid., p. 14.

35. Ibid., p. 14.
36. Ibid., p. 14.
37. Ibid., p. 14.
38. Ibid., p. 14.
39. Ibid., p. 14.
40. Ibid., p. 14.
41. Ibid., p. 14.
42. Ibid., p. 14.
43. Panna Lal 'Premi', "Meghwal Samaj–Kal-aur Aaj" in *Meghwal Darshan, 2000, Bikaner*, p. 15.
44. Ibid., p. 16.
45. For most important discussion of the origin of Meghwal Parishad in Bikaner and later on in other regions of the state and its objectives, see, in particular the pamphlet *Meghwal Samaj Se Appeal* published and circulated amongst community's fellows by proposed Meghwal Parishad Bikaner. The venue of meeting was Pragatisheel Khadi Samiti Bhavan, Junagarh-ke-Peechhe (Suchana Kendra), Bikaner, dated March 20, 1983. Time: 11.00 a.m. Printed by National Art Press, Bikaner. See, also *The Constitution of Rajasthan Meghwal Parishad, Bikaner.* Head Office: Pragatisheel Khadi Bhawan, Junagarh-ke-Peechhe, Bikaner, Rajasthan. Published on April 14, 1986.
46. Ibid.

13 Balai Uplift Movement in Delhi and Gujarat

The beginning of the movement dates from 1946, when Garib Saheb, who had been greatly influenced by Kabir's ideas, came to Delhi and began to work for the reform of his community. He founded a few organizations for the removal of social vices, bad habits and customs and the stigma of untouchability, through which he attempted to organize Balais in various 'bastis' of Delhi region. He visited several bastis throughout the region, holding 'kirtans', in which he tried to spread the message of social reform.

Another significant feature of Garib Saheb's movement was that it clearly admitted intellectual debt of Kabir Saheb and therefore can be considered as the first implementation of Kabir's ideas by the untouchable communities themselves.

In the next decade or so the Balai movement operated through several forms and in various provinces primarily in Rajasthan, Madhya Pradesh, Gujarat and Delhi. During this period Garib Saheb emerged as a unified leader. The impetus for agitation and mobilization among the Balais arose at the behest of Garib Saheb. He was a Kabir Panthi saint.

We may now consider the growth of different types of organizations among the Delhi Balais over a period of more than half a century.

Dilli Prantiya Sootrakar Sabha (DPSS), 1946

The first organization for Sootrakars was established by Garib Saheb, the great Balai reformer, on February 17, 1946[1] in Delhi. Subsequently, its branches were established in various bastis of Delhi. The report on Dilli Prantiya Sootrakar Sabha appeared in *Sootrakar* periodical on February 15, 1948 and it showed that in four areas namely, Railway Quarters Paharganj, Katra, Ram Nagar, Karol Bagh and Ajmeri Gate, branches of

DPSS were opened. The branches of DPSS were opened with Ganga Ram Doolaya, Sohan Lal, Ramnath and Govind Ram as Pradhans of their respective units. The head office of DPSS was opened at Railway Quarters Paharganj, New Delhi. *Sootrakar* periodical also shows that two persons namely, Goverdhan Das K.P. and Ramnath, played a prominent role in the formation of DPSS. The aims of the Sabha were to elevate the social, economic as well as spiritual conditions of the untouchables such as Balai, Sootrakar and other neglected communities by: (a) promoting education, (b) remedying their social evils and vices, and (c) preaching to them to integrate together. The Sabha was supported largely through individual donation as well as membership fee.

Dilli Rajya Balai Samaj Panchayat Kameti (DRBSPK) 1960

Like Bairwas and Raigars of Rajasthan the Balais of Delhi region also present a unique picture in many ways. There are old urban Balai residents living in Delhi from British days and Balai immigrants who came in waves especially to escape from the atrocities perpetrated upon the untouchables including Balais by Jagirdars, Jamindars, Thakurs and caste Hindus during the princely rule. In addition to atrocities, the incidents of harassments, humiliation and torture were also increasing in villages day by day and eventually a large number of Raigars, Bairwas and Balais migrated to Delhi, Madhya Pradesh, Maharashtra and Gujarat to save themselves from all this. Here they worked as casual labourers, factory workers, construction workers, etc.

After independence of the country in 1947, social workers, activists and political leaders from different parts of North India, such as Madhya Pradesh, Gujarat, Maharashtra and Rajasthan, speaking different languages and belonging to different sub-castes, shifted to Delhi.

The most significant factor in the process of socio-political awakening of Balais of Delhi and other regions was the emergence of Saint Garib Saheb as the most powerful Balai religious saint of Balai Samaj. When the entire country was under the British rule, saint Garib Saheb became the first social reformer in northern India. He was responsible for propagating the term 'Sootrakar' in place of Balai and remained the key social reformer of Sootrakars. He initiated the reform movement in several parts of northern India and remained in close contact with the rural Sootrakars. He was one of the chief patrons of Sootrakar movement in Rajasthan, Delhi, Gujarat and Madhya Pradesh and contributed to it a lot. He provided the platform and pleaded the diverse Chamar castes to come together.

Before 1960[2] the Balai social workers organized themselves into 'Akhil Bharatiya Rajya Balai Sabha' (ABRBS) and 'Dilli Prod Nav Yuvak Balai Jati Seva Samiti' (DNYBJSS) at Delhi. The Balais formed these organizations as reformatory and were committed to the all-round development of Balai Samaj and also to the values of humanness devoid of any kind of discrimination and exploitation. The leaders of organizations declared that the main objective of the organizations was to improve the pitiable social, economic and educational conditions of the masses, which mainly attracted the poor and landless Balais, but that they did not fight for their rights. A split occurred within the Balai Samaj between the existing organizations and social workers.

As a result of this, many active leaders of Balais came forward. The notable ones were:[3] Nand Ram Chhitroliya, Ram Chandar Idiwal, Behari Lal Lohia, Govind Ram Tatiwada, K.C. Godwana, Laxmi Narain Marodia, Moti Ram Chundawat, Prabhati Lal Chauhan, Ram Narain Narmad and Uttam Singh Bhatti. In 1960 these activists organized themselves and started a new organization called 'Dilli Rajya Balai Samaj Panchayat Kameti'[4] (DRBSPK). Thus, DRBSPK came into existence in the same year (i.e. 1960) with Nand Ram Chhitroliya as President, Behari Lal Lohia as General Secretary and Ram Chandar Idiwal as Treasurer. In addition, there were: Uppadhiyaksha and Treasurer-4, Office Mantri-1, Prachar Mantri-2, Mantri-1 and Lekha Nirikshak-1. Besides, there were 12 executive members. DRBSPK appealed to Balais to leave the ABRBS and DPNYBJSS which were controlled by selfish and vested interest persons, who were exploiting the poor and urged them to become the members of DRBSPK in more and more numbers.

DRBSPK under Nand Ram Chitroliya aimed:[5]

1. To work for radical changes in social and economic conditions of Balai Samaj.
2. To check the increasing tendency of crime in the society.
3. To fight against the bad customs, traditions, habits, superstition, etc.
4. To work for social harmony and brotherhood among the caste fellows. Also to implement programmes of socialism.
5. To work for all-round development of society or community.
6. To free them from the battalion of sensual and cunning people.
7. To free the community from foolish religious leaders.
8. To promote youths, intellectuals and the social reformers.

We get an idea of how ABRBS and DPNYBJSS at local level were defamed, with the growth of DRBSPK, from the two pamphlets published and circulated (both undated) by General Secretary Behari Lal Lohia amongst caste fellows.

Balai Jati Sudhar Sangh Delhi (BJSS), 1979

During pre- and post-independence period a few untouchable communities such as Bairwa, Raigar, Bhangi, Khatik, Koli, Meghwal, etc., had formed their own community organizations to introduce reforms in their own customs, traditions, food habits, rituals, traditional occupations, etc., and this was enthusiastically followed by their respective community men all over Rajasthan.

Now, it were the Balais of Delhi who also realized the need of reform movement at community organization. Why should we do so? Two reasons compelled them: The socio-economic backwardness and lack of an all-India organization. Although a few social workers and activists did try to awaken the consciousness among the caste fellows through campaigning against the social vices, touring several places and convening meetings at various places, they could neither unite themselves nor could they form any organization.

The real cause of their backwardness was the absence or lack of sincere efforts. It was their misfortune that apart from their terrible suffering, they had very little chances of progress and development. Yet it is also true that after 32 years of independence (in 1977), there had been tremendous progress amongst the untouchable communities. The united efforts had facilitated them. Too much had changed both in respect of touchables and untouchable. Thus, Balais realized that there was a lack of united efforts. If this could be solved, they could make progress, as the other untouchables communities did after 1947.

The Balais' real failure had been to work out this modus operandi with the community. The interaction between community fellows could be strengthened only by attracting the support of other communities of such strong caste organizations. It was perfectly possible to find a solution for Balai organization.

With such views in mind, in 1979 a few educated young Balais in Delhi took initiative to bring together their caste men. The first meeting of 34 like-minded progressive people was convened on January 14, 1979[6] at Baba Ram Deo Mandir, Anand Parbat, Delhi, under the leadership of

Dr Mange Ram Luniwal. Thus, 'Balai Jati Sudhar Sangh'[7] (BJSS) came into existence with Dr Mange Ram Luniwal as President, Nathu Ram Pidiyar as Vice-President, Chunni Lal Joiya as Secretary, Mool Chand Verma as Organizing Secretary and Manohar Lal Kalawat as Treasurer. Besides, there were six members. They were: Sohan Lal Verma, Mool Chand Maharana, Amarnath Verma, Mamraj, Ramji Lal and Kishan Lal. Thus, in this meeting a working committee consisting of 11 members was constituted to formulate a scheme for the all-round development of the society.

BJSS had emerged as a pivotal organization enlisting the cooperation of Balais from Delhi, Rajasthan etc. The establishment of BJSS in 1979 was a great event in the history of Balai movement. This organization made the Balais aware of their pitiable condition, their low social status as untouchables and necessity of reforms for social change and fighting against the atrocities in order to make an all-round progress. Thus, this organization supported the opening of branches of BJSS, whose main aim was to agitate and fight against the atrocities, untouchability and disabilities in different areas of Delhi and Rajasthan. This was the means of social mobilization.

BJSS also constituted a draft committee for framing its constitution with Sohan Lal Verma[8] as its chairman. Besides the chairman, there was one member in the Committee. The name of the member was Mool Chand Verma. The Committee made sincere efforts in preparing its constitution under the name of BJSS which was approved in the meeting of executive committee held on June 3, 1979 for registration. It was registered at Delhi under Registration No. S/10417 dated August 7, 1979. The Sangh had promised to ameliorate the lot of the community as also an all-round development of the community.

Here it will suffice to note a few selective objectives.[9]

1. In order to fulfil the aims of the organization, it was decided to launch a campaign against social vices and inculcate self-confidence amongst the caste fellows.
2. Needy Balai students should be helped morally and financially in their studies.
3. To use the knowledge of the elderly caste fellows to strengthen the community's solidarity and unity.
4. To provide help/assistance to those who are economically poor.
5. To persuade the caste men to become more and more members of the organization.

After the formation of BJSS, the members of the working executive committee concentrated its efforts on various fronts. The members of the executive committee went to various residential colonies/localities/basties of Balai in Delhi and also organized several meetings with local Balais for seeking their social and economic support. Besides, Balais were requested for their active participation in BJSS's activities and programmes. For instance, the members of executive committee visited[10] Anand Parbat, Thansingh Nagar, Nai Basti, Gadodia Road, Baba Pharidpuri, Taliwala Dera, Prem Nagar, Nehru Nagar, Ranjeet Nagar, Baljeet Nagar, Harijan Basti, New Moti Nagar, Karampura, Pachhim Puri, Panjabi Bagh, Railway Colony, New Delhi,, Railway Station, Paharganj and many others.

Everywhere these members were welcomed by caste fellows and they promised to extend their full support for this noble cause. Thus, they could enrol a large number of volunteers and could collect sufficient funds for BJSS. The income and expenditure statement of BJSS was published in the issue of the paper *Pragati*, Vol. 1,No. 1, 1980. Thus, for the year 1979–80 the total income from all sources, such as membership fee, annual subscription, donation, advertisement, interest etc., was Rs 8,355.40. Likewise for the year 1980–81, the total income from all sources was Rs 18,060.40. It was just more than double from the previous year. It shows the sound economic condition of the organization.

We also learn from the report of sangh that Krishan Lal Gora,[11] son of late Narain Gora, a resident of Delhi and a wealthy Balai who for the first time in the beginning of 1980 requested the executive committee of BJSS and expressed his willingness to award scholarships to meritorious Balai students of 7th, 8th and 9th standard in the memory of his late father, Narain Gora. The amount of scholarship was Rs 50 to be paid annually to each student. The executive committee, in its meeting held on January 13, 1980, welcomed this proposal and conveyed their consent. Krishan Lal Gora introduced this scheme to promote education amongst the poor Balais and in the interest of the Samaj. This scheme also motivated other Balais to do the same thing for the betterment of the Samaj.

Inspired by Krishan Lal Gora's initiative, a good number of wealthy Balais turned up to help the poor and needy meritorious students by providing them scholarship. According to *Ujjawal Path*[12] report (Vol. 6, No. 6. Year 1987), there were three more Balais—Surya Kumar Kataria,

Gopi Ram Baservadiya and Nanak Chand Sisodiya from Delhi to provide financial support through scholarship to Balai students. The scholarship ranged from primary standard to BA/BSc/BCom. BJSS greeted all the sponsors.

The trend was towards BJSS. In1987 *Ujjawal Path*[13] reported that three Balai donors—Sant Saran Das Narwara, Bharat Ram Mordhawaj and Ram Chand Sai donated Rs 552, 252 and 201 during 1984, 1985 and 1986 respectively. In addition, common Balais too were supporting BJSS financially.

During 1979[14] BJSS introduced certain positive programmes of socio-economic reforms as mentioned below:

(i) On certain auspicious occasions, the BJSS would encourage its members to donate some amount.

(ii) The committee also decided that the executive member would contribute Rs 2 per month to the Sangh, in addition to his regular subscription.

(iii) The committee would collect Rs 10 from each member as reserve fund. The same will be refunded when he withdraws his membership.

(iv) On December 23, 1979, a children's 'mela' was organized in public park at Anand Parvat, Thansingh Nagar. Mool Chand Maharana was the organizer. In all, 50 children took part in it. Due to the organizational efforts made by Mool Chand Maharana, two kinds of activities were held: (i) literary and (ii) games. Literary activities included essay writing, drawing and painting, singing of the songs, jokes and poems. Besides, baby show, race, etc., were held. Sweets, fruits etc., were distributed to children. It is significant to note that Smt Kaushalaya Malik a member, Nagar Nigam, New Delhi also encouraged the children's by attending it. Besides, a large number of Balais witnessed the children's mela. In the end, it was unanimously decided to distribute prizes to the winners at the time of the annual meeting of the executive committee. As a result of this, BJSS's President Dr Mange Ram Luniwal gave away the prizes to Pawan Kumar, Devendra Kumar Joiya, Pramod Kumar, Anjubala, Mukesh Kumar, Mahesh Chandra Joiya, Mohendra Kumar, Babi Babal, Raj Kumar and many others.

(v) The BJSS started a Hindi annual 'Patrika' called *Pragati* in Delhi with Mool Chand Verma as Editor, Sohan Lal Verma and Mool

Chand Maharana as Co-editors. Thus, these persons formed the forum of print media to propagate BJSS activities and bring about a greater consciousness among the Balais scattered over Delhi, Rajasthan and other regions of the country. On April 14, 1980 a release function was held at Baba Ramdeo Mandir in which President BJSS, Dr Mange Ram Luniwal released the first issue of *Pragati* at a huge gathering. Editors thanked all for the successful publication of its first issue.

The next big step that the BJSS undertook was to conduct elections of the new executive committee for the year 1980–81[15] during the month of December 1979 with the appointment of Bhure Lal Damolaya as returning officer as per Section 8 ka of the constitution of BJSS. All the 21 executive members were elected unanimously. Thus a new executive committee came into existence with Dr Mange Ram Luniwal as President, Nathu Ram Pidiyar as Vice-President, Sohan Lal Verma as Secretary, Mool Chand Verma as Organizing Secretary and Chunni Lal Joiya as Treasurer. Besides, there were four additional secretaries. They were: Amar Nath Verma, Radhe Shyam Malinda, Beli Ram Verma and Rajeshwar Lal. In addition to all this, there were 11 members. They were: KishanLal, Mamraj, Ramji Lal, Mangal Chand Verma, Puran Chand Bhati, Sohan Lal Jindal, Sita Ram Narwara, Sandu Ram Duharia, Sant Saran Das Narwara, Prabhu Dayal Damolaya and Girdhari Lal Badkodiya.

Soon after the formation of the new executive committee, the BJSS, under the chairmanship of Dr Mange Ram Luniwal, formed various committees[16] called Education Committee, Games Committee and Prachar Committee, headed by Surjan Singh Kekada, Mool Chand Maharana and San Ram Kalwas, respectively.

Besides launching reform activities for all-round development of Balai Samaj, the organization particularly emphasized on the enrolment of members in order to strengthen the BJSS. In 1980, BJSS published its first list of members in the paper *Pragati* in issue, Vol. 1, No. 1, 1980. From page 1–22, details of individual members, such as name of member, father's name with residential address, occupation and his/her official address, has been given. Thus, during 1979–80, 175 members were enrolled. Similarly, in 1980–81, the second list of members was published in *Pragati* in issue, Vol. 2, No. 2, 1980–81. This time nearly 120 members were enrolled. Not only did the organization raise the fund and membership, but it also decided to form a society called 'Balai Samaj Cooperative Thrift and Credit Society'[17] to support the poor and needy Balais. As a result of all this, a committee was constituted with Dr Mange Ram Luniwal as Chairman, Sandu Ram Duharia as Vice President, Beli Ram Verma as Secretary and Prahlad Chand as Treasurer to implement the above programmes.

The main problem which attracted the attention of these office bearers of the organization in the earlier years was the opening of the BJSS's office in Delhi. During the middle of July 1980 a few social activists connected with BJSS, particularly, Ramji Lal, Krashan Lal Nindawat, Puran Chand Nindawat and Dr Mange Ram Luniwal helped in solving the problem by submitting their proposals to the executive committee to provide space for opening the BJSS's office[18] in their respective houses. The four proposals of these social activists were:

(i) Ramji Lal surrendered his house located at Mangolpuri for office.
(ii) Krashan Lal Nindawat agreed to give 15 by 8 feet space from his plot located at Pharidpuri for office.
(iii) Puran Chand Nindawat announced that if BJSS constructed its own office in Mandir premises, he would donate Rs 501 and,
(iv) Dr Mange Ram Luniwal agreed to provide one room from his own house No. 48/16, Gali No. 10 situated at Mal Basti, Anand Parvat, Delhi.

On July 20, 1980, when such proposals were received, a meeting of the executive committee was summoned where all the four proposals were tabled and discussed in detail. After consultations, the executive committee accepted the proposal of Dr Mange Ram Luniwal for opening the office of BJSS. Thus, BJSS got its own, separate office and identity for the development of the activities of Balai movement.

The inauguration ceremony of the office of BJSS[19] was held at House No. 48/16,Gali No. 10, Nai Basti, Anand Parvat, New Delhi-5, on November 20, 1980 by its President, Dr Mange Lal Luniwal by garlanding the framed photo of Dr B.R. Ambedkar. A large number of people, including all the members of executive committee were present.

A notable feature during the presidentship of Dr Mange Ram Luniwal was a grand success of the socio-economic activities and programmes, as a vishal public function was held for launching of BJSS's mouthpiece, *Pragati*. Various literary and games activities were held. Aims and objectives of BJSS views of office bearers and common men on socio-economic issues were published in the paper *Pragati* which influenced the common man. Consequently, a large number of caste fellows became members of BJSS. In addition, the executive committee in all convened nine meetings for various issues. From 1980 onwards several other organizations[20] came into existence for Balais such as Samaj Sewa Dal at Delhi, Mahila Mandal, marriage bureau, opening branches of BJSS at various basties, Balkalayan Kosh etc. In the same year a few Vachnalayas (reading rooms) and Pustakalayas (libraries) were also opened for the community.

The second general election of BJSS for the year 1981–82,[21] was conducted under the guidance of Nathu Ram K.P. as returning officer. As like previous occasion, all the members were elected unanimously. It is significant to note that since the inception of BJSS Dr Mange Ram Luniwal had been the President. This time the new executive committee came into existence with Puran Chand Nindawat as President, Nathu Ram Pidiyar as Vice-President, Sohan Lal Verma as Secretary, Mool Chand Verma as Organizing Secretary, Chunni Lal Joiya as Treasurer and Bhagwan Das Narnolia, Joint Treasurer. Besides the above members, there were four additional Secretaries, namely Gopi Ram Besarvadia, Ramji Lal, Krashan Lal and Om Prakash Gotwal. There were 11 members also, namely: Manohar Lal Kalawat, Sandhu Ram Duhariya, Sohan Lal Jindal, Radhey Shyam Malinda, Amar Nath Verma, Sant Saran Das Narwara, Beli Ram Verma, Prabhu Dayal Damoliya, Het Prakash, Suraj Bhan Kolawat and Kalyan Sahay.

Rajasthan Balai Sewa Mandal (RBSM), Ahmedabad, 1956[22]

As noted earlier, the Balais of Gujarat had very close communal and organizational links with those in Rajasthan. There are approximately 2,000 Balais in Gujarat with approximately 1,000 in the city of Ahmedabad. The Rajasthan Balai Sewa Mandal, Ahmedabad which was established on January 26, 1956 became the centre around which Balais' social activists began to cooperate in making concerted efforts for the welfare of Balais. RBSM, Ahmedabad's President, Dalpat Ram Laxman Sorela, took the initiative in working for social and educational welfare and spiritual reformation of Balais. He was responsible for eradicating the bad traditions, customs, food habits, etc. The RBSM, Ahmedabad was registered under Registration No. E-2692.

In the history of Balai movement, 1973 was an important year. RBSM, Ahmedabad had emerged as a pivotal organization enlisting the cooperation of Balais from Rajasthan state. There was a natural urge on the part of the Balais to abolish the practice of holding large Gang Bhog feast. With this aim in mind a committee was set up under the chairmanship of Kalu Ram Patel. Other notable members were: Ram Lal Upadhiyaksh, PooranMal—Mantri, Hanuman Gulla—Up-mantri, Bhim Raj Gheesha, Prachar Mantri and Lal Chand, Sahyog Mantri. Thus Nukta Nishedha Samiti (NNS) came into existence.

A major programme of NNS was to stress on the abolishment of bad practices including the practice of holding large scale feast and whenever Balais held funerary feast, there was a demonstration and public agitation. The NNS decided to boycott such feasts, to excommunicate such violators and also impose a fine up to Rs 551. The NNS also decided to label and call them 'traitors' of Samaj.

While these issues were common to all the Balais in Gujarat, there were intra-provincial variations too. For instance, on August 27, 1974, under the chairmanship of Gopi Nath Tundwal, Sarpanch of village Kajipura, a meeting of Balai Samaj Sudhar Samiti Jawla (Jaipur) was held. The meeting passed many resolutions, the main was that there should be an immediate ban on the practice of holding large scale funerary feast and dowry system. When Nukta Nishedha Samiti, Ahmedabad came to know about the resolutions, RBSM supported the resolution passed by Balai Samaj Sudhar Samiti, Jawla, Jobner, Jaipur, because many poor Balais came under heavy indebtedness. Similarly, in the fight for the abolition of the practices of bad customs, traditions, food habits, etc., both Rajasthan and Gujarat Balais united to eradicate them.

On March 11, 1975 RBSM, Ahmedabad held its election meeting for formation of a new executive committee for the years 1975, 1976, and 1977 at Bheru Tekda-ka-Bagicha, Chamanpura, Ahmedabad under the Presidentship of Prema Chand Sorela, who was a social activist and reformer of Ajmer, Rajasthan. Thus, Dalpat Ram Laxman Sorela was elected Pradhan, Chhota Lal Jivan Ram as Up-pradhan and Balu Ram Bhuraji as Treasurer. In addition to this, there were 5 members. At Ahmedabad, on the day of Shiva Ratri, dated February 28, 1976, a large gathering was held which was significant because a good number of saints, sadhus, eminent persons of the samaj and social reformers assembled under the banner of RBSM. The Sammelan was chaired by

Swami Laxmana Nand, an eminent Balai saint of Rewari, Haryana. In his address, Swami pressed for imparting education and abolition of bad practices and customs for the progress of the samaj. Similarly, again, after an interval of two months another Vishal Sammelan was organized on Sunday, April 25, 1976. This time it was held at the ashram of Mahant Murdas, a Kabir Panthi at Chamanpura, Ahmedabad. Besides RBSM and NSS, and Garib Saheb Sewa Mandal, Ahmedabad also joined. The Sammelan was presided over by Ganga Ram Ved, an eminent Balai social activist of village Karad, Sikar, Rajasthan. Like earlier Sammelans, this Sammelan also reiterated the prohibition on holding funerary feasts.

During the middle of the year 1976, several things happened which encouraged the RBSM and roused Balais' consciousness to agitate against their miserable socio-economic conditions, low social status and discrimination against them. Also during the year 1976, Bhairu Lal Meghwal, an eminent political leader with distinct ideology and also editor of *Drastikon*, a Hindi fortnightly paper, Udaipur, Rajasthan, toured cities and towns of Gujarat including Ahmedabad and met the leaders of RBSM, social workers and activists. Bhairulal Meghwal was impressed by the achievements of RBSM. He encouraged the RBSM to continue their welfare programmes and reformatory activities as they will be useful for the benefit of the samaj. He asked the leaders of RBSM to campaign without external help.

Notes

1. For a discussion on Balai movement that stressed the role of both political and social organizations in the pre- and post-independence period and their socio-political consequences, see in particular Kishan Sahai Damolaya (ed.) *Sootrakar*, Delhi, Vol.1,No. 1,February 15, 1948, p. 18.
2. For detailed discussion of Balai movement that stressed the role of Dilli Rajya Balai Samaj Panchayat Kameti (social organization) in post-independence period and socio-religious consequences of movement, see in particular, Behari Lal Lohia, Maha-mantri, DRBSPK's two pamphlets "Dilli Rajya Balai Samaj Panchayat Kameti", and "Dilli Rajya (Balai Samaj) Panchayat Committee-ka-Alan",Undated.
3. Ibid.
4. Ibid.
5. Ibid.

6. Balai writers have given many analyses of the origin of Balai Movement, see particularly Mool Chand Verma (ed.) *Pragati*, Delhi, Vol. 1, No. 1, 1980. p. 13.
7. Ibid., p. 14.
8. Ibid., p. 14.
9. Ibid., p. 15–16.
10. Ibid., p. 16.
11. Ibid., p. 18.
12. For most important sources for socio-educational and other activities in Delhi region see *Ujjawal Path*, Vol. 6, No. 6, July 1987, published by Dr Mange Lal Luniwal (ed.). New Delhi, Thansingh Nagar, Anand Parvat, p. 13.
13. Ibid., p. 26.
14. *Pragati*, 1980, Ibid., pp. 15–24.
15. Ibid., p. 21–22
16. Ibid., p. 23.
17. *Pragati*,1980, Vol. 2, No. 2, Ibid., p. 14.
18. Ibid., p. 16.
19. Ibid., p. 16.
20. Ibid., p. 15.
21. Ibid., p. 23.
22. Shri Rajasthan Balai Sewa Mandal, Ahmedabad, Registered No. E-2692, Ahmedabad, gives an account of the meeting of the community fellows of Rajasthan Balais held at Ahmedabad, around early 1956 that banned social vices, published by Dalpat Ram Laxman Sorela, the founder Chief of 'Shri Rajasthan Balai Sewa Mandal, Ahmedabad' and distributed amongst community fellows. Undated. Also see pamphlet by Chhota Lal Jiwan Ram Bhalindia, Up-pramukh, Shri Rajasthan Balai Sewa Mandal, Ahmedabad and distributed amongst community fellows. Undated. Another pamphlet by Magan Lal K. Balöya, Vivasthapak, Suchna Mantri, RBSMA, Shri Rajasthan Balai Sewa Mandal, Ahmedabad, Undated.

IV
Religion

14 Dharmgurus' Contribution Towards Reform Movement of Chamars

The decade of 1940 saw the emergence of Untouchable Movement as a conscious, organized force in the social and political life of untouchable castes/communities in general and the Bairwas, Raigars and Chamars in particular. Though much ground for the advancement of the untouchables had been laid earlier in terms of education and social activities, the 1940s saw a qualitative leap forward.

At the national level the campaign against untouchables was marked by the promise made by Mahatma Gandhi to the untouchables as set out in Gandhi-Ambedkar Poona Pact in the year 1932. It was the period of advancing mass struggle and ideological upheavals in India when the untouchables began their major era of the organization under the leadership of Ambedkar. The untouchable struggle arose against the upper caste Hindus due to oppression and atrocities perpetuated by them and local organizations or campaign against untouchability were founded in many areas, though it was not until late 1940s that an all-India untouchable organization was established. The Congress' new mass-base was associated with the dominance of Gandhi and his call for social reform all linked with assertion of untouchables identity.

Harijan Sewak Sangh struggle, reformist trend embodied in Gandhi's Harijan movement, rise of Praja Mandal, Arya Samaj efforts and growing radical mass nationalism—all provided the ideological and organizational environment within which early untouchable movement took place. At the same time, untouchables' initiative put pressures on these active sections making the issue of untouchability a socio-political one. This process to some degree occurred everywhere. In case of

Chamars this was marked by the formation of "Meghwal Sudhar Sabha, Tiwri' in 1916 in Marwar state (now Jodhpur), 'Meghvansh Mahasabha, Pushkar', Ajmer in 1935, in Ajmer and 'Meghvansh Jati Sudharak Mandal Udaipur' in 1936, in Mewar state. Thus, we can get a better idea of pattern, analysing and organizing capacity of Chamars in Rajputana (now Rajasthan).

Dharmgurus' Contribution Towards Reforms Movement of Chamars

The period from the year 1805 to 1955, represents the formative period in the history of the Chamar movement. It was during this period that the individual efforts, dedicated to the upliftment of the Chamar as an untouchable community, were initiated and spearheaded by Dharmgurus under the leadership of Swami Uma Ram Maharaj, Swami Utam Ram Maharaj, Swami Gokuldas Maharaj, Swami Rusha Ram Maharaj, Swami Joga Ram Maharaj, Swami Ram Bax Maharaj, Garibdas Sahib and others, which began to acquire a socio-religious and educational consciousness. This period of development of the movement has two distinct stages, which were characterized by a different set of issues, leadership and style.

The first stage, dating roughly from the year 1805 to 1955 may be termed an era of self-reform. During this period, the organizations that were formed for reform in orientation and their major concern seems to have been the social upliftment and advancement of Chamar community. This advancement was to be effected through the medium of education, with the elimination of those practices and customs, which branded the Chamars as the untouchable community. Moreover, these individuals accepted the Hindu order as the social as well as ideological system and did not fundamentally question that order. Changes and progress among the Chamars were to occur within the Hindu framework and that progress demanded self-reform of the Chamars as well as the transformation of the attitude of caste Hindus, the destiny of the untouchables was seen as inseparable from that of the larger Hindu society. In the self-directed modernization of community lay the solution of untouchability. Untouchability was defined largely with references to cultural ideological criteria, the attitudinal and behavioural aspects of social life. Varna and Jati were accepted as principles of social organization, hence the progress of the untouchables was to occur within the social and ideological order of Hinduism rather than in opposition to it. It is important to note that these characteristics of Chamar movement at its inception were not unique but indeed were common to many untouchable castes movements emerging at this time. Self-reform within the Hindu framework was the shared perspectives of the movement among lower Castes and Untouchables that arose in Andhra Pradesh, Karnataka, Tamilnadu, as well as Kerala. And in their reformist stance, these movements were within the tradition of the caste Hindu reforms or modernizers who formed organizations such as Arya Samaj and Prarthana Samaj. In this respect, this phase of mobilization represented one possible response to the challenge posed by the West to all strata of Indian society.

By the year 1944, the Chamar movement however, moved towards a new direction with the displacement of the old leadership, the appearance of different issues and a new style in the conduct of the movement. The second phase of the movement saw the emergence and then the predominance of the political and social workers of Chamar as the leaders of the movement. With the ascendancy of educated Chamars, the previous goals of the socio-cultural regeneration of the Chamars community played a significant role. The Hindu framework was no longer acceptable as it was, and its parameters were no longer considered as binding on untouchable communities. Rather the social and ideological order of Hindu society was to be confronted. Untouchability was no longer seen merely as ritually defined, attitudinally conditioned and behaviourally manifested disability, but rather as a form of secular slavery whose imprint was felt in social life, particularly socio-economic. Finally, it was decided that it must be emphasized on the community that the development of Chamar movement did not occur in a vacuum, but was closely affected by social and political changes occurring in the broader environment.

Indian society as a whole was undergoing the process of social mobilization by way of its attendant dislocations with the elaboration of new modes of thought and action. Development in the Chamar community were both influenced by, as well as reflected the process of social mobilization. The origin of Chamar movement may be seen as an instance of that process. The larger political contact was characterized by the growth of Indian nationalist movement, the political awakening of other communities and the prospects for the devolution of power by the British, all of which affected the contours and direction of the Chamar movement.

Self-reform as the Solution of Untouchability

The origin of the Chamar movement and its early development may be seen as exemplifying the process of social mobilization. In Kar Deutsch's formulation "Social mobilization encompasses variety of changes—psychological, behavioural, sociological and political ... that characterize a society in transition from traditional to modern ways of life. These changes have a far-reaching effect on political behaviour and patterns of political action in these transitional societies. The scope of the politically relevant strata is widened and new non-traditional elites emerge. New modes of political interaction develop. The range of human needs that are considered politically significant expand".[1]

An examination of the early Chamar movement reveals that it did undergo the kinds of changes contained in the concept of social mobilization. The emergence of the new elite, which was influenced by modern ideas and was prepared to exhort its community to reject traditional values and roles, was particularly a crucial development in the Chamar community and in growth of the Chamar movement. The new Chamar elite, which was both a product as well as a beneficiary of modernization brought by the British, was the single indispensable feature in the inception of Chamar movement.

The beginning of the movement dates back from the year 1805 when Chamar Dharmgurus emerged in different parts of Northern India and began to work to reform their community. They travelled extensively throughout the regions and held religious gatherings in which they tried to spread the message in order to effect the social educational awakening of Chamar community. They also attempted to organize Chamars in the various regions of Northern India.

When a teacher evolves into a guru, he commands natural respect—not just respect but love and devotion too. The disciple becomes so devoted to the guru that he can sacrifice his life for the guru, though a true guru never expects any sacrifice. The guru shares his being, his love and light with his disciples, unconditionally.

Describing the role of the guru, Osho says, "The role of the guru is to give you a glimpse of the real—not teaching, but an awakening. The guru is not a teacher. The guru is an awakener".[2]

'Gu' means darkness and 'ru' means dispeller.[3] One who dispels your darkness is your Guru. The unique role played by Dharmguru must be considered against this socio-religious background. It was the influence and reputation of the Dharmguru as a 'Chamar Sant' that reached illiterate Chamars.

Dharamgurus of Chamars

Saint Uma Ram Maharaj: 1805

We have noted earlier that several other saints attempted to introduce certain reforms with regard to social vices, bad food habits and drinking of alcohol by Chamar communities to modern educational and employment opportunities. Saint Uma Ram Maharaj also made attempts to introduce certain domestic reforms amongst Chamars and to organize them to carry on his reform agitation.

Since Uma Ram Maharaj was associated with reform movement of Meghwal community, it is necessary to assess his contribution towards this reform movement.

Uma Ram was born in Vikram Samvat 1862[4] in Tanawada—a village situated in Jodhpur, the then princely state (now district Jodhpur). His father, Deva Ram Mehrda, was a poor Meghwal. From an account of events in Uma Ram Maharaj's life, given by one of his biographers, it had been described that Deva Ram Mehrda[5] was associated with religious activities. He took an active interest in inviting 'sadhus, sanyasis and saints' to his house for Satsangh and to deliver the sermon to community fellows. The family atmosphere provided a focus for religious activities. The family was also a training centre for children and both the brothers Uma Ram and Roopa Ram came under the influence of sadhus and sanyasis. In order to divert his attention from spiritual attitude Uma Ram was married at an early age. But even after his marriage he continued his spiritual activities.[6]

In order to lead a religious life, Uma Ram realized the importance of monks. Thus, he left the house. In the course of his wanderings he came in contact with Swami Bananath who was a well-known saint and was so impressed that he became his disciple.[7] He became an inmate of Bananath ashram at Ummaid Udyan, Jodhpur. Uma Ram was aged 26 years when he became a sanyasi.

From an account of events in Uma Ram Maharaj's life, it has been described that Uma Ram was considered to be an accomplished person (Siddha) capable of performing miracles. He acquired spiritual power of the gift of curing diseases of people. Thus, Uma Ram Maharaj emerged as a charismatic leader.

Swami Bananath Maharaj and Uma Ram Maharaj also attracted the attention of His Highness Jaswant Singh-II.[8] Both were invited by His Highness to his palace to participate in Dharm Shastra with pandits who came from Kashi.

कुण्डलिया

"पंडित परपंच त्याग दो, दूर करो सब छोड़
आत्मा की विधा बिना, कबहू न पावो ठोड़
कबहू ने पावो ठोड़, भाव अक्षर के मेटो
अन अक्षर निज स्वरूप, अपणा आप ही मेटो
उमाराम सत विद्या भाखी, सवी वासना तोड़
पंडित परपंच छोड़ दो दूर करो सब झोड़।[9]

Similarly, on other occasions, both were also invited to attend the Vishal Satsangh Samaroh at Darbar Palace. His Highness's family was influenced by the Swamiji and notably His Highness himself.

Swami Uma Ram Maharaj attempted to transform the community as a whole and to uplift the Chamar community by working out social and spiritual reform.

In order to make the social change effective, Uma Ram Maharaj Realized the importance of education. Thus, he toured all over Marwar region to promote and to encourage education amongst the Meghwal community. He went from hut to hut and from house to house pleading parents to send their children to schools.

Uma Ram Maharaj exhibited his talent by writing books in Hindi. The most notable work he wrote is *Anubhav Prakash*[10] a collection of Bhajans.

A large number of untouchables and caste Hindus were influenced by Uma Ram Maharaj and they became his disciples. Some of the disciples later became the Gadhiadhiyaksh of sects and worked hard for propagating and spreading the message of Uma Ram Maharaj. They were:

(i) Swami Kishna Ram Maharaj, Jodhpur.
(ii) Swami Ganesh Ram, Pokaran.
(iii) Ashu Ram Maharaj, Jodhpur.

Swami was active as a socio-religious reformer in Vikram Samvat 1888 and he died in Vikram Samvat 1952.[11] During a period of about 64 years, the kind of socio-religious changes he ushered in were remarkable. When he died, he was of the age of 90 years.

Swami Uttam Ram Maharaj: 1986–1977

Uttam Ram was a great social activist of Jaisalmer. He was born in the year 1969 in a poor family of Mitu Ram Gadi (Bunkar by caste). His mother's name was Khatu Devi.[12] The most significant event during Uttam Ram's childhood was the occurrence of the great famine during 1883,[13] which resulted in a series of migrations. For instance, a large number of inhabitants of Jaisalmer, especially Chamar, Meghwal, Balai, Bunkar and Salvi (all untouchable communities) migrated to different parts of the country, such as Sindh, Punjab and Gujarat in search of work. Mitu Ram Gadi and his wife Khatu Devi, along with their five children (sons-Hukma Ram and Uttam Ram, daughters Ajabai and Parvati Bai) moved to Sindh (now in Pakistan) and settled down their permanently. After some time, father Mitu Ram Gadi passed away. This created nervousness amongst the members of the family which made them realize that they should do some work to earn their livelihood and therefore decided to start weaving and spinning work. At that time Uttam Ram was aged only 14 years when his family migrated to Sindh in Vikram Samvat 1944,[14] he became the disciple of Swami Vishveshwar Das 'Doodhadhari' and in Vikram Samvat 1946,[15] he left the house. In the course of his wanderings he came in contact with Swami Achala Ram Maharaj and was so impressed that he became his disciple in Vikram Samvat 1960.[16] Uttam Ram Maharaj envisaged the need for a socio-religious organization to reach the masses. He established an ashram and thus the famous 'Uttam Ashram' came into existence at Sindh Meerpur in Vikram Samvat 1980.[17] Uttam Ram Maharaj not only maintained close contacts with the spiritual activities but also engaged himself in reform activities, in order to devote his time and energy to campaign against the social vices, such as child marriage, death feast and removal of untouchability. He also stressed the need for education with a view to overcome the traditional outlook and securing non-traditional employment.

Uttam Ram Maharaj himself attained mastery in Hindu language and has written many works in Hindi. The most notable works were:[18] *Anubhav Vani Granth*, *Uttam Bhajan Prakash* and *Avdhoot Gyan Chintamani*. In *Uttam Bhajan Prakash*, there are 300 Bhajans.[19] Similarly, there are 400 stanzas,[20] Poetry in *Avadhoot Gyan Chintamani*.

In 1947, when partition took place, Uttam Ram Maharaj shifted to Jodhpur. In order to make the social and religious changes effective,

Uttam Ram Maharaj realized the importance of having an ashram. Thus, he established a new ashram[21] at Kaga marg, Nagauri gate, Jodhpur and this gave Meghwals and other untouchables an opportunity to participate in reform campaign. The ashram took care of social activities to uplift social life.

Uttam Ram Maharaj was active as a socio-religious reformer in Vikram Samvat 1946 and he died in Vikram Samvat 2038.[22] During a period of about 92 years, the kind of changes he ushered in were remarkable. He was 108 years old, when he died.

Swami Pusha Ram Maharaj: 1873–1952

In western Rajasthan, another Sootrakar saint was Swami Pusha Ram Maharaj. Swami Pusha Ram Maharaj was born on Thursday, Bhadrapad Sudi 10, Vikram Samvat 1930[23] in village Nausar, Tehsil, Bhopalgarh, district Jodhpur. His father, Kalla Ram Kataria, a poor Sootrakar, was living in a traditional style. His mother's name was Sugni Devi. Throughout his childhood and youth, he lived with sadhus, sanyasis and saints of different sects. In the course of his wanderings he came in contact with Swami Ishar Ram Maharaj who was a famous saint of Marwa-Mundwa region and was so impressed by him that he became his disciple in Vikram Samvat 1964 (1907). Swami Pusha Ram Maharaj was dedicated to spreading of God Hanuman's message.[24] The first Hanuman's Mandir, which Swami got constructed, was located at village Roll in Nagaur district. It is believed that some one misbehaved with Swami during his stay at Roll. As a result Swami left the village and moved to another village, Roopasar Bas Tausar near Nagaur city.[25] Here, Swami built another Hanuman Mandir and this was used as a centre for community activities, the most, important being the launching of reform agitation. For instance, the description of social vices, prevailing at that time show that Untouchables were overwrought by social evils, such as child marriage, drinking of alcohol, eating of meat, death feast, Bahu Vivaha (polyandry) and evils of untouchability. Swami criticized them bitterly and urged his community fellows to abandon all this. It is believed that Swami acquired spiritual power of gift of curing the diseases of men.[26]

Swami was active as a socio-religious reformer and he died on Ashad Sudi 2, Vikram Samvat 2009[27] (i.e., June 24, 1952).

Swami Goverdhan Saheb 1884–1979

From an account of events of the ancestors of Saint Goverdhan Saheb's family as given by one of his biographers, Acharya Guru Prasad K.P. (2002), it will be seen that the saint's grandfather, Mohan Jiloya, was residing in village Jilo (Pitan) in the then princely state of Jaipur.[28] Once, the Thakur Saheb passed some remarks on Mohan Jiloya which pained him. It was mainly due to the humiliation and insult thus caused that Mohan Jiloya decided to leave the village and very soon moved to another princely state, i.e., Alwar.[29] He started living in village Giruri in Bansoor Tehsil, Alwar state. Due to Thakur Pansingh's encouragement and patronage, Mohan Jiloya started agriculture work at Giruri.[30]

Mohan Jiloya had two sons—Mangat Ram and Bhola Ram. Mangat Ram usually looked after the agriculture work, while Bhola Ram used to drive chariots of Gulab Singh, Nihal Singh and Sadul Singh all sons of Thakur Pansingh. Mangat Ram was married to Bhuri Devi. After a few years, in 1884, Bhuri Devi gave birth to a male child on the next day of Diwali, i.e., Goverdhan Puja day and this made the parents name the child 'Goverdhan'.[31] Hence, the child was called Goverdhan. Mangat Ram was a famous singer and exhibited his talent by composing songs in the local dialect. This talent of his, earned him personal and deep rooted jealousies of many men. As a consequence, someone gave him poison (सिन्दूर) in Petal. It was this poisoning which largely caused his death. At that time the Sootrakar Samaj allowed levirate and sororate to protect the family from breaking up. The members of family allowed Bhola Ram to marry Bhuri Devi and to lead the family. The Samaj also supported this decision.

When Goverdhan was a child he used to carry his cows and she-goats to the forest for grazing. Once, while grazing the cattle in the jungle he met Charan Das Maharaj who was a famous sadhu.[32] Charan Das Maharaj had his own abode in the jungle and received water from Gwallas. Water was a problem for Charan Das Maharaj.

In order to get rid of the problem Charan Das Maharaj impressed upon his three sons the need to dig small wells for sweet water. All the three sons dug different wells one after the other, but no sweet water could be found. As a result of this, Charan Das Maharaj now asked Goverdhan to dig another small well. With the order of Charan Das Maharaj, Goverdhan started digging a small well and through his hard work, sweet water emerged. Charan Das Maharaj was very happy with this success and so he blessed Goverdhan.[33] Thus, Goverdhan started sitting at the abode of Charan Das Maharaj from morning to evening. Under Charan Das Maharaj's influence, Goverdhan also received religious teaching.

Due to his son's religious aptitude the parents were worried and tried to woo him (Goverdhan) away from Charan Das Maharaj. Similarly, while his parents were obsessed, during 1901–1902,[34] the villagers of Giruri were facing acute drought and famine. Water ponds were drying up, animals were dying and villagers were moving to other places. All these circumstances compelled Bhola Ram to move somewhere else. After some time, Bhola Ram, along with his wife and Goverdhan, went to Delhi[35] for his livelihood. Bhola Ram was now searching for a government job. His efforts for a job took a positive turn when railway authorities appointed him as a 'casual labour' on daily wages.[36] When Goverdhan became a youth, he was also appointed in the Railways.

Acharya Guru Prasad K.P. mentioned that Goverdhan had become attendant of Lord Vegaran, a railway authority at Delhi.[37] After staying for a few years in Delhi and before Lord Vegaran returned to England, youth Goverdhan was promoted as railway mate.[38] A railway quarter was allotted to Bhola Ram at Sabji Mandi[39] railway station.

When Goverdhan attained marriageable age he was married to Shiv Kumari, the elder daughter of Kalu Dayal Kadela who had migrated from Jodhpur and settled down permanently in Delhi. After one and a half year Shiv Kumari died. Goverdhan was therefore, remarried to Badam Bai, younger daughter to Kalu Dayal Kadela. Badam Bai gave birth to two sons Acharya Guru Prasad K.P. and Satya Guru Prasad and daughter Guru Daya Bai.[40]

Even after his marriage and remarriage his religious aptitude and activities continued. During this period Goverdhan came in contact with Balai Saint, Kalu Das, who was a Kabir Panthi at Mojad (now Mojmabad). But Goverdhan could not receive any significant gain from his guru.[41] He craved to satisfy his spiritual thirst. Having failed in self-satisfaction, Goverdhan turned his attention to another Saint Bhopal Das[42] who was chief of Tulsi Panth. Every year a festival was organized at the Samadhi called 'Tulsi Saheb' at which hundreds of pilgrims came to Hathrash Kila to get the blessings of Saheb. Goverdhan Maharaj took leading part in it.

Goverdhan Maharaj learned Vedant, throughout his long career, he could not have spiritual satisfaction. In the course of his wandering he came in contact with Garib Saheb,[43] who visited Delhi during 1938–39.

Garib Saheb was the first untouchable saint to have shown an intellectual ability in interpreting and discussing the religious issues with Muslim Maulvis and eminent Arya Samaji scholars such as Pandit Ramachandra Dehlavi[44] at Delhi. This attracted the attention of Goverdhan Maharaj and was so impressed that he became his disciple.[45] He became a staunch follower of Garib Saheb and worked hard for spreading and propagating the teachings and philosophy of Garib Saheb among the community fellows. He also organized several Vishal Satsang Samarohs at Delhi. Besides organizing community Sammelans, Kabir Jayanti and propagating the message of Garib Saheb, Goverdhan Maharaj played an important role in Sootrakar movement in North India launched by Garib Saheb.[46]

Soon Goverdhan Saheb gained all-India fame as sadhus, sanyasis and saints from distant places visited him at Delhi. Acharya Ram Swaroop Saheb and Shanti Saheb—both from Burhanpur, Madhya Pradesh, Acharya Raghav Saheb from Kashi and Acharya Granth Muninam Saheb from Dayar Bera came to Goverdhan Saheb[47] at Delhi. Goverdhan Maharaj toured all over Rajasthan, Madhya Pradesh and Uttar Pradesh and left a large number of followers for propagating the message of Kabir Saheb. He died on 10 February, 1979.[48]

Yogeshwar Budhanath Maharaj: 1898–68

Budha was one of the illustrious sons of Balai community, who was born in Unboliya gotra family. His native village was Chhoti-Dungari in district Jaipur.[49] It may be mentioned here that through out his childhood Budha was a devotee of Lord Shiva. It is believed that Lord Shiva descends on earth and ventures around the globe during the month of Shrawan. Devotees—both men and women observe long fast during this month and offer milk and flowers and Belpatra (Plant leaves) etc., on the temple Shivlings.

From the very beginning, Budha was interested in listening to Bhajans and lived with sadhus and sanyasis and listened to their sermons. Once it is said, Bhuranath,[50] who was a famous saint of Nath Panth at that time, went to the village, Chhoti-Dungari and stayed there for a brief period. Budha was so impressed by him that he became his disciple. Thereafter, he became Budhanath Maharaj from Budha. After the death of his guru, Bhuranath, Budhanath gave up his family life and became a sadhu. Soon after this, he made extensive tours by visiting places of pilgrimage in North India and meeting great sadhus. He visited Shamdha, in district Alwar to see Gaddiadhiyaksh Yogeshwar Gopalnath Maharaj.[51]

From an account of events in Budhanath's life, given by one of his supporters, Hanuman Sahai 'Rojra' 2002, it will be seen that Budhanath Maharaj was associated with diverse kinds of socio-religious activities with regard to reform campaign. He took an active interest in collecting funds for either building temples or renovating water ponds. For instance, every year the head priest organized an annual Mela at village Narena, near Phulera, district Jaipur in honour of late Baba Rajrishi Ransi Maharaj,[52] which was attended by a large number of Balai sadhus, swamis and sanyasis and other pilgrims from different places. In Narena, there was a small water pond which provided drinking water facilities to common people, but shortage of water disrupted the pilgrims. In the year 1963, it was Budhanath Maharaj who took a special interest in digging the water pond deeper and renovating it.

Besides building temples or renovating water ponds, Budhanath Maharaj also took active interest in removing the superstitions amongst his followers. He made extensive tours in the rural areas, propagating his views and encouraging people to give up social vices.[53] He stressed the importance of education.

He attained mastery over local language and wrote a few works in Hindi.[54] The most notable work was 'Garbh Chetavni', 'Pativrata', 'Updeshika', 'Pragya Bajibodh' and 'Atam Sanhita'. He died on April 20, 1968 at Jaipur.[55]

Swami Joga Ram Maharaj: 1902–1988

Joga Ram was born on Shrawan Shukla 6, Vikram Samvat 1956[56] in Dava, a village situated in tehsil Nokha-Mandi, district Bikaner.

उन्तीस सौ उनसाठ मांही लाल जी जानक तांई।
जननी जी तीजां बाई, जोगाराम जाये है।।
बांटी है बधाई लाल, बाज्यो कांसी हंदो थाल।
लोक भय मालो माल, हेत हरसाये है।।
छोटा भाई पन्नाराम, बहिन है धूडी नाम
पिता जी परम धाम, विसराय पाये है
शादी वक्तु के सध पुत्र पुत्री दोय अंग
रंग में विरंग रंग, माताजी सिध्याये है
(Quoted from: स्मारिका : व्यक्तित्व–कृतित्व
स्वामी जोगाराम जी महाराज जन्म शताब्दी (1902–2003)

आत्मा राम उपाध्याय, 2003 पेज 15)

His father, Lalu Ram Chahiliya[57] was a poor Chamar. His mother was Tija Bai. His brother was Panna Ram and sister was Dhuri Bai. Throughout his childhood and youth he evinced keen interest in religious activities[58] such as participating in religious gatherings, Satsangh Samarohs, sermons delivered by saints, sadhus and sanyasis. Worried by his religious aptitude, the strategy that his parents adopted was to get him married. Thus, Joga Ram was married to Batu Bai.[59] When they started their married life, Batu Bai gave birth to a female child. Once Yogi Varagyanath, who was a well-known sadhu of Nath sect, visited Dava village and remained there for a brief period in the midst of people, living with members of the low untouchable castes and eating at their houses. During this period, he came in contact with Yogi Varagyanath. After coming in contact with Yogi Varagyanath, Joga Ram decided to leave the family life. Thus, Joga Ram emerged as a sanyasi by Vikram Samvat 1987.[60]

उगणिसे समत में साल सितीयासी मांय।
घर गांव छोड़ गये, धीरजन धाये।।
जोधपुर शहर में, गुरुद्वारे आप आये।
कृपा भाई कृष्ण हुकी, पद रज पाये।।
कुछ निद बाद माय, दिक्षा दीनी गुरु राय
अध्ययन की रूचि पाय, रणछाराम धाये।
मास भर पास रहे, शब्द एक सिखायान
लखन राम जी आऐ, करांची जो रहाये है।।

(Quoted From स्मारिका : व्यक्तित्व एवं कृतत्व–स्वामी जोगाराम महाराज जन्म शताब्दी (1902–2003) आत्माराम उपाध्याय, 2003, p. 16)

In the course of his wanderings, he came in contact with Swami Kishna Ram Maharaj at Jodhpur. It is believed that on Magsar Mah, Krashna Paksh 11, Vikram Samvat 1687,[61] he became the disciple of Swami Kishna Ram Maharaj.

Joga Ram Maharaj was illiterate as the untouchables were denied admission to schools. He acquired elementary education from his Guru Kishna Ram Maharaj. For further studies, he went to Balotra,[62] district Barmer. For a brief period, living with Saint Ranchha Ram Maharaj, he learned some elementaries but was not satisfied. During the same period, another saint, namely Laxman Ram[63] from Pali district, arrived at Balotra and stayed there for a brief period. Joga Ram Maharaj demonstrated his curiosity about education under an eminent scholar. This attracted the attention of Saint Laxman Ram Maharaj[64] who advised Joga Ram Maharaj to go to Swami Uma Ram Maharaj's ashram at Karachi (now in Pakistan). Joga Ram Maharaj became an inmate of the ashram at Karachi. Swami Uma Ram Maharaj taught Sanskrit to Joga Ram Maharaj. From an account of events in Joga Ram Maharaj's life given by one of his biographers it will be seen that Joga Ram Maharaj once took up a challenge to pass Sanskrit examination. When he appeared in the Laghu Sidhant Komudini examination, he was declared successful.

This incident demonstrated that Joga Ram Maharaj had an ability to get education. He travelled from Nokha-Mandi, Bikaner to Jodhpur and then to Balotra, Barmer. Thereafter, he went to Karachi.

While Joga Ram Maharaj was studying at Swami Uma Ram Maharaj's ashram at Karachi, a sad incident occurred at Jodhpur. His Gurudeo, Swami Kishna Ram Maharaj expired. In order to attend both Bhandara ceremony in the memory of late Swami Kishna Ram Maharaj and religious ceremony of Swami Bhoja Ram Maharaj as Gaddi-Adhiyaksh at Swami Kishna Ram Maharaj's abode at Hanuman-ji-ki-Bhakari, Jodhpur, he left Karachi and reached Jodhpur.[65] After a short stay at Jodhpur, Joga Ram Maharaj returned to Karachi.[66]

As stated earlier after the sudden demise of Swami Kishna Ram Maharaj (SKRM), Swami Bhoja Ram Maharaj became the Gaddi-Adhiyaksh and was later made in charge of SKRM's ashram where he organized several socio-religious activities and launched social reform agitation. On Magh Badi 10, Vikram Samvat 1998[67] (i.e., on Monday January 12, 1942) he died at Jodhpur.

Yogiraj Naval Nath and Swami Achla Ram Maharaj[68] envisaged the need of a suitable successor for Gaddiadhiyaksh and in Swami Joga Ram Maharaj they found suitability. A 'Vishal' meeting of the disciples was convened under their leadership and thus, a sincere, dedicated and famous Saint Joga Ram Maharaj was chosen unanimously for the Gadhiadhiyaksh.[69] He was informed accordingly.

When Swami Joga Ram Maharaj came to know about all this, he immediately withdrew himself from studies in order to devote his time and energy to strengthening and spreading the socio-religious reforms that SKRM had initiated. He reached Jodhpur. Thus, on January 28, 1942,[70] he became the Gaddiadhiyaksh in the presence of huge gathering and emerged as a dynamic leader by the 1942s.

Swami Joga Ram Maharaj was active as socio-religious reformer in 1940s and he passed away on September 17, 1988. During a period of about 50 years, the kind of changes that he ushered in, were remarkable. He made a direct attack on social evils, bad food and drinking habits, especially drinking alcohol and eating meat. Since the caste was associated with traditional unclean occupation, Swami Joga Ram Maharaj advocated the need for Chamars to give up their occupation of removing the dead cattle and skinning them.

Joga Ram Maharaj realized that Chamar, Meghwal and Balai had been exploited economically by upper caste Hindus, especially Jagirdars, Jamindars, and Thakurs. Hence, he appealed to his community men to stop forced and free labour, viz., 'Begar'.[71] A large number of Community followers were influenced by Joga Ram Maharaj who successfully encouraged them to leave all this. These reforms with regard to traditional occupation and economic exploitation 'Begar' created a lot of problems for them. Upper caste Hindu became restless and vindictive. At several places violence took place. Untouchables were oppressed. For instance, the description of social vices and their consequences show that in the year 1953[72] a 'Vishal' Satsangh Samaroh was organized at Napasar village in Bikaner district under the presidentship of Joga Ram Maharaj. The 'samaroh' provided an opportunity for community activities including imparting knowledge of clean occupations as well as training for weaving and spinning for the poor and unemployed Community fellows. Joga Ram Maharaj considered weaving and spinning as the real job which would educate people into removing the stigma of untouchability.

Besides imparting training, Joga Ram Maharaj appealed to community men to lead a spiritual life. Ganga Ram Goyal, Hazari Ram, Moda Ram, Mulka Raj Thind, Panna Lal Barupal, Govind Goyal and Damodar Ojha also supported this campaign.[73] Chhotulal Vyas, a Brahmin active social worker of Harijan Sewak Sangh also played an important role. Joga Ram Maharaj made extensive tours encouraging his community fellows to follow his new message.

Joga Ram Maharaj as social activist wanted the support of social workers in western Rajasthan against the atrocities and oppressions perpetrated by Jagirdars, Jamindars and Thakurs on untouchables. It was for this reason that on April 4, 1955,[74] Joga Ram Maharaj arranged a 'Vishal' meeting at Kaku village, tehsil Nokha Mandi, district Bikaner.

Joga Ram Maharaj presided over the meeting. A large gathering of the community men, women, children and social workers assembled at village Kaku. The spirit of the Sammelan was to agitate against atrocities and oppressions. Maharaj announced the launching of the agitation. He made a bold statement attacking upper caste Hindus and called it a serious thing that untouchables were cruelly beaten up.

Next day on April 5, 1955,[75] another Vishal meeting was arranged at village Pachu, tehsil Nokha Mandi, district Bikaner. Swami addressed the gathering extolling the importance of agitation.

As a result of Maharaj's efforts and specific course of action by supporters of reform, the orthodox upper caste Hindus threw open the public wells, water tanks and ponds to untouchables.[76] The few untouchable leaders who participated in the meeting were treated as sympathizers. They were: Panna Lal Barupal, Member of Parliament; Prabhu Dayal Raigar, MLA; Govind Ram Goyal, Ramji Maharaj and Kalu Ram Indolia.[77]

After three years, Maharaj and his supporters launched another agitation. The agitation was to demand the right of entry for untouchables into temples. Maharaj toured all over western Rajasthan and appealed to his caste fellows to attend the Sammelan slated to be held in Jodhpur. With all these preparations a stage was set for the Sammelan to begin on March 26, 1958.[78] Maharaj convened a Vishal Sammelan at Ramdwara Hanuman-ji-ki-Bhakri, Jodhpur. A large gathering of community men, women children, social workers and followers assembled. Member of Parliament from Bikaner, Panna Lal Barupal was the chief guest. Eminent saints[79] like Swami Gopal Ram, Swami Ramanand, Saint Lada Ram, Seth Kistur Chand, and Moti ji Mehta also participated and supported the propagation of the 'Removal of Untouchability programme including temple entry agitation in Rajasthan. Maharja pleaded for removal of restrictions regarding admission to schools, entry into hotels and temples. The Sammelan also passed several resolutions of which the most important were:[80]

(i) To ban child marriage and death feast immediately.
(ii) To reduce extravagant expenditure and to pay more attention on child education.
(iii) To encourage the parents to send more children to schools.
(iv) To encourage the community fellows to give up traditional occupation and adopt the non-traditional occupations.

From an account of events with regard to temple entry agitation given by one of Maharaj's biographers, it will be seen that Shivji Kumavat, a non-Brahmin resident of Hanuman-ji-ki-Bhakri and also disciple of Maharaj was associated with reform activities. He took active interest and provided funds for suçcess of the Sammelan. He felt a lot of joy because of the positive effect it had on untouchable masses. He was so happy that on the same day he died[81] at the Sammelan due to cardiac arrest.

After a few months of the Sammelan a delegation under the leadership of Panna Lal Barupal, MP[82] and Joga Ram Maharaj met Pandit Jawaharlal Nehru, the then Prime Minister of India, at New Delhi and presented him a memorandum apprising about the atrocities and oppressions perpetrated by upper caste Hindus in Rajasthan.

In order to devote his time and energy to the strengthening and spreading of socio-religious reformations, Maharaj continued his activities of reform. From 1950 onwards, Maharaj[83] visited New Delhi several times to see great political leaders such as Pandit Jawahar Lal Nehru, Sardar Vallabh Bhai Patel, Govind Ballabh Pant and Babu Jagjivan Ram and apprised them of his ongoing socio-religious programmes and also attracted their attention towards the miserable conditions of untouchables in Rajasthan. These political leaders were so impressed that they assured Maharaj to initiate any programme for welfare of untouchable communities.

Besides reform activities, Maharaj also constructed new buildings and renovated the old ones. The most important building was Swami Kishna Ram Maharaj's Ramdwara[84] at Jodhpur. The records of Swami Kishna Ram Maharaj show that large number of pilgrims arrived here every year to attend religious functions. For instance, every year it organizes Swami Kishna Ram Maharaj's anniversary which is attended by hundreds of Swami's followers, sadhus, sanyasis and disciples belonging to different sects. Ramdwara provides lodging and boarding facilities to devotees and visitors. Hanumanji-ki-Bhakri, where Swami Kishna Ram Maharja built Ramdwara in 1880 and lived until 1932 is now facing the problem of accommodation. In the year 1978 Joga Ram Maharaj took special interest in renovating the old one. In addition, he constructed quite a few new rooms, one Satsangh Bhawan and upper storey. These were built with a view to propagating the message of Swami Kishna Ram Maharaj and carrying out action-oriented programmes, such as prohibition and encouraging education.

After the completion of construction work on February 22, 1980[85] a Vishal Satsangh Samaroh was held at Hanumanji-ki-Bhakri. A large gathering of the community men, women, children, sadhus and disciples of different sects assembled. A procession was also taken out through the main bazaar of the city. The most significant feature of the procession was the ride of Maha Mandaleshwar Swami Kewlanand Maharaj on an elephant. Besides building Satsangh Bhawan, Maharaj also built a few temples[86] in different parts of Rajasthan. For instance, in the year 1986 Maharaj built Satsangh Bhawan and temple at village Pachu, district Bikaner.

Drought and famine were common phenomena in Rajasthan. Every year hundreds of animals died due to scarcity of water and fodder. It was because of this that Maharaj envisaged the need for fodder to save the cattle during such critical periods. Hence, at the tail end of his life he opened in 1987[87] a depot at his native village Dava to supply fodder to cattle and on September 17, 1987[88] he died at Jodhpur. On September 18, 1988 he was buried near his guru's Samadhi at Nagauri gate Jodhpur. It has become a centre of pilgrimage for the Meghwals. A marble statue of Swami Joga Ram Maharaj was installed on September 18, 1988 and several services are offered to Maharaj's idol (Pratima).

Swami Ram Bax Maharaj: 1905–1975

Apart from Gokul Das Maharaj, Swami Ram Bax Maharaj also took lead in spreading social reforms. Born in 1905[89] in an ordinary family of Balai he brought about a new cultural awakening among the Balais of Nagaur district. In his early childhood, Swami evinced keen interest in attending religious gatherings and listening to religious Bhajans (songs). He went from house to house and village to village to hear the sermons of all saints belonging to different sects. In the course of his wanderings he came in contact with Swami Gokul Das Maharaj, who was a well-known Saint of 'Alakh' Sect, Domara and was considered to be an accomplished person (Siddha) capable of performing miracles. Ram Bax was aged 20 years[90] when he became Swami Gokul Maharaj's disciple.

Swami Ram Bax Maharaj himself had attained mastery over Hindi and Pingal languages and had written many works in Hindi. The most notable work was 'Shree Kranti'[91] in two parts. He was the first untouchable to have shown intellectual ability in writing Chhand (stanza), Kundaliya, Saveya, Dohe, Dhanaxariya etc.

Since the community was associated with traditional occupations, Swami Ram Bax Maharaj advocated the need for Chamars to give up their occupation of removing of dead animals and skinning them. Swami realized that Chamars had undesirable religious and social customs and norms.[92] He made a direct attack on social vices, especially on food habits. He appealed to his community fellows to stop such practices. At the time of marriage and birth of a male child in a family, liquor and meat were usually served to relatives and Chamars considered it prestigious to continue these customs. Hence, they (Chamars) spent a large sum of money on it, which Swami considered unnecessary and meaningless.

The other ceremonies which Swami considered unnecessary and wasteful were Charas, Bhang, opium, Ganja etc.,[93] which were served at the time of marriage and on any happy occasions. It was also served when in-laws or guests were invited or visited the house. These reforms with regards to domestic rituals reduced the costs and eliminated unnecessary expenditure. In one of his Dohas (couplet), Swami appealed his community fellows to give up the social vices for advancement of the community. They are:

एकैक कुरीति को, खोद–खोद बाहर काडो।
मेरे प्यारे भाईयों मिल, सुरीति समझाय दो।।
बीती जा रही अवस्था, अब प्रोढ़ो को समझाय दो।[94]
गांजा, भांग, बीड़ी, चाय, चरस पीवे अमल खाय।
काया के लगादी लाय, दारुडी की बास में।।
साधु स्वामी सेवडा वैरागियो की कौने गिने।
"रामबक्ष" निशरडा धुवाड़ो खेंचे सांस में।।[95]

Swami considered child marriage and untouchability harmful for the whole society.

In an attempt to awaken the masses Swami toured all over Rajputana, the neighbouring cities and towns[96] like Delhi, Punjab, Ahmedabad, Bombay (now Mumbai), and Indore. Swami was active as socio-religious reformer in 1920s and he took his last breath in 1975.[97] During a period of about fifty years, the kind of changes he ushered in were remarkable.

Saint Anand Saheb: 1907–1988

Anand was born in Ramjipura, a village situated in Jaipur, the then princely state of Rajputana. His father, a poor Bunkar, was enjoying his family life in traditional style. Looking at his spiritual aptitude, his father got Amand married at an early age. Even after his marriage his spiritual aptitude and religious activities continued. In the course of his wanderings Anand came in contact with Garib Saheb, who was a well-known saint amongst the untouchables in general and Balai in particular and was so impressed by him that he became his disciple.[98]

Saint Anand Saheb received his spiritual education from his guru—Garib Saheb. He had also attained mastery[99] over Kabir's Bijak, 'Garib Saheb's Jinda Bodha Prakash' and other works of Kabir Saheb. Saint Anand Saheb made extensive tours, propagating his new message, visiting places of pilgrimage in northern India and meeting great people. He visited several important places, such as Kashi, Burhanpur and Banaras,[100] acquired spiritual power and also wrote many works in Hindi.[101] The most notable works were: Amar Bodha Prakash, Part I and Part II, Prakash Bodha Part I and Part II, Anand Bhajnawali, Madak Roodwall Khandan and Sadguru Kabir Sar Sidhant.

In Amar Bodha Prakash, Saint Anand Saheb has discussed Amaratva (immortality).

संत आनन्द साहिब
भारत में फैली पोपों की धूंधकार (टेर)
जागे भाट, ब्राह्मण, वंचक, पाखंडियों का नहीं है पार।।
साधू नहीं स्वाधूं जग में, भेष बनाकर पिरे लबार।।
दूध मलाई गिरी छुंवारा, शटरस भोजन खाने तैयार
कोटिन में कोई बिरला योगी मन इन्द्रियों को मार।।
खासा मलमल शाल दुशाला, तन पर हो गजरा हार
तेल फुलेल सुगंध लगावे त्रिया समयों करे सिंगार
नाटक चाटक खेल तमाशा, झाड़ा पूंका करे उतार
छेल छबीले बनके धूमें, लूट रहे संसार ।।2।। भारत
मूंड हिलावे देव भरावे, परचा देवे बेशूमार
हूँ–हूँ करके ढ़ोंग मचावे, नाचे कूदे दे फटकार।।
पूवा–पापड़ी बकरा मांगे, जागरणों दो अब की बार
पूरण काम हो तेरा देव भरे भण्डार।।3।। भारत
चूंडा मूंडा देत भवानी, डोरा गंडा देश बणाय
कपड़ा लाल रेशमी धागा, इंतजाम पूरा हो जाय
भूत प्रेत फिर पास ने आवे, जंतर मंतर नाथ बचाव
निर्भय हो जगत से, खेलो मानो बचन हमार।
पूजा पाठ मसान जमावे कलवा सेवे करते घात
जादू टोना मूठ चलावे, फूंक फांक करते दिन रात

कल्पित मान जन्म क्यू खोवे, वहाँ कछु नहीं आवे हाथ
"आनन्द दास" साक्षी चेतन बीजक गुरूदास सार।।5।। भारत

(Source: Tika Ram Bagotia (ed.) Santo-ke-jiwan Parichaya-*Ismarika*, Jaipur 2002, p. 22)

Similarly in Parakh Bodh Prakash, Saheb had described 'Parakh' Through Anand Bhajnawali, Saheb tried to explain the importance of Kabir Saheb. Saheb had also bitterly criticized and condemned social vices such as dowry, drinking of alcohol, dead feasts, child marriage etc., in his "Madak Roodiwad Khandan". Thus, Saheb gave Balai, Bunkar, Meghwal and Chamar an opportunity to live in non-brahminical Hinduism which has been denied to them for centuries. However, Saheb was certain that the Balai, Bunkar, Meghwal and Chamar might adopt the way of the Brahmins as much as they would, but they would not be allowed to participate in their religious institutions. Hence, Saheb established separate institutions which gave them a sense of achievement, rather a sense of respect for doing things better than the Brahmins. Saheb died in village Kaachseda.

Garib Saheb: 1913–1970

Garib Saheb[102] (henceforth called Saheb) was born on March 9, 1913 in Bhojpura Kala, a village situated nine miles away from Phulera tehsil in Jaipur district, Rajasthan. Born on Mahashivratri, Saheb was named as Shivlala. He showed wisdom and spiritual bent of mind from his early childhood itself. His father, Nanak Das a, poor untouchable Balai, was doing traditional work. Throughout his childhood, Saheb used to visit an eminent saint of Dadu sect at an ashram which was situated near his home. Thus, he came under the influence of the religious teachings of the saint at the age of 12.[103] All of a sudden he disappeared for penance and meditation and reached Indore, Madhya Pradesh. In the course of his wanderings, he came in contact with Ratna Saheb who was well-versed in Kabir Darshan (philosophy) and was considered to be a highly influential saint. A large number of persons belonging to lower castes became his followers.[104] It is believed that Saheb was influenced by Ratna Saheb and joined his ashram at Indore.

Saheb received his religious education from his guru Ratna Saheb at Dehradun. Thereafter, he went to Nagpuri Burhampur in Madhya Pradesh and under the guidance of the then Acharya of Kabir Panth, he studied Kabir's major work 'Beejak Mahagranth'. Then he went to Banaras and there he passed "Sahitya Ratna". Saheb became learned in Kabir's socio-religious philosophy. Thus Saheb emerged as a socio-religious reformer by the year 1942.[105]

Saheb remained active as socio-religious reformer from 1942 and died on October 2, 1970.[106] During a period of about twenty-eight years, the kind of changes he ushered in were remarkable. He formulated his system of thought, oriented towards socio-religious transformation and maintained the reformation of Hinduism, which was necessary and remained attached to it for the upliftment of lower castes. He advocated Manav-dharam, i.e., religion of mankind.[107] He believed that god lives in man and not in idols. He made an attack on the caste system, especially on the supremacy of the Brahmins.

Saheb demonstrated that caste was not an essential factor in acquiring all kinds of knowledge. He himself had attained mastery over Kabir's teachings and had written 9 books in Hindi.[108] The most notable work is *Jinda Bodh Prakash*. It was published in 1955. Other works are: *Manav Dharam Darshan* (1943), *Mera Yogya Shastra* (1943), *Tajhe Bhagwan Ki Bhent* (1946), *Jan Kranti Sandesh* (1957), *Sadguru Bhakti Bihar* (1957), *Saar Sabha Mert* (1958), *Jan Jagran Sandesh* (1969) and *Sawartit Swaroop Baashya* (1975) (published posthumously).

He was the untouchable who has shown deep interest in preaching and propagating Kabir Beejak, the supreme text of Kabir's social and religious philosophy. Saheb was of the opinion that people have a right to study all religious books and opposed idol worship. As stated earlier, Saheb opposed the 'Begar' (forced labour). The following incident related to Saheb's achievement was narrated in the dissertation (1996) of Anita Chacko,[109] an M.Phil student at the Department of Sociology, University of Rajasthan. Apparently, Saheb was once resolved to mobilize the downtrodden masses and created a feeling against the oppressed and suppressed by caste Hindus. For instance, in 1942[110] Saheb organized a huge gathering in which a large number of Chamars, Balais etc., participated to demonstrate their grievances. The procession started from Chandpole gate and reached Ram Niwas Garden. There Saheb led a delegation to submit a memorandum to His Highness the Maharaja of Jaipur, Sawai Man Singh, requesting him to solve their problems particularly the Begar. It is said that Saheb was the first untouchable who influenced, His Highness through his reform work. This attracted the attention of His Highness. As a result of welfare activities, His Highness offered some financial support to Saheb to continue welfare programmes, but he refused. Saheb requested His Highness to do away with exploitative feudal system prevailing in the princely state of Jaipur and thereby help in liberating the exploited section of society. As a result of agitation His Highness initiated a few steps to abolish the pratice of 'Begar'.

The *coronation, Silver Jubilee celebration of* Maharaj Sawai Man Singh of Jaipur (also the then Rajpramukh of Rajasthan) was held on April 9, 1948 at Albert Hall, Rambagh. The great Saint Garib Saheb who was leading the reform movement, in Rajasthan and was popular for his sermons and teachings presented "अभिनन्दन" to the Maharaja on this occasion for the betterment of untouchable castes/communities. An *Ismarika* entitled "ग्यारहवीं षताब्दि में स्थापित श्री समष ऋषि गद्दी स्थान बिचून, जयपुर की सहस्त्राब्दिः स्मारिका" edited by Acharya Guru Prasad K.P., Uttam Nagar, New-Delhi 2003 contains "अभिनन्दन पत्र" of Sootrakar Samaj.

"अभिनन्दन पत्र" dated April 9, 1948 from Sootrakar Samaj presented by Garib Saheb to Maharaja Sawai Man Singh:

श्रीमान् महाराजाधिराज, राज राजेन्द्र, सर आमदे, राज सहाय हिन्दुस्तान, मेजर जनरल, हिज हाइनैस श्री मानसिंह बहादुर जी, सी.एस.आई., जी.सी.आई.ई., एल.एल.बी. की सेवा में

"अभिनन्दन पत्र'

आज समस्त भारत और जयपुर राज्य के सूत्रकार श्रीमान् के सुशासन की रजत जयंती पर श्रीमान् को हृदय से बाधाई देते हैं।

राज राजेन्द्र! आपका शासनकाल जयपुर राज्य और इतिहास में ही नहीं, बल्कि भारत में आदरणीय रहेगा। श्रीमान् के शासन के 25 वर्ष में जयपुर राज्य ने राजनीति, शिक्षा, उद्योग धन्धों, सामाजिक तथा आर्थिक सुधारों और हर एक क्षेत्र में जो उन्नति की है उसकी मिसाल अन्यत्र बहुत कम मिलती है। आज जयपुर उत्तरी भारत में शिक्षा का महान केन्द्र है। जयपुर नगर सुन्दरता में भारत का सबसे सुन्दर गुलाबी नगर है। आज जयपुर राज्य में सैंकड़ों की तादाद में कल–कारखाने खुले हुए है। जयपुर राज्य शांति और न्याय के लिए प्रसिद्ध है जहां शेर और बकरी एक जगह पानी पी सकते हैं, भारत विभाजन के समय भी उत्तरी भारत में जयपुर ही एक ऐसी जगह थी जहां पर हर एक की जानो–माल की पूरी रक्षा होती रही है। श्रीमान् ने हाल ही में यहां पूर्ण उत्तरदायित्व वाली सरकार कायम की है। श्रीमान् के शासनकाल की जितनी भी प्रशंसा की जाय उतनी कम है।

रघुकुलभूषण! आपके राज्य में हम करीबन तीन लाख सूत्रकार बलाई बसते हैं। हम हमेशा से शांतिप्रेमी और राजभक्त रहे हैं और हम तमाम अन्य समाजों की भी अपने शिल्प से सेवा करते आये हैं और खास करके गांवों के आर्थिक जीवन में हमारा बहुत बड़ा भाग है। प्रायः हम लोग कपड़ा बुनने का कार्य करते हैं और हमको इस बात पर गर्व है कि

हमारे हाथ की बुनी हुई खादी आज भी भारत देश के प्रमुख नेताओं और देशभक्तों की पोशाक है और स्वर्गीय बापू जी की तो यह बहुत ही प्रिय वस्तु रही है। आज जयपुर के सूत्रकार मशीन द्वारा बुने हुए कपड़े से भी सुन्दर कपड़ा बना सकते हैं।

प्रजापालक! हम श्रीमान् का ध्यान हमारी कुछ परिस्थितियों पर भी दिलाना चाहते हैं। जयपुर राज्य के बेगार पर प्रतिबन्ध होने पर भी कुछ गांवों में जोर जबरदस्ती से हम लोगों से बेगार ली जाती है और कहीं–कहीं पर रोका गया है। हमें आशा है कि श्रीमान की सरकार कड़ाई के साथ इनका इन्तजाम करेगी। जयपुर राज्य के सूत्रकारों को एक बड़ी तकलीफ इस बात की भी है कि उनको मिल का सूत बहुत ही थोड़ी मात्रा में मिलता है और इसके कारण हमारी बेकारी बढ़ गई है। जयपुर राज्य से जो हाथ बुनी खादी बाहर जाती है, उसकी निकासी पर राज्य का भारी मसहूल (टैक्स) होने के कारण, हमारा माल भी बड़ी तादाद में बाहर नहीं जा पाता है, इससे भी हमारे रोजगार में बड़ी कमी आई है। राजस्थान चर्खा संघ ने जब सूत लेने का नियम बनाया था तबसे उनकी भी खादी की बिक्री कम हो गई है। इन बातों पर श्रीमान् की सरकार को गम्भीरता से विचार करना होगा। शिक्षा के क्षेत्र में भी हमारे सूत्रकार समाज की बहुत बुरी हालत है और हम लोग श्रीमान् की सेवा में दया व उदारता के पात्र है।

नरेशाधिनरेश! हम श्रीमान् को बधाई देते हुए हमारे इष्टदेव रामदेव जी महाराज, व डालीबाई और धारू जी मेघवाल की रजत प्रतिमा तथा स्वर्ण डोरा वेष्ठित रजत नारियल आपकी राज्यरोहण की रजत जयन्ती पर श्रीमान् को प्रेमपूर्वक भेंट कर रहे हैं। हमारी यह एक तुच्छ भेंट है किन्तु इसको श्रीमान् हमारी भक्ति का नमूना चिन्ह मानकर स्वीकार करेंगे, ऐसी हमे आशा है। न्यायपरायण श्रीमान् हम श्रीमती महारानी साहिबा, श्रीमान महाराज कुंवल साहब की व समस्त राज परिवार की चिरायु होने की ईश्वर से कामना करते हैं।

हम है, श्रीमान के प्रजाजन अखिल भारतीय सूत्रकार महासभा के पदाधिकारी तथा सदस्यगण एवं जयपुर रियासत के हरिजन

जयपुर

9 अप्रैल, 1948

Maharaj and Rajpramukh Sawai Man Singh of Jaipur responded and enthusiastically appreciated the gesture of Saint Garib Saheb.

महाराजाधिराज का मान–पत्र के उत्तर में भाषण

आज सूत्रकारों और अन्य हरिजनों (दलितों) से मिलकर मुझे बड़ी खुशी हुई है। जो राजभक्ति आज दिखलाई गई है और राज परिवार के लिये जो शुभकामनायें दी गई है उसके लिये मैं आभारी हूं।

मुझे यह जानकार संतोष है कि मेरी सरकार ने हरिजनों (दलितों) की भलाई के लिए जो कुछ अब तक किया है उसे सराहा गया है। मुझे विश्वास है कि मेरी सरकार की नीति वहीं रहेगी याने सूत्रकारों और हरिजनों (दलितों) दिनो–दिन तरक्की करते रहेंगे।

हरिजनों के लिये 'दलितों' शब्द नाम में लाना मैं अनुचित समझता हूँ। पुराने जमाने में सभी जातियों को समाज में उचित स्थान दिया जाता था क्योंकि जैसे हमारे शरीर के अलग–अलग अंग है उसी प्रकार हरिजन भी समाज के जरुरी अंग हैं।

पिछली लड़ाई के वक्त में सूत ना मिलने के कारण सूत्रकारों को कुछ कठिनाइयाँ उठानी पड़ी है, परन्तु अब हालत सुधर गई है और मैं आशा करता हूँ कि जो भी कमी है वह पूरी हो जायेगी।

सब जानते हैं कि हमारी देश की स्वतंत्रता की प्राप्ती के समय यह हुक्म जारी किया गया है कि को–ऑपरेटिव सोसाइटीज की मार्फत भेजे गये माल पर कोई चूंगी न लगाई जाय और आज अगर दूसरे जरिये से भी खादी जायेगी तो भी उस पर मामूली चुंगी लगेगी। मैं समझता हूँ कि रियासत में सूत्रकारों को काफी फायदा होगा।

इसके अलावा अभिनन्दन–पत्र में जिन विषयों पर खास तौर से ध्यान दिलाया गया है, मुझे विश्वास है कि मेरी सरकार उन पर पूरा विचार करेगी और जल्दी ही मुनासिब कार्यवाही शुरूकर देगी। मैं यह जानकर बहुत खुश हूँ कि सूत्रकार और हरिजन अपने रहन–सहन सुधारने और पढ़ने–लिखने की पूरी कोशिश कर रहे हैं। यह बहुत ही अच्छा है क्योंकि इनमें तरक्की करने से ही और बातों में सफलता मिलेगी। मैंने यह तय किया है कि सूत्रकारों और हरिजनों की प्रगति के लिए एक फण्ड में कुछ देना मुनासिब होगा। इसकी मंजूरी मैने दे दी है वह एक लाख रूपया आपको मिल जायेगा। आप लोगों को दी गई यह बाबा रामदेव जी महाराज का स्मृति की मूर्ति और अभिनन्दन मैं प्रेम से स्वीकार करता हूँ और यह फिर कहना चाहता हूँ कि मुझे सूत्रकारों और हरिजनों से मिलकर बहुत खुशी हुई है।

Another notable incident which is associated with Saheb during 1960s was Kabir's birth anniversary celebration programme in Delhi.[111] Dr Sarvapalli Radha Krishnan, the then Vice-President of India, presided over the function. On June 21, 1960 Saheb attended the function and spoke to the gathering about Kabir's socio-religious philosophy. During this programme Saheb met the Vice-President also

Saheb realized that Chamars, Balais and the other castes had undesirable religious customs and norms. He appealed[112] to his followers to stop animal sacrifice in their traditional temples. The other habits which Saheb considered bad and wasteful were drinking of alcohol and eating of meat. Saheb also encouraged them for Sanskritization. He advocated monogamy as against polygamy.

In order to make the socio-religious changes effective, Saheb toured all over Rajasthan and the neighbouring states. Thus, he created a socio-religious awareness and this gave Chamars, Balais and others, an opportunity to participate in socio-religious philosophy of Kabir, which had been denied to them for centuries. Saheb was certain that even if untouchable Chamars, Balais etc., adopted the ways of the Brahmins, they would not be allowed to participate in their religious institutions. Hence, he advocated Kabir Darshan which gave them a sense of achievement and fulfilment and in some respect of doing things better than Brahmins. Saheb condemned the system of idol worship. He believed that man himself was god and by serving human beings one realized god. He asked his followers to stop idol worship.

Saheb made extensive tours, visiting places of pilgrimage in northern India and meeting great people for propagating Kabir's message. He brought about a high degree of identity among Chamars and Balais, who shared Kabir's ideology. There are today four 'mutts' or 'ashrams'. 'mutt' or 'ashram' is the seat of a sanyasi, generally called Saheb, who is incharge of the study and teaching of other religions in general and Kabir's teachings in particular. The first 'mutt' established after Saheb's death in 1970[113] was at Azad Nagar, Kishangarh, Ajmer. In 1975[114] his disciples established another one at Kota. They also established two 'mutts' at Phulera, in the year 1976 and 1977 respectively.[115] His followers established a fourth one at Bhojpura village where he spent his early life in 1985–86.[116] Besides these, there is one 'mutt' in Indore, Madhya Pradesh (1985–86)[117] and another in Ahmedabad, Gujarat (1985–86).[118] In each of these 'mutt' or 'ashram' there is an untouchable sanyasi devoted to the study of Saheb's work and who will follow and propagate Kabir's teachings.

Saheb emphasized the need for women upliftment through spread of education and advocated their equal social and religious rights.[119]

From an account of the literary contribution of Saheb's disciples given by Chacko in her dissertation (1966), it is evident that his disciples were associated with religious activities to write more and more on 'Manav Dharma'. For instance, Acharya Swami Chaitanya Das Beejak Pathi wrote[120] 'Manav Dharma Updesh' (1975), 'Shri Sadguru Bhakti Padh Prakash' (1976) and 'Shri Sadhguru Bhakti Vihar' (1983). Mahant Atmadass also wrote "Manav Bodh Prakash" (1983).[121]

Saheb encouraged modern education because it had a liberating effect on Hindu customs. In his sermons he stressed the importance of girls' education. He considered education essential because it would educate the people to stop caste differences.

On October 2, 1970, Saheb died at Bichun. It is necessary to mention here that for nearly 15 years, on account of non-availability of a suitable person, the Gaddi remained vacant. However, on the request of the followers, Acharya Gojit Saheb ascended[122] the Gaddi on December 13, 1985. Acharya Gojit hails from Madhya Pradesh. Like Garib Saheb, he also believes in humanism, equality and liberty.

Acharya Gojit envisaged the need for an organization to reach the masses. He encouraged his disciples and others to form an organization and thus the famous 'Acharya Swami Garib Saheb Vikas Sansthan' (ASGSVS) came into existence at Bichun in 1986–87, which was registered in the year 1988–89 under the registration No. 319.[123]

ASGSVS is dedicated to spreading of Kabir's and Saheb's messages. ASGSVS, which has its headquarters at Bichun manages mutts of ashrams. Every year on 9th March, the birth anniversary of Saheb is celebrated at Bichun and other places at which hundreds of pilgrims come to Bichun to partake in the blessings of Saheb. Bichun, where Saheb lived until 1970, has become a centre of pilgrimage for Balais, Chamars and other untouchables. The Samadhi of Saheb was constructed with marble stones and services are offered to Saheb's Samadhi. Pilgrims make wishes and offer prayers to Saheb. Thus, even after his death, the spiritual regeneration amongst the Chamars, Balais etc., continues.

Balinath Maharaj: 1926

The main leader of social reforms amongst the Bairwas was Balinath Maharaj.[124] He was born in Samvat 1926 in Mandavari village, tehsil Lalsot in Jaipur district. His father was Kishan Ram and his mother was Sundar Bai. His parents named him 'Nand Ram'. Nand Ram was a handsome boy. His personality attracted the attention of Bairwas of nearby villages and the ladies there wanted to marry him.

When Nand Ram came to know about plans for his marriage with Champa of Basipada, he disappeared and went into forest. After an intensive search for five days he was traced out and brought back home. After a brief period, he was ultimately married to Champa, a resident of village Basipada, near Gangapur city, Sawai Madhopur district.[125] It is said that when he was married, he was only 11 years old. After two years of marriage, his mother died due to an epidemic. It was a great shock to his father. His father could not bear her loss and after an interval of one year he also expired. Thus, throughout his childhood and youth Nand Ram did not have the affection of his parents. This incident changed his whole life. All of a sudden he again disappeared from home for meditation. In the course of his wanderings he reached Shoranji. Here he came in contact with a person named Gangaguru.[126] For a brief period Nand Ram lived with him. He had a daughter and he wanted to marry his daughter with Nand Ram. When Nand Ram knew about all this, he immediately ran away.

In order to learn spiritual knowledge, he reached Kashi. In Kashi he came in contact with Pandit Gangadhar,[127] who was a literary person with a wide knowledge of Sanskrit. Nand Ram remained here for six years and learned Sanskrit but he was not happy. Later he returned to Mandavari.

In the course of his extensive tours he visited Saint Tunginath's ashram[128] near Mandavari village and was impressed by his teaching. Tunginath was a Gaur Brahmin from Sirsa Bhivani. Nand Ram accepted Tunginath as his guru and became his disciple. Tunginath rechristened him 'Balaknath'.[129] Balaknath served his guru whole-heartedly. Balaknath was the first untouchable to become his disciple. Thus, Tunginath set an example and asked his followers not to observe caste discrimination. Tunginath not only made a Bairwa his disciple, but also kept him in his ashram. Thus, Balaknath became an inmate of Tunginath's ashram at Mandavari and was later made incharge of the ashram.

With guru's permission Balaknath went on a pilgrimage to Onkeshwarnath temple at Ujjain.[130] During his journey he met a few great saints such as Hiranand Bharti at Badnagar. From Badnagar he went to Gadnal where he remained for nearly three years in the mountains.[131] From Badnagar he went to Amreshwaran Mahadev, Mountain in Sawai Madhopur district. There he lived for six years.[132] His heritage ashram is still in existence and is known as 'Anpurna'.

At the tail end of Tunginath's life Balaknath returned to Ashram. On his return after nearly a decade or so, Tunginath became very happy. Looking towards his old age and declining health, Tunginath expressed his desire amongst the Mahants and other members of the ashram that Balaknath be considered to succeed him after his death. When Tunginath died, the followers of the Nath sect fully supported Balaknath and according to guru's wishes, organizers of the sect organized a big religious gathering called 'Bhandara' and they invited Balaknath to become the "गद्दीध्यक्ष" and when he reached there, he was made "गद्दीध्यक्ष". From that day he was called 'Balinath'.[133]

For quite a few years Bairwa caste had been suffering from social evils and vices, so Balinath realized the need to reform the internal socio-religion. He made extensive tours and visited places of pilgrimage in India, propagating his new message and meeting the people. He visited Lahore,[134] Punjab, Karachi and Delhi and Madhya Bharat. He also attracted the attention of Bairwas towards their social and economic backwardness. He appealed to his people to abandon the Mrityubhoj (death feast), child marriage, dowry, begar (forced labour), drinking of liquor and eating of meat.

In his early years as a social reformer, Balinath went from village to village, and from house to house to meet caste fellows and discussed these problems with them. He appealed for a social regeneration of the masses. While these sporadic efforts did not achieve the character of the movement, Balinath's new reform created widespread and spontaneous excitement. A few influential persons in villages and towns collected volunteers, formed a group and spread the message of Balinath. They asked the people to give up the worship of evil spirits, to abstain from the places where alcohol and meat were served. The Balinath realized that Bairwas had undesirable religious customs and norms. He appealed to his followers to stop animal sacrifice. The main object of Balinath was to promote and encourage the socio-religious reforms and industrious habits amongst the Bairwa community. Thus, he brought about a new social awakening among the Bairwas of Rajasthan.[135]

A few caste Hindus were not happy with Balinath's informative activities, particularly Thakurs. When Balinath was camping at Jhalai, Rajasthan, Thakur Kalyan Singh harassed and insulted him. Thakur asked him to leave the place immediately. Without uttering a single word, Balinath left that place (Jhalai). From an account given by B.L. Nagar,[136] chief editor of 'Bairwa Saint Siromani Maharashi, Balinath Maharaj Bairwa Divas Swarn Jayanti Samaroh, 1976 of the events in Balinath's life, it will be seen that Thakur Kalyan Singh immediately fell down in Balinath's feet and tendered his apology with folded hands. Balinath pardoned him. On Thakur's request, Balinath made him his disciple. Balinath was considered to be an accomplished person (Siddha) capable of performing miracles.

Balinath was active as a socio-religious reformer and he breathed his last in Samvat, 1982. During a period of about thirty years, the kind of changes he ushered in were remarkable. Mandavari where Balinath lived until samvat 1982, has become a centre of pilgrimage for the Bairwas. Every year on 31st December, disciples organize a function in honour of

Balinath which is attended by Bairwas, Sanyasis and others belonging to different castes. Pilgrims make wishes and offer prayers to Balinath which are usually fulfilled.[137]

Baba Khivadas: 1936–2001

Baba Khivadas also took the lead in bringing awakening among the untouchables. He was born in Vikram Samvat 1993 (in the year 1936) in village vithura, tehsil Ladnu, district Nagaur in a poor family of Khuma Ram.[138] His mother's name was Choti Devi. Baba could not receive education as untouchables were not admitted to schools. However, his aptitude towards education continued. In Vikram Samvat 2022 (i.e., March 23, 1996) after the Bhandara ceremony of late Saint Ladu Ramji Maharaj, Baba Khivadas was made Chief Mahant of Dhoona Sangaliya in the presence of a huge gathering.[139]

In an attempt to establish schools, Aushadhalyas, Mandirs and Bhavans, Baba Khivdas travelled all over Rajasthan. He encouraged modern education because of the liberalizing effect it had on customs. Baba Khivadas took a special interest in opening educational institutions. According to the description given by one of his biographers, it is apparent that during 1995–1997, Baba Khivadas constructed a college called 'Baba Khivadas College' on Sikar-Didwana Road. The college was spread over 37 bighas land.[140] On November 29, 1997 the college was inaugurated by the then Higher Education Minister, Lalit Kishore Chaturvedi, Government of Rajasthan.[141] Baba Khivadas considered educational institutions the real temples which educate people to sink social vices and caste differences.

Whenever the followers of Sangaliya Panth meet they greet each others by saying "jai saheb". He died on August 12, 2001.[142]

Relationship with Other Movements and Communities

The change in attitude and strategy from submissiveness to assertion and from acquiescence to defiance represented a direct challenge to the caste system or Jati Vyavastha, which sought to maintain it, as well as an assault on the ideology and principles which underlay that order. This change was supported by all sections of the untouchable communities. The 'All-India Bairwa Mahasabha'[143] for instance launched a campaign against untouchability and caste disabilities for untouchable Bairwa's in Rajputana, Madhya Pradesh, Delhi and Uttar Pradesh. The reasons behind launching this reform movement for overall improvement in the conditions of untouchables was to demand equality in socio-religious, educational and economic spheres.

Other untouchable communities in the then Rajputana princely states such as Chamars, Meghwals, Bhambhis and Raigars,[144] developed their own association in 1940 separate from Bairwa movement. The tone, style and kind of issues promoted by these associations are reminiscent of Bairwa movement in the early 1940s.

It is not surprising that each of the untouchable communities, however, small or large had developed their own organizations, as the rivalry and distinctions among them are of long standing. It is a testament to the potency and pervasiveness of the idea of caste amongst the untouchable communities themselves that notions of pollution and purity shaped their interrelationship. Chamars consider themselves as the most 'pure' of the untouchables, and thus do not interdine or intermarry with either the Raigars or the Bhambhis. While the Chamars, Bhambhis and Raigars as well, consider themselves to be 'pure' yet they have very limited commensality. The residential patterns of all these communities are also based on segregation, there being a Chamar Mohalla (basti), Raigar Mohalla as well as Bhabhi Mohalla, in any given village.

These ritual differences among untouchable communities were parallel to the socio-economic differences as well. The Chamars seemed to be economically secure. They had their own traditional occupation of removing the dead animals, skinning them and leather working which were essential to the village. They were heavily represented in the ranks of agricultural labour as were the Meghwals and Bhambhis. They had direct connection with the village administration and were thus considered village servants. The Chamars also had their own traditional occupations. They were skin or leather dyers and their products were economically necessary to the village. The advent of British rule had an advantageous effect on these (leather communities such as Meghwal, Bhambhi, and Chamar) communities, as the establishment of leather factories in India improved the working conditions of these communities. By the 1940s, therefore the Chamars, Meghwals, Bhambhis and Balai's became the most advanced communities.

The Chamars had produced a leader with education political skills or stature of Amrit Lal Yadav. Chamar organization developed the confrontational ideology and strategy of Bairwa (former Chamar community) movement in its early reform phase. The Dharmgurus of Chamar Samaj called upon their community fellows to initiate a process of self-reform and modernization, to cleanse themselves of baneful social practices and above all to educate themselves. In this endeavour both the Raigars and Chamars recognized the dearth of qualified leaders and educators in their own communities. Furthermore, neither the Chamars nor Raigars or Bairwas' organizations developed the political thrust as of Mahar movement in Maharashtra, but remained by and large socio-cultural groups dedicated to the internal self-reform. Instead, Chamars, Meghwals, Bhambhis and also Raigars gravitated towards the Congress realizing their social and political interests and aspirations through this party.

The divergence in the political orientations of Chamar movement on the one hand and the Raigar movement on the other, may be explained by differing socio-economic development of the two communities under traditional caste systems. The Chamar community was far more affected by the process of socio-political mobilization than were either the Raigars or Bhangis. This process expanded the range of politically aware and politically silent Chamars—a more or less modernized elite to a much greater extent than among other untouchable communities including the Raigars.

The development of Chamar elites which had been influenced by modern ideas (such as Prajamandal agitation, Rajputan Harijan Sewak Sangh's socio-cultural activities, national movements and political awakening in the then princely states), subversive of the established social and religious order was certainly crucial in the early politicization of Chamar movement and direction, it was to take under Babu Jagjiwan Ram. The stunted development of Raigar movement reflects the show and uneven progression of social mobilization among the Raigars and the other untouchable communities.

The development of the Chamar movement occurred more or less in isolation from the other untouchable communities of Rajputana now Rajasthan. It also did not form close ties with other untouchable movements. Despite their common heritage in the ideas and example of Dr Ambedkar, the Chamars and the other untouchable communities came closer over some fundamental issues. Yet at an earlier period, Prajamandal agitation, Rajputan Harijan Sewak Sangh activities, national movement etc., had been active in promoting the social and educational progress of the untouchables. The Maharaja of Jhalawar was the first in removing social disabilities imposed on untouchables. The Maharaja had also opened the temples and schools to untouchables in his state.

In the earlier and later stages of the untouchable movement, they elicited cooperation from Prajamandal, Rajputana Harijan Sewak Sangh, social and political leaders attached with the national movement, Arya Samaj and other organizations against untouchability.

Indeed, during the reform movements of the following year, conflict between high caste Hindus and untouchable movements became quite evident. During this period there were attacks and pillage of homes and property of the Chamars, Meghwals, Balais and Raigars in rural areas. The untouchables were also physically assaulted and their houses pillaged by the upper caste zealots, who were on rampage against the untouchables in the villages. All this revealed that the dominant castes in rural areas opposed the attempts made by the untouchables to alter their socio-economic status. The efforts made by untouchables to transform their position ran counter to the established interest and ideology of caste Hindus, that of the Jagirdars, Jamindars, Brahmins, Gujjars, Jats, Ahirs, Yadavs,—the resulting equations was one that was detrimental to the Chamar and Raigar communities as untouchable caste.

Notes

1. Karal Deutsch quoted by Jaya Shree Gokhale in *From Concession to Confrontation: The Politics of an Indian Untouchable Community*, Mumbai, Popular Prakashan, 1993, p. 65.
2. Swami Chaitanya Keerti, "The Guru Awakens and Heals the Mind" in the *Times of India*, New Delhi, July 5, 2001.
3. Ibid.
4. संतों के जीवन परिचय – स्मारिका, टीकाराम–सम्पादक बागोतिया, प्रकाशक – महंत लालचन्द बुदगाया, कबीर पंथ, जयपुर 2002.
5. Ibid., p. 30.
6. Ibid., p. 30.
7. Ibid., p. 30.
8. Ibid., p. 30.
9. Ibid., p. 31.
10. Ibid., p. 32.

11. Ibid., p. 32.
12. संतों के जीवन परिचय, पृ. 39.
13. Ibid., p. 39.
14. Ibid., p. 39.
15. Ibid., p. 39.
16. Ibid., p. 39.
17. Ibid., p. 39.
18. Ibid., p. 39.
19. Ibid., p. 39.
20. Ibid., p. 39.
21. Ibid., p. 39.
22. Ibid., p. 39.
23. संतों के जीवन परिचय, पृ. 40.
24. Ibid., p. 40.
25. Ibid., p. 40.
26. Ibid., p. 40.
27. Ibid., p. 40.
28. संतों के जीवन परिचय, पृ. 19.
29. Ibid., p. 19.
30. Ibid., p. 19.
31. Ibid., p. 19.
32. Ibid., p. 19.
33. Ibid., p. 19.
34. Ibid., p. 19.
35. Ibid., p. 20.
36. Ibid., p. 20.
37. Ibid., p. 20.
38. Ibid., p. 20.
39. Ibid., p. 20.
40. Ibid., p. 20.
41. Ibid., p. 20.
42. Ibid., p. 20.
43. Ibid., p. 20.
44. Ibid., p. 20.
45. Ibid., p. 20.
46. Ibid., p. 21.

47. Ibid., p. 21.
48. Ibid., p. 21.
49. संतो के जीवन परिचय वहीं पृ. 50.
50. Ibid., p. 50.
51. Ibid., p. 50.
52. Ibid., p. 50.
53. Ibid., p. 50.
54. Ibid., p. 50.
55. Ibid., p. 50.
56. Meghwal writers have written and published a few important incidents of socio-religious activities of the community saints carried out by them in different regions of Rajasthan. The evidence readily available to us are from small essays published in the form of *Ismarika* in Hindi and small booklets. In order to maintain the objectivity in presentation of the facts on which this description is based, we have depended on *Ismarika* and small booklet. For instance, see, 'संतों के जीवन परिचय – स्मारिका', सम्पादक टीकाराम बागोलिया, प्रकाशक – महंत लालचन्द बुदगाया, कबीर पंथ, जयपुर 2002, p. 24. Also see Atmaram Upadhyay, *Ismarika*: व्यक्तित्व एवं कृतित्व–स्वामी जोगाराम जी महाराज जन्म शताब्दी (1902–2003) Jodhpur, Hanuman Bhakri, Nai, Sarak, 2003.
57. Ibid., p. 24.
58. Ibid., p. 24.
59. Ibid., p. 24.
60. Ibid., p. 24.
61. Ibid., p. 24.
62. Ibid., p. 24.
63. Ibid., p. 24.
64. Ibid., p. 24.
65. Ibid., pp. 24–25.
66. Ibid., p. 25.
67. Ibid., p. 25.
68. Ibid., p. 25.
69. Ibid., p. 25.
70. Ibid., p. 25.
71. Ibid., p. 26.
72. Ibid., p. 26.
73. Ibid., p. 26.
74. Ibid., p. 27.

75. Ibid., p. 27.
76. Ibid., p. 27.
77. Ibid., p. 27.
78. Ibid., p. 27.
79. Ibid., p. 27.
80. Ibid., p. 27–28.
81. Ibid., p. 27.
82. Ibid., p. 27–28.
83. Ibid., p. 28.
84. Ibid., p. 28.
85. Ibid., p. 28.
86. Ibid., p. 28.
87. Ibid., p. 28.
88. Ibid., p. 28.
89. संतों के जीवन, पृ. 15.
90. Ibid., p. 15.
91. Ibid., p. 15.
92. Ibid., p. 15.
93. Ibid., p. 15.
94. Ibid., p. 16.
95. Ibid., p. 16.
96. Ibid., p. 17.
97. Ibid., p. 17.
98. संतों के जीवन, पृ. 22.
99. Ibid., p. 22.
100. Ibid., p. 22.
101. Ibid., p. 22.
102. A full account is provided in "Garib Saheb: An Untouchable Saint: His Life and Mission' by Anitha Chaiko (M.Phil Dissertation. Submitted in the Department of Sociology, University of Rajasthan, Jaipur, 1996) (unpublished).
103. Ibid., p. 53.
104. Ibid., p. 54.
105. Ibid., p. 56.
106. Ibid., p. 61.
107. Ibid., p. 59.

108. Ibid., p. 77.
109. Ibid., p. 56–57.
110. Ibid., p. 56.
111. Ibid., p. 57.
112. Ibid., p. 63–75.
113. Ibid., p. 10.1.
114. Ibid., p. 10.1.
115. Ibid., p. 101.
116. Ibid., p. 101.
117. Ibid., p. 101.
118. Ibid., p. 101.
119. Ibid., p. 105.
120. Ibid., p. 99.
121. Ibid., p. 99.
122. Ibid., p. 98.
123. Ibid., p. 102.
124. For studies of various dimensions of the vision and socio-religious activities of Maharashi Balinath, see Meghna Purohit, "Awakening the Masses: Maharshi Balinath Guru Maharaj" (M.Phil. dissertation submitted in the Department of Sociology, University of Rajasthan, Jaipur, 2000) (unpublished.). यह भी देखे, बैरवा संत शिरोमणि महर्षि बालीनाथ जी महाराज बैरवा दिवस स्वर्ण जयंती समारोह स्मारिका, 31 दिसम्बर, 1976 दिल्ली, '31 दिसम्बर बैरवा दिवस क्यों महान है ?' बैरवा जाति नई दिल्ली, जयपुर 1995.
125. विस्तृत जानकारी हेतु देखें, 'समाधि' बैरवा संत शिरोमणि महर्षि बालीनाथ जी महाराज, 1976 (पेज नम्बर अंकित नहीं है).
126. Ibid.
127. Ibid.
128. Ibid.
129. Ibid.
130. Ibid.
131. Ibid.
132. Ibid.
133. Ibid.
134. Ibid.
135. The most important source for the early socio-religious movement and situation of Bairwas in Rajasthan is Meghna Purohit, "Awakening the Masses: Maharshi Balinath Guru Maharaj" (M.Phil dissertation, submitted in

the Department of Sociology, University of Rajasthan, Jaipur, 2000.) (unpublished). यह भी देखें, प्रहलादराय "सामाजिक नियोग्यताओं के विरूद्ध दलितों का संघर्ष – 1946–47" एवं "दलितों का मुक्ति संग्राम" बैरवा ज्योति, नई दिल्ली, अक्टूबर, 1990, पृ. 7–9 एवं अक्टूबर, 1990, पृ. 5–9.

136. "समाधि" बैरवा संत शिरोमणि महर्षि बालीनाथ जी महाराज, 1976.

137. Ibid.

138. संतों के जीवन, वही पृ. 18.

139. Ibid., p. 18.

140. Ibid., p. 18.

141. Ibid., p. 18.

142. Ibid., p. 18.

143. For more details, see Shyam Lal, *Untouchable Movement in India*, Jaipur, Sublime Publication, 2002.

144. For details see, Shyam Lal, *Untouchable Caste in India*, Jaipur, Rawat Publications, 2006.

V
Caste Paper

15 The Meghwals' Mouthpiece

During the pre-independence period the Chamars were involved in social reform movement, but their political participation was limited. Being untouchables, most of the Chamars were politically inactive. Only a few persons were active, who participated in the independence movement. The formation and growth of the Rajasthan Meghvansh Mahasabha (RMM) during the British Raj cannot be attributed to a single factor. The need for such an organization was felt by different leaders and at different times. With the advent of independence, a large number of Meghwal leaders felt the necessity of publication of caste periodical for all-round development of Meghwal activities as also one of the important mediums of communication between the community organizations and caste men. The community journals would provide a platform for reform movement and community organizations would expound its views on socio-political issues. It will also give a living picture of the community.

However, along with socio-economic and political activities, social activists could also see the necessity for publication of a powerful community paper to bring to the notice of the general communities and government as also to well-wishers of untouchables, their miserable conditions and to propagate the philosophy of religious saints and to motivate their vast following. Such an attempt would help crystallize the ideology and work out a programme of action for fighting against the various kinds of social evils, discrimination and deprivation.

As mentioned earlier, Swami Gokuldas Maharaj's attempt to organize an 'All Rajasthan Mcghvansh Mahasabha' to carry forward an agitation and soon after the formation of RMM, he infused enthusiasm among the workers, which made them realize that community newspaper would be essential for their progress in an educationally backward community and therefore decided to launch the paper.

In the history of Meghwal movement, the year 1935 was an important year. RMM emerged as a pivotal organization enlisting the cooperation of Meghwals from Ajmer. There was a natural urge on the part of RMM to publish its own newspaper. With this aim in mind, the first issue of *Prakash*—a monthly newspaper was published in the year 1948 from Domara,[1] Ajmer. The first issue was published under the editorship of Swami Seva Das Maharaj. RMM published a few issues of *Prakash*. After this RMM could not continue its publication as it had to face financial crisis. Hence, it stopped its publication.

These were the views of Meghwal leaders 60 years ago, at the time of inception of the RMM. But during the last six decades various welfare and economic institutions had grown up. The traditional occupational structure had undergone considerable changes. The percentage of educated persons had gone high. In the 15th election of parliament, people had cast their votes. In short, the conditions of 1935s had undergone considerable change in the year 2009. Hence, an obvious question arises, why Rashtriya Mahasangh has not been able to launch the publication of its own paper even today, viz., 2009. The author raised this question with some of the Meghwal leaders. In reply, some showed reservations, while others blamed the inactiveness of Rashtriya Meghwal Mahasangh, some leaders expressed their grievances that nobody in the organization listened to their views.

However, most of the Meghwals felt the necessity of the community periodicals for giving a live picture of the community and to expound its views on the socio-political issues. After independence of the country in 1947, a year later, in 1948 one of the most radicals of the untouchable reformers, Garib Saheb started a newspaper called *Sootrakar*[2] comprising more than 20 pages from Delhi. The first editor was Kishan Sahay Doomolya from Delhi. He was fierce in his criticism of upper caste hegemony and superiority and preached the equality of all. He viewed the different names—Bhambhi, Balai, Bunkar, Meghwal, Sootrakar and others as regional names and these categories should be integrated into Meghwal category. He tried to translate the views of Garib Saheb into practice. Garib Saheb was dedicated to integrate the scattered segments of Chamar communities into Meghwal community and to that end in view, he toured several regions and urged the social activists to integrate themselves. In the paper the proceedings of Rajasthan Sootrakar Balai Sammelan, poems, short essays, life sketches of a few elites of Sootrakar samaj were published. The paper had also published incidents of atrocities on untouchables by upper caste Hindus particularly Jagirdars, Jamindars and Thakurs. The paper had also published news on Gandhi's assassination in the same edition. On January 31, 1948 under the chairmanship of Garib Saheb a condolence meeting was held.

While the promotion of social reforms within the untouchable communities remained a goal of Meghwal movement in 1947, the importance of the issue seemed to have changed. In the earlier period, reform had been seen as the panacea which would in the long run cure the ills of Meghwal community. The position that the Meghwal movement now adopted was, that the untouchables' lack of their own newspaper was a matter of concern. To highlight their socio-economic and political issues, the untouchables would have to publish their own paper. Thus, the seventh decade of 20th century showed signs of the beginning of more interest in the field of publication of newspapers.

After the year 1969, a number of community's newspapers, following the pattern of local initiative and leadership were published throughout the regions. The first regionwide paper *Hakdar*[3] was published in the year 1969 at Bikaner. Meghwal Panna Lal Premi, a noted social activist and untouchables' educator, launched the paper called *Hakdar* through which he attempted to organize the Bhambhis, Meghwals, Balais, Chamars etc., of various regions of Rajasthan into one category. He wrote short essays in which he tried to spread the message that Bhambhis, Chamars, Balais, Meghwals, Sootrakars were not different categories but one in spite of regional artifact. In this way Premi tried to rationally analyse the origin of various names. *Hakdar* is published on the 1st and 15th of every month in Bikaner and a yearly subscription for readers costs Rs 100 while life membership subscription is Rs 2,000. The printing cost of an issue is Rs 800. As it is totally dependent on its subscribers for survival and publishes no advertisement, the paper has frequently appealed to its readers for financial help. The cost of bringing out a paper every fortnight is approximately Rs 2,000. As no figures on publication are available, it seems that the collection through subscription is not sufficient to cover its cost. In spite of financial hardship, it is still continuing. In this sense the paper contributed to the social mobilization of Meghwal community. Panna Lal Premi is the founding member and Chief Editor of *Hakdar*.

One noted organization 'Akhil Rajasthan Balai (Meghvanshi) Mahasabha' started the publication of *Megh Sandesh*,[4] a community paper for the Meghwal community from Deoli, Tonk district in the year 1975. Ugam Chand was the editor. Another Meghwal Dhan Raj Singh Katariya, a prominent social activist also started publishing a paper called *Bhomiya*[5] from Jaipur in the year 1979. From 1980 onward, Balai Samaj assumed a vigorous active role in the publication of community paper. During the year 1980, 'Balai Jati Sudhar Sangh', New Delhi published *Pragati*[6] in Delhi in order to publicize the activities of Balai movement as well as to integrate the Balai community better. Mool Chand Verma, a well educated and eminent social activist was the editor.

Similarly, in the year 1982 another noted social organizations called Yuva Pragati Manch, Bhambhi (Sootrakar) Indore, Madhya Pradesh launched the publication of *Nav Prabhat*[7] (monthly) in Indore, Madhya Pradesh *Meghveer*, a monthly, had been published in 1987[8] in Bikaner by Pannalal 'Premi'. Similarly in the year 1988, the Meghwal Samaj of Jaisalmer, launched the publication of *Goldendoot*[9] in Jaisalmer under the editorship of Gemra Ram Devra. *Dr Ambedkar aur Bahujan*,[10] a weekly, had been published in 1991 in Suratgarh by Satya Pal Meghwal. The paper's importance for the development of Meghwal movement in particular and untouchables in general lies in three areas. First, its publicizing and sponsorship of conferences and meetings held by members of the Meghwal community all over Rajasthan. Second, its presentation and promotion of socio-political issues with respect to Meghwal community and its news on the nature of caste atrocities and untouchability. *Dr Ambedkar aur Bahujan,* directly created a climate of opinion which could be favourably utilized by any leader. In this sense the paper contributed to social mobilization of the Meghwal community.

Another paper dedicated to the cause of the social upliftment of Meghwal (untouchables) was *Parivartan: Prabhakar*,[11] a fortnightly paper published in the year 1993 by Dr Kusum Meghwal, M.A., Ph.D., a retired officer in Udaipur. She devoted the major part of her energies in creating Dalit literature and also to the advancement of the untouchable communities. In *Meghwal Mandal Udaipur, Ismarika 1999* published by her, which provided much information about the Meghwal movement, in southern Rajasthan, Kusum Meghwal wrote that inspiration for her work came from witnessing the efforts of her father and grandfather. Indeed she dates the beginning of her resolve to better the lot of the untouchables to her meetings with Meghwal leaders and social workers.

In Jodhpur Meghwal activists were not content merely with holding meetings but publicizing the needs for social reforms. In 1994, one poor social worker from Meghwal community, Jeth Mal Panwar, graduate from Jai Narain Vyas University, Jodhpur, started a monthly paper, *Meghwal Jagrati*[12] in order to publicize the activities of the Meghwal Samaj, as well as to better integrate the Meghwal community. *Meghwal Jagrati* was an interesting and significant publication for the development of Meghwal movement; it published essays which were of concern primarily to Meghwal community and thus served a valuable communication for the development of Meghwal movement. It also initiated debate and exchange of opinion among its readers on the topical issues of the day and in general afforded an opportunity for literate Meghwals to learn about their community and the directions in which it was moving. The paper operated on a rather small budget and experienced day-to-day financial difficulties. Another Meghwal, Rajeev Dangi also published a weekly paper *Megh Times*[13] from Jaipur, in the year 1995.

Similarly, in the year 1995, another educated social activist from Jatav community, Harish Chandra Kardam, Sahityaratan, Jodhpur, started a quarterly paper *Jatav Times*[14] in order to publicize the socio-economic and educational activities of untouchable communities in general and Jatav, Chamar and Balai in particular, as well as to better integrate the samaj. *Jatav Times* was an interesting and significant publication for development of Jatav and Meghwal movement. It published short essays, poems, short biographical sketches 'contributions' of Jyoti Rao Phoole and Ambedkar for the betterment of the conditions of the downtrodden, weaker sections of society and empowerment of women. It also concentrated on the role of the educated in bringing the social and political awakening and changes.

In Ajmer region, the Balai community had shown considerable vitality in producing a leadership and organizational aptitude which sprang up in numerous localities and took initiative in directing its social and educational development. What is particularly noteworthy about Balai movement in this region is that it was a product of Swami Gokul Das Maharaj.

Hanuman Prasad Kataria notes that many Balai social workers had been inspired by Swami Gokul Das Maharaj's social work, particularly his campaign for the protection of the interest of Balai Samaj. During the year Balai Gulab Chand Jindal took active interest in social, educational and cultural matters, he wrote several articles on the subject to reform his community. A few decades later, he also launched a periodical, which was circulated largely in Ajmer region. Thus, on October 10, 1997, a release function of *Balai Darpan*[15] a quarterly Patrika, was arranged at Railway Centre, Naka-Madir, Ajmer, which was released by Yogacharya Shyam Anand Giri and Dr Raj Kumar Jaipal. Interesting, Jindal is also a literary person and used his talents to arouse consciousness of his community. He wrote many articles on untouchable saints, short essays and poems etc., on the conditions of Balai, Meghwal, Sootrakar etc.

Another important publisher at Jaipur, Babu Lal Verma by caste Balai, started the *Udai Megh*[16] a weekly newspaper in the year 1998. He started this paper in order to highlight the social, economic and educational conditions of the untouchable communities as well as to better integrate the Balai, Bhambhi, Sootrakar, and Meghwal. communities together. The paper devoted itself exclusively to "ameliorate and uplift the untouchable communities in Rajasthan". Indeed, *Udai Megh* is distributed largely in Rajasthan but a few copies of the paper are also sent to Indore and Madhya Pradesh. A single copy costs Rs 2. A yearly subscription costs Rs 150 while life subscription is Rs 1,100. As it is totally dependent on its subscribers for survival and takes no government advertisements, the paper frequently appeals to its readers for financial help. The cost of bringing out a paper every week is Rs 2,000 and while no figures of its published copies are available, it seems that its total collection from the subscribers is not sufficient to cover its cost. Babu Lal Verma's venture into publicational aspect of the newspaper, however, did not seem essentially different from earlier publications on Meghwal movement.

In 1985, Bhambhis (Sootrakar) of Indore and Madhya Pradesh, formed the Bhambhi-Sootrakar Samaj (BSS), an association which was to be dedicated to the cause of upliftment of the Bhambhis which would also provide an organizational forum for their social activities. Two decades later, in the year 2002, BSS started a newspaper the *Sootrakar Sandesh*[17] in order to highlight the activities of Bhambhi-Sootrakar movement as well as to properly integrate the Bhambhi-Sootrakar communities. The paper gave wide coverage to the meetings, resolutions, socio-economic and educational matters. The aim of the paper, as expressed in the early issues was to rouse the consciousness about the evils of the community for developing self-consciousness and how social reforms could be brought about in the community, as also to highlight their grievances and problems through this paper. In their social, political and educational aspects they are still backward as they were centuries ago. Thus, the paper tried to foster in them caste consciousness and unity in order to assert political power. Govind Guru Doomoliya was the Chief Editor and Mukesh Mehrda was the Managing Editor, respectively.

The Meghwal, Balai, Bhambhi and Sootrakars are reported to have published the following periodicals:

1. *Prakash* (1948) by Swami Seva Das Maharaj from Ajmer state.
2. *Sootrakar* (1948) by Kishan Sahay from New Delhi.
3. *Hakdar* (1969) by Panna Lal 'Premi' from Bikaner, Rajasthan.
4. *Megh-Sandesh* (1975) by Ugam Chand from Deoli, district Tonk, Rajasthan.
5. *Bhoomiya* (1979) by Dhanraj Singh Kataria from Jaipur, Rajasthan.
6. *Pragati* (1980) by Mool Chand Verma from New Delhi.
7. *Nav Prabhat* (1982) by R.D. Mehrda from Indore, Madhya Pradesh.
8. *Meghveer* (1987) by Panna Lal 'Premi' from Bikaner, Rajasthan.
9. *Goldendoot* (1988) by Gemra Ram Devra from Jaisalmer, Rajasthan.
10. *Dr Ambedkar aur Bahujan* (1991) by Satya Pal Meghwal from Suratgarh, Rajasthan.
11. *Parivartan: Prabhakar* (1993) by Dr Kusum Meghwal from Udaipur, Rajasthan.
12. *Meghwal Jagrati* (1994) by Jethmal Pawar from Jodhpur, Rajasthan.
13. *Megh Times* (1995) by Rajeev Dangi from Jaipur, Rajasthan.'
14. *Jatav Times* (1995) by Harish Chandra Kardam from Jodhpur, Rajasthan
15. *Balai Darpan* (1997) by Gulab Chand Jindal from Ajmer, Rajasthan.
16. *Udai Megh* (1998) by Babu Lal Verma from Jaipur, Rajasthan.
17. *Sootrakar Sandesh* (2002) by Govind Guru Doomoliya from Indore, Madhya Pradesh.

These periodicals are published by different individuals and local organizations from different places and states and are still being published except a few.

Out of these periodicals some are published as weekly or fortnightly while others are monthly or quarterly with 4 to 20 pages. The periodicals generally contain the news on education, social and economic attainment of Meghwals, news of Meghwal activities at various places, enquiries from the readers, short essays, stories and poems on current topics of general interest, problems of community and its other related fields. The editorial describing the activities of Dr Ambedkar, criticizing political parties also appeared in the periodicals. In its news section the atrocities perpetrated by caste Hindus on Scheduled Castes, indifferent attitude of government officials to safeguard the rights of SCs/STs, poems depicting socio-economic conditions of Balai, Sootrakar, Meghwal and other untouchable communities and similar other items are reported prominently. Political news—local, national or international often appeared in the periodicals. Occasionally, sufficient number of copies on the occasion of festivals, conventions or various problems are published. The periodicals propagated the views of influential leaders during the elections. It asked the Meghwals and other untouchable castes to vote for a particular political party, explaining the policy and programmes of that party. At the same time grievances of individuals of a section of Meghwal community are also expressed. The periodicals are often mailed to the person concerned in order to influence or inform him regarding the community's views and problems.

The columns of these periodicals are open to any type of contribution. These caste periodicals discharge the function of establishing and reinforcing contact between widely depressed caste men and news items constructed by the scholars published in the periodicals, reflect the aspirations and achievements of caste men and their problems. There are some examples of typical articles that have been published in the periodicals, they are on the explanation of the word, Meghwal, Balai and the like, origin of Meghwals with reference to the religious texts, the fusion and fission of different castes of Meghwal caste cluster, necessity of periodicals, etc.

These papers carry diverse material in its issues devoting its space on matters relating to the caste problems and welfare, elite biographies, work of caste leaders, atrocities on Meghwal, Chamar, Balai in particular and SCs/STs in general. Some of the space is filled up by the editor who may discuss subjects covering religion, politics, social, economic reservation, etc. Besides, the papers also publish matters relating to matrimonials, diseases and their treatment, issues related to public litigation, legal advice, caste problems and welfare activities, inter-subcaste commensual rules, child marriage, preparation of directory of caste men etc., figure prominently. The papers carry 80 per cent material in its issues endorsed by writers from Rajasthan.

The financial condition of these papers is not sound. Most of the issues contain an appeal for enrolling new members and raising funds for the papers. The papers have reminded again and again that if caste men do not help the papers financially, they will have to stop their publications. *Hakdar* had two types of subscription in 2006. The yearly subscription is Rs 100 and life membership is Rs 2,000. In spite of low subscription, the members had not remitted their subscriptions for a long period. Out of the listed subscribers, almost all are from Rajasthan.

Among other caste periodicals, *Meghwal Jagrati* had two types of subscription in 1985. They are: per issue Rs 1.50 and annual subscription Rs 18.

Notes

1. For details, see *Balai Darpan*, Ajmer, Vol. I, No. 2, January-March, 1998, p. 7. Also see Swami Gokul Das Maharaj, *Meghvansh Itihas*, Ajmer, Vikram Samvat 2050, Sewa Das, Rishi *Jiwan Darshan: Yug Purush Swami Sri Gokul Das Maharaj*, Ajmer, 2005
2. The most detailed account on the socio-economic and educational and political conditions of the Balais in Delhi, Rajasthan and other neighbouring states is given by Kishan Sahay Doomolaya, (ed.). *Sootrakar*, in his 20-page issue, Vol. I, No. 1, February 15, 1948.
3. Ganesha Ram Danva (ed.), *Meghwal Darshan*, 2000, Bikaner, July 2000, p. 48. Also see, issues of Hakdar, Bikaner.
4. For most important discussion of the origin of 'Akhil Rajasthan Balai (Meghvanshi) Mahasabha' and publication of *Megh Sandesh*, see in particular 21-page issue, *Megh Sandesh*, Deoli, Tonk, Vol. 1, No. 1.
5. See, issues of *Bhomiya*, Jaipur.
6. The most detailed account on the socio-economic and educational and political conditions of the Balais in Delhi is given by Mool Chand Verma, Editor in his 28-page issue *Pragati*, Vol. 1, No. 1, 1980. Also see, issues of *Pragati* 1980–81.
7. See issues of *Nav Prabhat*, No. 4, July 1982, Also see, No. 3, March, 1984.
8. *Meghwal Darshan*, 2000, Bikaner, Ibid., p. 49. Also see, issues of *Meghveer*, 1987.
9. Mana Ram Baloch (ed.) *Meghwal Digdarshika*, 2001, Jaisalmer, April 2002, p. 131.
10. See, issues of *Dr Ambedkar aur Bahujan*, Hanumangarh.

11. See, issues of Parivartan: Prabhakar.
12. The detailed account of the publication of *Meghwal Jagrati* and some other relevant information of it were provided by Jeth Mal Panwar, editor, in his conversation with the author, May 20, 2004. See also issues of *Meghwal Jagrati*, 1994 onwards.
13. Conversation with Navin Dangi, the father of editor, Jaipur, June 18, 2004.
14. See issues of *Jatav Times*.
15. Conversation with Dr Gulab Chanda Jindal, editor, *Balai Darpan*, Ajmer, March 2005. See also *Balai Darpan*, Vol. 1, No. 2, January-March, 1998.
16. Conversation with Rakesh Verma, the son of Babu Lal Verma, editor, *Udai Megh*, Jaipur, July 25, 2005. See also, issues of *Udai Megh*.
17. For background and publication of *Sootrakar Sandesh* the most important source, *Sootrakar Sandesh*, Vol. 1, No. 2. August, 2002.

Index